Educating Children With Learning and Behavior Problems

Educating Children With Learning and Behavior Problems

Martin A. Kozloff

Center for Applied Social Science and
Department of Sociology
Boston University

A WILEY-INTERSCIENCE PUBLICATION

John Wiley & Sons   New York • London • Sydney • Toronto

Library of Congress Cataloging in Publication Data:

Kozloff, Martin A
  Educating children with learning and behavior
problems.

  "A Wiley-Interscience publication."
  Includes bibliographies.
  1. Mentally handicapped children—Education.
2. Problem children—Education. 3. Behaviorism
(Psychology) I. Title. [DNLM: 1. Behavior therapy
—In infancy and childhood. 2. Child behavior disor-
ders. 3. Education, Special. 4. Learning disorders.
LC4015 K883b]

LC4661.K65   371.9   74-11304
ISBN 0-471-50630-3

Printed in the United States of America

10 9 8 7 6 5 4 3

For my parents, Rae and Louis

"He who saves a single life, it is as though he has saved the entire world."

Talmud

Preface

This book was written for teachers, parents, speech and language therapists, clinicians, and school administrators working to educate children
with a variety of learning and behavior problems—the autistic child, the
mentally retarded child, the child with speech or language problems, the
oppositional child. It can be used as a *handbook* to help the reader plan
and run educational programs for children, or it can be used to help *train*
teachers, parents, and therapists. A few words about how the book came
into being are in order.

After working with children, teachers, parents and parent organizations,
and schools and school systems for the past six years, two things stand
out. First, few people agree on what a *comprehensive* program for educating children with a variety of learning and behavior problems should be.
Moreover, few people have developed such a comprehensive program for
themselves, no matter what the approach. Some, for example, are experts
at teaching speech, others at teaching motor skills, and a third group at
teaching self-help skills. But when asked where they would start a child's
educational program, which behavior or skill they would work on next,
and which behavior or skill they would concentrate on after that, few
people give a satisfactory answer. It seems as though we have been so
stunned by some of our children's problems, or have been working so
hard to plan and run teaching programs for various behaviors and skills,
that we have not had the time to stand back from the day-to-day job of
teaching and ask ourselves what we are doing, where we are going, and
how we can bring some order to the whole effort.

Second, it is often very hard to obtain usable information on how to
educate children with learning and behavior problems. People working

within different approaches often see each other as mortal enemies, do not understand each other's terms, and do not trust each other enough to sit down and work out an educational program broad enough to embrace the special strengths of all groups. At the same time, a great deal of information that could be used by those who spend the most time with children (parents and teachers) is tucked away in professional journals. And, although working within a university makes it easier to obtain just about any periodical, journal articles, with the exception of those written by very rare individuals (who are not named here, but whose works are referred to at the ends of chapters), leave the reader with only a vague image of the actual methods used to teach a child.

This book is a synthesis of both my own experience in teaching children, parents, and teachers, and the most often replicated and well documented methods for teaching children within the behavior modification approach. With the exception of several of the methods described in Chapter 14, "Chores and Self-Help Skills," all of the teaching methods have been used and tested by my staff and me in various settings over the past six years.

The basic methods for teaching Learning Readiness skills (eye contact, good sitting), Large and Small Motor skills, Motor Imitation, Verbal Imitation, and Functional Speech were worked out, tested, and revised between 1966 and 1971 in the Autism Program (a laboratory school for autistic and autistic-like children, directed by Robert L. Hamblin, Ph.D., now chairman of the Department of Sociology at the University of Arizona), which was funded by the Office of Education through contracts awarded to CEMREL, Inc., St. Louis, Missouri, and the Social Science Institute at Washington University, St. Louis, Missouri. Those methods are described and documented in *The Humanization Processes* (Robert L. Hamblin, David Buckholdt, Daniel Ferritor, Martin Kozloff, and Lois Blackwell: John Wiley and Sons, 1971) and in *Reaching the Autistic Child* (Martin A. Kozloff: Research Press Co., 1973).

Since then, the basic methods have been further tested and revised, and new ones added, as a result of my work with individual families, in short-term teacher training programs, and in a weekly recreation-education program for adolescents with learning and behavior problems, sponsored by the Massachusetts Association for Mentally Ill Children.

The last step leading to this book was the testing of still new teaching methods and, most important, the developing and testing of a *comprehensive educational program* that would bring together all of the methods and would help the reader (teacher, parent, therapist, school administrator, trainer) to plan and run educational programs for children. To date, this book (and the educational program and teaching methods in it) has been tested and revised three times in parent training programs conducted pursuant to a grant from the Experimental and Special Training Branch, National Institute of Mental Health. In those parent training programs, parents met each week as a group to discuss the chapter assigned for the week and the teaching programs they were running at home. Home visits were made each week by me and by my research assistants, serving as behavioral consultants, to coach, videotape, and reinforce the parents as they used the chapters to plan and run their home teaching programs. A detailed description of the organization and operation of the parent training programs can be found in "A Comprehensive Behavioral Training Program for Parents of Autistic Children" by Martin A. Kozloff, in D. Upper and D. Goodenough (Eds.), *Behavior Modification in Educational Settings: Proceedings of the Fourth Annual Brockton Symposium on Behavior Therapy*, published by Roche Laboratories, Nutley, New Jersey, 1973.

In addition, earlier versions of the book have been used by parents, teachers, and speech therapists not participating in the training programs, and in training programs for parents of mentally retarded children, conducted by Donald Anderson, Ph.D., and his staff, of the Delta House project, Cambridge, Massachusetts.

A number of persons or organizations made important contributions to this book. Support for the work was furnished by Grant No. MH 12873, awarded to the Boston University Center for Applied Social Science by the Experimental and Special Training Branch, National Institute of Mental Health. I thank George Psathas, Ph.D. (formerly Director of the Boston University Center for Applied Social Science and presently Professor of Sociology in the Department of Sociology at Boston University), whose encouragement and help in the planning of the grant made this book possible. I am grateful also to the Department of Sociology at Boston University for the use of facilities in our parent training programs.

Thanks go also to Barbara Bruno, who provided several valuable ideas, and to Leopold O. Walder, Ph.D., and Robert G. Wahler, Ph.D., who served as consultants for the project. Their reading of and comments on earlier versions of the book provided corrective feedback and needed reinforcement.

I will always be indebted to the parents who participated in our training programs. This book, at first written for them, was possible only because of them and their hard work.

Special thanks are due my research assistants past and present: Gregory E. Hudson, Virginia Hudson, John Peters, and Shelley Leavitt. They helped in the planning and running of the parent training programs and in the writing of the early versions of several chapters. In addition, they served as behavioral consultants for the families noted in later chapters.

I thank my secretaries—Laura O'Donovan, Pam Baker, and Lori Gulley—who kept things afloat and typed the manuscript.

Finally, deepest appreciation is due my wife and son, who put up with me during the writing of this book.

MARTIN A. KOZLOFF

Boston, Massachusetts
April 1974

A Few Tips for the Reader

Please read all chapters slowly. It is better to learn the ideas than to finish quickly.

Some chapters have assignments at the end. It is very important to do all of an assignment as well as you can because (1) you will get a better understanding of what you are reading; and (2) the assignment will help you to plan educational and teaching programs for the children. Also, if you are reading and using this book with others (parents, teachers, a friend, your husband, or your wife), it is a good idea to talk about what you are reading and how to do the assignments. But in the end you should write out the assignments by yourself.

Finally, if you are having trouble with a chapter, go back to an earlier one to see whether it clears things up.

M. A. K.

Contents

Tables

Figures

CHAPTER ONE

The BEHAVIOR
MODIFICATION Approach

1. CHILDREN WITH LEARNING AND BEHAVIOR PROBLEMS

This chapter will give you a new way to think about, talk about, and *look at* children with *learning* and *behavior problems*. We want you to know how we see the problems of your children or the children you are teaching, and what we think all of us together can do for them. And we want you to know the reasons for what we will be asking, teaching, and helping you to do in the rest of the book.

Let us begin with a look at three children with learning and behavior problems. Billy, Tommy, and Nancy may not be exactly like the children with whom you are involved, but they are enough like your children that they will ring a bell.

Billy

The first child is Billy. He is 7 years old. For the first year or so of his life he seemed to be developing normally. He smiled, babbled, ate well, watched his parents when they talked to him, and did not have any more illnesses or problems than most other children. When Billy was almost 2 years old, however, his parents noticed that he did not talk very often. This really did not worry them very much because they knew that many children learn to talk a little later. But by the time he was 3 years of age, his parents saw that he was not learning to do many other things. For example, instead of playing with his toys, Billy spent much of his time wandering around the house, shaking small bits of string, looking at shiny

1

objects and at his fingers. They also saw that Billy did not pay much attention to them. He did not *look at* them very often when they were talking to him and he did not *do* what they asked him to do.

By then, Billy's parents were very worried and started making the rounds of physicians, psychiatrists, and clinics. Each time, they were told that something was probably wrong with Billy. One professional said that Billy was "autistic." Another said that he might be "aphasic." A third said that he might be "brain damaged." And a fourth said that she could not be sure what type of disorder Billy had. Although these people tried to help Billy's parents by giving them advice and support, Billy did not get much better.

What is happening now in Billy's family? Of course, Billy's parents keep looking for help and do all they can to teach him to talk, play, cooperate, and take care of himself. But they know that their hard work is getting them nowhere. Billy is not *learning* as fast as his parents think he can learn, and he is doing things, such as the following, that are very upsetting.

1. Billy does not *look at* them very often when they call his name or talk to him. He does not *watch* what other people are doing, even when they are trying to show him how to do something. He stays by himself in his own room for 2 or 3 hours during the day, and when he is with other people he does not *join in* their activities. Instead, he looks at his hands or at shiny objects, or walks around the room without looking at others. He does not seem to notice or care when his parents and teachers try to praise him for doing something well, and he gets stiff or whines when they cuddle him.

2. Billy does not spend his time during the day *playing* like other children. He does not know how to kick, throw, catch a ball, or ride a tricycle. He is not very good at hopping and broad jumping, and he cannot play ring-around-the-rosy, tag, or other children's games. But if he really *wants* something, he climbs on chairs and kitchen counters to get it.

3. Billy also seems to have a hard time with *small objects*. For instance, he cannot copy a circle or square, work puzzles, stack blocks, cut with scissors, color with crayons, or use a hammer and nails. He sometimes has trouble picking up small objects from the table or moving them from one hand to the other. It may look as if Billy cannot use his hands and fingers very well to play like other children, but he is very good at spinning ashtrays, opening packages, and taking things apart.

4. Billy's parents see that he does not try to *imitate* them or do what they are doing. For example, he never pretends that he is sweeping the

floor when his mother does. He does not play "pat-a-cake," stamp his foot, pat his tummy, or clap his hands when his parents show him how. When they ask him to imitate these movements, Billy either tries once or twice and then walks away, or he does not try at all. Most of the time when his parents are trying to show hom how to do something, Billy turns his head the other way.

5. Billy's parents worry the most about his *speech*. Billy can say a few words, like "baby" and "cookie," but he does not *use* those words to talk with people. He just says them once in awhile. Most of the time he makes sounds like *Oooo* or *Eeee*. And when his parents try to teach him to talk ("Billy, say 'Mama'"), Billy does not look at them or move his mouth to imitate. So, instead of *asking* for things he wants, Billy either gets them himself or pulls and pushes his parents. If he does not get what he wants, he whines, throws a tantrum, or slaps and bites himself.

Billy may not talk, but he surely seems to understand most of what he hears. If his mother says the name of his favorite food, he comes right into the kitchen and pushes her to get it for him. When his father tells him in a loud voice to sit down, he does it. And if someone says, "Do you want to go for a ride?" he runs to the door.

6. Billy does not *take care* of himself. He cannot take off his shirt by himself or put on his clothes. He does not brush his teeth, wash and dry himself, or comb his hair. Also, he does not correctly use the toilet very often—only when his parents take him into the bathroom and stay with him.

7. Billy never helps around the house either. He does not do *chores*, like making beds, washing the dishes, or taking out the trash. When he is asked to do a simple task, like putting away his coat, he just walks away without trying.

8. On top of all of the things that Billy *does not do*, there are many things that Billy does *too much*. For example, he spins ashtrays and lids, gets into and messes up drawers and closets, makes strange faces, holds his hands and arms in strange positions, and shouts many times during the day. Instead of playing, he spends most of his time wandering around the house, sitting and watching television or listening to music, rocking back and forth, tearing up papers or scattering things on the floor—often peeking out of the corner of his eye to see whether his parents are looking at him.

You can see that Billy has problems in many *skill areas*. He does not make eye contact with other people, watch what they are doing, or cooperate with things they ask him to do (*learning readiness skills*). He does not know how to learn by watching and then repeating what others do (*motor imitation skills*). He does not repeat (imitate) what other people say (*verbal imitation*), and he does not use the words that he can say to ask for things or answer questions (*functional speech skills*). He does not help around the house or take care of himself (*chores and self-help skills*). And many of the things he does are strange and disruptive (*problem behaviors*).

Billy Is Not Alone

Of course, most children with learning and behavior problems do not have problems in as many *skill areas* as Billy. Also, their problems may be much easier to correct. Tommy and Nancy are examples.

Tommy

Tommy is 9 years old. He can speak well for his age, makes eye contact with others, imitates what they do and say, and can do chores. Tommy's problem involves mostly *cooperation* and *disruptive behavior*. When he does not get his way—for example, if he has to wait before he can go outside, if he strikes out in softball, or if he does not like what his mother fixed for supper—he throws a tantrum, cries, hollers at his parents, or hits other children.

In school, Tommy does not pay attention to his work for very long. He is always leaving his seat, walking around the room, teasing and bothering the other children, and doing things that upset his teachers. As a result, he is not learning as much as he could in school and is behind the other children.

Tommy behaves in the same way at home. He seems to be moving all the time, never playing with his toys for more than a few minutes, and often doing things that get his parents angry, like pulling his sister's hair, kicking the furniture, or running away when he is called. He knows how to do chores, but when his mother asks him to take out the trash or clean his room, he puts up such a fuss that she leaves him alone.

Nancy

Nancy is 5 years old. Her parents say that she was developing normally in all areas. Now that she is in kindergarten, though, her teachers and parents see that she has problems in some of the *skill areas*. Nancy is able to speak. She understands everything that is said to her. She knows how to play, perform chores, and take care of herself. *But she does not!* Just about the only time she speaks well is when she really wants something. The rest of the time she whispers, points, or gets things for herself.

When no one is near her on the playground, she plays on the swings and sliding board, but as soon as the other children come near, Nancy walks away and stands by the fence or by the teachers. In fact, Nancy spends a great deal of time by the teachers. She is always holding up her doll for them to see, or getting them to look at the tiny scratches and bumps on her knees—the kind that children always have. When the teachers are not paying much attention to her, Nancy comes to them and starts to cry about her little scrapes.

At home, Nancy always tries to be near her parents. Even when she is having a good time watching a television program, if her mother leaves the living room Nancy will get up to find her. Nancy's parents used to ask her to do simple chores, but she acted so helpless that they stopped asking her.

STOP READING NOW, AND TAKE A BREAK FOR A FEW MIN-UTES. THINK A NICE THOUGHT, OR DO SOMETHING YOU LIKE TO DO. THEN COME BACK AND START THE NEXT SECTION.

2. WHAT IS WRONG WITH CHILDREN LIKE BILLY, TOMMY, AND NANCY?

Some people who try to help children like Billy, Tommy, and Nancy think that they may have *emotional problems*. The children do not talk, play, and do things with other people because they are afraid and "insecure." Others think that these children may have some kind of problem in their *bodies*. Their body chemistry may be out of balance, or their nervous systems may not be working right.

So far, it has been shown that programs which try to correct some problem of such children's emotions or bodies have *not* been very successful, especially with children like Billy. They just do not get much better. But, since the early 1960's, people using a method of *teaching* called *behavior modification* have been able to help. In fact, they have been able to teach parents how to help educate their own children and have given teachers powerful educational tools. This does not mean that behavior modification has the whole answer, but it has made a big start. Let us see what behavior modification is all about.

3. BEHAVIOR MODIFICATION

The words "behavior modification" are new, but the method is very old. In fact, Helen Keller's teacher, Anne Sullivan, was an expert user of behavior modification. Anne Sullivan did not try to *cure* her blind, deaf, and mute student, Helen Keller. She *taught* her. She *changed* or modified the child's behavior so that Helen could talk, read, and do very important things with other people.

Behavior modification started after 50 years of work had been done by psychologists who studied how animals, including human beings, *learn.* They found out three very important things. First, they found out that *a person will learn to do the things he is rewarded for doing.* A child will learn to talk or to throw a tantrum to get his parents' attention. And an adult will go to work to earn money. Second, they found out that *a person will stop doing things that he is no longer rewarded for doing.* A child will stop throwing tantrums when he no longer gets attention for them. And an adult will stop going to work if he stops getting paid. And, third, they found out that *a person often learns best when he is taught in small steps.* If you want to teach someone how to run, first teach him how to walk. And if you want to teach a child how to work a puzzle, first teach him how to put in one piece.

These three facts were important because by using them you could help a person to *change his behavior.* If he did not know how to do something, you could teach him by *going in small steps* and by *rewarding him while he learned.* And if a person's problem was that he did a certain behavior *too much,* you could help him by setting things up so that he *no longer was rewarded* for that behavior, but was rewarded for a different one. This is exactly what was done by people who started using behavior modification.

They helped people to overcome their fears by rewarding them for doing the things they were afraid of. They helped children like Tommy and Nancy, who were having a hard time in school and at home, by showing teachers and parents how to reward the children for learning even a little bit at a time. And they helped children like Billy by setting up schools where the children would be rewarded over and over for slowly learning how to talk, play, and take care of themselves, and would not be rewarded for any of their unwanted behaviors.

4. HOW BEHAVIOR MODIFICATION SEES CHILDREN LIKE BILLY, TOMMY, AND NANCY

In this section, we want you to learn what behavior modification sees as being wrong with children like Billy, Tommy, and Nancy. *What is wrong with them is their behavior.* If we are going to help these children, *we must help them to change their behavior.* Your child (or the child you are teaching) may not talk, play, cooperate, look at you, or sit still long enough for you to teach him. These are *behaviors he needs to learn to do better and to do more often.* And your child may throw tantrums, mess up the house, holler, and whine. These are *behaviors he needs to do less often and needs to learn to replace with more helpful behaviors.*

Are you a little worried that we are talking only about *behavior?* Are you wondering why we have not talked about *labels* that the child may have been given (autistic, brain damaged, hyperactive, oppositional) or the *causes* for his problem behavior? Let us talk about labels first.

Your child may have been given a label, perhaps even several labels. Does the child's label help him to cooperate, talk, or play? Does it help you to *teach* him? Is there any value to these labels? There is value to labels if they really mean that children with different labels need different kinds of special programs. But, as things are now, the labels do not tell us very much about the children. *In fact, the labels that a child is given tell us nothing more about him than we can already see with our own eyes. The child's problem is not his label. It is his behavior.*

A child is given a label because of the behaviors he is doing too often (disruptive behavior) or not doing often enough (talking, cooperating). So let us not worry about labels. Let us think, instead, about changing the behaviors that may be happening too often or not happening often enough. Let us help the child to change his behavior by *teaching* him.

Now let us talk about *causes.* Some people try to find out when, how, and why a child's development got off the track in order to explain the way he is now. They are looking for causes. They may give him all kinds of tests to see whether something is wrong with his brain or with his body chemistry. They may ask all kinds of questions to see whether something happened to him when he was very young that stopped him from learning and developing in a normal way.

Is there any value in looking for causes? Yes, there might be. If we learn that a child has something wrong with his body chemistry, a special diet or drug may be able to correct the problem and give him a second start. We might also be able to keep more children from being hurt in the same way. But, so far, no one can tell just what it was that started a child off on the wrong foot. No one knows for sure why a child did not learn to talk, play, cooperate, or pay attention.

Anyway, even if we knew why a child began to move in the wrong direction, we would still have to help him to change his behavior now. Isn't that true? Knowing why a child did not learn to talk is not going to change the fact that he does not talk now. Look at it in the other way. *You do not always have to know why a child did not learn to talk in order to teach him how to talk.* You do not have to know how a person got a cut on his finger in order to fix the cut. And if the cut is bad enough, there may not be time to find out.

So let us not spend our time trying to find out what *might* have happened a long time ago. It is better to concentrate on the child's *behavior now* and work to *change it.*

STOP READING NOW, AND TAKE A BREAK FOR A FEW MINUTES. WALK AROUND THE BLOCK OR FIX YOURSELF A SANDWICH.

5. WHAT IS BEHAVIOR

If we are going to help you to change a child's behavior, we had better make sure that we all know what "behavior" is. The idea to learn in this section is that *behavior is movement.* The two are the same thing. Whenever we use the word "behavior," we are talking about movements of the body. We give names to many kinds of behavior or ways of moving the body. When we move our lips, tongue, jaw, throat, and breathing muscles together in just the right way, we call this talking or *verbal behavior.* When we move our eyes so that they are aimed at the eyes of someone else, we call this *eye contact behavior.* When a child moves his eyes, arms, and legs together in certain ways, this might be called *playing behavior. Tantrum behavior* is also a certain way of moving the body. Maybe you use the word "tantrum" when a child yells, swings his arms about, and jumps up and down. Yelling, swinging the arms, and jumping are all *movements* of the body.

6.   WHAT BEHAVIOR IS NOT

Remember: *behavior is movement.* What we want you to learn now is that *we use the word "behavior" only when we are talking about movements that we can really observe (see or hear).* If we cannot observe the behavior we are trying to change, how can we ever tell whether it is changing in the way we want it to? So, whenever we are talking about what a child is doing or what we are going to help him change, we must make sure that we are talking about things that we can all *observe* (*see* or *hear*).

"Billy does not *want* to learn!" Does this tell us about behavior? No, it does not, because the word "want" *does not* tell us about *movements* that we can really see. How can we help Billy *want* to learn if we cannot see what "want" is? The answer is that we cannot help him. "Billy *turns his head to the side* when his father says, 'Look at me.'" This *does* tell us about Billy's behavior because it is talking about *movements* that we can see. In fact, if we are going to teach Billy to *look at* his father when his father asks him to, we can *see* and *count* the number of times Billy looks at his father. In this way, we can tell how fast Billy is learning.

7.   A LITTLE TASK

Before you read any more, do the following task. For 5 minutes, *observe* the behavior of the child you will be teaching by using this book. Do not talk to him. Sit or stand across the room from where he is and watch the *movements* he is making. Watch the way he moves his hands and eyes. What does he touch? What does he look at? Listen to the sounds that he makes. Listen well enough so that you could write them down. Watch his eyes when he makes sounds. Does he look at anyone then? You may not be able to do this task right now. You may have to wait until someone else is around. But do not read any more until you have done this.

8.   WHAT DO WE CHANGE WHEN WE CHANGE ANY BEHAVIOR?

If you watched the child closely, you saw many behaviors you would like to change. And if you watched him all day, you would see so many behaviors to change that you would want to give up. But don't! What we want you to learn now is that, when you teach the child or change his behavior, you can change it in only four ways: teach him to do it *better* (or with *more skill*); *increase* it; *decrease* it; or teach him to do it *at a certain time or place*. Let us use Billy, Tommy, and Nancy as examples.

Behaviors to Teach the Child to Do Better

First of all, there are many behaviors that Billy does not *know how* to do very well. He does not know how to kick, throw, or catch a ball. He does not balance himself on one foot very well. He does not know how to ride a tricycle. And he does not know how to talk very well. These are all behaviors that Billy needs to learn how to do *better* or with *more skill*.

Before you read any more, write down three behaviors of your child that you think he must learn to do *better* or with *more skill*. You do not have to limit yourself to behaviors you saw earlier. Remember: write down only *movements* that can be *observed*.

1.

2.

3.

Behaviors to Increase

There are some behaviors that Billy and Nancy know how to do, but they do not do them often enough. For instance, Billy knows how to *look at* his mother and father when they are talking to him (because they have seen him do it), but he hardly ever does it. Also, Billy has a little skill at *play behavior*, but he plays for only a few minutes a day. So what Billy needs to learn is to *look at* his parents *more often* and to *play* for a *longer time*. Nancy, on the other hand, knows how to talk, but she hardly ever does. She knows how to play with other children, but she does so for only a few minutes at a time. In other words, we would *increase* the number of *times* that Billy looks at his parents and the number of *minutes* that he plays each day. And we would *increase* the number of *times* that Nancy talks each day and the number of *minutes* that she plays near or with other children.

Before you read any more, write down three behaviors of your child that you think should be *increased*. Remember: write down only *movements* that can be *observed*.

1.

2.

3.

Behaviors to Decrease

There are other behaviors that Billy and Tommy do *too much* and that need to be *decreased*. For instance, Billy spins ashtrays, shouts, throws tantrums, takes food from the cabinets, and makes strange faces *many times* each day. Tommy, on the other hand, teases and fights with children in his class, and it takes him a long time to finally settle down at bedtime. So these are behaviors that we want Billy and Tommy to do less often and for less time. These are behaviors to *decrease*.

Before you go on, make a list of three behaviors of your child that you think should be *decreased*.

1.

2.

3.

Behaviors to Learn to Do at a Certain Time or Place

Finally, there are some behaviors that Billy and Tommy do in the wrong *place* or at the wrong *time*. For example, Billy goes to the bathroom in his pants. He needs to be taught to do this *somewhere else*—in the toilet. Also, Billy walks around the house when his parents tell him to come over to them. Billy is walking around at the wrong time. He needs to learn to walk around at some other time and not when his parents are calling him. Tommy takes off his clothes at night and leaves them on the floor. It is okay to take off one's clothes at night but not to leave them on the floor. Tommy needs to learn to put his clothes somewhere else— in a hamper or drawer.

Before you read any more, make a list of three behaviors that your child should *learn to do at the right place or at the right time.*

1.

2.

3.

9.   WHAT YOU HAVE LEARNED SO FAR

Here is a list of the ideas you should have learned so far:

1. At this time the child's most important problem is his *behavior.*
2. This book will teach you how to *change* your child's behavior.
3. Worrying about *labels* or about *causes* that happened long ago may not help us to change the child's behavior now.
4. Behavior means *movements* that can be seen or heard (*observed*). Anything that we cannot observe is not behavior. You cannot tell whether something is changing the way it should if you cannot observe it.
5. When we change behavior we can change it in *four ways*: give the child *more skill; increase* the *number* of times or the *amount* of time he does the behavior; *decrease* the number of times or amount of time he does the behavior; or teach him to do the behavior at a *certain place* or *time.*

10.   WHAT BEHAVIORS OF THE CHILD NEED TO BE CHANGED?

In a way, this is a silly question. You already know some behaviors the child needs more skill at, what behaviors he needs to do more often, what behaviors he needs to do less often, and what behaviors he needs to learn to do at a certain time and place. So what is the problem? Simply this. It is not all that hard to change a certain behavior. What is hard is making sure that the change is really going to help the child in the long run.

Too often, educational programs for children and training programs for parents and teachers do not select in a logical way the behaviors to be changed. Sometimes parents and teachers spend too much time and effort in first trying to teach the children hard behavior skills, like speech, because weaknesses in that skill area are easy to see. *But children must learn the simpler behaviors first.* Remember the idea that persons learn best in small steps? Also, teachers and parents may spend too much time trying to decrease behaviors that occur too much, like tantrums. *But it is more important to increase "good" behaviors than to try to decrease "bad" behaviors.* And, third, some people spend too much time working on *one behavior* at a time. They forget that *children become bored this way.* (So do the people teaching them.)

The educational program in this book is different from most others. Before we start, we want you to know how and why it is different. Keep these next three facts in mind. First, *children often learn behaviors in a number of small steps.* For example, they crawl before they walk and they babble before they say words. So, when we teach children, we should *follow those steps.* Second, even if you become very upset by some of the behaviors that your child does too much, *you cannot "get rid of" or decrease "bad" behaviors unless you replace them with "good" behaviors that you teach the child.* "Replace" is the key word. And, third, *children learn best when they are learning many different behaviors at once.*

Now let us look more closely at these three facts and see what they mean for this program.

11.   WE MUST FOLLOW A SKILL SEQUENCE

When you pick behaviors to teach, you have to remember that *learning a skill means building up and putting together simpler behaviors.* Some behaviors, like speech (*verbal behavior*), are very complex—have many behaviors in them—and take a long time to learn. In fact, before a child can even start to learn most skills, he needs to have already learned other *basic* behaviors and skills, like *watching, listening to,* and *imitating* people. So, if someone tries to teach a child to speak, and that child does not yet look at, listen to, and imitate people very much or very well, that child will not learn to speak. He does not have the *basics.* He does not *know how to learn.* Instead, he will hate learning because it will be so unrewarding. The teacher will also hate teaching him.

What we are saying is that *a child usually learns a skill slowly by going through a number of smaller learning steps.* Each time he masters a step, it is easier for him to master the next. If the teacher or parent misses teaching him a step, it is much harder for the child to learn any new steps—in fact, it may be impossible. So, when we choose behaviors to teach the child, we are going to choose from a *skill sequence.* In that way, we can be sure that the behaviors we teach in each step of the child's education will help him in the next steps.

In Chapter 4 you will learn more about the skill sequence. You will also learn about the Behavior Evaluation Scale, which will help you to figure out where any child is in the skill sequence and what behaviors he needs help with in that sequence. Then you will be ready to plan a whole educational program for the child.

12. WE MUST REPLACE "BAD" BEHAVIORS WITH "GOOD" BEHAVIORS

One thing is sure: It is almost impossible to get rid of or decrease a "bad" behavior unless you are teaching the child a "good" behavior to replace it. We know how very hard it is to put up with a child's tantrums, but unless he learns *another way* to obtain what he wants you will have an even harder time trying to get rid of his tantrums. So *you must always choose some "good" behavior to teach the child before you try to get rid of or decrease a "bad" behavior.*

13. WE MUST TEACH CHILDREN MORE THAN ONE BEHAVIOR AT A TIME

Some people who teach children like Billy, Tommy, and Nancy work on one behavior at a time. When they are working on *eye contact behavior,* for example, they work on nothing else. This makes it easy to find out just how fast the child is learning eye contact, because only one behavior is being observed. Unfortunately, it also causes terrible problems. The children get *bored* because they are doing only one thing at a time; they *do not learn anything else in the meantime* because they are not rewarded for learning anything else; and *when they are away from the person who has been teaching them, they stop doing what they were taught.*

Children always learn more than one behavior at a time. Each day the young child is learning to walk, use his hands and eyes, and talk. In this way, the behaviors mastered in one skill area help the child to learn and master behaviors in the other skill areas. So in this book we will teach you how to work with children in several skill areas at once. In this way, you and the children will stay excited by the teaching activities, and the children's education will follow the way most children learn.

14. WHAT IS IN THE REST OF THIS BOOK?

The one goal of this book is to help you plan and run *teaching programs* for children with learning and behavior problems, so that they can learn to play normal parts in their families, schools, and communities. Since people often learn skills best in small steps, we will teach you what you need to know one step at a time. What you learn in one chapter will help you to learn what is in the next. Here is a list of the things you will be learning in the rest of the book.

1. In order to set up and run a teaching program, you must know how and why behavior changes—in other words, how people *learn*. So the first topic is learning (Chapter 2).

2. *Rewards* are the most important part of a teaching program (because rewards help people to learn). So the next topic is rewards: what they are and how to use them (Chapter 3).

3. When you have learned about the most basic part of a teaching program—the rewards—you will be ready to *plan* a child's whole *educational program*, by finding out which skills he needs help with, how much help he needs in each skill area, and in what *order* you should work on the different skills (Chapter 4).

4. But before you start a teaching program, you need to learn how to *observe* and *measure behavior* so that you can keep track of the child's progress and find out how well the teaching program is working (Chapter 5).

5. Next we will teach you just how you can set up the *first* teaching program: what rewards and teaching methods to use (Chapter 6).

6. Then you will learn how to spot and correct *problems* in any teaching program that are keeping the child from learning the way he should (Chapter 7).

7. Finally, we will teach you about setting up *advanced teaching programs* for the harder skills, such as verbal behavior (Chapter 8).

A number of other chapters come after Chapter 8. In them you will find very clear directions on how to teach behaviors in the many skill areas. You will be using these chapters and the appendices to plan and run your teaching programs.

NOW THAT YOU HAVE FINISHED READING THIS CHAPTER, TAKE A BREAK FOR A FEW MINUTES. RELAX, WATCH SOME TELEVISION, OR HAVE A SNACK. THEN GO TO THE NEXT PAGE AND START YOUR FIRST WRITTEN ASSIGNMENT.

ASSIGNMENT: A LIST OF BEHAVIORS TO CHANGE

This assignment is very important. It is the start of an educational program for your child that we will plan together. Here is the assignment. Pick one child that you will be teaching by using this book. List ten of the child's behaviors that you think need to be changed. When you make your list, start with the behavior that you think needs to be changed first. The second behavior on the list should be the one that you think should be changed second, and so on down the list. Also list five behaviors which the child is doing well enough and which do not need to be changed. Each person doing this assignment should make his or her own list, even if all lists are for the same child.

Behaviors That Need
to Be Changed

Behaviors That Do Not Need
to Be Changed

1.

1.

2.

2.

3.

3.

4.

4.

5.

5.

6.

7.

8.

9.

10.

REFERENCES AND EXTRA READINGS

Allen, K. E., Hart, B. M., Buell, J. S., Harris, F. R., and Wolf, M. M. "Effects of social reinforcement on isolate behavior of a nursery school child." *Child Development*, 1964, **35**, 511-518.

Bender, L. "Schizophrenia in childhood: Its recognition, description and treatment." *American Journal of Orthopsychiatry*, 1956, **26**, 499-506.

Bernal, M. E., Duryee, J. S., Pruett, H. L., and Burns, B. J. "Behavior modification and the brat syndrome." In R. Ulrich, T. Stachnick, and J. Mabry (Eds.), *Control of Human Behavior, Volume II: From Cure to Prevention.* Glenview, Ill.: Scott, Foresman, 1970. Pp. 161-170.

Bettelheim, B. *The Empty Fortress.* Toronto: Collier-Macmillan, 1967.

Churchill, D. W., Alpern, G. D., and DeMyer, M. K. *Infantile Autism.* Springfield, Ill.: Charles C. Thomas, 1971.

DesLauriers, A. M., and Carlson, C. F. *Your Child Is Asleep,* Homewood, Ill.: Dorsey Press, 1969.

Eisenberg, L., and Kanner, L. "Early infantile autism, 1943-1955." *American Journal of Orthopsychiatry*, 1956, **26**, 556-566.

Forness, S. R., and Macmillan, D. I. "The origins of behavior modification with children." *Exceptional Children*, 1970, **37**, 93-99.

Hamblin, R. L., Buckholdt, D., Ferritor, D. E., Kozloff, M. A., and Blackwell, L. J. *The Humanization Processes.* New York: John Wiley, 1971.

Harris, F. R., Johnston, M. K., Kelly, C. S., and Wolf, M. M. "Effects of social reinforcement on regressed crawling of a nursery school child." *Journal of Experimental Child Psychology*, 1964, **55**, 35-41.

Hart, B. M., Allen, K. E., Buell, J. S., Harris, F. R., and Wolf, M. M. "Effects of social reinforcement on operant crying." *Journal of Experimental Child Psychology*, 1964, **1**, 145-153.

Kanner, L. "Autistic disturbances of affective contact." *Nervous Child*, 1943, **2**, 217-250.

Kozloff, M. A. *Reaching the Autistic Child*. Champaign, Ill.: Research Press, 1973.

Leff, R. "Behavior modification and the psychoses of childhood: A review." *Psychological Bulletin*, 1968, **69**, 396-409.

Levitt, E. E. "The results of psychotherapy with children: An evaluation." *Journal of Consulting Psychology*, 157, **21**, 189-196.

Levitt, E. E. "Psychotherapy with children: A further evaluation." *Behaviour Research and Therapy*, 1963, **1**, 45-51.

Lovass, O. I. "Some studies on the treatment of childhood schizophrenia." In J. M. Shlien (Ed.), *Research in Psychotherapy*, Vol. III. Washington, D.C.: American Psychological Association, 1968. Pp. 103-122.

Lovaas, O. I., Koegel, R. Simmons, J. Q. and Long, J. S. "Some generalizations and follow-up measures on autistic children in behavior therapy." *Journal of Applied Behavior Analysis*, 1973, **6**, 131-166.

Ney, P. G., Palvesky, A. E., and Markely, J. "Relative effectiveness of operant conditioning and play therapy in childhood schizophrenia." *Journal of Autism and Childhood Schizophrenia*, 1971, **1**, 337-349.

Nordquist, V. M., and Wahler, R. G. "Naturalistic treatment of an autistic child." *Journal of Applied Behavior Analysis*, 1973, **6**, 79-87.

Patterson, G. R., Jones, R., Whittier, J., and Wright, M. A. "A behavior modification technique for the hyperactive child." *Behavior Research and Therapy*, 1965, **2**, 217-226.

Patterson, G. R., and Brodsky, G. D. "A behaviour modification programme for a boy with multiple problems." *Journal of Child Psychology and Psychiatry*, 1966, **7**, 277-295.

Rimland, B. *Infantile Autism*. New York: Appleton-Century-Crofts, 1964.

Rutter, M. (Ed.). *Infantile Autism: Concepts, Characteristics and Treatment*. Baltimore: Williams and Wilkins, 1971.

Sherman, J. A., and Baer, D. M. "Appraisal of operant therapy techniques with children and adults." In C. M. Franks (Ed.), *Behavior Therapy: Appraisal and Status*. New York: McGraw-Hill, 1969. Pp. 192-219.

Thompson, T., and Grabowski, J. (Eds.). *Behavior Modification of the Mentally Retarded*. New York: Oxford University Press, 1972.

Wahler, R. G. "Oppositional children: A quest for parental reinforcement control." *Journal of Applied Behavior Analysis*, 1969, **2**, 159-170.

Wener, C., Ruttenberg, B. A., Dratman, M. L., and Wolf, E. G. "Changing autistic behavior: The effectiveness of three milieus." *Archives of General Psychiatry*, 1967, **17**, 26-35.

CHAPTER TWO

How PARENTS, TEACHERS, and CHILDREN Teach One Another

1. SOME IMPORTANT IDEAS FROM CHAPTER 1

You learned several important ideas from Chapter 1. You learned that there are many *behaviors* of your child that need to be *changed*, that *behavior is movement*, and that when we *teach* someone we are helping him to *change* his *behavior*. You also learned that behavior can be changed in four ways: it can be done *better* or with *more skill*; it can be *increased* (done more often or for a longer time); it can be *decreased* (done less often or for a shorter time); or it can be changed so that it happens at a *certain time or place* (the *right* time or place). *(Please read pages 9 through 12 again in Chapter 1 before you go on.)*

When we use the word "learning," we are talking about these four kinds of *changes in behavior*. When a person *learns* something, his behavior has changed. He has learned to do the behavior better, more often, less often, or at a certain time or place.

By now you may have done some thinking about which behaviors of your child you would like to change. We hope that you are eager to get started. But before we can get started in any teaching program for your child, there are a few more things that you must know. You must know *how people learn* (*how behavior changes*). Otherwise, you might not be very sure of yourself in using the methods we will be teaching you. Also, your efforts might not be as successful as you want them to be.

So in this chapter we are going to teach you how all people learn. We are also going to teach you how learning happens in the family and classroom. In other words, we want you to see how *parents* and *teachers teach children* and how *children teach their parents* and *teachers*. When you have finished this chapter, you should be able to read short stories in which parents, teachers, and children are teaching each other (*changing each other's behavior*) and be able to say *what behavior* the parents, teachers, and children are learning, in what way the behavior being learned is going to *change*, and what is *causing* the behavior to change. Once you have a pretty good idea about how behavior is learned, you will be ready to start helping your child's behavior to change in an educational way.

2. AN EXAMPLE OF LEARNING OR BEHAVIOR CHANGE

One of the important behaviors that children learn as they grow up is how to *touch* things. Let us look at a child learning *touching behavior* and see how she learns it. The child's name is Cathy. She is 1 year old and spends most of her time crawling around the floor.

One day when Cathy was crawling around the living room she *saw* a bright red rug. She *moved* her hand and *touched it. It felt nice and warm* on her skin.

Saw red rug———→Moved hand and touched it———→Felt nice and warm

So she touched it a few more times. The next day when she saw the red rug she touched it, and again it felt good. After that, she touched the red rug whenever she was near enough to see it.

Cathy also *heard* the ticking of the big grandfather clock by the wall. She crawled over to the clock and *touched* it. The wood *felt smooth*. She *liked* the feeling and touched it a few more times. Everyday after that, whenever she heard the ticking she would crawl over to the clock and touch it.

Cathy learned to touch many things around the house in this way. In fact, she began touching just about everything she could get her hands on. *Is Cathy's touching behavior changing?* Yes, it it. *It is increasing.* Not only is she touching the red rug and the grandfather clock more often, but she is touching *other things more often* as well. She is also *getting better* or *more skilled* at touching things because she is getting more and more *practice*.

But why is Cathy's touching behavior increasing? To answer this question, think about the way Cathy touches things. While she is crawling around, something first catches her attention. She *sees* or *hears* something. When she sees the bright red rug, it is as if she were getting a *signal* to touch the rug. And so she *moves* her hand and *touches* it. *After* Cathy touches the rug, something *always happens* to her. Touching an object is always *followed* by something. So far, when Cathy touches things her behavior (touching) is followed by a *good feeling*. In other words, *right after she touches things she is rewarded* by a good feeling. That is the reason why she *keeps on* touching things and why her touching behavior is *increasing. A person learns to do what he is rewarded for doing.*

IF A BEHAVIOR IS REWARDED IT WILL INCREASE.

For a long time Cathy opened a little cabinet door by pulling the knob.

Saw knob ————————→Pulled knob ————————→Door opened
(*Signal*)   (*Behavior*)   (*Consequence*: Reward)

Her mother put a lock on the door so that pulling the knob would not open the door. The next time Cathy saw the knob, she pulled it as she always did, *but nothing happened.* She kept on pulling it many more times, but *still nothing happened.*

Saw knob————————→Pulled knob————————→Door did not open
(*Signal*)   (*Behavior*)   (*Consequence*: No reward)

After a while Cathy *stopped* pulling the knob and crawled away to touch something else.

Did her behavior change? Yes it did. *It decreased.* Why? Because her behavior (pulling the knob) *was no longer rewarded.* At first, when she pulled the knob the door would open (the reward for pulling the knob). Later, when she pulled the knob *nothing happened.* Her pulling behavior was *no longer followed* by a reward. It was as if her pulling behavior were being *ignored.*

BEHAVIOR THAT IS NO LONGER FOLLOWED BY A REWARD (OR IS IGNORED) WILL SLOWLY DECREASE.

Cathy also used to touch the oven door on the stove. Whenever she *saw* the big white stove (*signal*), she would reach out and touch the oven door (*behavior*). She did this because each time after she touched the door she got a nice cool feeling on her hand (*reward*). But one day, the stove was hot. *Ouch!*

Saw stove————————→Touched oven door————————→Felt pain
(*Signal*)   (*Behavior*)   (*Consequence*:
                                                      Punishment)

She burned her fingers. Later, when she was back in the kitchen and she saw the big white stove, do you think she touched it?

Did Cathy's behavior change? It certainly did! *It decreased*—and very fast. She did not try over and over to find out what would *happen after* she touched the oven door, as she did with the knob. She stopped touching the oven door altogether.

The reason Cathy's behavior of touching the oven door decreased is that she learned that this behavior is *followed by punishment*. For Cathy, punishment *followed the behavior immediately* and *was severe. A person stops doing what he is punished for doing.*

BEHAVIOR THAT IS PUNISHED DECREASES VERY FAST.

As you see, Cathy's touching behavior has changed in several ways. She is getting *better* at it. *Some* of her touching behavior is *increasing. Some* of it is *decreasing.* And she is learning to do her touching only *at a certain time or place.* She is learning to touch only *certain* things and *not* to touch other things, like white oven doors (because it hurts) and cabinet door knobs (because nothing happens).

So far, we have talked about what *happened* to Cathy *after* she touched things. We saw that her behavior increased when it was followed *over and over* by reward, decreased slowly when it was *no longer* followed by reward, and it decreased very fast when it was followed by punishment. We also saw that Cathy learned to touch certain things (when touching was followed by reward) and not other things (when touching was followed by nothing or by punishment).

But what starts Cathy touching something? Why will Cathy be crawling around one second and touching something the next? And why will she touch one thing and not another? The answer is the *signals* that Cathy is getting while she crawls around. Cathy *has been rewarded* when she touches the red rug and the grandfather clock. So, when she *sees* or *hears* these things now, they are a *signal* for her to touch them. (Read the last two sentences again.) She knows that if she touches them it will feel good; she will be rewarded.

The same goes for the white stove. She has been punished for touching it, so the sight of it has become a *signal* for punishment. When she sees the white stove she knows that *if* she touches it she *will* be punished. It is almost as if the sight of the white stove tells her the *rule* for how to behave near stoves: "Touch the stove, and you will be hurt. Do not touch the stove!"

You can see that *signals really control a person's behavior.* The white stove is a strong signal for Cathy. It is a strong signal that *if* she touches the stove (*behavior*) she *will* be punished. So Cathy's touching behavior is *controlled by* the sight of the white stove. When she sees it, her touching behavior stops. Cathy's touching behavior is also *controlled by* the sight of the bright red rug. The red rug is a *signal* to Cathy that *if* she touches it she *will* be rewarded by a nice fuzzy feeling on her hand. So, when Cathy sees the red rug, she touches it.

But something will be a signal (and will control behavior) only if it is backed up by the reward or punishment it used to be a signal for. What do you think will happen if Cathy touches a piece of metal on the grandfather clock and gets a small electric shock? Will the ticking of the clock still be a *signal* to Cathy that she will be *rewarded* by a nice feeling *after* she touches it? No, it will no longer be a signal for reward. If Cathy keeps getting shocked when she touches the clock, the ticking that used to be a signal for reward will *become* a signal for punishment, and Cathy will touch the clock less and less often.

When the ticking of the clock was a signal for reward, it *controlled* Cathy's behavior in one way: when she heard the ticking, she touched the clock. Now that the ticking is a signal for punishment, it will control her touching behavior in another way: when she hears the ticking, she will not touch the clock.

Cathy likes to bang her blocks against the glass TV screen. What will happen if Cathy's mother says to her, "Do not bang on the TV screen or you will have to leave the room," and Cathy keeps banging on it but her mother does not make her leave the room as she said? Cathy will learn that her mother's voice is *not* a signal, and Cathy will not listen to her mother. So her mother's voice *will not control* Cathy's banging behavior. The only way Cathy's mother will be able to make her voice a signal that will control Cathy's banging behavior is to make sure that when she says, "Do not bang on the TV screen or you will have to leave the room," and Cathy bangs on it, Cathy has to leave the room.

SOMETHING BECOMES A SIGNAL (OR STAYS A SIGNAL) ONLY WHEN THE BEHAVIOR IS FOLLOWED BY THE CONSEQUENCE THAT *USED* TO FOLLOW OR *IS SUPPOSED* TO FOLLOW THE BEHAVIOR.

TIME TO REWARD YOURSELF!

3. REVIEW OF IMPORTANT IDEAS

Keep two ideas in mind before you go on. Here is the first idea:

WHENEVER A PERSON STARTS SOME BEHAVIOR (MOVEMENT),
THIS OCCURS BECAUSE HE GOT SOME *SIGNAL*.

You step on the brake pedal of your car (behavior) because you *see* a red light, or you *see* a car cutting too close to you, or a passenger *asks* you to slow down, or you *hear* a police siren. All of these are *signals* to step on the brake and slow down, or you will be punished. You put on your sunglasses (behavior) because someone tells you the sun is bright or because you see and feel the bright light of the sun. These are signals to put on your sunglasses so that you will be rewarded by *avoiding or getting away from* the painful sunlight. And a child learns to *say* the word "apple" (behavior) when he *sees* an apple (signal) because then his father says, "Very good. You are right! (Social Reward) It is an apple," or because his father gives him the apple (Food Reward). In other words, seeing an apple becomes a signal to the child that *if* he says the word "apple" he will be rewarded. When someone says, "Supper is ready," most of us come to the supper table. The reason we come is that we are signaled by what the person said. We are signaled that *if* we come to the table we will be rewarded by being able to eat.

The second idea is this:

BEHAVIOR IS ALWAYS *FOLLOWED* BY SOMETHING THAT HAP-
PENS TO THE PERSON.

A child might say, "Cookie, please!" (behavior), and his mother might give him a cookie (reward for saying, "Cookie, please"), or she might say, "Stop nagging and go to your room" (punishment), or she might not do or say anything at all (gives no reward and ignores child). A mother might cook a nice supper (behavior), and her son might throw it on the floor (punishment for the mother), or he might tell her that it was a great meal (reward for the mother), or he might eat his meal and leave the table without a word (gives no reward and ignores mother's good cooking behavior).

All of these things that happen to a person after he has behaved in some way are called "consequences." A person does something, and it has *consequences* for him. He may be rewarded, punished, or ignored. Why is this idea of consequences important? The *consequences* of a person's behavior are important for him because they can change his behavior.

If a father asks his son questions and the *consequence* for the father is that his son *never answers* (the father's question behavior is ignored, not rewarded), what will happen to the question behavior of the father? If you think that it will decrease, you are right! He will ask questions of his son less and less often. His behavior will decrease just as Cathy's behavior decreased when she found out that pulling the knob would not open the door.

What if the *consequence* for the child who says, "Cookie, please" is that he usually gets a cookie? If you think that he will say, "Cookie, please" more and more often, you are right! His behavior ("Cookie, please") will *increase* because the *consequences* of saying it are *rewarding*. And what if the *consequence* for the mother who prepares nice meals is that her child keeps dumping his food on the floor? What will that *punishing consequence* do to her behavior (cooking nice meals)? Of course! She will cook nice meals for him less and less often. Her behavior will decrease.

Can you guess what would happen if the mother set it up so that *every* time the child threw his food on the floor the *consequence* for him was that he had to clean the floor and wait until the next meal before he could eat? Do you think that his food throwing behavior would *decrease?*

So you see that *consequences change behavior*. Behavior that is *often* rewarded will *increase*. Behavior that is *never* or *no longer* rewarded (*ignored*) will *decrease*. And behavior that is *punished* will also *decrease*.

Table 2-1 puts all of these ideas together. Study it very carefully.

4. LEARNING IN THE FAMILY AND THE CLASSROOM

In this section we are going to use many examples from all kinds of families and classrooms to show you how parents, teachers, and children teach each other (*change each other's behavior*). While you are reading the examples, look for four things: *signals, behavior, consequences,* and *behavior changes* that you think will happen. Also, try to see that *both* the child and the parent or teacher are learning some behavior in every example.

1. Eric goes into the bathroom and turns on all the faucets. He splashes water out of the toilet bowl and dumps all the toilet paper into the sink. He takes off his shoes, fills them with water, and pours the water all over the bathroom floor. Eric's mother hears the sound of the splashing and running water. She runs into the bathroom and hollers at Eric to get out of there and never do that again. Eric scoots out of the bathroom with a little grin on his face.

Table 2-1. Signal, Behavior, Consequence, and Behavior Change

Signal →	Behavior →	Consequence →	Behavior Change
Child sees red rug.	Child touches the rug.	It feels good (child is rewarded).	Child touches red rug more often (touching increases).
Father sees red traffic light.	Father steps on the brake pedal.	Does not get ticket (father is rewarded).	Father's braking behavior when he sees a red traffic light increases.
Mother says, "Come to supper."	Child comes and sits at the table.	Gets to eat supper (child is rewarded).	Child's coming to table and sitting when called increases.
Mother says, "Let's play 'Simon Says.'"	Child throws a tantrum.	Mother ignores tantrum (child is not rewarded).	Child's tantrum behavior around mother decreases.
Child throws a tantrum.	Mother goes about her business (ignores tantrum).	Child's tantrum stops (mother is rewarded).	Mother ignores tantrums more often (ignoring of tantrums increases).
Child sees mother leave the kitchen.	Child makes a big mess in the kitchen.	Child misses his favorite TV program because mother makes him clean the whole kitchen (natural consequence of making a mess).	Child's making messes decreases.
Teacher asks child what he wants to eat.	Child says "Apple."	Child gets apple (child is rewarded).	Child answers more and more questions like that one (answering increases).
Child answers a question.	Teacher rewards child.	Child's answering behavior increases (teacher is rewarded for rewarding child).	Teacher rewards child more often for answering questions.

2. Karen's father pulls the car into the driveway, gets out of the car, and opens the door for Karen. Karen does not look at her father. She does not make any move to get out of the car. It is hot outside. Karen's father tells her to come out, but Karen just sits there. Finally, Karen's father carries her out of the car and brings her inside the house.

3. Joey climbs on top of the cabinet during lessons. His teacher is afraid that he will fall off and hurt himself, and the noise he makes disrupts the class. She tells Joey to come down. He grins and looks at her. Finally, she goes to the cabinet and carries Joey down from it, telling him that he must never climb up there again. He sits still for a little while.

4. Frankie often gets up at 3 o'clock in the morning. He yells and whines. His father cannot stand the noise, so he goes to Frankie and asks him what he wants. Frankie whines that he wants water. His father tells him to stop whining and gets Frankie a glass of water. When Frankie falls asleep again, his father leaves the room and goes back to bed.

5. Kim runs around the classroom while the teacher is trying to give the class a lesson. When the teacher cannot stand the running around any longer, she goes after Kim and brings her back to the group. Kim's legs go limp, and the teacher has to almost carry her back. Kim smiles while this is happening.

6. Tracy is in the kitchen with her mother, who is trying to prepare supper. Every time her mother turns her back, Tracy opens the refrigerator or the cabinets to sneak food. Her mother keeps stopping her and tells her to wait for supper. Tracy stops for a few moments and then goes right back to food-snitching, watching out of the corner of her eye to see what her mother will do now. Finally, her mother gives her some crackers so that Tracy will stop getting into food and let her cook in peace.

Do you see that in each of these examples the child's behavior is followed by a *consequence* that is *rewarding* for him? The behaviors of all the children were followed by *attention* and, in the cases of Frankie and Tracy, by *food rewards* as well. When Frankie hollers, his father comes to him and gets him water. When Karen refuses to get out of the car, her father carries her out. When Kim runs around, the teacher goes to her and brings her back.

After a while, if the children continue to be rewarded for these behaviors, they will *increase*. Eric will be running into the bathroom many, many times each day because it gets attention for him, and Joey will be climbing on just about everything in the classroom. So we know that, if the children keep being rewarded for these behaviors (if these behaviors keep being followed by attention or food), the children will do these behaviors more and more often.

But what *signals* Karen to stay in the car? And what signals Joey to climb on the cabinets? EACH child is going to start his behavior *at that time or place when it is very likely that the behavior will be followed by the reward it has gotten before*. Karen has learned that her father is sure to help her out of the car on very hot days. So hot days will be a signal for her to just sit there when her father tells her to come out. Joey, on the other hand, has learned that when his teacher is not around or when he is just sitting still he is *not* very likely to get attention. But he has learned that he *is* likely to get attention for climbing when he is with his teacher, and especially when she is busy giving a lesson. So being in the room with his teacher while a lesson is on is Joey's signal to start climbing.

Why does Joey's teacher keep rewarding him with attention after he starts climbing, when it is attention that is increasing his climbing? The answer is that Joey *has taught her to give him attention*. Because his climbing disrupts the class and because she is afraid he will fall, she tries to *stop* him. And what happens when she tries to stop him by giving him plenty of attention? *He does stop*—for a little while. In other words, when Joey's teacher gives him attention, *she is rewarded when he stops*. The *consequence for her* when she gives him attention is that she is rewarded. So her behavior—giving Joey attention when he climbs—increases.

That is what is happening in all of the examples so far. When the parents or teachers give the children attention (or food), the children *stop* the behavior that the parents or teachers cannot stand. This rewards the adults for giving the children attention and food.

As you can guess, the *signal* for the parents or teachers to give the children attention or food is the children's behavior. The signal for Tracy's mother to finally give her food is Tracy's continual attempts to snitch food. As a result Tracy's behavior seems to be *controlling* her mother's behavior. Her mother has learned that if she gives Tracy food and attention (mother's behavior) Tracy will stop (mother's reward). The signal for Kim's teacher to chase after her is the sight and noise of Kim running around. Kim has learned to control her teacher's chasing behavior by running around the room, because that is the teacher's signal to chase. And the signal for Frankie's father to get up and go to his son might be a certain kind of whine coming from Frankie, because he has learned that if he goes to Frankie when the child is whining in a certain way, Frankie is more likely to *stop* whining and go back to sleep. Frankie is also learning which kind of whine is the best, because a certain whine (a loud, long one) controls his father's behavior. A certain whine brings his father.

Does it seem to you that things are going around in a circle? Well, they are! Parents and teachers teach children, and children teach parents and teachers how to teach them. Parents, teachers, and children are changing each other's behavior at the same time.

The first six examples were about behaviors of a child that a parent or teacher might want to decrease, but were accidentally *increasing*. In the next few examples, let us look at how parents, teachers, and children teach each other "good" behaviors.

7. Judy hardly ever asks for what she wants. Instead, she usually pulls or pushes her teachers to get her things she wants, or she points to them. One day Judy is on the playground with her teacher, Mrs. Oaks. She is standing by the drinking fountain, pointing to the faucet. Mrs. Oaks does not pay any attention to her pointing. Judy stops pointing and looks up at Mrs. Oaks, who then says, "say 'water.'" Judy says, "Wa-er." Mrs. Oaks quickly tells Judy how well she said it and helps her to get a drink.

8. Jimmy hardly ever does anything for himself, and he never does any chores in the house. Around supper time one day, his mother notices that he is holding a plate. She tells him to come over to the table. Jimmy does. When he gets to the table, still holding the plate, his mother puts a big spoonful of his favorite food on it and he sits down to eat it.

9. With so much to do around the house, Mrs. Blake hardly has a minute to spare to sit down and work with Billy. One day Mr. Blake comes home and finds his wife working with Billy on speech. He is so pleased that she has found the time that he does the dishes that night. Mrs. Blake is so pleased with Mr. Blake that she makes him a midnight snack.

10. Jack almost never watches what other people are doing. One afternoon when his mother is shelling peanuts, she looks up and sees that Jack is watching her. She quickly gives him a big smile and hands him a peanut.

The same things are happening in examples 7 through 10 as were happening in 1 through 6. Some of the children's, parents', or teachers' behaviors are being *followed* by a reward, which should make the behaviors increase. For instance, if Judy's teacher continues to *require* that she *attempt to ask* for things and then gives her what she asks for, Judy's asking behavior will increase. The same goes for Mr. and Mrs. Blake. If he continues to reward her for *working* with Billy, she will work with Billy more and more often.

Do you see that the parents and teachers are also being rewarded? Since Judy's teacher likes to hear her ask for things, each time that Judy asks for something she is rewarding Mrs. Oaks for *teaching* her to ask.

In the same way, Jack's mother enjoys seeing him watch what people are doing. So each time that he watches people, Jack is rewarding his mother for *giving* him those peanuts.

As our last examples, let us look at behaviors that are being decreased.

11. Every time that Bobby's teacher, Mr. Stokes, sits down with Bobby to work on speech, Bobby throws a tantrum and makes it impossible to teach him.

12. Joey's teacher decides that Joey is getting attention for climbing on cabinets. She decides to *remove* that attention. Every time he starts to climb, she acts as if nothing were happening. She does not stop what she is doing, and she does not go over to him. She *ignores* his climbing and gives a great deal of attention to children who are sitting. She also gives Joey attention when he is sitting.

13. Karen's father decides that Karen is able to get out of the car by herself. Instead of telling her to come out of the car and instead of helping her out, he just parks the car as usual, gets out, and goes into the house.

14. Eric has several favorite television programs. His mother tells him that if he plays in the bathroom water he will miss the next one of his favorite programs that comes on. Each time he plays in the bathroom water after that, she calmly removes him from the bathroom and puts him in his room until the program is over. She also rewards him for playing with his toys instead of water.

In these examples you see that the behavior of Eric, Karen, Joey, and Mr. Stokes is *not* being rewarded. Each time that Mr. Stokes tries to *teach* Bobby, he is *punished* by Bobby's tantrums. After a while, he will stop trying to teach Bobby. What is Bobby learning? He is learning how to make Mr. Stokes stop trying to teach him. He is learning that throwing a tantrum is followed by a reward: Mr. Stokes will stop the session. So, whenever Bobby's teacher sits down with him at the table or says, "Come here," this is a *signal* for Bobby to throw a tantrum.

What is happening to Karen, Eric, and Joey is a little different. They are no longer getting a reward that they *used* to get. The *consequence* of their behavior for them is that they are *ignored*. Their behavior is *not followed* by anything that is rewarding. And, in Eric's case, a reward (television) is taken away. It may take a week or so, but Karen will get out of that hot car, Joey will stop climbing (as long as he keeps getting attention for *sitting*), and Eric will play in water less and less and with toys more and more.

So, by *ignoring a "bad" behavior and instead rewarding a "good" be-havior, the "bad" behavior will begin to decrease and the "good" be-*

havior to increase. We know that *ignoring* problem behaviors ("bad" behaviors) is a lot to ask right now. Some behaviors are hard to live with, and ignoring them makes you feel that you are letting the child "get away" with them. But you really are not letting him "get away" with anything. By ignoring "bad" behaviors, and instead rewarding good behaviors, you are helping him to learn "good" behaviors with which to replace the "bad."

Do you remember the things that were *signals* for Joey to climb and for Karen to stay in the car? Joey would start to climb when he was not getting attention in a lesson with his teacher. That was the signal for him to get attention by climbing. But now that his teacher is ignoring climbing and rewarding sitting, being with her during a lesson will stop being a signal to climb and will become a signal to sit. The same goes for Karen. Being in the car on a hot day was a signal for Karen to act helpless. Now that she is being ignored for acting helpless in the car on a hot day, these things will stop being signals to act helpless and will become signals to get out of the car.

Do not forget that signals are changing for the parents and teachers too. It used to be that Joey's climbing was a signal for his teacher to give him attention. But now that she ignores climbing and is rewarded for ignoring it (because Joey climbs less and sits more), whenever he does climb it is a signal for her to ignore him. Also, when Eric plays in water, it is no longer a signal for his mother to chase after him. Now it is a signal for her to put him in his room and turn off the television.

TAKE A BREAK FOR A FEW MINUTES. YOU DESERVE IT.

5.   WHAT YOU HAVE LEARNED IN THIS CHAPTER

1. An easy way to see how behavior happens and how it can be changed is this:

Signal ——————→ Behavior ——————→ Consequences

This means that all behavior is *started* by some signal and *followed* by some consequence. Signals and consequences have an effect on behavior; they change it.

2. So far, we have talked about three kinds of *consequences: reward, punishment,* and *ignoring.* Each of them affects (*changes*) behavior in a different way.

a. Rewards *increase* the behavior they follow, especially if they are given *quickly* and *often*. Also, the more often the person does the behavior, the more *practice* he gets. This practice helps him to do the behavior *better* and *better* or *with more skill*.

b. Punishments *decrease* the behavior they follow, especially if they are given quickly and often.

c. Ignoring a behavior (the behavior is not followed by anything) *decreases* it, but only if the behavior keeps on being ignored and another behavior is being rewarded instead.

3. So you see that *consequences* change behavior in three or the four ways talked about in Chapter 1: *increase it* (rewards); *decrease it* (punishment, ignoring); teach the person to do it *better* or *with more skill* (rewards).

4. *Signals* are things that happen *before* a behavior, like touching, and either start the behavior (Cathy seeing the fuzzy red rug) or keep it from starting (Cathy seeing the hot white stove).

a. If something always comes *before* a certain behavior and that behavior is followed over and over by the same consequence, that something will become a *signal* for the consequence. In this way, the sight of the red rug became a signal for Cathy to touch the rug and be rewarded.

b. A signal keeps on being a signal only as long as the behavior is followed by the same consequence. The ticking of the grandfather clock will be a signal to touch the clock only as long as Cathy keeps being rewarded for touching the clock.

c. So signals change behavior in the fourth way: *Signals tell the person the right time and place for the behavior.* The right time and place for touching is when Cathy is near the red rug; the wrong time and place is when she is near a white stove.

6. A FIRST LOOK AT TEACHING

Now that you have learned some basic ideas about *signals, behavior,* and *consequences* and about how signals and consequences change a person's behavior, you are ready to think about using these ideas to change your child's behavior by setting up a *teaching program.*

When you get right down to it, teaching involves three steps. (1) Teaching the child *signals.* Some signals will be to keep behaviors from happening, and some signals will be to start behaviors. For example, you want the child to learn not to climb on the table when you say, "Do not climb!" And you want the child to learn to look at you when you call his name or when you say, "Look at me!" (2) Giving the child *many chances* to *try* to do what you want to teach him. This means giving him materials to work with, a place and a time to do the behavior, and many chances to practice. (3) Giving *consequences,* so that behaviors you want the child to learn will increase and be done with more skill, and behaviors you want him to replace will decrease.

With some behaviors, like *eye contact,* the job of teaching is almost as simple as the three steps listed above. When teaching becomes more difficult, the reason is not so much because the three steps are harder as because there are so many more behaviors to use the three steps on. Therefore, for the first few weeks that you are running a teaching program using this book, you will be teaching only a few simple behaviors, so that by the time the child is ready to learn harder behaviors you will be ready to teach him.

Your assignment for this chapter will be done when you have answered the questions on the next few pages. You can discuss the questions and possible answers with others (in fact, it is a good idea), but the answers should be your own. Write them in the spaces provided. When you are finished, turn to Appendix 1. There you will find our answers to the questions and reasons for them. If your answers do not agree at all with those in Appendix 1, or if you do not understand an answer, reread this chapter and Chapter 1. The answers are there. *Please do not go on to Chapter 3 until you have correctly answered the questions.*

REVIEW QUESTIONS

How Parents, Teachers, and Children Teach One Another

1. For two weeks, Jimmy's mother has been popping bites of sugar-coated cereal into his mouth each time he makes eye contact with her.
   a. What is the consequence for Jimmy when he makes eye contact with his mother?

  b. What is the signal for Jimmy's mother to give him a bite of food?

  c. How do you think Jimmy's eye contact behavior will change?
        (Underline one.)
        Increase   Decrease   Stay the same
  d. If Jimmy's eye contact does not increase, what will happen to his
        mother's behavior of rewarding him for making eye contact?
        (Underline one.)
        Increase   Decrease   Stay the same

2. Sandy whines when he wants something. His teacher cannot stand
   hearing him whine, and so she usually tells Sandy over and over again
   to stop whining. If Sandy does not stop, his teacher usually gives him
   what he was whining for. Then Sandy stops.
   a. Sandy stops whining after his teacher gives him what he wanted.
         When Sandy stops whining he is (punishing; rewarding; ig-
         noring) his teacher for giving him what he wanted. (Under-
         line one)
   b. What is the signal for Sandy's teacher to give him what he wants?

   c. If Sandy's teacher does absolutely nothing when Sandy whines
         (ignores the whining), after a while Sandy's whining behavior
         will probably (stay the same; increase; decrease). (Underline
         one.)
   d. What do you think might be a signal for Sandy to start whining?

3. When Mr. Blake comes home, he sees the trash piled high in the
   waste basket. Mrs. Blake asks him to take out the trash, and he says
   he will do it after supper. But he never does. One day she tells him
   that she will prepare supper after he takes out the trash.
   a. If Mr. Blake takes out the trash, supper will be his (punishment;
         reward). (Underline one.)
   b. If Mr. Blake takes out the trash for about a week and gets his
         supper after he does this each evening, the sight of the trash piled
         high in the waste basket will be a signal for him to do what?

   c. If Mr. Blake keeps taking out the trash each evening but Mrs.
         Blake stops fixing his supper and does not thank him for taking

out the trash, Mr. Blake's behavior of taking out the trash will probably (stay the same; decrease; increase). (Underline one.)

4. During the day, Billy often gets into the kitchen cabinets, takes things out, and scatters them around the floor. His mother does not like this behavior, and she often goes after him, telling him to stop and taking him out of the kitchen. He usually stops for a little while. Once in a while Billy plays with his toys. His mother does not go over to him and give him attention very often when he is playing.

   a. What is the usual consequence for Billy when he messes up the kitchen cabinets?

   b. What is the usual consequence for Billy when he plays?

   c. How do you think Billy's behavior of messing up the kitchen cabinets will change?

   d. How do you think Billy's playing behavior will change?

   e. What is the signal for Billy's mother to go after him in the kitchen?

   f. What is the usual consequence for her when she goes after Billy and takes him out of the kitchen?

   g. How do you think Billy's mother's behavior of going after him in the kitchen will change?

5. Billy's mother decides to try something for 2 weeks. Every time Billy starts to mess up the kitchen, she takes him to his room and makes him stay there for 15 minutes. She does not tell him anything; she just puts him in his room. And every time Billy starts to play, she goes over to him and tells him how well he is playing, hugs him, or smiles at him.

   a. What is the consequence for Billy of messing up the kitchen?

b. How do you think his behavior of messing up the kitchen will change?

c. What is the consequence for Billy of playing?

d. How do you think his play behavior will change?

e. What is the signal for Billy's mother to put him in his room?

f. What is the signal for Billy's mother to hug and praise him?

g. If Billy's play behavior increases, what do you think will happen to his mother's behavior of praising him and hugging him for playing?

h. If Billy's behavior of messing up the kitchen does not decrease after a while, what do you think will happen to his mother's behavior of putting him in his room for messing up the kitchen?

GOOD JOB! CHECK OUT YOUR ANSWERS IN APPENDIX 1.

REFERENCES AND EXTRA READINGS

Allen, K. E., Henke, L. B., Harris, F. R., Baer, D. M., and Reynolds, N. J. "Control of hyperactivity by social reinforcement of attending behavior." *Journal of Educational Psychology*, 1967, **58**, 231-237.

Allen, K. E. "The behavior modification approach to preschool education." Paper presented at the Southwest Regional Conference for Head Start Program Directors, Phoenix, November, 1969.

Bandura, A. *Principles of Behavior Modification.* New York: Holt, Rinehart and Winston, 1969.

Benson, F. A. (Ed.). *Modifying Deviant Social Behaviors in Various Classroom Settings. Monograph No. 1.* Eugene, Ore.; Department of Special Education, University of Oregon, February, 1969.

Bijou, S. W., and Baer, D. M. *Child Development I: A Systematic and Empirical Theory*. New York: Appleton-Century-Crofts, 1961.

Deese, J., and Hulse, S. H. *The Psychology of Learning*. New York: McGraw-Hill, 1958.

Ferster, C. B., and Perrott, M. C. *Behavior Principles*. New York: Appleton-Century-Crofts, 1968.

Guess, D., Smith, J. O., and Ensminger, E. E. "The role of nonprofessional persons in teaching language skills to mentally retarded children." *Exceptional Children*, 1971, **37**, 447-453.

Holland, J. G., and Skinner, B. F. *The Analysis of Behavior*. New York: McGraw-Hill, 1961.

Mira, M. "Results of a behavior modification training program for parents and teachers." *Behaviour Research and Therapy*, 1970, **8**, 309-311.

Patterson, G. R., and Guillion, M. E. *Living with Children: New Methods for Parents and Teachers*. Champaign, Ill.: Research Press, 1968.

Reese, E. P. *The Analysis of Human Operant Behavior*. Dubuque, Iowa: Wm. C. Brown, 1966.

Reynolds, G. S. *A Primer of Operant Conditioning*. Glenview, Ill.: Scott, Foresman, 1968.

Smith, J. M., and Smith, D. E. P. *Child Management: A Program for Parents*. Ann Arbor, Mich.: Ann Arbor Publishers, 1966.

Wahler, R. G., Winkel, G. H., Peterson, R. F., and Morrison, D. C. "Mothers as behavior therapists for their own children." *Behaviour Research and Therapy*, 1965, **3**, 113-124.

CHAPTER THREE

REWARDS:
What They Are
and How
to Use Them

This is the most important chapter in the book because rewards will be the most important part of your teaching programs. You will be using rewards both to increase good behaviors and to decrease bad behaviors by replacing them. In this chapter we want you to learn *what* rewards are, what *kinds* there are, how things *become* rewards, and how to *use* and *find* rewards.

Since this is a long chapter, read only half of it at a time. At the end of each half, there are some review questions to answer. Remember that it is more important to understand the reading and be able to answer the questions than to finish reading quickly. Take your time, and be sure to reward yourself as you go along. The assignment at the end of the chapter will help you to plan later teaching programs.

1. WHAT IS A REWARD?

We have all used the word "reward" many times. You know what rewards do: when a behavior is followed by a reward over and over, that behavior will *increase*. So *a reward is something that will increase the behavior it comes after or follows.* Knowing this, we can try to increase a *target behavior* by setting things up so that something that is rewarding follows the target behavior. (The *target behavior* is the one that you have decided to change in a teaching program.) We can increase the number of times

38

a child cooperates with requests by making sure that his cooperative behavior is followed by something that is rewarding for him. And we can increase eye contact behavior by making sure that eye contacts are followed by something that is rewarding to the child. It is also important in the beginning to *reward the target behavior immediately and every time it happens.* Now let us look at different *kinds* of rewards.

2. SOME THINGS ARE BORN (PRIMARY) REWARDS

When a *hungry* baby turns his head to the bottle and gets a mouthful of sweet milk, his behavior (turning his head to the bottle) has been rewarded (by the mouthful of milk). When a *thirsty* child asks for a glass of water and gets one, his behavior (asking for water) has been rewarded (by the water). When it is cold outside and you put on your coat and feel warm, your behavior (putting on the coat) has been rewarded (by feeling warm). And when you put on your sunglasses in the bright sunlight, your behavior (putting on the sunglasses) has been rewarded (by escaping the painful sunlight).

All of these things (getting food when we are hungry, getting water when we are thirsty, getting warm when we are cold, and getting away from the sun when it is in our eyes) have *always* been rewarding to us. That is the way we are built. So we call them *primary rewards. Any* behavior the baby tries out that gets rid of the sun in his eyes will be rewarded. He can squirm, turn his head, close his eyes tight, or cry until someone closes the window shade. All or any of these behaviors will be rewarded if followed by getting the sun out of his eyes. And he will try these behaviors *again* when the sun is in his eyes (the *signal*). Also anything that a hungry baby does (crying, reaching) that is followed by or gets him food will be rewarded. And he will repeat that behavior (crying or reaching) when he is hungry (the signal to cry or reach). In other words, behavior that is rewarded will happen again (*increase*).

How much will a very hungry or thirsty person do in order to get food or water? He will do a great deal, won't he? So these kinds of rewards (*Primary Rewards*) are very *strong.* As long as a person is hungry or thirsty, *any* behavior that is followed by or gets him food or water will *increase* very fast. It does not take a baby very long to learn to cry when he is hungry, does it? That is so because getting food is such a strong reward for crying when he is hungry.

But will food, water, and these other Primary Rewards *always* be rewarding? When is food not a reward? When is water not a reward? Of course! These things are rewarding only at certain times—when we are hungry and thirsty. So, even though they are very *strong* and will make behavior increase *fast*, they will do this only as long as the person has not yet had his fill of them—that is, is hungry or thirsty.

So there are two sides to *Primary* Rewards. They are *strong* rewards. And because they are strong, *any* behavior that gets or is followed by them will increase fast. But they are rewards (and will increase behaviors) only as long as the person has not had them for a while or has not had his fill. As soon as the person has had enough or is full (*satiated*), they are no longer rewards, and the behavior that used to get them will *stop*.

3. MOST REWARDS ARE MADE (LEARNED), NOT BORN

If food, water, being warm, and having the sun out of our eyes were the only things that rewarded our behavior, we would not have very much behavior. About all we would know how to do would be to get food, get water, get warm, and get the sun out of our eyes. But we know how to do all sorts of things, so there must be many other rewards for us besides *Primary* Rewards.

Examples of Other Rewards

If someone tells you how nice you look in a new outfit and you wear that outfit again, chances are your behavior (wearing the outfit) was rewarded by the *praise* you got (a *Social* Reward). If you do some work and are paid for it, and you do the same kind of work again, it is likely that your behavior (working) was rewarded by the *money* (a *General* Reward). If a child messes up the bathroom by splashing water all over, his mother yells at him, and he splashes water again when he has the chance, it is a good bet that he is rewarded by being yelled at (attention—another kind of *Social* Reward). And if you finish a job you do not like to do (washing dishes) and then go for a ride or read a book, and you do the same job again in the future, chances are that your behavior (washing dishes) was rewarded by going for a ride or reading (*Activity* Rewards). Keep these three terms in mind—*Social* Rewards, *General* Rewards, and *Activity* Rewards.

Do you think anyone is born being rewarded by praise (a *Social* Reward)? Probably not. At least we know that you can praise a new-born baby all day for a certain behavior, and the behavior you are praising will not increase. The same thing goes for money (a *General* Reward), driving, and reading (*Activity* Rewards). We learn to be rewarded by them, so we call them all "learned rewards," instead of *Primary* Rewards.

TAKE A BREAK. REWARD YOURSELF.

4. HOW ARE REWARDS LEARNED?

Sometimes people become uneasy when they think about using food (a *Primary* Reward) as a reward to increase talking, playing, or cooperating with children who do not talk, play, or cooperate. And they are right to be uneasy. Food rewards, as you know, are rewarding only when a person is hungry. Besides, you cannot walk around all your life with a bag of candy to reward the child!

The problem is that many children are just not rewarded by things that reward other people. Some children are not rewarded by praise, for instance. Their behavior will not increase if it is followed by praise. They do not seem to care. And they are not rewarded by money or anything like money (tokens, check marks, or points). Their behavior will not increase if it is followed by these things. They do not seem to know what it is all about. And they may not be rewarded by or get any satisfaction from being able to finish a puzzle or play a game (activities). So the question is: How can you teach a child to be rewarded by the kinds of *Social, Activity,* and *General Rewards* that are used in everyday life?

We must find an answer to this question! And here is the reason why. You already know that you can increase behaviors with *Primary Rewards* like food. But what will happen to the behavior you have increased with a Primary Reward once the child has had enough of it? The behavior will decrease! Or what will happen to that same behavior when the child is with other people who will not reward his behavior with food? Again, the behavior you worked so hard to increase will decrease. *To keep a child's behavior going, he must learn to be rewarded by the things that people are usually rewarded by—Social, Activity, and General Rewards.* Let us look at the way people learn to be rewarded by things. First, we will consider *Social* Rewards.

Social Rewards

A baby is not born being rewarded by his mother's smiling at him, talking to him, or praising him (things that are *Social Rewards* to most of us now). If she smiles at him or talks to him after he makes baby sounds, his sounds *will not increase*, because her smiling and talking are not yet rewards for him. But, after a while, his mother's smiling and talking *will become* learned rewards (*Social* Rewards). And, once they are rewards, if his mother smiles at him or talks to him *after* he makes sounds, he will make sounds more often. His sounds will *increase* just as if she were rewarding his sounds with food (a *Primary* Reward). In fact, once her smiles and talking are rewards, they will increase almost *any* behavior of his that they follow. If she smiles or talks to him after he giggles, wiggles, or makes eye contact, these behaviors will increase.

The reason that her smiling and talking will become *learned* (*Social*) *rewards* is that over and over again—day after day—she will smile or talk to him *just before (and while) he gets some Primary Reward*, such as food, water, or having his wet diaper changed. (Please read this sentence again.)

The diagram below shows what we mean. Notice that it is just like the *signal–behavior–consequence* diagrams in Chapter 2, but with an important difference. Something has been added *between* the *behavior* and the rewarding consequence, and that something is going to become a rewarding consequence itself—a learned reward.

Baby smiles, makes ⟶ Mother smiles or talks ⟶ Baby gets food, water,
sounds, or makes eye   to him   or a clean (more com-
contact   fortable) diaper—Pri-
                                                                            mary Rewards

(*Behavior*)   (Not Learned Re-   (*Consequence*)
                                            wards Yet)

In other words, the baby learns to like being smiled at and talked to, because he finds out that *after* he is smiled at and talked to he will get something he *already likes*—a Primary Reward such as food, water, or being made comfortable. In fact, almost anything (working tasks, talking, cooperating) that is followed over and over by things that are already rewarding can become a learned reward. (Please read the last sentence again.)

So far we have talked about *Social* Rewards and how they are learned. You know that Social Rewards are such things as smiles, praise, and hugs from other people—in other words, *attention* from others. They are only rewarding *now* because we *used* to get them just before or right along with Primary Rewards. For example, we used to be fed by our parents who were smiling at us, talking to us ("It's a cute, cute baby. Yes, it is"), and hugging us at the same time we were eating (Primary Reward). So we learned to enjoy being smiled at, talked to, and hugged. Social Rewards can become very strong rewards. In fact, in everyday life, *Social Rewards are the usual or "natural" rewards that increase our behaviors and keep them going.* Our friends do not reward us with food and water. They reward our behaviors with a pat on the back, a smile, or a kind word.

Social Rewards are great. They are *easy* to use, they are always there to be used (it does not take much to praise someone), and they can reward (and increase) many behaviors. Most important, once a child learns to enjoy them, you can begin to use Social Rewards instead of the Primary Rewards (like food) which you might have had to use at first to get his good behaviors on the increase. But, just as with Primary Rewards, there is a catch to using Social Rewards: they can be used too much. You can have your fill of praise and smiles if you get them for too long or too often. When that happens, the behavior that has been followed by praise and smiles will decrease. We all know people who give us so much sugary praise that we try to stay away from them. Once a child becomes sick of praise, his behavior that is being rewarded by praise will decrease too. So, although we will always use Social Rewards in a teaching program, we must find others as well. Let us turn now to *General* and *Activity Rewards* and see how they become *learned* rewards.

General Rewards

General Rewards are such things as money, poker chips, tokens, points, and check marks for good work. These things have *no real value* in themselves, and yet we enjoy getting them. They are *rewards* for us. *They will increase the behaviors that get them for us.* For example, money rewards us for working; poker chips reward us for sharp card playing; and tokens, points, and check marks were probably used in school to reward us for doing our lessons.

If these things have no real value, why are they rewards? Why will we do certain behaviors to get them? Why will they increase almost any behavior that gets them? The answer is that *getting them is followed by getting something else that is already a reward.* In other words, we can *use* money, poker chips, or tokens to *buy* other rewards.

Work on a job ───────→ Get pieces of paper ──→ Use money to buy
                          called money   other rewards
(*Behavior*)   (*Rewarding*
                                                        Consequence)

So tokens, money, poker chips, and many other things that have no value
in themselves become *General* Rewards in the same way that smiles and
praise become *Social* Rewards—they are followed by things that are already rewards for us. (This is an important sentence.)

The reason we call poker chips, money, and tokens *General* Rewards
is that they can be followed by, or used by us to get, *almost any kind of
reward we want*. Money can be used to buy food (*Primary Reward*),
company (*Social Reward*), or bowling (*Activity Reward*). Because *General Rewards* can be used to buy so many other rewards, people almost
never have enough of them. Unlike ice cream (Primary Reward) and
praise (Social Reward), it is next to impossible to have your fill of (be
satiated on) money, tokens, or poker chips. When you are too full of the
food you bought with your General Reward (money), you can use the
rest of your money to buy a different reward (bowling).

Like *Primary* and *Social Rewards*, though, *General Rewards* have a
weak spot. Money, tokens, and poker chips are rewards *only as long as
they can be used to buy other rewards*. If there were nothing at all to buy,
how long or hard would you work for pieces of paper called money? The
same goes for children. If you are using tokens to reward them for working and learning, and you forget to let them *exchange* their tokens for
other rewards or for things that *they* enjoy, they will stop working for
tokens. In Chapter 8 we will talk about ways to teach children to be
rewarded by and to use General Rewards, such as tokens.

Activity Rewards

If you were to make a list of all of your behaviors during a day—from the
first thing you might do in the morning to the last one right before you
fall asleep—you would see that your behaviors are hooked together in a
very long *chain*. For example, first you sit up in bed, then you put on your
slippers, then you walk to the bathroom, then you splash water on your
face, . . . then you get dressed, then you eat breakfast, . . . and so on.
In a way, *each behavior in the chain is like a rewarding consequence for
the behavior which came before it*. For example, getting to splash water
on your face is the rewarding consequence for walking to the bathroom;

being able to walk to the bathroom is the rewarding consequence for sitting up in bed (the hardest behavior of all). In other words, each behavior in the chain—each link—is rewarded when you do the *next* behavior in the chain.

Some of the behaviors in the long chain of daily living are behaviors that we enjoy doing or look forward to, for example, listening to the radio, watching television, playing cards, reading the newspaper, looking out the window, going for a drive, daydreaming, calling a friend on the telephone, taking a nap, and hundreds more. If we had the chance, we would do these behaviors a great deal, and some of them we do a great deal anyway (looking out the window). So let us call them *high behaviors,* because they are highly likely to happen. Soon you will see that these high behaviors can also be *Activity Rewards.*

On the other hand, some of the behaviors in the long *chain* are behaviors that we may not care to do as much, for instance, getting out of bed in the morning, doing the laundry, washing dishes, mowing the lawn, doing a lesson, or going to work. If we could, we would rather do something else. We would rather do the *high* behaviors. So let us call these behaviors *low behaviors,* because if we could choose between doing a high and low behavior, the low behavior would be *less* likely to happen. If you had a choice between removing wallpaper (a *low* behavior for you) and playing cards (a *high* behavior), which would be more likely?

Now, the important point is that *doing a low behavior first will be rewarded by getting to do a high (more enjoyable) behavior next.* (Please read this sentence again.) In other words, *high* behaviors can be (and often are) *naturally used* as *Activity Rewards* to *increase low* behaviors. If, for instance, we *often* do the laundry (*low* behavior) first and then do something we really like to do (a *high* behavior such as going to a movie), then going to a movie is an Activity Reward for doing the laundry. And doing the laundry will *increase.* In the same way, you could increase dishwashing (*low* behavior) by following it over and over with on Activity Reward such as television watching (*high* behavior). And, for a child, cleaning his room (*low* behavior) can be increased by having him first do *a little* room cleaning before he can go outside to play (*high* behavior). Or, asking for things without whining (*low* behavior) can be increased by following good asking (asking without whining) with an *Activity* Reward (getting a piggy-back ride—a *high* behavior).

In other words, *anything* that a person does very much or would like to do (*high* behavior) can be used as an *Activity Reward* for *first* doing a *low* behavior. If the low behavior is rewarded *often enough,* it will increase. The key words are "often enough." Rewarding a *low* behavior one time may not increase it. The child needs practice in learning the behavior and finding out that it will be rewarded.

Whenever Activity Rewards are used as in the diagram below:

Mother says, "*AS SOON*
AS you put on your shoes
   (*LOW* behavior), *YOU*   Child puts on   Child goes
CAN go outside——————→shoes——————————→outside
   (*HIGH* behavior)
   (*Signal*)   (*Behavior*)   (*Consequence*—
                                                           ACTIVITY REWARD)

we call this *Grandma's Law* (Homme, 1967), because that is how grand-mothers get us to do (increase) so many *low* behaviors. "*As soon as* you eat your spinach (*low*), *you can* play outside with Grandpa (*high*)." So Grandma's Law means making sure that *a lot* of a *high* behavior—*Activity Reward*—follows *a little* of a *low* behavior. The nice thing about Grandma's Law is that there are so many Activity Rewards that can be used. There are many high behaviors that we hardly ever think of, but if we watch what children *do* we can see the *high* behaviors. Remember: anything that a child usually does or wants to do can be made an Activity Reward for his *first* doing *a little bit* of a *low* behavior that you want to *increase*. If a child always seems to be kicking over the wastebasket in class, use Grandma's Law. Let him kick the wastebasket during free time, after he does some of his lessons. Before you read any more, think of five ways you could use Grandma's Law with your child (or a child you are teaching) to *increase* a *low* behavior.

HOW ARE ACTIVITY REWARDS LEARNED?

First of all, keep in mind that anything that is already a *high* behavior (happens a good deal) can be used as an Activity Reward by having it follow a *low* behavior. Some behaviors, though, cannot yet be used as Activity Rewards because they are *low* behaviors. For instance, the child might not like to play outside or go for walks. Then you could not use these activities as rewards. Instead, you would have to *teach* the child to enjoy these activties and make them *high* behaviors. The way to do that is to *reward the child many times for doing these behaviors.*

When you think about it, many of our *high* behaviors now—the activi-ties we look forward to—were not always high behaviors. We might not have always enjoyed bowling or gardening. And how many of us really enjoyed those first weeks of learning to read? But bowling or gardening or reading may be enjoyable now. We might even do some behavior first (washing dishes) in order to get to do these *high* activities. How did they become more enjoyable? Why are we doing them more often now than before? The answer is that *we were rewarded over and over for doing them.* We might have hated doing the dishes as children, but when our parents made us wash them *before* we could listen to the radio (*Activity* Reward, Grandma's Law), or praised us for doing a good job (*Social* Reward), or gave us our 15-cent allowance (*General* Reward) when we had finished, doing the dishes increased and maybe even became less of a bother.

So, if we are rewarded *often enough* for some *low* behavior, not only will it *increase* but we may come to actually *enjoy* it. For instance, we might not have cared for bowling at first. But, after our friends praised us for getting strikes and spares, we started enjoying it. Bowling then became an *Activity Reward itself* for other behaviors. Now we might even wash the dishes in order to go bowling.

So the beauty of using Activity Rewards and *Grandma's Law* is that, once you have taught a child to enjoy an activity (by rewarding him for doing it), you can use that activity to reward him for some other behavior. At first, you may have to teach the child to play with puzzles by rewarding him with food and praise (*Primary* and *Social* Rewards). But once he seems to enjoy playing with puzzles and you notice that he spends more time playing with them on his own (once this becomes a *high* behavior), you can try to use Grandma's Law: "As soon as you put your plate in the sink (*low* behavior), you can play with your puzzles (now a *high* behavior).

As you will soon see, Activity Rewards and Grandma's Law will help you to switch from the food rewards that you may have to start with, to more *natural rewards,* such as activities that the child enjoys.

GOOD JOB! GIVE YOURSELF AN ACTIVITY REWARD.

"Control" as a Learned Reward

So far in this chapter, you have seen how important rewards are for increasing "good" behaviors (which is the whole reason for *teaching*). If you were asked what good it does the child to increase certain of his behaviors, such as cooperating, paying attention, talking, or helping around the house, you would probably give one of these answers or something like it:

1.   The child will have a better chance of getting more education.
2.   The child will have a better chance in life as an adult.
3.   The child and his family will have a more pleasant time living to-
     gether.
4.   It is a good thing for a child to learn what he is able to learn.

Of course, all of these answers are great! But rewarding a child while
he learns a behavior teaches him something more—it *teaches the child
how to get rewards.* Are you going to teach a child to talk just for the
sake of talking? Certainly not; you will be teaching him to talk because
of what talking will *do for him.* He will be able to bring people to him,
have his questions answered, get the things he needs to stay alive
(*Primary* Rewards), and do the things he wants to do (*Activity* Rewards). By learning to talk, in other words, the child learns how to gain
what he wants and needs—namely, the things we have called *rewards.*
The same goes for *any* other behavior you teach him. Knowing how to
play will bring the child other people to play with (*Social* Rewards), as
well as the enjoyment of playing well (*Activity* Reward).

So you see that all of the behaviors we do very often and all of the
behaviors you will be teaching the child have something in common. They
give us some *control* over the objects, events, and people (the *scene*)
around us. They bring us the Primary, Social, General, and Activity
Rewards that we want and need. In fact, *being able to control things is
a strong learned reward in itself.* We like to see things come out the way
we want them to. It is rewarding to see our behavior have an *effect.*

Remember examples 1 through 6 in Chapter 2, in which children were
getting attention (Social Rewards) and food (Primary Rewards) for all
kinds of "bad" behaviors? When you think about it, those children were
controlling (having an *effect* on) their parents and teachers—getting their
parents and teachers to give them attention and food. The little smiles
and grins of the children, and the way they sometimes watched out of
the corners of their eyes when their "bad" behaviors made people jump,
were good signs that the children were rewarded as much by their *control*
as by the food or attention.

Of course, parents and teachers are also rewarded by being able to
control things. It is rewarding, for example, to see your child's behavior
change the way you wanted it to after you put in long hours of teaching.
You smile when your child learns a hard behavior as much because you
have taught him (had an *effect* on his behavior) as because you are
happy for him.

*To sum up, one purpose of teaching is to give the child a better way to
control, have an effect on, and gain rewards from the scene around him.*

You are teaching him "good" behaviors to replace the "bad" behaviors he may have been using to control others and obtain rewards.

5. SUMMARY OF IMPORTANT IDEAS YOU HAVE LEARNED SO FAR

1. Rewards are one kind of *consequence*. They *increase* the behaviors they follow.

2. One kind of reward is called a *Primary Reward*. These rewards are the things we are born being rewarded by, such as food, water, and being made comfortable. Primary Rewards are *strong* rewards; the behaviors they follow increase *fast*. However, Primary Rewards increase behavior only when a person is *deprived* of them. As soon as the person is "full" of the Primary Reward (*satiated*), the behavior decreases.

3. Most of the things that reward our behaviors in everyday life are *not* Primary Rewards. They are *learned* rewards. Like Primary Rewards, learned rewards *increase* the behaviors they follow. There are three kinds of learned rewards. *Social* Rewards are things like praise, smiles, and hugs (all *attention*). *General* Rewards are things like money and tokens; they are "general" because they can be used to "buy" *many* other kinds of rewards. *Activity* Rewards are things we like to do (*high* behaviors). Activity Rewards can be used to increase *low* behaviors (*Grandma's Law*).

4. *Social, general,* and *activity* Rewards become rewards when they are followed over and over by something that is already a reward. For example, praise (a *Social* Reward) becomes a reward to a child when it is followed many times by food or by some activity the child enjoys. *General* Rewards become rewards when the person learns that he can *use* them to buy other rewards. Many *activities* become rewards when we are rewarded for doing these activities. A child can learn to enjoy playing on a swing set if he is rewarded for it. Then playing on a swing set can be used as an *Activity* Reward for another behavior.

5. Learning a behavior means that the behavior has *increased* or that the child now has *more* skill. It also means that the child can *use* the behavior to have an *effect* on or *control* things and events around him, hopefully in ways that are *better* for him and for those he lives and learns with.

This is enough reading for today. Before you read any more, answer the questions on the next few pages. They will help you to remember the ideas you have learned so far in Sections 1 through 5. As in Chapter 2, you can talk to others about the questions and possible answers, but answer the questions yourself. After you have answered them as well as you can, check your answers in Appendix 1. If you still have problems with the questions, please read Sections 1 through 5 again to find the correct answers and the reasons for them. *Please do not go on until you have answered the questions correctly.*

REVIEW QUESTIONS ON SECTIONS 1 THROUGH 5:

Rewards

1. Primary rewards (are learned like anything else; have always been rewards for a person). (Underline one.)
2. Primary rewards are rewards (only as long as a person has not had enough of them; all the time). (Underline one.)
3. If you try to reward someone's behavior with a primary reward and he has already had enough of it, the behavior will (increase, decrease, stay the same). (Underline one.)
4. Something becomes a learned reward when it is_____ over and over by something that is already a reward (Fill in the blank.)
5. Which one of the examples below will help to make praise a learned reward? Let us say that going outside is already a reward for Billy. (Circle one.)
    a. Billy finishes a chore His mother lets him go outside. Then she praises him.
    b. Billy finishes a chore. His mother praises him. Then she lets him go outside.
6. People (can; cannot) become satiated with or have their fill of Social Rewards such as praise. (Underline one.)
7. General Rewards, such as money and tokens, (have value; do not have value) in themselves. (Underline one.)
8. Money and tokens become General Rewards when the person finds out_____. (Fill in the blank.)
9. Since General Rewards can be used to get many other rewards, (it is easy; it is hard) to become satiated with or to have enough of them. (Underline one.)

10. How can you teach a child to enjoy an activity (to make it an Activity Reward)? (Write a short answer in the space provided.)

11. Write out Grandma's Law, using activities from the columns below. Make up two Grandma's Laws. Use the space provided after (*a.*) and (*b.*)

High Behaviors	*Low Behaviors*
Going for a walk	Doing a chore
Eating cherry pie	Eating spinach

   a.

   b.

12. When you use Grandma's Law, (a lot; a little) of a *high* behavior is supposed to follow (a lot; a little) of a *low* behavior. (Underline one in each set of parentheses.)

13. Jimmy did not always enjoy reading. Now he does. Give an example of how reading could be used as an Activity Reward. (Write a short answer in the space provided.)

14. Learning a behavior also means learning how to_____ the scene around you. (Fill in the blank.)

15. Learning a behavior also means learning how to gain_____. (Fill in the blank.)

VERY GOOD! NOW TAKE A LOOK AT THE ANSWERS IN APPENDIX 1.

6.　WHICH REWARDS DO I USE? AND HOW OFTEN DO I USE THEM?

At this point you may be saying to yourself, "There are so many different kinds of rewards. All of them increase behavior. But which one do I use

to increase a *target behavior* (a behavior you have decided to change)?
Do I use the same reward all the time for that behavior? And how often
should I reward the behavior? Every time it happens? Once in a while?"
These are very important questions. Knowing *what* rewards are and knowing *how* to use them are two different things. Therefore in the next sections we will talk about *which* rewards to use, *when* to use them, and *how
often* to use them. You must be able to answer the above questions before
you plan any teaching program.

7. REWARDS AND REWARD SCHEDULES IN THE BEGINNING OF A TEACHING PROGRAM

In a child's educational program, you will be working to change behaviors
he needs help with in the different skill areas. Let us repeat an idea from
Chapter 1: You pick (*pinpoint*) target behaviors to teach the child on
the basis of his *behaviors now* (which ones he needs to do with more
skill, more often, less often, or at the right time and place), not on the
basis of any *labels* he may have.

With some children, your first teaching program will be in the most
basic skill area, called *learning readiness*. There the children will be
learning target behaviors, such as *eye contact, good sitting*, and *cooperation* with simple requests. After the children have mastered the Learning
Readiness skills, you will be starting teaching programs for target behaviors in the more *advanced* skill areas, for example, *Looking, Listening,*
and *Moving skills, Motor Imitation,* and *Verbal Imitation.* With other
children, who already have the basic Learning Readiness skills, you might
be starting their education in the Motor Imitation skill area; when they
have mastered that, you might move ahead to Verbal Imitation and
Functional Speech.

A general rule to follow at the *start* of the child's *first* teaching program
and at the *start* of *later* teaching programs for *hard* behaviors is this:

USE A *STRONG* REWARD
and REWARD THE TARGET BEHAVIOR *EVERY TIME* IT HAPPENS.

Let us use *eye contact* as an example. Eye contact is one of the Learning
Readiness skills. It is a "must" behavior. Unless the child looks at you
when you ask him to, when you are talking to him, and when you are
showing him how to do something, you will not be able to teach him
anything!! So you have to make sure that the child has good eye contact
before you work on target behaviors in any other skill area. With some

children, eye contact will be the *first target behavior;* after it has increased enough, you will move on to other target behaviors.

Knowing how important eye contact is, what could you do if a child
refused to make eye contact when you asked him to, or did not make eye
contact very often simply because he did not seem to *notice* or *care* that
you were there? You would have to reward him *every time* he made eye
contact, and you would have to use a *strong reward.* If praise were not a
very strong reward for the child, praising him every time he made eye
contact would not increase his eye contact very much, if at all. So you
would have to use a stronger reward—perhaps a *Primary Reward* such
as his *favorite food.* And to make sure that the food (*Primary*) reward
was as strong as possible, you might even run teaching sessions at mealtime, when he would be very hungry. Of course, you would have to make
sure that the child was not snacking between meals or getting the food
rewards for free.

The same rule should be followed *later* in any child's education when
you are starting a new teaching program for a hard target behavior. If
the target behavior is very *weak* (the child has never done or hardly ever
does the behavior, and he does not do it with much skill), you must
start the new teaching program by using a *strong* reward and by rewarding the weak target behavior *every time it happens.*

In other words, when you start a new teaching program, especially
one in which the new target behavior is a hard one for the child, you
want him to try to do something he may have never done before or never
done very well. And he has probably never been rewarded for that behavior, either. So, when he does *try* to do the new target behavior, he
must be given a strong reward, and he must, *at first,* be rewarded every
time.

To get you using a term we have not talked about yet, when a target
behavior is rewarded *every time it happens,* we say that it is being rewarded on a *Continuous Schedule.* In other words, the rewards are *always*
there when the behavior happens. As you will soon see, there are other
kinds of *reward schedules* besides a *Continuous Schedule* (*reward every
time the behavior happens*).

8. MAKING BEHAVIOR MORE NATURAL: REWARDS AND REWARD SCHEDULES LATER IN ANY TEACHING PROGRAM AND LATER IN THE CHILD'S EDUCATION

Using a very *strong reward* (such as food) and a *Continuous Schedule*
(the target behavior is rewarded *every time*) may be all right at the

very start of a child's education and at the start of new teaching programs for hard behaviors. In fact, some children make no progress at all unless their teaching programs, *at first*, have *strong rewards* and a *Continuous Schedule* of rewards. But you cannot keep on using strong, primary rewards like food, which you might have had to start with. And you cannot keep on rewarding the behavior on a Continuous Schedule. Maybe you are asking yourself, "Why not? If these things work so well to get a target behavior started (on the increase), why can't you keep on using them?" Well, there are three good reasons.

What Does "Normal" Mean?

Jill and Mike are 8 years old. Jill never had any behavioral problems and never needed any special education. Mike, on the other hand, did not talk very well and had other behavioral problems. He got some special education, and was rewarded with food (*strong, Primary Reward*) on a *Continuous Schedule* as he learned to talk and play. Now he behaves just like Jill. Jill is called a "normal" child. Is Mike a "normal" child now, too? You might think so; his behavior *looks the same* as Jill's.

But what if being rewarded *once in a while* (*Intermittent Schedule*) with *Social* and *Activity Rewards* is enough to keep Jill's behaviors going and to teach her new behaviors, while Mike *still* needs food (*Primary*) rewards on a *Continuous Schedule* to teach him new behaviors and to keep his old ones going? No, Mike *cannot* be called a "normal" child yet. He may *behave* like any other child, but the rewards and reward schedules his behaviors need are not *normal;* they are not the kinds of *natural rewards* and *natural schedules* that are usually used in everyday life.

To be "normal" means that *both* (1) the *behavior* and (2) the *rewards* and *reward schedules* that keep the behavior going are "natural." You can say that your child has "normal" speech only when (1) he speaks like other children, and (2) his speech is kept going with the same kinds of *rewards* and reward *schedules* that are usually (*naturally*) given for children's speech.

So, you see, not only are you working to teach "normal" behavior, but also you are working to get the children's new behavior under the *control of natural rewards and natural schedules.*

Enough Is Enough!

The second reason is simple. We talked about it before. *Primary Rewards* and a *Continuous Schedule* are great to *increase* a target behavior *fast,*

but they will also make the child *full* (*satiated*) fast. And you know
what happens to the behavior then: it *decreases fast!* So, to prevent the
child's behavior from decreasing because he is full of the reward
(*satiated*), you must switch to different rewards and *intermittent* (once
in a while) schedules. You switch once the behavior has *increased so
much* that it no longer needs to be rewarded every time and to be given
such a strong reward.

You Have Only Two Hands

After a few months of teaching the child, you will be working on three
or four target behaviors *at once*. You will be increasing the newest target
behavior and keeping the older ones going. Can you imagine rewarding
the four target behaviors *every time* (on a *Continuous Schedule*) with
food (or any other kind of reward)? If you were using food as a reward
for all four behaviors, the child would be full (satiated) in 10 minutes.
Even if you did not use food, you could not *keep up* with all of the behaviors you were trying to reward every time. They would be happening
too fast for you to reward or even see every one of them.
  So there is no getting around it. You have to

SLOWLY MOVE AWAY FROM PRIMARY REWARDS
AND CONTINUOUS REWARD SCHEDULES ·
once
ANY TARGET BEHAVIOR HAS INCREASED ENOUGH
and once
YOU HAVE STARTED TO KEEP TWO OR THREE BEHAVIORS
GOING AT THE SAME TIME.

Instead, you need to

MOVE TOWARD MORE NATURAL REWARDS
(SOCIAL, GENERAL, AND ACTIVITY REWARDS)
and toward
MORE NATURAL SCHEDULES
(INTERMITTENT—ONCE IN A WHILE—SCHEDULES). ·

Now let us talk about how to use more natural rewards and schedules to
keep behaviors going once they have increased, and to teach *NEW*
behaviors once the child has mastered several target behaviors.

Using a Natural Schedule of Rewards

Once a behavior has increased enough on a *Continuous* (every time) *Schedule,* it is time to *slowly* get the behavior on a schedule that rewards the behavior about as often as other children are rewarded for the same behavior in daily life. No one is rewarded every time he makes eye contact, works a puzzle, or asks for something. We are rewarded once in a while. In other words, most behavior is on an *Intermittent Schedule of rewards.* And that is what you must do after a target behavior increases— get the child off of a *Continuous (every time) Schedule and onto an Intermittent (once in a while) Schedule.*

In the next few pages we will talk about the four main kinds of *Intermittent Schedules.* Until you use them, it is very easy to become confused by their names. So do not get upset if you feel you do not know them after we talk about them. It takes time and practice. Just try to remember their names for now and think of examples for each one. We will talk about them more when it is time to use them. They will be easy to understand then.

Here are some examples of behaviors being rewarded on *Intermittent Schedules.* Instead of rewarding the child every time he makes eye contact, we could start to reward eye contact two out of three times, then slowly move to about once out of two times, and still later, about once out of three or four times. Or, instead of rewarding the child each time he puts in a puzzle piece, we could reward him for putting in two, three, or four pieces, or for finishing two, three, or four puzzles. Or maybe, instead of rewarding him for every piece he puts in, we could reward him after he has been working for 1 minute, and for 2, 3, 5, and 10 minutes.

Notice that in these *Intermittent Schedules,* we can reward the child *after he does the behavior a number of times* (two, three, four eye contacts) or *after he has done the behavior for an interval or length of time* (2, 3, 5 minutes working at puzzles). So we have *number schedules* and *interval schedules.* Which kind of schedule is a gambler rewarded on when he is playing a slot machine? If you think it is a *number* schedule, you are right. The gambler is rewarded after playing the slot machine, a *number* of times. On the other hand, our work on the job is usually rewarded on an *interval* schedule. We get our pay check (*General* Reward) after we have worked an interval of a week, 2 weeks, or a month.

Sometimes a target behavior is rewarded after the *same number* of times the behavior happens or after the *same interval* of time has gone by since the last reward. In other words, the *number* of times or the *interval* is *fixed.* Getting paid each time a month goes by is a *Fixed Interval Schedule.* The *interval* that must go by before a reward will be given is the *same (fixed)* each time. Can you think of another one of your behaviors that is rewarded on a *Fixed Interval Schelude?*

On the other hand, rewarding the child *every time* he has finished putting four pieces in a puzzle would be a *Fixed Number Schedule.* The *number of times* the behavior must happen for a reward to be given is always the *same*—four puzzle pieces put in. Can you think of a behavior of yours that is rewarded on a *Fixed Number Schedule?*

But a target behavior may not be rewarded after the *same (fixed)* number of times or the *same (fixed)* amount of time *(interval)* has gone by. Instead, the *number* of times the behavior must happen or the length of the *interval* that must go by can *change after each reward is given.* When the *number of times* the behavior must happen changes after each reward, we say that it is on a *Changing Number Schedule.* The gambler playing a slot machine is on a *Changing Number Schedule.* The *number of times* he must work the machine (put in his money and pull the handle) *changes* every time he is rewarded. He never knows how many pulls it will take to be rewarded the next time.

On the other hand, when the *length of time (interval)* between rewards changes after each reward, we say that this is a *Changing Interval Schedule.* If, during the same teaching session, the teacher rewards the child for working after 2 minutes, then 10 minutes, then 3 minutes, then 5 minutes, . . . , the child is being rewarded on a *Changing Interval Schedule.*

LET'S SUMMARIZE

1. *Continuous Schedule:* Reward is given every time target behavior happens (reward after each eye contact).
2. *Fixed Number Schedule:* Reward is given each and every time the target behavior happens a certain (*fixed*) number of times (child is rewarded each time he finishes two puzzles). A *Continuous Schedule* is really a *Fixed Number Schedule,* isn't it? The number of times the behavior must happen is fixed at one.
3. *Fixed Interval Schedule:* Reward is given the first time the target behavior happens after the end of an interval of time, and the *length* of the interval is always the *same* (a pay check every month).
4. *Changing Number Schedule:* Reward is given after the target behavior happens a number of times, but just how many times *changes* after each reward (gambler on a slot machine does not know just how many times he has to work the machine before it pays off).
5. *Changing Interval Schedule:* Reward is given the first time the target behavior happens after the end of an interval of time, but the length of the interval *changes* after every reward (child is rewarded after

doing his lessons a certain number of minutes, but the number of minutes changes after each reward).

As we said before, it is hard to keep all of these schedules in mind until you use them. So, in the spaces below, think of an example of each one from everyday life. In other words, write down a behavior that is rewarded on each of the schedules, and state what the reward is.

1. Continuous Schedule:

2. Fixed Number Schedule:

3. Fixed Interval Schedule:

4. Changing Number Schedule:

5. Changing Interval Schedule:

FINE. Now go on to the next section.

You know that once a target behavior has increased enough it is time to move away from a *Continuous Schedule* and toward an *Intermittent Schedule*. But which one? Later chapters will tell you all you need to know in order to decide, but here are two tips.

1. If a *Fixed Schedule* is used, the child (or anyone) will soon learn just *how many times* (*Fixed Number*) or *how long* (*Fixed Interval*) the behavior must happen before the reward. As a result he will *pause* or take a break after the reward. In fact, the higher the number of times or the longer the fixed interval, the longer the pause will be. So with a *Fixed Schedule* the behavior is not very smooth. It slows down and speeds up again after each reward. How do you feel and how much do you work on Monday? The end of the *Fixed Interval* and the reward (the weekend) are very far away.

2. But *Changing Schedules* do not let a person know when the target behavior has been done enough times (*Changing Number*) or for long enough (*Changing Interval*). So there is not so much of a *pause* after the reward, because the reward can come at any time. Behavior in *Changing Schedules* is much smoother.

With these two tips in mind, when you move away from a *Continuous Schedule*, it is a good idea to move toward one of the *Changing Schedules*. This keeps the child on his toes and his behavior going strong. Since the number of times or the interval of time is not fixed, he cannot tell just when he will be rewarded. The number of times the behavior must happen or the interval between rewards keeps changing. As a result, he is more likely to learn and work at a steadier pace. Again, for many behaviors you should

MOVE TOWARD CHANGING SCHEDULES,

in which the behavior is rewarded fairly often (to keep it going strong), but always after a different *number* of times or a different *interval* of time.

WHEN IS THE RIGHT TIME TO MOVE TO AN INTERMITTENT SCHEDULE?

At the end of Chapter 1, we talked about teaching you how to keep track of (*measure*) the child's behavior during a teaching program. We will do that in Chapter 5. But, for now, we can say that the *chart* you make of the behavior you are measuring will tell you when it is time to move to an

*Intermittent Schedule. When the chart shows that the target behavior has
increased and is leveling off, it is time to slowly reward the behavior less
and less often.*

The CHART in Figure 3-1 shows how a child's *eye contact* increased
each day during teaching sessions that were 20 minutes long. Food was
used as a reward.

Do you see that the behavior has its ups and downs each session, but
keeps increasing overall? Also notice that between sessions 13 and 17 the
number of times that eye contact happens each session is starting to level
off at around thirty. This is the time to begin to use an Intermittent Schedule to reward the behavior less and less often.

THE MOVE TO A MORE NATURAL (INTERMITTENT)SCHEDULE MUST BE MADE
SLOWLY

Although the idea is to get the child to the point where he is rewarded
about as much as anyone else for the same target behavior, you cannot cut
down on the rewards too fast. Move from a Continuous to an Intermittent
Schedule *very slowly.* If you make too big a jump by cutting out too many
rewards all at once, the target behavior will go way, way down. If your
chart of the number of times the behavior happens each session shows that
the behavior is starting to decrease when you start intermittent rewards,
you should *go back* to *more rewards* for a while and then start to give
fewer and fewer rewards again, but more slowly.

SUMMARY OF WHAT YOU HAVE LEARNED ABOUT NATURAL SCHEDULES

1.   Very few behaviors are rewarded on a *Continuous Schedule* in daily
     life. *Intermittent Schedules* are more natural.

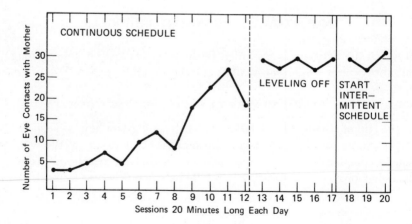

2. There are four main types of Intermittent Schedules: *Fixed Number* (behavior must happen the same number of times each time for a reward); *Fixed Interval* (behavior is rewarded after a certain amount of time has passed since the last reward, and the amount of time is always the same); *Changing Number* (number of times behavior must happen for a reward to be given changes after each reward); *Changing Interval* (behavior is rewarded after a certain amount of time has passed since the last reward, and the amount of time that must pass changes after each reward).
3. When the target behavior has increased and started to level off (as shown by your *chart* of the behavior), it is time to move to one of the Intermittent Schedules.
4. Often, the best Intermittent Schedules to move toward are the *Changing Number* and *Changing Interval* schedules. They keep the child on his toes and his working and learning pace high and steady.
5. When you move away from a Continuous Schedule, do it *slowly*, that is, cut down on the rewards a little at a time. If the behavior decreases when you do this, go back to rewarding the behavior more often and then start to cut down on the rewards again, but more slowly.

Using More Natural Rewards

Another way to keep behavior going in a more natural way is to use *natural rewards*. The rule to follow is this: *Move from Primary Rewards (Food) to Social Rewards (praise) to Activity Rewards (anything the child likes to do)*. In other words, when your *chart* shows that the child's behavior has increased and has started to level off, you should use *Social Rewards* like praise and hugs more and more instead of food. Instead of a bite of food every time for eye contact, give the child a big smile, a hug, or a few seconds of roughhousing. And only once in a while use food if it is still needed.

But you always want to get the child off food and onto Social and Activity Rewards. *So, use Activity Rewards as much as possible. Have the child use his new behavior to get to do things he likes.* For example, once eye contact has increased, have the child make eye contact *before* you let him open the refrigerator, or before you play with him, or before he can go outside, or before you let him take a bath. Or, if you have increased the number of times the child makes sounds during the day, *slowly* use food less and less, and instead reward his sounds with natural Activity Rewards. For example, have him make a sound before you open the door for him, or before you hand him his toy, or before he can have some more ice cream.

The idea is to *require the child to use his new behaviors to get to do the things he likes to do*. Getting to do the Activity Rewards will "naturally" reward his behavior.

Grandma's Law is a good example of using natural Activity Rewards. When you tell the child, "As soon as you put on your coat, you can go outside," you are having him do a new behavior (dressing himself) to get to do a rewarding activity (playing outside). This is a much more natural way to reward him for learning to put on his coat than giving him a bite of food.

Using Natural Chains

Behaviors do not usually happen all by themselves. *Behaviors are usually hooked up or chained to other behaviors*. We talked about *chains* before and the large number there are during the day. For instance, after you *get out* of bed, you *wash* yourself, then you get *dressed,* and then you *eat* breakfast. Or, when you are cleaning the house, you might *wipe* the table, then *wash* the dishes, *dust* the furniture, and then *read* a book. Or you might *peel* the onions, then *cut* the potatoes, then *put* the roast in the oven, and then hear your spouse say, "Great supper!"

Do you see how all of these behaviors, like washing yourself and peeling onions, are *hooked up* to other behaviors in a *chain?* And what is at the *end* of each of these chains? Some kind of *reward*—a *Primary* Reward (breakfast), an *Activity* Reward (reading), or a *Social* Reward (praise). *The reward at the end of the chain keeps you doing the whole chain day after day.* And when you are doing a certain chain, each behavior in the chain gets you closer and closer to the reward at the end. In fact, *each behavior in the chain is rewarded by the next behavior in the chain, because the next one is a little closer to the reward.* It is much more rewarding to walk into the kitchen before breakfast than it is to get out of bed, because walking into the kichen is *closer* to the reward at the end of the chain—eating breakfast.

So you can see that by hooking up your child's new behaviors in chains, so that the chains end in some reward, these behaviors will be kept going in a natural way.

Using chains is a little like using Grandma's Law. Grandma's Law hooks up two behaviors: the child puts on his coat and then goes outside. You can set up even longer chains in the same way. *Have the child do one behavior before he can do another one. And he must do both of them before he is rewarded.*

For example, the child may already have good eye contact and make sounds. Then, instead of rewarding *each* of these behaviors, hook them up so that he has to make eye contact and then make a sound *before* he is rewarded. Or, if he enjoys going outside (*Activity Reward*), have him (1) wash his face and then (2) dress himself before he can (3) go outside. Or, during a teaching session, make sure that he is (1) looking at you before you (2) let him work a puzzle that he will be (3) rewarded for finishing.

In setting up a chain, remember that *the child should already be able to do the behaviors in the chain.* For example, if you want to hook up eye contact and making sounds, you should have already increased both of these. Also, remember that *the chain should end in some kind of reward —strong rewards at first,* and later *Social and Activity Rewards.*

Now that you know which rewards to use and when to use them, it is time to talk about how to *find* rewards.

9. FINDING REWARDS IN THE HOME AND SCHOOL

By now, you know that food is probably a strong reward for any child. Maybe attention is also a reward. *The more rewards you have, the more you can change a child's behavior.* For this reason it is impotrant to *find* things that are rewarding to the child so that you can *use* them.

What Turns the Child On?

One way to find out what is rewarding to a child is to watch what he does when he gets certain things. What does he do when you praise him by telling him what a good boy he is? Does he smile, wiggle with pleasure, or come over to you? *If he does, praise is probably a reward for him.* What does he do when you yell at him or tell him to stop some behavior? Does he grin or go back to what he was doing? If he does, being yelled at or told to stop is probably a reward, and it would be a good idea not to give him those rewards for "bad" behaviors.

Reward Menu

Another way to find out what a child is rewarded by is to tell him about or show him pictures of many things, for instance, foods, children playing outside, people riding in a car, or a child in the bathtub. This is called a "reward menu" (Addison and Homme, 1966). By teaching the child to *point* to the pictures on the menu, you can find out what will be rewarding to him at the moment, and you can then reward good behaviors with the things he picked on the menu. For example, you can show him the reward menu—pictures of many things he might enjoy—and tell him that "as soon as" he does some behavior (perhaps a chore) he can have what he pointed to.

Grandma's Law

We talked about Grandma's Law before. With Grandma in mind you can find many *Activity Rewards* for your child. Watch what he does during the day. You may see that he eats more than he washes his hands, wanders around more than he plays, spins objects more than he works puzzles, watches television more than he follows directions, or knocks things over more than he does chores. In fact, if you take *any* two of his behaviors, you will find that he always does one of them more than the other. *Of any two behaviors, one is a high behavior and one is a low behavior, and you can use the high behavior as an Activity Reward for doing the low behavior.*

So the message is to watch the child and note which behaviors he does more than the others. Those he does more (*high behaviors*) can be used as *Activity Rewards* for *low behaviors*, by setting up Grandma's Law.

SUPER JOB! GO HAVE A PIZZA AND A FUDGE SUNDAE.

To help firm up the ideas you learned in Sections 6 through 9, answer the questions on the next few pages as you did before. Reread the sections or talk with other people if you want to, but the final answers should be your own. When you have finished, turn to Appendix 1 to see if your answers agree with ours. If some do not, *please* go back and reread the parts of Chapter 3 that will help you to answer the questions. Do not read any more until you have answered the questions correctly.

REVIEW QUESTIONS ON SECTIONS 6 THROUGH 9:

Rewards

1. What is the general rule about rewards and reward schedules to use at the *start* of a child's first teaching program and at the start of later teaching programs for hard behaviors?
   a. Use a_____reward. (Fill in the blank.)
   b. Reward the target behavior_____ it happens. (Fill in the blank.)
2. One way to make a reward *stronger* is_____
   _____.(Fill in the blank.)
3. In a *Continuous Schedule* the target behavior is rewarded (once in a while; every time it happens). (Underline one.)
4. You must move away from Primary Rewards and a Continuous Schedule and toward more *Natural rewards* and *Intermittent Schedules*. Give three reasons why. (Write short answers in the space provided.)

   a.

   b.

   c.

5. An *Intermittent Schedule* is one in which the target behavior is rewarded (every time it happens; once in a while). (Underline one.)
6. There are four main kinds of *Intermittent Schedules*. (Fill in the blanks or underline.)
   a. In a *Number Schedule,* the behavior is rewarded after it happens a certain number of_____ .
   b. In an *Interval Schedule,* the behavior is rewarded after a certain amount of _____ has gone by since the last reward.
   c. In a *Fixed* Schedule, the number of times the behavior must happen or the amount of time that must go by before the reward is given (changes after each reward; stays the same after each reward).
   d. In a *Changing Schedule,* the number of times the behavior must happen or the amount of time that must go by before the reward

is given (changes after each reward; stays the same after each reward).

7. If a schedule is *fixed*, the person (cannot figure out; can figure out) when the behavior has been done enough times or for a long enough time to be rewarded. (Underline one.)

8. In a *Fixed* Schedule, the behavior (is steady; goes down after the reward and then up again as the reward gets closer). (Underline one.)

9. In a *Changing* Schedule, the person (cannot figure out; can figure out) when the behavior has been done enough times or for long enough to be rewarded. (Underline one.)

10. In a *Changing* Schedule, the behavior (is steady; goes down after the reward and then up again as the reward gets closer). (Underline one.)

11. It is better to move toward (Changing; Fixed) Schedules. (Underline one.)

12. The right time to move away from *Continuous Schedules* and toward more natural, *Intermittent* Schedules is when the behavior (is increasing; has leveled off; is decreasing). (Underline one.)

13. When you move to an *Intermittent* Schedule, you should cut out rewards (slowly; as fast as you can). (Underline one.)

14. A *natural* reward for asking for an apple would be (getting a piece of candy; getting an apple; getting praise for saying "'Apple'" so well). (Underline one.)

15. To *naturally* reward a child for making eye contact with her, a teacher would (give the child praise and an M & M for making eye contact; use his eye contact as a signal to go over to him or talk to him). (Underline one.)

16. Grandma's Law is a way to use_____ rewards. (Fill in the blank.)

17. In a *chain* of behaviors, each behavior in the chain gets a person _____ to the reward at the end. (Fill in the blank.)

18. In what order would you have the child do the three behaviors (chain them) in each column below? Put 1, 2, and 3 next to the behaviors that should come first, second, and third in each column.

Child asks for ice cream cone.	Child is given a token.
Child gets ice cream cone.	Child sits and watches teacher.
	Child answers question.
Child makes contact with mother.	

19. By watching what a child does the most during the day, watching how he reacts to praise and other things, and telling him about or showing him pictures of things, you can find out _____

(Fill in the blank.)

Please check your answers in Appendix 1. When you have done so, reread any parts of Chapter 3 that you need to correct your answers. Then go on to the last assignment for this chapter. Since it is a very important one that will help you to plan a child's educational program, take a break before you start it.

ASSIGNMENT: FINDING AND USING REWARDS

As you know, rewards are the most important part of any teaching program. This assignment will help you begin to set up teaching programs for a child by asking you to pick some of the rewards to use. There are two parts to the assignment.

Part One: Reward List.   The assignment at the end of Chapter 1 asked you to pick one child and make a list of his or her behaviors. Using the same child, make a list of the things which are *rewards* for the child *now*. Be *specific*. For example, do not list "food" under Primary Rewards, but list the *kinds* of foods which the child likes, such as vanilla ice cream, peanuts, grape soda pop, or french fries. The same goes for Social Rewards. Writing down "praise" does not tell you very much (What is "praise?") Remember that behavior is *movement*, such as hugging, smiling, or saying, "Hey, terrific job!" What movements of people are Social Rewards for the child? What does someone have to *do* to really "light him up?" For Activity Rewards, "playing" would not be specific enough. But "working with puzzles," "splashing water in the bathroom sink," or "going for a ride" would be. Finally, list anything that is a General Reward for the child. Has he ever earned a penny to put in a gumball machine? Has he ever worked for points, tokens, or check marks?

BE SURE THAT THESE ARE REALLY REWARDS!!

Before you call anything a reward, ask yourself these three questions:

1. Does it *follow* a behavior? Is it a *consequence*?
2. Does it *increase* or *keep* a behavior *going*? (This is a "must." If a certain consequence does *not* increase a behavior or keep it going, it

is not a reward. If you are not sure whether a certain consequence increases a behavior or keeps it going, you are only *guessing* that the consequence is a reward. Number 3 below will help you to at least make a *good* guess.)

3. Does the child *smile,* grin, or laugh when he gets a certain consequence? (This is a good sign that it is a reward.)

Now fill out the Reward List (Table 3-1) on the next page.

Later in the child's education, add any *new* rewards to this list. Also, *make blank copies* of this table so that you can fill it out for other children. Now please go on to Part Two of this assignment.

Part Two: What Rewards Have Behaviors Been Getting?   In Chapter 2, we looked at the behaviors of many children and talked about the rewards those behaviors were getting. We want you now to do the same thing for the child you have picked. For your assignment in Chapter 1, you made a list of behaviors that needed to be changed and behaviors that did not need to be changed. Take those same behaviors and write down what rewards, *if any,* they have been getting. If you are a teacher and have not known or seen the child for very long, ask his parents or other people who have taught him. Better yet, observe the child now when he is with his parents and teachers. If you are a parent, spend time (a day or more) observing the child to see just what rewards his behaviors are getting.

On the left-hand side of the page, write down the same behaviors you listed at the end of Chapter 1. Next to each behavior, write down the *specific* rewards it has been getting. There may be more than one reward. Again, ask yourself the three questions to decide whether a certain thing (*consequence*) is a reward for a behavior:

1. Does it *follow* the behavior?
2. Does it *increase* the behavior or *keep* it *going?*
3. Does the child *smile,* grin, or laugh when he gets the consequence?

You will find that things you would not think are rewards really are rewards for the behavior, because, over time, they have increased the behavior or have kept it going. For example, a behavior such as messing up kitchen cabinets may have been followed by people going after the child and telling him, "Get out of there this instant!" If the child still does this behavior, yelling at him may be a reward. Remember that a behavior can also be rewarded if it gets the child out of having to do something. For example, if the child throws a tantrum or whines and the *consequence* is that he does not have to do what he was asked, his tantrum or whining was rewarded. Finally, if a certain behavior (for instance, eye contact) has *not* been getting rewarded (perhaps because it has not been noticed), write down that it is *not rewarded.*

Table 3-1. Reward List

Primary Rewards

Social Rewards

General Rewards

Activity Rewards

Rewards That Behaviors Have Been Getting

Behaviors That Need *to be Changed* (from Chapter 1)	*Rewards These Behaviors Have* *Been Getting*
1.	1.
2.	2.
3.	3.
4.	4.
5.	5.
6.	6.
7.	7.
8.	8.
9.	9.
10.	10.

Behaviors That Do Not Need *to Be Changed* (from Chapter 1)	*Rewards These Behaviors Have* *Been Getting*
1.	1.
2.	2.
3.	3.
4.	4.
5.	5.

When you have finished this assignment, go on to the next page.

What You Should Have Learned from This Assignment.   The point of this assignment was not only to give you lists of possible rewards to use in later teaching programs, but also to help you see how certain behaviors have been rewarded over the years and how others have not. Look back at your list and ask yourself the following questions:

1. *Have any of the behaviors that needed to be decreased ("bad" behaviors) been getting rewarded?* Is it possible that over the months or

years the very behaviors that no one can stand have been rewarded by *attention* (going after the child, telling him to stop, picking him up and carrying him away), by *giving him what he wanted* (handing him the cookie to shut him up, letting him stay up a little longer to stop his whining), or by *letting him get out of doing things* he does not "want" to do (letting him get out of doing chores or lessons because no one can put up with his whining, fussing, or lack of attention)?

If your answer is, "Yes, I guess I (we, people) have been rewarding these behaviors," you are human! Who can stand tantrums and whining day after day without finally giving in or giving up! But now you know that there are other ways of handling behaviors you cannot stand. You can teach the child other, *better ways* to get things he wants; you can *ignore* disruptive behaviors (hard as it seems now!) and you can decrease problem behaviors in many other ways. Chapter 15, "Replacing Problem Behaviors," tells you how to set up programs for doing just that.

2. *Have the behaviors that needed to be increased been getting rewarded?* Have the behaviors the child needs the most work on—the weakest behaviors that are important for him but that hardly ever happen—been getting rewarded? Have they been getting rewarded with *strong* rewards and on a *Continuous* Schedule? If so, great! If not, you now know that *they should be. The weaker a behavior is, the stronger the reward should be and the more often the behavior should be rewarded.*

So, when you start teaching programs for those *weak* behaviors, you are going to have to start using strong rewards (check your reward list in Part One of this assignment) and a Continuous Schedule.

3. *Have the behaviors that the child is doing well and that do not need to be changed been getting rewarded?* Most behaviors cannot be taken for granted. They will keep happening (stay strong) only if the person gets some kind of reward—only if they lead to some kind of pleasant consequence (for example, praise or an enjoyable activity)—at least once in a while (*Intermittent Schedule*). Remember: behaviors that are ignored or no longer rewarded will decrease. Are there any behaviors that have been taken for granted (not rewarded) because the child did them well enough or often enough? If so, again you are human. With so many "bad" behaviors to keep you jumping and so many weak behaviors to increase, how could you keep on the lookout to reward the behaviors that did not need so much help?

Well, now you know that keeping a behavior going does not take a great effort. You can use an *Intermittent Schedule* (to keep the behavior going strong by rewarding it once in a while); you can use *Grandma's Law;* and you can *chain* the behavior to other behaviors, so that the reward at the end of the chain will keep the behavior strong.

DO YOU FEEL AS IF YOU NEED TO BE REWARDED ABOUT NOW?
YOU SHOULD! SO DO SOMETHING NICE FOR YOURSELF. In
the next chapter, we will be setting up the basis for a whole educational
program.

REFERENCES AND EXTRA READINGS

Addison, R. M., and Homme, L. E. "The reinforcing event (RE) menu." *National Society for Programmed Instruction Journal*, 1966, **5**, 8-9.

Baer, D. M., and Wolf, M. M. "The entry into natural communities of reinforcement." Paper presented at the annual meeting of the American Psychological Association, Washington, D.C., 1967.

Ferster, C. B., and Skinner, B. F. *Schedules of Reinforcement.* New York: Appleton-Century-Crofts, 1957.

Ferster, C. B. "Behavior therapy with children." *Psychological Record*, 1966, **16**, 65-71.

Ferster, C. B. "Arbitrary and natural reinforcement." *Psychological Review*, 1967, **17**, 341-347.

Gallimore, R., Tharp, R. G., and Kemp, B. "Positive reinforcing function of 'negative attention.'" *Journal of Experimental Child Psychology*, 1969, **8**, 140-146.

Homme, L. E., DeBaca, P., Devine, J. V., Steinhorst, R., and Rickert, E. J. "Use of the Premack principle in controlling the behavior of nursery school children." *Journal of the Experimental Analysis of Behavior*, 1963, **6**, 544.

Homme, L. "A behavior technology exists—here and now." Paper presented at the Aerospace Education Foundation's "Education for the 1970's" Seminar, Washington, D.C., 1967.

Homme, L., Csanyi, A. P., Gonzales, M. A., and Reches, J. R. *How to Use Contingency Contracting in the Classroom.* Champaign, Ill.: Research Press, 1969.

Honig, Werner (Ed.). *Operant Behavior: Areas of Research and Application.* New York: Appleton-Century-Crofts, 1966.

Hudson, E., and DeMyer, M. K. "Food as a reinforcer in educational therapy of autistic children." *Behavior Research and Therapy*, 1968, **6**, 37-43.

Lovaas, O. I., Freitag, G., Kinder, M. I., Rubenstein, D. B., Schaffer, B., and Simmons, J. Q. "Establishment of social reinforcers in two schizophrenic children on the basis of food." *Journal of Experimental Child Psychology*, 1966, **4**, 109-125.

Osborne, J. G. "Free-time as a reinforcer in the management of classroom behavior." *Journal of Applied Behavior Analysis*, 1969, **2**, 113-118.

Patterson, G. R. "Responsiveness to social stimuli." In L. Krasner and L. P. Ullmann (Eds.), *Research in Behavior Modification.* New York: Holt, Rinehart and Winston, 1965. Pp. 157-178.

Premack, D. "Reinforcement theory." In D. Levine (Ed.), *Nebraska Symposium on Motivation: 1965.* Lincoln, Neb.: University of Nebraska Press, 1965. Pp. 123-180.

Schoenfeld, W. N. (Ed.). *The Theory of Reinforcement Schedules.* New York: Appleton-Century-Crofts, 1970.

Skinner, B. F. *Science and Human Behavior.* New York: Free Press, 1953.

Smock, C. D., and Holt, B. G. "Children's reactions to novelty: An experimental study of 'curiosity motivation.'" *Child Development,* 1962, 33, 631-642.

CHAPTER FOUR

Planning
an EDUCATIONAL
PROGRAM

The first three chapters gave you some important ideas. Chapter 1 talked about behavior and the ways it can change. Chapter 2 talked about how behaviors are learned. And Chapter 3 was about rewards, reward schedules, and the ways in which rewards increase behaviors. This chapter and the next four will help you to (1) plan an educational program; (2) pick behaviors to work on; (3) plan and run teaching programs; and (4) keep track of the child's progress.

1. WHAT IS AN EDUCATIONAL PROGRAM?

Parents and teachers of children with behavior and learning problems do not usually ask, "What do these children need to learn?" They have been working hard for years to teach the children to talk, play, take care of themselves, cooperate, and take part in classroom and family events. Instead, parents and teachers usually ask, "Where is the best place to *start* with these children? What is the first *behavior* to work on?" and "What is the best *way* to teach our children the skills they need to learn?" It does not take a world-famous child psychiatrist to tell you that a child does not talk, cooperate, or sit still long enough to learn during a lesson. You have *seen* behaviors he needs help with.

Most people want to jump in and start teaching once they have found a new way to see behavior and some useful methods for changing it. This is great! But slow down. Before we jump in, let us make sure we have a plan in mind (and on paper) of just *which* behaviors we are going to help the children learn. It is true that we can see *many* behaviors that need changing, but have we seen them *all*? And what is the line-up? Which behaviors should be changed first? Which second? And which third? We must not pick behaviors to change in a helter-skelter way. That will only make it harder for the children to learn anything. So, before we start teaching the children, we will plan an *educational program*.

Please turn back to Chapter 1 and read Sections 10 and 11 again. They cover only a few pages.

First, let us get our words straight. When we talk about a child's "educational program," we mean the whole list of *target behaviors* to change and the *order* in which we plan to change them. A "teaching program," on the other hand, is the *way* we teach (change) and measure a certain target behavior we have *pinpointed*. In other words, an *educational program* has many *teaching programs* in it. And the *teaching programs* follow one another is some *order* or *sequence*.

To plan an *educational program,* we have two jobs: (1) to carefully pick (*pinpoint*) *target behaviors* to change in *teaching programs*; and (2) to decide on the proper order or *sequence* for working on the target behaviors. Let us handle the two jobs one at a time. First, which target behaviors should you work on in a child's educational program?

2.   HOW DO I FIND OUT WHICH BEHAVIORS A CHILD NEEDS HELP WITH?

Sections 10 and 11 of Chapter 1 had two important ideas to help pinpoint target behaviors for a child's educational program. Those ideas were (1) children learn most skills in *small steps,* from easy to hard; and (2) before a child can start in a skill area, he must first learn *basic behaviors* from other skill areas. For example, *verbal imitation* is a skill that children learn in small steps. First they learn how to imitate (repeat) simple sounds, then harder syllables, then words, phrases, and sentences. So a child masters Verbal Imitation skills in small steps, starting with easy behaviors (imitating sounds) and working up to hard behaviors (imitating sentences).

But before a child begins to learn Verbal Imitation—before he learns to imitate even simple sounds or words well—he has to learn *basic behaviors* in *other skill areas*. For example, he must make *eye contact, look at* people's mouths, *listen* to what they say, and know how to shape his

mouth into different *mouth positions*. Unless he has already learned these
basic behaviors from other skill areas, you could work on Verbal Imitation
for months with no results.

What Are "Skill Areas?"

This brings us to *skill areas*. A *skill area* is a group of behaviors with
similar movements. And the behaviors are listed in *small steps*, starting
with easy ones and going to hard ones. For example, the skill area called
"Looking, Listening, and Moving" is about Large and Small Motor activities. It starts with a simple behavior (bending and standing up), moves to
a harder behavior (pedaling a tricycle), and goes on to still harder behaviors (pointing to objects by name or cooperating on a task with others).
  Here is why skill areas are important. Children with behavior and learning problems may need help with many, many behaviors. By grouping
similar behaviors into skill areas, and by lining them up from simple to
hard, it is easier to teach children in the "normal" way that people learn—
in *small steps*.

What Are the Different Skill Areas?

The many behaviors children may need help with (behaviors they need to
do with more skill, more often, or at the right time and place) are grouped
into six skill areas. There is also one area that lists problem behaviors that
may need to be replaced and decreased. Here is what the skill areas are
about.

A.   LEARNING READINESS SKILLS

This is the most basic skill area. Some of the *target behaviors* in this area
are *basic behaviors* that a child needs before he can go on to *any* other
skill area. Examples of basic behaviors in this skill area are making eye
contact, cooperating with simple requests, and sitting down to work at a
task. A child must learn them before he will be *ready* to learn *anything*
else. How could you teach a child to imitate hard words (Verbal Imitation
skills) if he did not even look at you, cooperate, or sit down? So, for some
children, target behaviors in this skill area will be the *first* ones in their
educational programs.

B.   LOOKING, LISTENING, AND MOVING SKILLS

There are many movements and activities in this skill area. They are
important in two ways. First, a child can spend his time *playing* at Large

and Small Motor activities, for example, working puzzles, stacking blocks, and riding a tricycle. By giving him *more skill* at these activities, and by *increasing* the amount of time he spends at them, you can help *replace* problem behaviors (such as "getting into things" or wandering around).

Second, Large and Small Motor activities are *basic behaviors* for most of the other skill areas. Unless a child is skilled at moving his body, using his hands and fingers, and looking at what he is doing, he will not learn to *imitate* movements of other people (Motor Imitation skills) and he will not learn Chores and Self-Help skills very well. So, when a child has mastered basic behaviors in the Learning Readiness skills area, the *next* target behaviors in his educational program can be chosen from the Looking, Listening, and Moving skills area.

C.   MOTOR IMITATION

How do children learn the thousands of behaviors they can do? Nobody sits down and teaches them each and every behavior. The answer is that children learn most behaviors by *watching* and *repeating (imitating)*. They learn how to set the table, wash their hands, and put on their coats by *watching* other people do these behaviors. Of course, they get a little coaching along the way. And they learn to talk by *watching* and *listening* to other people talk.

It is just plain impossible to teach a child every behavior he needs to learn, one by one. It would take more than a lifetime. A shortcut is needed. A child must learn some skill that will help him to learn other behaviors and skills faster and more on his own. *Motor imitation is that shortcut.* After you teach a child to imitate your movements, he will be able to learn hard motor activities by watching and repeating.

Motor Imitation is also a *basic behavior* for some of the harder skill areas, for example, Verbal Imitation and Functional Speech. So, for some children, the Motor Imitation area will come after they work on Looking Listening, and Moving and before they work on Verbal Imitation and Functional Speech. Motor Imitation skills will also help the child to learn Chores and Self-Help skills.

D.   VERBAL IMITATION SKILLS

Learning to imitate the way people move their hands, arms, and legs (Motor Imitation) also helps a child learn to imitate the way people talk—move their lips, tongue, jaw, and vocal cords (Verbal Imitation). Just as you cannot each a child every kind of movement or task by hand, one by one, so you cannot teach him all the different sounds, syllables, words, and phrases by hand, one by one. He needs a shortcut. Verbal Imitation is the shortcut for learning *how* to talk.

So, if a child does not know *how* to talk, you will be running teaching programs for target behaviors such as imitating sounds, syllables, words, and phrases. Once the child learns how to imitate some sounds, syllables, and words *(basic behaviors)*, he will be ready to work on Functional Speech.

E.   FUNCTIONAL SPEECH SKILLS

Learning *how* to talk is only one side of speech. Learning what words, phrases, and sentences *mean* and *when* to *use* them to communicate with people is the other side.

There are many, many kinds of Functional Speech, for example, asking for, naming, describing, and identifying things, answering questions, understanding and using pronouns ("I," "you," "me," "he"), prepositions ("on," "in," "under"), opposites ("hot" "cold"), colors, shapes, and sizes. Each is a target behavior in the Functional Speech area.

F.   CHORES AND SELF-HELP SKILLS

Chores and Self-Help skills give the child a way to spend his time and take part in family and classroom life. They give him new motor skills and a feeling of success. Target behaviors in this skill area are different kinds of Chores and Self-Help tasks for the child to learn, from easy to hard.

But, to learn Chores and Self-Help tasks, the child must already have some skill at using his body. Hence a good time to work on Chores and Self-Help skills in the child's educational program is after you have worked on basic behaviors in the Learning Readiness and Looking, Listening, and Moving areas.

G.   PROBLEM BEHAVIORS

Of course, this is not really a "skill" area. You do not want to teach the child to do problem behaviors better or more often. Instead, this area lists many kinds of problem behaviors to replace and decrease, for instance, yelling, tantrums, spinning objects, and getting into things.

This area is last for a very good reason. We want you to think about "good" behaviors to teach rather than "bad" behaviors to decrease.

Here is what you have learned so far about *skill areas:*

1.   Many behaviors children may need help with are grouped into skill areas.
2.   Behaviors in each skill area have *similar movements.*
3.   Behaviors in each skill area are listed from *easy to hard,* so that a child learns behaviors in a skill area step by step (the "normal" way).

4. Some behaviors in each skill area are called *basic behaviors*. Before a child can start in a harder skill area, he must learn basic behaviors in easier skill areas.
5. Behaviors that a child needs help with in each skill area will be *target behaviors* in *teaching programs*.

TAKE A SHORT BREAK IF YOU NEED ONE.

Now let us talk about how to *find out* which behaviors a child needs help with, so that you can *PINPOINT* them as *target behaviors* for *teaching programs*.

The Behavior Evaluation Scale (BES)

The Behavior Evaluation Scale (BES) makes pinpointing target behaviors very easy. The Behavior Evaluation Scale is given in Appendix 2, and here is what it does. It lists many behaviors (about ninety) that a child with learning and behavior problems may need help with and groups these behaviors into the skill areas we just talked about. By answering questions about each behavior in the BES, you find out (1) *which behaviors* the child needs help with; and (2) *what kind* of help he needs (more skill, more often, right time and place, or less often).

Filling out the BES is the first step in planning a child's educational program. And you will be using the BES each time you pinpoint the *next* target behavior or skill area to work on.

Behavior Evaluation Table (BET)

The BES is too long to keep thumbing through every time you want to pinpoint the next behavior to change. And you surely cannot remember all the items. You need to see at a glance which behaviors the child needs help with; you need something that sums up the BES. The Behavior Evaluation Table (BET) in Appendix 3 does just that. The BET is a list of all the behaviors in the BES, grouped into the same skill areas. After you *circle* all the behavior items in the BES that the child needs help with, circle the same ones on the BET.

Take a few minutes now to read the first few pages of the "Introduction" to the BES (Appendix 2), and skim through it to get a feel for the skill areas, the behaviors in them, and the questions that are asked.

As stated above, the BET is in Appendix 3. You should *make a copy* of it for each child you will be working with. At the end of this chapter is a copy of the BET already filled out for a child. Look at it now. Note that the BET has the same items as the BES, but lets you see at a glance all the skill areas and the behaviors in them that the child needs help with.

Notice that some items in the BES and BET have asterisks (**) in front of them and are written in CAPITAL LETTERS. These are the *basic* (most important) *behaviors* in the skill area. Of course, you can work on *all* of the behaviors in a skill area, but those in CAPITAL LETTERS are the ones to shoot for; they are your goals.

How Much Can One Person Do?

About now, you may be asking yourself that question. All the new words we are using and all the things we are saying that you will be doing may make you feel like quitting while you are ahead. *But don't!* You will see (as other parents and teachers have seen) that planning a child's education with the BES and BET is really no harder than filling out a laundry slip or following a recipe in a cookbook. You just need some practice.

PAT YOURSELF ON THE BACK OR HAVE SOMEONE ELSE DO IT FOR YOU. THEN DRINK ANOTHER CUP OF COFFEE.

3. IN WHAT SEQUENCE (ORDER) SHOULD THE TARGET BEHAVIORS BE TAUGHT?

One job in planning an educational program is finding out which behaviors the child needs help with. They will be *target behaviors* in *teaching programs*. The BES and BET help you to pinpoint behaviors the child needs help with. Now let us deal with the second task—planning the best *sequence* to follow in teaching the target behaviors. Just as you must carefully pinpoint target behaviors, so you must carefully plan the order or sequence for teaching them.

You already have part of the answer to what the *sequence* should be like. We said that (1) it is best to follow the sequence by which children *"normally"* learn; (2) hard skills are often learned best in *small steps;* and (3) before a child can start learning in most skill areas, he must learn *basic behaviors* in other skill areas.

Tables 4–1 and 4–2 help to put these ideas together. Using the two tables, the BES, and the BET, you have just about all you need to plan a child's educational program. Let us first look at Table 4–1, the *skill sequence table.*

Skill Sequence Table (Table 4-1)

The Skill Sequence Table (Table 4–1) lays out all the skill areas in a sequence. Arrows show how to move from one skill area to another during a child's education. Please follow the arrows while we talk about the sequence.

The *skill sequence* starts with *basic behaviors* from the Learning Readiness skills area: Spontaneous Eye Contact (A1); Eye Contact on Request (A2); Cooperation with Simple Spoken Requests (A4); and Sitting Long Enough to Work at Some Task (A5). These are first in the skill sequence because a child needs to know them before he will learn much of anything else.

The other box at the top right is something that should be done at the start of an educational program—namely, to reward many "good" behaviors, no matter how simple they are, and to ignore problem behaviors as much as you (and everyone else) can. You will find that, if you work on behaviors in the first five boxes, children will also start smiling, coming to people, paying attention, and cooperating more and more.

Of course, many children do not have to start their educational programs with all four of the *basic* Learning Readiness skills. If a child's eye contact is already strong, or if he already sits long enough to work at tasks, you might start his educational program by working on Cooperation with Simple Spoken Requests (A4). In fact, if he has *already learned all four* of the *basic* Learning Readiness skills (A1, A2, A4, A5), you might start his educational program in the Looking, Listening, and Moving skills area or even in the Motor Imitation skills area. In other words, a child's educational program does not have to start with the four *basic behaviors* from the Learning Readiness skills area (A1, A2, A4, A5), *but he must learn them before he goes anywhere else.*

When the child has learned the four basic behaviors from the Learning Readiness skills area, or if he has already learned them, his educational

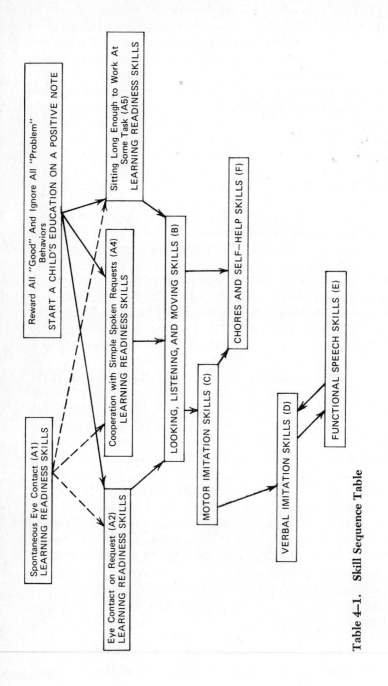

Table 4–1. Skill Sequence Table

program moves to the Looking, Listening, and Moving skills area. There he learns activities to use in playing, and he also learns other basic behaviors that will help him in harder skill areas in the sequence.

After the child has learned some Looking, Listening, and Moving skills, his education can move to the Motor Imitation area *and* to Chores and Self-Help skills. In the Motor Imitation area he learns how to move his body (arms, legs, lips, tongue) as others do. This will help him to learn harder Chores and Self-Help tasks *and* Verbal Imitation skills.

When the child has learned to imitate many movements, especially mouth movements and positions, he is ready to start on Verbal Imitation. If the child does not make many sounds on his own often, and does not use his sounds to get things he wants, work on these behaviors first. Then you can start teaching him to repeat or imitate sounds, words, or phrases after you. When he has learned to imitate some sounds and simple words, move to the Functional Speech area and teach him what his words *mean* and when to *use* them to talk to people. As he learns what words mean and when to use them, teach him *how* to say *new* sounds, words, and phrases by Verbal Imitation. In other words, when you are working on speech, you go back and forth between teaching the child *how* to say sounds, words, and phrases (Verbal Imitation) and teaching him what they *mean* and when to *use* them (Functional Speech).

WORK IN SEVERAL SKILL AREAS AT ONCE

Just because you start working on the next skill area in the child's educational sequence, this *does not* mean that you stop working on the earlier ones. You move to new and harder skill areas when the child has learned *basic behaviors* in the earlier skill areas. *But there are many behaviors in each skill area besides the basic behaviors.* For instance, when you start on Motor Imitation, *keep working* on Looking, Listening, and Moving skills, where the child can be learning *harder* activities.

AS YOU MOVE TO *NEW* SKILL AREAS IN THE CHILD'S EDUCATIONAL PROGRAM, *KEEP WORKING* IN EARLIER SKILL AREAS TOO, ON THE HARDER TARGET BEHAVIORS IN THOSE AREAS.

Work on different skill areas either at different times or, better, in the same session.

How Do You Know When the Child Is Ready for A Skill Area in the Sequence?

The Skill Sequence Table tells you where to go next, but not *when* the child is *ready* for a skill area. *Basic behaviors* are the key to finding out if the child is ready to work in a particular area of the skill sequence.

A child must learn *basic behaviors* in *easier* skill areas *before* he can learn very much in harder skill areas, because harder skills are *built on* easier behaviors. The Learning Readiness area is an example of this. A child must learn *basic behaviors* in this area (A1, A2, A4, and A5) *before* he can learn much in *any* harder area of the skill sequence. How could a child learn to imitate what you say (Verbal Imitation skills) if he did not look at you, sit still, or cooperate with simple requests? So *before you start in any skill area, and before you move on to the next skill area in the skill sequence, you must find out if the child is ready for that area.*

The way to find out if the child is ready is simple. The Table of Basic Behaviors (Table 4-2) shows you how. Remember that some items on the BES and BET have asterisks (**) in front of them and are written in CAPITAL LETTERS? These are the *basic behaviors*—the most important target behaviors—in each skill area. And *some of them are basic behaviors a child must learn before he can start in other skill areas.* Table 4-2 tells you *which basic behaviors* from the easier skill areas a child must learn before he can start in, or move to, a harder skill area. Please read Table 4-2 now, very, very carefully.

Table 4-2. Basic Behaviors Child Must Learn Before He Can Work in Each Skill Area[a]

A. Learning Readiness Skills
    This is the most basic area. The child must learn *Basic Behaviors* A1, A2, A4, and A5 before he can learn much of *Anything* else.

B. Looking, Listening, and Moving Skills
    Before he works on Looking, Listening, and Moving the child must learn:
    (A1)   Spontaneous Eye Contact
    (A2)   Eye Contact on Request
    (A4)   Cooperation with Simple Spoken Requests
    (A5)   Sitting Long Enough to be Rewarded for Working at a Task

---

C. Motor Imitation Skills
    Before he works on Motor Imitation, the child must learn:
    (A1)   Spontaneous Eye Contact
    (A2)   Eye Contact on Request
    (A4)   Cooperation with Simple Spoken Requests
    (B13)   Skill at Many Large Motor Activities

Table 4-2.   Basic Behaviors Child Must Learn Before He Can Work in Each Skill Area[a] **(continued)**

(B14)	Looks at Objects, Parts of the Body, Face, Mouth
(B21)	Skill at Many Small Motor Activities
(B22)	Good Work Habits, such as Sitting, Listening, and Working
(B24)	Uses Eye Contact to Get Natural Rewards

D.   Verbal Imitation Skills
Before he works on Verbal Imitation, the child must learn:

(A1)	Spontaneous Eye Contact
(A2)	Eye Contact on Request
(A4)	Cooperation with Simple Spoken Requests
(B14)	Looks at Objects, Parts of the Body, Face, Mouth
(B22)	Good Work Habits, such as Sitting, Listening, and Working
(B24)	Uses Eye Contact to Get Natural Rewards
(C4)	Imitates Mouth Movements and Positions
(C7)	Imitates Some Models Even If Not Rewarded

E.   Functional Speech Skills
Before he can work on Functional Speech, the child must learn:

(A1)	Spontaneous Eye Contact
(A2)	Eye Contact on Request
(A4)	Cooperation with Simple Spoken Requests
(B14)	Looks at Objects, Parts of the Body, Face, Mouth
(B22)	Good Work Habits, such as Sitting, Listening, and Working
(B23)	Points or Matches by Name
(B24)	Uses Eye Contact to Get Natural Rewards
(C4)	Imitates Mouth Movements and Positions
(C7)	Imitates Some Models Even If Not Rewarded
(D3)	Makes Many Different Sounds on His Own, Often
(D6)	Makes Eye Contact and a Sound at the Same Time to Get Things
(D7)	Imitates Basic Sounds
(D8)	Imitates Syllables
(D9)	Imitates Simple Words

F.   Chores and Self-Help Skills
Before he works on Chores and Self-Help skills, the child must learn:

(A1)	Spontaneous Eye Contact
(A2)	Eye Contact on Request
(A4)	Cooperation with Simple Spoken Requests
(B14)	Looks at Objects, Parts of the Body, Face, Mouth

G.   Problem Behaviors
Before you can decrease problem behaviors, you must be increasing "good" behaviors in other skill areas to replace problem behaviors.

[a] The box for each skill area tells you *which basic behaviors* from earlier skill areas the child must learn before he can work in that skill area.

BASIC BEHAVIORS THE CHILD MUST LEARN BEFORE HE CAN WORK IN
EACH SKILL AREA

Table 4-2 tells you *which basic behaviors* from earlier skill areas must be
learned before the child *starts* working in a harder skill area. For example,
Table 4-2 tells you that before a child *starts* on Motor Imitation, he should
have learned *basic behaviors* such as the following:

(A1)   Spontaneous Eye Contact.
(A2)   Eye Contact on Request.
(A4)   Cooperation with Simple Spoken Requests.
(B13) Skill at Many Large Motor Activities.
(B14) Looks at Objects, Parts of the Body, Face, and Mouth.
(B21) Skill at Many Small Motor Activities.
(B22) Good Work Habits, such as Sitting, Listening, and Working.
(B24) Uses Eye Contact as a Signal to Get Natural Rewards.

Do you see how these *basic behaviors* help the child to learn Motor
Imitation? How could a child learn to imitate your movements if he did
not make eye contact, look at what you were doing, cooperate, have good
work habits or motor skills? You would be wasting your time—and his. So
the rule to follow is:

BEFORE YOU START WORKING ON A SKILL AREA, CHECK
TABLE 4-2 TO SEE *WHICH* BASIC BEHAVIORS THE CHILD MUST
LEARN FIRST. IF (OR WHEN) HE HAS LEARNED THOSE BASIC
BEHAVIORS, YOU CAN START ON THE SKILL AREA. BUT IF HE
STILL NEEDS HELP WITH *ANY* OF THOSE BASIC BEHAVIORS,
YOU MUST WORK ON THEM SOMEMORE. (The chapter on that
skill area tells you how.)

BUT HOW DO I KNOW IF OR WHEN THE CHILD HAS LEARNED THE
BASIC BEHAVIORS?

This brings us right back to the beginning. To find out if the child has
already learned the *basic behaviors* he needs before he can work on a
certain skill area,

LOOK AT HIS BEHAVIOR EVALUATION SCALE (BES) AND
BEHAVIOR EVALUATION TABLE (BET).

The items you *circled* are behaviors he needs help with. If any of the
items you circled are *basic behaviors* that Table 4-2 says he needs before
he can start on the skill area you picked, help him with those *basic behaviors* in a teaching program. On the other hand, when you are working
on a *basic behavior* in a teaching program, and want to find out if the

child has learned it well enough yet, the chapter on the skill area for that behavior tells you what "well enough" means. Since you will be *measuring* the child's behavior as you teach him, you will know just how well he is doing.

TAKE A BREAK. YOU DESERVE IT.

4. STEPS TO FOLLOW WHEN PLANNING AN EDUCATIONAL PROGRAM

Here is a list of steps to follow when you are planning a child's educational program.

1. *Fill Out the Behavior Evaluation Scale (Appendix 2) and the Behavior Evaluation Table (Appendix 3) for the Child.* Study his BET. Does he need a great deal of work in the Learning Readiness area? How are his Verbal Imitation and Functional Speech skills? How many problem behaviors need to be replaced? If the child has little or no speech and many problem behaviors, it is a good bet that his educational program has to start with *basic behaviors* in the Learning Readiness area.

On the other hand, if the child has a good deal of Functional Speech, Looking, Listening, and Moving skills, and Motor Imitation skills, you may only need to work on increasing attention to his work, cooperation, and replacing problem behaviors.

2. *Pick a Skill Area to Start Working On.* Look at the Skill Sequence Table (Table 4-1) for a skill area that you think the child is ready for. Then check Table 4-2 to see which *basic behaviors* are needed for that skill area. Next look at the child's BET to see if he has learned the *basic behaviors needed* (they are *not* circled) or if he still needs help with them (they *are* circled). If he has learned them *all*, begin working in that skill area.

But if the child's BES or BET tells you that he has *not* learned *all the basic behaviors* needed for the skill area you picked, try an *easier* skill area—one closer to the *top* of Table 4-1. Again, check Table 4-2 to see which *basic behaviors* are needed for the second skill area you picked. And check the child's BES or BET again to see if he has learned them. If he has learned them *all*, start working in the second (easier) skill area you picked. If he has not learned all the *basic behaviors*, pick another (still easier) skill area. You should finally start with a skill area

FOR WHICH THE CHILD HAS ALREADY LEARNED ALL THE
BASIC BEHAVIORS LISTED FOR THAT AREA IN TABLE 4-2, AND
WHICH IS CLOSER TO THE TOP (EASIER PART) OF THE SKILL
SEQUENCE TABLE (TABLE 4-1), but HAS BEHAVIORS IN IT
THAT THE CHILD STILL NEEDS HELP WITH (these will be target
behaviors for teaching programs in that area).

If the child is not ready for *any* of the harder skill areas (because he
has not yet learned *all* of the *basic behaviors* needed for *any* of them),
start his education in the Learning Readiness skills area.

3. *Pinpoint a Target Behavior to Change in That Skill Area.* After you
have picked the first skill area to work on, *pinpoint* a *target behavior* in
that skill area. Do this by looking at all the behaviors in that skill area
listed on the BET. They are listed with simpler behaviors at the *top* of
each skill area, moving down to harder behaviors.

By filling out the BET for a child, you know which behaviors he needs
help with. You will have put *circles* around each one.

FROM THE BEHAVIORS THE CHILD NEEDS HELP WITH IN THE
SKILL AREA YOU PICKED, PINPOINT THE EASIEST ONE (CLOS-
EST TO THE TOP OF THE BET) AS YOUR FIRST TARGET
BEHAVIOR IN THAT SKILL AREA.

In other words, *start* with the *easiest skill area* on the Skill Sequence
Table (Table 4-1) that the child is ready (has *all* the basics) for. The
first *target behavior* to pinpoint and work on in that skill area should be
the *easiest* one (nearest the top of the list on the BET) that he needs
help with.

4. *Find Out What Kind of Help the Child Needs with the Target
Behavior.* After you pinpoint a target behavior, look back at the child's
Behavior Evaluation Scale (BES) to find out *what kind of help* he needs.
Does the behavior have to be done with more skill? Done more often
(increased)? Done at a certain time or place?

5. *Take a Baseline on the Behavior You Pinpointed.* After you pinpoint a target behavior, *measure* it for a few days *before* you start any
teaching program, to see if the child *really* needs help with it as you
thought. We call this the *baseline period.* For example, you might pinpoint "spontaneous eye contact" because you think the child "rarely" or
"never" makes eye contact. But if you *count* the number of eye contacts
the child makes for a few hours each day during the baseline (before
you start a teaching program to increase eye contact), you may find out
that he makes eye contact more often than you thought. If so, pinpoint

a new target behavior. We will talk more about baselines in the next chapter.

6. *Read about How to Teach the Target Behavior in a Later Chapter.* All the target behaviors are grouped into skill areas. Each chapter after Chapter 8 is about one of the skill areas. So, when the baseline shows that the child needs help with a target behavior, your next step is to *READ HOW* to teach the target behavior in the chapter about the skill area. This will help you to plan a teaching program. The BET tells you which skill area a target behavior is in. For example, if you pinpoint (A4), Cooperation with Simple Spoken Requests, and the baseline shows that this behavior needs to be increased, read how to increase cooperation in Chapter 9, "Learning Readiness Skills," because cooperation is in the Learning Readiness skills area.

7. *Write the Teaching Program Plan.* After you read how to teach the target behavior in one of the later chapters, write down *exactly* what your teaching program for that target behavior will be. In other words, being *businesslike,* put on paper *how* you will teach the target behavior. What rewards will you use? Which reward schedule? Where and when will you do the teaching? How will you measure the target behavior? By keeping the *teaching program plan* handy, you will know just what to do and you will not be asking yourself, "How should I reward this behavior?" The teaching program plan will be like a recipe to follow when cooking a meal. It makes the job neat and easy. Chapter 6 talks about how to plan and write a *teaching program.*

8. *Run the Teaching Program.* When the teaching program plan is on paper, you are ready to run the teaching program. Chapters 5, 6, and 8 have tips on how to plan and run teaching programs and measure how well they are working.

9. *Revise the Teaching Program Plan or Go On to the Next Target Behavior.* As you will see in the next chapter, *measuring behavior* is part of *any* teaching program. By *counting* the target behavior, you find out *if* or *how much* it is changing as planned.

If the target behavior *is not changing* as it should, you must find out what is wrong with the teaching program, and *revise* it. Chapter 7 talks about spotting problems and revising teaching programs. On the other hand, if the target behavior *is changing* as planned, it is time to plan a teaching program for a *new* target behavior. Chapter 8 will help you to plan *advanced* teaching programs.

Pinpoint the next target behavior in the same way you pinpointed the first one. *Look in the same skill area of the BET and pinpoint one of the next harder behaviors down the list.* In other words, when the first target behavior has changed enough, move down the list for that skill area in the BET and pinpoint a behavior that is *a little harder*.

Keep two things in mind when you pinpoint a new target behavior. First, you must *keep the old target behaviors going by rewarding them on Intermittent Schedules and with more natural rewards* (Grandma's Law). Second, work on other *behaviors in the same skill area, even if the child does not need help* (they are not circled). In other words, *give him practice on behaviors he does not really need help with*. In fact, you can (and should) work on any behaviors *you think of, even if they are not on the Behavior Evaluation Scale or Table*.

10. *Start Programs to Replace Problem Behaviors*. If the worst problem behaviors are still strong by the third or fourth week of the child's educational program, even though you have been rewarding *all* good behaviors and ignoring problem behaviors, pinpoint a few problem behaviors to replace and decrease. Use Chapter 15, "Replacing Problem Behaviors," to help plan a teaching program for this purpose.

11. *Pick the Next Skill Area*. When the child has learned many of the *basic behaviors* in the first skill area, it is time to pick a new and harder skill area to work on *along with* the first one. Remember what we said before: You do not just stop working in a skill area altogether. You spend some time working on target behaviors in two or more skill areas, either at *different times* or, better, during the *same* teaching session. This will keep you (and the child) from becoming bored.

To pick the next skill area, *look at the Skill Sequence Table* (Table 4-1) to see which skill area comes after the one you have been working on. When you have picked it, repeat steps 2 through 10.

12. *Update the Child's BET*. As the child's education goes along, *check off* behaviors on the BET that he has learned. You will find that children get better even at behaviors you do not work on in a teaching program. Check these off too. And if a child has trouble with a behavior you did not circle when you first filled out his BES and BET, circle it then.

So there are twelve steps in planning an educational program. Table 4-3 sums up these steps and shows you how to move from one step to another.

Please remember this table of steps to follow and keep it handy. You will be using it, along with the Skill Sequence Table (4-1), the Table of Basic Behaviors (4-2), the BES, and the BET all through the child's education.

GOOD JOB. TREAT YOURSELF TO AN ACTIVITY REWARD.
Then come back to the assignment for this chapter.

Table 4-3.   Steps to Follow in Planning an Educational Program

1. Fill out the BES and BET.

2. Use the Skill Sequence Table (4-1), the Table of Basic Behaviors (4-2), the BES, and BET to *pick a skill area to start with.*

3. Use the BET to *pinpoint a target behavior to change in that skill area.*

4. Use the child's BES to find out *what kind of help* he needs with the target behavior you pinpointed.

5. Take a *baseline* on the target behavior. Then *decide* if the target behavior really needs to be changed in a teaching program. (Chapter 5 tells you how to take a baseline.)

6. *Read* part of the chapter on how to teach the target behavior you pinpointed.

7. *Write the teaching program plan* for the target behavior you pinpointed. Use Chapter 6 and the chapter on the target behavior to help you write the teaching program plan.

8. *Run* the teaching program according to the *plan.* (Chapters 6 and 8 have tips on how to run teaching programs.)

9. If the target behavior changed as planned, use the BET to *pinpoint another target behavior.* Chapter 8 tells you how to run an *advanced teaching program* for the new target behavior. If the target behavior did not change as planned, *read Chapter 7* to find out what went wrong, and *revise the teaching program plan.*

10. Start programs to decrease and *replace problem behaviors* that are hurting the child's educational program. (Chapter 15, "Replacing Problem Behaviors," tells you how.)

11. *Pick the next skill area,* using the Skill Sequence Table (4-1), the Table of Basic Behaviors (4-2), and the child's BES and BET. (Then *repeat steps 2 through 10.*)

12. *Update* the child's BET by *checking off* the items the child has learned. Also *circle* or *add* any *other behaviors* the child needs help with.

ASSIGNMENT: PLANNING AN EDUCATIONAL PROGRAM

Now let us plan a child's educational program. Give yourself a week to do the assignment, and take a break after each part.

Part One: Practice Using the BET: This part gives you practice following Steps 2, 3, and 9 of the Table of Steps to Follow (Table 4-3). At the end of this chapter is a sample BET already filled out for a child (Step 1). There are circles around behaviors he needs help with in each skill area. Your assignment is to use that BET to (1) pick the first skill area to work on with the child, and (2) pinpoint the first two target behaviors to work on in *each* skill area. Section 4 of this chapter will help you. Just follow Steps 2, 3, and 9.

Write your answers in the spaces below. When you are done, turn to Appendix 1 to find the answers. If yours do not agree, please reread Section 4 of this chapter and correct your answers before you go on to Part Two.

1. First Skill Area to Work on (give name and number from BET):
2. First and Second Target Behaviors to Work on in Each Skill Area (give names and numbers from BET):
    A. Learning Readiness Skills
        First, work on:_____
        Second, work on:_____
    B. Looking, Listening, and Moving Skills
        First, work on:_____
        Second, work on:_____
    C. Motor Imitation Skills
        First, work on:_____
        Second, work on:_____
    D. Verbal Imitation Skills
        First, work on:_____
        Second, work on:_____
    E. Functional Speech Skills
        First, work on:_____
        Second, work on:_____
    F. Chores and Self-Help Skills
        First, work on:_____
        Second, work on:_____
    G. Problem Behaviors
        First, work on:_____
        Second, work on:_____

GOOD JOB. NOW FIND THE ANSWERS IN APPENDIX 1.

Part Two: Review Your List of Behaviors. Remember the list of behaviors you made at the end of Chapter 1? For this part of your assignment, take another look at that list. Ask yourself these questions: Does the child have the *basic behaviors* he needs to work on the behaviors you listed? Does your list follow the *skill sequence* (Table 4-1)? If you listed problem behaviors to decrease, did you also list "good" behaviors to *replace* them with? These are the kinds of questions you must ask yourself from now on when you plan a child's education.

Part Three: Filling out the BES and BET. For the third part of the assignment, fill out the Behavior Evaluation Scale (BES) for a child you will be working with using this book. The "Introduction" to the BES tells you how to fill it out and use it. When you have finished, fill out the Behavior Evaluation Table (BET) in Appendix 3. Do this part of the assignment slowly and carefully. It may take you a week. Then come back and do Part Four.

Part Four: Using the BES and BET. When you have filled out the BES and the BET, (1) pick the first skill area to work on with the child, and (2) pinpoint the first target behavior to work on in that skill area. Write them below. *Make sure to pinpoint a target behavior to increase—* a behavior the child needs to do *more often or for a longer time.* We will worry about replacing problem behaviors later.

1.   First Skill Area to Work on (give name from BET):

2.   First Target Behavior to Increase in That Skill Area (give name and number from BET):

Now, check up on yourself by going over Steps 1 through 4 of Section 4 above. Does the child have all the *basic behaviors* needed for the skill area you picked, as listed in Table 4-2? If not, pick an *easier* skill area. And did you pinpoint the *easiest* target behavior that needs to be *increased* in that skill area?

VERY GOOD! YOU HAVE JUST FINISHED THE MOST IMPORTANT PART OF A CHILD'S EDUCATION. The next chapter, Chapter 5, brings you one step closer to starting a child's first teaching program.

Sample Behavior Evaluation Table (BET)

A. Learning Readiness Skills

** (A1) SPONTANEOUS EYE CONTACT
** (A2) EYE CONTACT ON RE-QUEST
(A3) Responds to his name
** (A4) COOPERATES WITH SIMPLE SPOKEN RE-QUESTS
** (A5) SITS TO WORK AT SOME TASK
(A6) Approaches others

(A7) Smiles at others
(A8) Responds to praise

B. Looking, Listening, and Moving Skills

Large Motor Skills

(B1) Bend and stand
(B2) Balance when walking
(B3) Walks backwards
(B4) Kicks ball
(B5) Throws ball
(B6) Jumps in place
(B7) Balances on one foot
(B8) Broad-jumps
(B9) Hops on one foot
(B10) Heel-toe walks
(B11) Catches ball
(B12) Pedals tricycle
** (B13) SKILL AT MANY LARGE MOTOR ACTIV-ITIES; SPENDS MUCH TIME AT THEM

Small Motor Skills

** (B14) LOOKS AT OBJECTS, PARTS OF THE BODY, FACE, MOUTH

(B15) Moves objects from one hand to the other
(B16) Picks up objects with thumb and index finger
(B17) Stacks blocks
(B18) Works simple puzzles
(B19) Imitates drawing line
(B20) Imitates drawing circle
** (B21) SKILL AT MANY SMALL MOTOR ACTIVITIES; SPENDS MUCH TIME AT THEM
** (B22) GOOD WORK HABITS, SUCH AS SITTING, LISTENING, AND WORKING AT A TASK
** (B23) POINTS OR MATCHES BY NAME

Social Skills

** (B24) USES EYE CONTACT TO GET NATURAL RE-WARDS
(B25) Plays with others
(B26) Cooperates on a task
(B27) Takes or waits his turn

C. Motor Imitation Skills

Imitation of Movements

** (C1) IMITATES LARGE MO-TOR MODELS
** (C2) IMITATES SMALL MO-TOR MODELS
** (C3) IMITATES OBJECT PLACEMENTS
** (C4) IMITATES MOUTH MOVEMENTS AND PO-SITIONS
(C5) Plays imitation games
(C6) Imitates complex move-ments

Sample Behavior Evaulation Table (continued)

Generalized Imitation

°° (C7) IMITATES SOME MOD-
ELS EVEN IF NOT RE-
WARDED

(C8) Moves body as others do
on his own

(C9) Imitates chores or tasks on
his own

°°(C10) IMITATES MOTOR
MODELS OF MANY
PEOPLE

D. Verbal Imitation Skills

Easing into Verbal Imitation

(D1) Pays attention to the
speech of others

(D2) List of sounds child makes

°° (D3) MAKES MANY DIFFER-
ENT SOUNDS ON HIS
OWN, OFTEN

(D4) How does the child make
sounds?

(D5) Makes more sounds if you
imitate him

°° (D6) MAKES EYE CONTACT
AND A SOUND AT THE
SAME TIME TO GET
THINGS

Verbal Imitation

°° (D7) IMITATES BASIC
SOUNDS

°° (D8) IMITATES SYLLABLES

°° (D9) IMITATES SIMPLE
WORDS

°°(D10) IMITATES PHRASES
AND SIMPLE SEN-
TENCES

°°(D11) IMITATES VERBAL
MODELS OF MANY
PEOPLE

E. Function Speech

Kinds of Functional Speech

°° (E1) NAMES OBJECTS OR
PICTURES

°° (E2) ASKS FOR THINGS HE
WANTS

°° (E3) IDENTIFIES AND DE-
SCRIBES WHAT HE
SEES AND HEARS

°° (E4) ANSWERS SIMPLE
QUESTIONS

°° (E5) SAYS "HELLO" AND
"GOODBYE" COR-
RECTLY

°° (E6) USES PHRASES AND
SIMPLE SENTENCES
TO NAME, ASK, DE-
SCRIBE, ANSWER
QUESTIONS

°° (E7) IDENTIFIES AND DE-
SCRIBES ONE AND
MORE THAN ONE
(PLURALS)

°° (E8) UNDERSTANDS AND
USES PREPOSITIONS

°° (E9) UNDERSTANDS AND
USES PRONOUNS

°°(E10) UNDERSTANDS AND
USES OPPOSITES

°°(E11) USES WORDS ABOUT
TIME (BEFORE/AFTER)

Handling Special Problems

°°(E12) USES THE FUNC-
TIONAL SPEECH HE
KNOWS HOW TO USE

°°(E13) USES FUNCTIONAL
SPEECH INSTEAD OF
ECHOING OR PARROT-
ING

°°(E14) USES FUNCTIONAL
SPEECH IN MANY

Sample Behavior Evaluation Table (continued)

PLACES AND WITH
MANY PEOPLE

((G4))   Hits, bites, kicks others
(G5)   List of destructive behaviors

F. Chores and Self-Help Skills

Chores

°° (F1)   DOES SIMPLE TASKS
°° ((F2))   DOES MORE COMPLEX
TASKS AND CHORES
ON HIS OWN, OFTEN

Self-Help Tasks

(F3)   Feeds himself with the
right utensils
(F4)   Undresses himself
(F5)   Dresses himself
(F6)   Washes and dries face and
hands
((F7))   Brushes his teeth
(F8)   Toilet trained
°° ((F9))   DOES MANY SELF-
HELP TASKS ON HIS
OWN, OFTEN

G. Problem Behaviors

Destructive Behaviors

(G1)   Bangs head
(G2)   Bites or scratches himself
((G3))   Throws tantrums

Getting Into Things

((G6))   Gets into or messes up
things

Strange Behaviors

(G7)   Rocks himself
(G8)   Spins himself
(G9)   Spins things
((G10))   Stares at fingers or objects
(G11)   Flaps hands or arms
(G12)   Makes strange faces
(G13)   Strange postures
((G14))   Demands or does rituals
(G15)   List of strange behaviors

Reaction to Certain Consequences

(G16)   Physical punishment
((G17))   Verbal punishment
((G18))   Time out
((G19))   Ignoring
°° (G20)   PROBLEM BEHAVIORS
ARE BEING REPLACED
WITH GOOD BEHAV-
IORS FROM OTHER
SKILL AREAS

REFERENCES AND EXTRA READINGS

Cartwright, G. P. "The relationship between sequence of instruction and mental abilities of retarded children." *American Educational Research Journal*, 1971, **1**, 143-150.

Cohen, H. L. "Educational therapy: The design of learning environments." In J. M. Schlien (Ed.), *Research in Psychotherapy*, Vol. III. Washington, D.C.: American Psychological Association, 1968. Pp. 21-53.

Gagné, R. M. *The Conditions of Learning* (Second Edition). New York: Holt, Rinehart and Winston, 1970.

Haring, N., and Phillips, E. *Educating Emotionally Disturbed Children.* New York: McGraw-Hill, 1962.

Hess, R. D., and Bear, R. M. (Eds.), *Early Education.* Chicago: Aldine, 1968.

Hewett, F. "A hierarchy of educational tasks for children with learning disabilities." *Exceptional Children,* 1964, **31**, 207-214.

Hewett, F. "Educational engineering with emotionally disturbed children." *Exceptional Children,* 1967, **33**, 459-467.

Hewett, F. *The Emotionally Disturbed Child in the Classroom.* Boston: Allyn and Bacon, 1968.

Moore, O. K., and Anderson, A. R. "Some principles for the design of clarifying educational environments." In J. Aldous, T. Condon, R. Hill, M. Straus, and I. Tallman (Eds.), *Family Problem Solving: A Symposium on Theoretical, Methodological, and Substantive Concerns.* Hinsdale, Ill.: Dryden Press, 1971, Pp. 90-133.

Ney, P. G. "Effect of contingent and non-contingent reinforcement on the behavior of an autistic child." *Journal of Autism and Childhood Schizophrenia,* 1973, **3**, 115-127.

Piaget, J., and Inhelder, B. *The Psychology of the Child.* New York: Basic Books, 1969.

Quay, H. C. "The facets of educational exceptionality: A conceptual framework for assessment, grouping, and instruction." *Exceptional Children,* 1968, **35**, 25-31.

Reynolds, M. C., and Balow, B. "Categories and variables in special education." *Exceptional Children,* 1972, **38**, 357-366.

Thorndike, E. L. *Human Learning.* Cambridge, Massachusetts: The M.I.T. Press, 1966. (first printing 1931).

CHAPTER FIVE

MEASURING BEHAVIOR, or How to Keep Track of What's Going On

In Chapter 4 you learned the twelve steps for planning a child's educational program. Most important, you learned how the Skill Sequence Table (4-1), the Table of Basic Behaviors (4-2), the BES, the BET, and the Table of Steps to Follow (4-3) will help you all through a child's education. Your assignment for Chapter 4 was to fill out the BES and the BET for a child; pick the first skill area to work on with him; pinpoint the first target behavior in that skill area to plan a teaching program for; and find out in what way the target behavior needed to be changed. In other words, by this time you have done Steps 1 through 4 of the Table of Steps to Follow (Table 4-3).

In this and the next chapter we will talk about setting up and running your first teaching program for the target behavior you pinpointed (Steps 5 through 10 of Table 4-3). This chapter is about a very important part of *all* the rest of the steps and of *any* teaching program—*measuring behavior*. In other words, in teaching programs you must do two things:

CHANGE THE TARGET BEHAVIORS YOU PINPOINTED

and

MEASURE HOW MUCH THE TARGET BEHAVIORS ARE CHANGING.

Measuring behavior is a *must* for *good teaching*. It lets you know *if* or *how much* the target behavior is changing as it should in your teaching programs. Measuring behavior simply means *counting*. For example, if a teaching program is to *increase* the number of times the child *asks for things* (Functional Speech), you would *count how many times* he correctly asks during the day. Or, if a teaching program is to *increase the amount of time* the child *plays* with his toys (Looking, Listening, and Moving), you would *count the number of minutes* (or hours) he plays each day. Or, if a teaching program is to *decrease the number of times* the child throws a *tantrum* (problem behavior), you would *count the number of tantrums* each day.

We all know that helping the child learn (helping him change his behavior) is the whole reason for teaching him. Are you worried that measuring behavior will make teaching even harder? This is an important question. In the next few pages we will answer it.

1. WE ARE MEASURING THINGS ALL THE TIME

When we are dieting, we use a scale to see if our weight is *decreasing*. In winter, we look at the thermometer to see if the furnace is *increasing* the temperature of the house as it should. If our child gets a high fever, we take his temperature to see if the aspirin we are giving him is *decreasing* his fever.

In all of these examples, we *do* something: we go on a diet, turn on the furnace, and give the child aspirin. We want to make a *change: decrease* our weight, *increase* the heat in the house, and *decrease* our child's fever. But we also *measure how much change* we are getting, by weighing ourselves and by using thermometers in the house and in our child.

BY MEASURING WHAT WE ARE TRYING TO CHANGE (WEIGHT, TEMPERATURE), WE CAN FIND OUT IF WHAT WE ARE DOING (DIETING, GIVING ASPIRIN) IS WORKING AS IT SHOULD.

Look at what can happen if we do not measure our child's temperature in some way. We might (1) keep giving him aspirin even though his fever is rising; (2) keep giving him aspirin even though his temperature is down to normal; or (3) stop giving him aspirin even though his temperature is not down to normal yet. In other words, we could be making bad mistakes in our "program" (giving aspirin) to decrease our child's fever. And our mistakes might harm the child. The point is that we might make the same mistakes in *teaching programs* to change *behavior* if we do not *measure* what is happening. Let us see how.

2. HOW MEASURING BEHAVIOR WOULD HAVE HELPED
MRS. BLAKE AND BILLY

Mrs. Blake's son, Billy, made eye contact with her only two or three times a day. She planned a great *teaching program* to *increase* the *number of times* an hour that Billy made *eye contact* with her each day. She was going to praise him (Social Reward) and quickly give him a small bite of sugar-coated cereal (Primary Reward) every time (Continuous Schedule) he made eye contact with her. She tried the program for 1 week and was sure that Billy's eye contact behavior had increased enough. So she started to reward his eye contacts less and less often (Intermittent Schedule) and began working on a new target behavior.

That was too bad! Because Mrs. Blake was wrong: Billy's eye contacts had not increased as much as she *thought*. So, when she began to reward him less often for eye contact, the number of eye contacts he made went all the way back down to two or three times an hour. (Behavior that is no longer rewarded decreases!) *Mrs. Blake forgot to measure the target behavior. She did not count the number of times Billy made eye contact with her during the day.* If she had counted Billy's eye contacts (the *target behavior*), she would have found out that her program was not working so well. *She would have found out that she should reward eye contacts a little longer or try a different reward to increase Billy's eye contacts.*

This is how many *times* each day Billy really made eye contact with his mother between 2:00 and 3:00 P.M., *before* she started the reward program and *after* she got it started.

Baseline Period Before Program				During Reward Program				
Mon.	Tues.	Wed.	Thurs.	Fri.	Sat.	Sun.	Mon.	Tues.
2	3	2	3	4	5	4	5	5

Does it look as if Billy's eye contacts have increased very much now that his mother is rewarding them with bites of sugar-coated cereal? He *is* making eye contact a little more than before, but *not* so much more that Mrs. Blake should cut down on the rewards.

Billy also threw *tantrums*—six or seven times a day. And he threw them when he was bored and did not know what to do with himself. Mrs. Blake planned to *decrease* the number of Billy's tantrums (the *target behavior*) by *replacing* them with playing behavior. She decided to *ignore* all tantrums, as if they were not even happening, and to spend an hour in the morning and afternoon teaching Billy how to play—a better way to spend his time than throwing tantrums.

After a week, Mrs. Blake was ready to quit. Billy seemed to be having as many tantrums as before she started her program to replace tantrums with playing. In fact, she got so "hung up" on Billy's tantrums (always on the lookout for one) that she hardly had any energy left for teaching him to play. She also felt that Billy was not spending any more time playing now than he had before she started her teaching program.

Too bad again! Because Billy's tantrums had *decreased*. He was really having tantrums only about two times a day now and playing much more than he used to. But Mrs. Blake did not know this. She did not *count the number of tantrums* Billy threw. And she did not *count how many minutes he played each day*. If she had counted the number of times Billy threw tantrums and the number of minutes he played each day, she would have *seen* that her program was working nicely, that she did not have to worry about Billy's tantrums, and that she could spend more of her time and energy teaching him "good" behaviors.

This is how many times Billy threw tantrums and the number of minutes he played each day *before* Mrs. Blake started the program and during the program:

	Baseline Period Before Program				During Teaching Program				
	Mon.	Tues.	Wed.	Thurs.	Fri.	Sat.	Sun.	Mon.	Tues.
Tantrums	6	8	7	7	4	2	3	2	2
Playing	10	5	7	15	15	20	35	21	40

You can see that Billy is having tantrums *less* often and playing *more* often now that his mother is *ignoring* tantrums and *rewarding* playing. This does not mean that Billy is ready to move on to harder behaviors. It means that Mrs. Blake's teaching program *is working* and that she should let it keep working to increase Billy's playing and decrease his tantrums. The teaching program is doing its job.

What do these examples tell us? They tell us that

COUNTING THE TARGET BEHAVIORS YOU ARE TRYING TO CHANGE WILL TELL YOU WHETHER YOUR TEACHING PROGRAM IS WORKING AS IT SHOULD.

This gives you a better idea about *what to do next*: to *keep on* with the same program a while longer, to *stop* what you are doing and try something else that might work *better*, or to start the child on the *next* step of his educational program because he is *ready* for it.

3. MEASURING BEHAVIOR WILL MAKE TEACHING EASIER

This may be hard to believe, but it is true. Do problem behaviors (such as whining, throwing tantrums, or hitting) get you wound up inside? Do you ever get so upset that you try to end those behaviors by going to the child, telling him to stop, or giving him what he wants? If so, it would be pretty hard for you to decrease those behaviors by *ignoring* them, wouldn't it? *But if you take the time to measure (count) those behaviors each time they start, you will have something to do that will cool you off.*

If a child starts another tantrum, and instead of thinking, "Oh, God, if this keeps up I'll lose my mind," and rather than trying to stop him, you just take your sheet of paper and write down that he is starting a tantrum, or click your wrist counter, it will be much easier to ignore what he is doing. Counting behavior lets you stand back. It gives you the time you need to think about what to do next, how to handle the behavior. When you are tense, a child's "bad" behaviors can keep you busy all day trying to stop him. But if you are *watching and counting his Problem Behaviors instead,* you will not get so tied up. More important, you will feel that you are *changing* his behavior. And you will be!

Also, some hard behaviors, such as Verbal Imitation, may take a rather long time before they increase a great deal. You may feel "down," thinking that nothing is happening. But if you are counting the target behavior, you will see that the child *is* making progress. It may be slow at first, but it is there. This will keep you feeling good about yourself and about your teaching programs, and will make it easier to keep on, even if the going is slow at the time.

4. MEASURING BEHAVIOR WILL KEEP YOU ON YOUR TOES

Let us say you plan to *increase* the number of times a child makes sounds, by rewarding him with praise and a small bite of food every time he makes a sound. *When a behavior is very weak (does not happen very often), it is important, at first, to reward it every time it happens (Continuous Schedule).* Do you think you would notice every time the child made a sound? Do you notice every car that drives by? You might try to hear every sound he made, but you would still miss many of them. Too many other things are happening at the same time. *But if you were counting his sounds* (by making a mark on paper or by clicking a counter), *you would be more likely to notice each time he made a sound.* You would be more on the lookout for the target behavior that is to be rewarded, in the same way that you would notice all the cars that went by if you were to count them.

You have seen how important it is to measure the child's target behaviors in your teaching programs. *It is also very important to measure your own behaviors.* Let us use an example from everyday life to see why.

Mrs. Jones went on a diet to lose weight. She weighed herself every day to see if the diet (her program) was working. The scale told her that she was not losing weight, so she stopped the diet.

Mrs. Jones thought that the diet was not working. Why did she think that? Well, she was measuring the target behavior (her weight)! And she was right in thinking that she did not lose weight. But how do we know that she followed her diet? She did not measure *how much she ate* (her dieting behavior)! Maybe she did not lose weight because she was really eating as much as before her "diet" started. *Her diet might have worked better if she had measured her weight (target behavior) and how much she ate (dieting behavior).*

The same thing goes for teaching. To find out how much a child's behaviors are changing, you must measure his behaviors. And to find out *how well you are following the teaching programs you plan, you must measure your own behaviors.* Measuring the target (child's) behavior in a teaching program will only tell you *if* the target behavior is changing, but not *why* it is or is not changing. It may *not* be changing because the teaching program itself has some problems in it (Chapter 7 talks about these) or because *you* are not doing what the teaching program calls for.

For example, you may have a teaching program to increase the number of minutes the child plays with his toys each day, by rewarding him after he has played a certain number of minutes, a number that changes after each reward (Changing Interval Schedule). If the behavior does not increase, is the reason that there was something wrong with the program itself (toys too hard?) or that you did not reward the child as often as you were supposed to? The only way to find out if *you* are following the teaching program is to count your own teaching behaviors, for instance, how many times you reward playing. This will also keep you on your toes to reward the target behavior.

Counting will also help you to change some of *your* own behaviors that you might want to change. You do not want to give a child attention when he is whining, but it is sometimes hard to stop yourself in time. You might not even notice that you do it. But if you count the number of times you give a child attention for whining, you will start to *notice* yourself doing this, and will be able to replace that behavior (giving attention) with some other behavior (like ignoring).

5. WHAT YOU HAVE LEARNED SO FAR

By this time you should have learned five things:

1. Measuring a child's behavior will let you know how the behavior is changing, so that you can tell if the teaching program is working as it should.

2. Once you have an idea of how well the teaching program is working, you can decide whether to (*a*) continue it; (*b*) stop it and try something else because it is not working well enough; or (*c*) stop it and go on to the next step of the child's education.

3. Measuring the child's behavior will help you to "stand back" so that you can really see what is happening and have time to think of what to do. It will help you to be less tied up by problem behaviors. And it will help you to see that the child's behavior is changing day to day and week by week even if it does not seem to be.

4. Measuring the child's behavior will keep you on the lookout for the target behaviors you are trying to change, so that you can reward them, ignore them, "time out" (see page 106) the child for them, and so forth.

5. Measuring your own behavior will keep you on the lookout for your own behaviors, so that you will be more likely to reward the target behaviors you are supposed to reward, ignore the behaviors you are supposed to ignore, and so forth.

REWARD YOURSELF BEFORE YOU GO ON TO THE NEXT SECTION.

6. HOW DO YOU MEASURE BEHAVIOR?

We have said so much about measuring behavior that you may think it is very hard. You will find, though, that in a few days it becomes natural. And when it shows you that the child is learning, you will begin to like doing it.

Here is what you do when you measure behavior.

1. *Pinpointing*: This means *picking* a behavior to measure and *defining* it so clearly that you or anyone else can easily *see* it.
2. *Counting*: This means *watching* the behavior you pinpointed when it happens (*occurs*) and marking down (*recording*) the number of

times it happens or the number of *seconds* or *minutes* that it lasts.
3. *Charting*: This means *writing* down what you counted each day so
    that you can see how the behavior changed day by day.

Now let us look at these three items more carefully.

7. PINPOINTING

Pinpointing means picking or choosing behaviors to measure (*count*),
and defining them so that you are sure of just what you will be counting.
But what behaviors should you pinpoint? Take a look at Table 2-1 on
page 26 of Chapter 2. You are going to pinpoint three kinds of behaviors:

Signals you give the——→ *Behaviors* of the child——→ *Consequences*   you
child   give the child

Behaviors of the Child (Target Behaviors)

You already have a good idea of the child's behaviors that you want to
pinpoint. They are the behaviors you circled on your BES and BET for
the assignment at the end of Chapter 4. In other words, *you will be pinpointing behaviors of the child that you want to change (teach him to do
better, increase, decrease, OR teach him to do at a certain time or place).*
     What could be simpler? You want to change behaviors like eye con-
tact, cooperating, playing, making sounds, imitating (repeating sounds
and words), and asking for things. Therefore these are target behaviors
to pinpoint first, so that you can measure them during your teaching program.

Behaviors of the Parent and Teacher (Teaching Behaviors)

The behaviors of yourself to pinpoint are the kinds of *signals* you use
to start or stop the child's behaviors and the kinds of *consequences* you
follow his behaviors with, such as rewards, ignoring, or time out (see
page 106). As you know, the signals and consequences that you use teach
a child (change his behavior). If you do not pinpoint and count your own
behaviors—signals and consequences you give the child—you will not be
able to find out *why* a teaching program is working or why it is not working.
     Let us be a little more clear about the behaviors of yourself that you
will be pinpointing and counting.

SIGNALS

Signals, you remember, are all the things you do to start or stop certain behaviors of a child. (*Reread page 24 in Chapter 2 before you go on*). Here is a list of signals you use now or might use later:

1. Directions, commands, or requests: Telling the child "Come here" or
2. Grandma's Law: Saying, for example, "As soon as you (finish the "Let's sit down and work" or "Pick up the red block" or "Point to the picture of the dog."
   puzzle; put on your coat) you can go outside."
3. Questions: Asking the child questions like "What color it this?" or "What do you want to eat?"
4. Modeling: Showing the child some behavior for him to imitate or repeat, like a word ("Say 'CAT'") or some movement (like pat-a-cake).
5. Ringing a bell or a timer: Using a bell or timer as a signal to sit down at the table and start working at some task, or as a signal that the child will soon be rewarded if he keeps on working. There are many ways in which you can use bells or timers to start the child's behavior.

CONSEQUENCES

You also remember that consequences are the things that happen to the child *after* he does something. (*Reread pages 24 and 25 in Chapter 2 before you read any more here.*) Here is a list of consequences you use now or might use in the future:

1. Reward: This means following the child's behavior with something that will *increase* it, like food, praise, hugs, things he likes to do (activities), or anything else that will increase a behavior it follows.
2. Ignoring: This means that the child's behavior is followed by nothing rewarding. It means that his behavior is not followed by any reward it used to get, like attention, so it will *decrease*. It means that you behave as if nothing had happened. (But remember: you can ignore "bad" behaviors and you can ignore "good" behaviors. Both kinds will decrease if you ignore them. So be careful *not* to accidentally ignore "good" behaviors.)
3. Time out: Time out is a short period of time when the child has no chance of getting any kind of reward. Time out might mean putting the child in his room or in a special "time out room," making him come inside the house, or making him sit in the corner. If a problem behavior is followed over and over by a time out period, it will decrease (as long as another "good" behavior is being rewarded).

4. Punishment: This means following a certain behavior with a consequence that will decrease it, like a spanking, taking away television or music time, or saying something like "No" in a loud voice.

Defining Behaviors

You cannot really *count* anything unless you know just what you are looking for. You need to *define* the behaviors you plan to change and count in your teaching programs.

Defining a behavior means saying what you are going to be seeing or hearing. In other words, defining a behavior means describing what it looks or sounds like—as *movement*. A good word to use is "observable." The behavior that you are pinpointing and that you want to count and change has to be *observable. People must be able to see it or hear it.*

The "behaviors" on the left-hand side of Table 5-1 are *not observable*. They are *not* movements that anyone can see or hear. So they cannot be counted. And if they cannot be counted, you cannot find out if they have changed. The behaviors on the right-hand side of the table, however, *are observable*. They are defined so that anyone can see or hear them, count them, and change them.

Do you see that the behaviors on the right-hand side of the table are defined by *movements* that can be *observed?* You can see and hear tantrums; you can see a child smile; you can hear him repeat words. So you can *count* and *change* them. But what does "self-control" look like? What does a "good mood" look like? Would we all agree on what a good mood

Table 5-1. Definitions of Behavior

Not Observable Behavior	Observable Behavior
1. Child needs *self-control.*	1. Child *throws* five *temper tantrums* a day.
2. Child *likes* other people.	2. Child *comes over* and *touches* friends and relatives, *smiles* when he is with them.
3. Child is not in a *good mood* to learn.	3. Child *whines* or *turns* his head the other way when he is given directions or requests.
4. Child's speech is *improving.*	4. Last week child *imitated* five words. This week he imitated ten words.
5. Child is *aggressive.*	5. Child *hits, kicks, bites,* or *pinches* other people.

looks like? Of course not! But we could agree on whether or not a child was whining.

> WHENEVER YOU PINPOINT A BEHAVIOR TO CHANGE, YOU MUST WRITE DOWN A *DEFINITION* FOR THAT BEHAVIOR. THE DEFINITION MUST *DESCRIBE* THE BEHAVIOR AS *MOVEMENTS* THAT CAN BE SEEN OR HEARD. ALWAYS ASK YOURSELF IF THE BEHAVIOR YOU ARE PINPOINTING CAN BE OBSERVED. IF NOT, LOOK MORE CAREFULLY AT THE BEHAVIOR AND DEFINE IT AGAIN AS MOVEMENTS.

8. COUNTING BEHAVIOR

After you *pinpoint* a target behavior, you can *count* it. To count behavior all you do is *watch it* (*look for it to happen*) and then *mark down* (*record*) what you observed.

What Am I Watching for in the Behavior I Observe?

There are always a few things that you can watch for in any behavior you have pinpointed. One thing is *how often* (how many *times*) it happens (*occurs*) during the time you are watching for it. For instance, you can count

1. the number of times the child makes eye contact with people during one certain hour of the day;
2. the number of times you reward him for playing during the day;
3. the number of times he gets up from the table during supper;
4. the number of times you tell him to sit down (reward him with attention) when he gets up from the table;
5. the number of times he gets into packages and makes messes in the kitchen;
6. the number of times you make him clean up the kitchen when he makes messes; or
7. the number of times he imitates words during his half-hour teaching session with you each day.

> IF YOU ARE TRYING TO INCREASE *HOW MANY TIMES* A PIN-POINTED BEHAVIOR HAPPENS, WATCH AND COUNT THE NUMBER OF TIMES IT HAPPENS.

The second thing you can watch for is the number of seconds, minutes, or hours (*how long*) the behavior *lasts* when it happens. For example, you can count

1. the number of minutes the child plays during each day;
2. the number of hours he watches television instead of playing;
3. the number of minutes he whines after you put him to bed;
4. the number of minutes he pays attention during lessons; or
5. the number of minutes you spend playing with him or teaching him
    each day.

IF YOU ARE TRYING TO CHANGE THE *AMOUNT OF TIME* (how long) A TARGET BEHAVIOR LASTS, WATCH AND COUNT THE NUMBER OF SECONDS, MINUTES, OR HOURS THAT IT LASTS EACH TIME IT STARTS. THEN *ADD* UP THE NUMBERS YOU COUNTED.

When Should I Watch and Count Behavior?

Usually, you watch and count behavior every day, during teaching sessions and outside of them. For most target behaviors, you will be running teaching sessions to give the child a lot of practice on the target behavior, *so count behavior during teaching sessions.* On the other hand, you need to count behavior *outside* of sessions also. For example, to find out if the child is using speech at other times and places besides sessions, you have to watch for and *count the target behavior (speech) outside of sessions.* Also, some behaviors may not happen during sessions (for example, problem behaviors during meal time, whining at bedtime, or playing with other children on the playground). You have to watch for them and count *whenever* they happen.

How Much Time Should I Spend in Watching and Counting Behavior?

If you want to increase a behavior that happens only *one time* a day, is 10 minutes of watching and counting enough? Of course not. You will surely miss it. On the other hand, if a certain behavior happens hundreds of times a day (speech, strange noises), do you have to watch and count for 8 hours a day? No again. If it happens that much, 1 hour will be enough to tell you if it is changing. So *how much time you spend depends on how much the target behavior happens now.* If it does not happen very often, watch for it and count a *large part* of the day. For instance, if the child plays for only a few minutes a day, be on the lookout for playing, and count how many minutes he plays *all day*, or else you will miss the few minutes he spends at this behavior.

Behaviors that happen just at a certain time (meals, bedtime) need to be watched and counted only during those times. Finally, behaviors that happen *very often* and at just about *any time* of day (tantrums, head-banging, speech), do not need to be watched and counted all day. One hour or so will be enough. For instance, if the child makes noises all day —about thirty times an hour—and you plan to decrease the number of times he makes those noises, watching and counting for *1 hour each day* will be as good as counting all day to tell you if the behavior is decreasing.

We can sum up as follows:

1. Count behaviors *during* sessions.
2. Behaviors you work on during sessions should also be counted *outside* of sessions.
3. The *more* a behavior happens outside of sessions, the *less* time you need to watch and count.
4. The *less* a behavior happens outside of sessions, the *more* you need to watch and count.
5. Some behaviors only happen at a *certain* time or place. Count them then.

Should I Watch and Count for the Same Amount of Time Each Day?

This is important. Let us say that Billy's mother spent 3 days counting the number of times Billy did very simple chores on his own, such as putting his plate or cup in the sink, closing the door after he went out, or hanging up his coat. The first day she counted five times that he did simple chores on his own; the second day she counted ten; and the third day she counted fifteen. It looks as if Billy's chore behavior is increasing, doesn't it? But *what if Billy's mother spent more time watching and counting each day?* What if she watched and counted for 1 hour the first day, 2 hours the second, and 3 hours the third day? Is Billy's chore behavior increasing? Or did his mother just *see* more of it because she *watched longer?* How can we find out?

All we have to do is *divide the number of times the chore behavior happened by how much time she watched.* This gives us the *rate* of Billy's chore behavior—the number of times he did *chores per hour.* The little table below shows how to find the *rate* of Billy's chore behavior.

Day:	Monday	Tuesday	Wednesday
Number of Chores Done	5	10	15
Number of Hours Watched	1	2	3
Rate of Chore Behavior	$\frac{5 \text{ chores}}{1 \text{ hour}} = 5$ chores per hour	$\frac{10 \text{ chores}}{2 \text{ hours}} = 5$ chores per hour	$\frac{15 \text{ chores}}{3 \text{ hours}} = 5$ chores per hour

You can see that *the rate is the same.* Each day, Billy did simple chores at the *rate of five per hour.*

Here is another example. Mr. Blake was working with Billy on simple puzzles during teaching sessions. He was trying to increase Billy's *attention* to his work. Whenever Billy was paying attention, Mr. Blake turned on a stopwatch, and when Billy stopped paying attention, he turned off the stopwatch. So, at the end of each session, Mr. Blake knew how many minutes Billy had paid attention. The stopwatch told him that Billy paid attention for more minutes each day. But sessions lasted for a different number of minutes each day! One day the session was 10 minutes long; the next day 15 minutes; and another day 30 minutes. Was attention increasing, or did Mr. Blake just have more time to count it?

To find out if Billy's attention was increasing, Mr. Blake

DIVIDED THE NUMBER OF MINUTES THE BEHAVIOR (AT-TENTION) HAPPENED *BY* THE NUMBER OF MINUTES IN THE SESSION.

This gave him the *rate* of attention. Study the table below to see how Mr. Blake found the *rate.*

Day:	Monday	Tuesday	Wednesday	Thursday
Number of Minutes Billy Paid Attention	7	10	15	15
Number of Minutes in Session	10	15	30	45
Rate of Attention	$\frac{7}{10}=70\%$	$\frac{10}{15}=67\%$	$\frac{15}{30}=50\%$	$\frac{15}{45}=33\%$

You see from the table that the *number of minutes* Billy paid attention was larger each day. But *sessions were longer, too.* So did attention increase? No, it did not! When you look at how much time Billy paid *attention per minute,* you see that it was decreasing. The rate of attention, or *the percentage of time* he paid attention, fell from 70 percent, to 67 percent, to 50 percent, down to 33 percent.

The point is this: If you watch and count for the *same amount of time* each day, the numbers you count *will* tell you how much the behavior is changing. But if you watch and count for a different amount of time each day, the numbers *will not* tell you how much the behavior is changing. So

TRY TO WATCH AND COUNT FOR THE *SAME* AMOUNT OF TIME EACH DAY.

Try to count for the same number of minutes during sessions each day. Outside of sessions, watch and count for the same number of minutes or hours each day.

If you *change* the number of minutes or hours you watch each day, you must find the *rate* of the behavior by

DIVIDING THE NUMBER OF TIMES (OR HOW LONG) THE BEHAVIOR HAPPENED *BY* THE NUMBER OF MINUTES OR HOURS YOU WATCHED.

Checking Up on Yourself (Reliability)

No matter how hard you try, you will miss some behaviors to count, either because you looked away for a second or because you were too busy working with the child. That is all right, but it is important to have *someone else* watch and count with you once in a while to give you a check on what is going on. When another person watches and counts the *same behavior at the same time*, we call this a *reliability check*.

Every few days, or *at least once a week*, have *another person* stand near you or in another room, and have him watch and count the same behavior as you are, for the same amount of time. Then, at the end of the session, *compare your counts*. If the numbers you counted are the same, that is great; it is called *100 percent agreement*. If the numbers are *not* the same, you must find out the *percentage of agreement*. This is easy to do. Just *divide the bigger number into the smaller one*. For example, if one of you says that the behavior happened twenty times and the other counted eighteen times, divide twenty into eighteen (18/20), which gives you *90 percent agreement*. Or, if one of you says that the behavior lasted 10 minutes and the other that it lasted 5 minutes, divide ten into five, which gives you *50 percent agreement*.

Make *reliability checks* like this for *each behavior* you are counting. Shoot for at least *80 percent agreement*. Write down the behavior and the percentage of agreement each time you make a reliability check. If the percentage of agreement falls below 80 percent, talk it over with the second person. Make sure that you are watching the *same behavior*, that you have the *same definition*, and that you are counting at the *same time*. Then try again the next day.

How Do I Count Behavior?

Once you have pinpointed the target behavior (or a teaching behavior), and have decided *when* and for *how much time* each day to watch and count, you are ready to start watching and counting. There are many fancy ways to mark down (*count*) what you see, but it is just as good to use a pencil and a pocket notepad. Use one page for each day, with half a page for the target behavior and half for any of your behaviors (teaching behaviors) you want to count. Put a hash mark (/) in the spaces for the target behavior and teaching behavior each time they happen. The table below shows what a page might look like.

> Name of Child: Tommy Adams
> Name of Teacher: Mr. Smith
> Time Session Started and ended: 9:20 to 9:40 (20 minutes)
> Target Behavior: Giving correct name of household objects
>   //// //// //// // (17)
> Teaching Behavior: Rewarding correct naming
>   //// //// //// (15)

You can also use a golf counter or grocery store counter. These counters are sold at sporting goods stores and dime stores. Have one for each behavior, and just click the counter each time a behavior happens.

To count how many minutes or hours a behavior lasts, use a wristwatch, wall clock, or stopwatch. If you use a wristwatch or wall clock, write on your note pad how long the behavior lasts *each* time. If you use a stopwatch, just run it while the behavior is happening and turn it off when the behavior stops. To count behaviors that happen only a few times a day (going to the bathroom, bedtime problems, doing chores), you can use a *large calendar*. Hang it on the wall, and mark what happened in the box for each day.

Examples of Behavior Counts

Two examples of *behavior counts* made by a teacher and a parent are given below. In each one a *teaching program plan* is given first, and then the behavior counts made before and during the teaching program. Please look back at the Table of Steps to Follow (Table 4-3) in Chapter 4 to see how the teaching program plans follow those steps.

"Teaching Program Plan for Increasing Child's Spontaneous Eye Contact"

Name of Child: Jimmy Smith
Name of Teacher: Mrs. Oaks

Skill Area for This Teaching Program: Learning Readiness (A).

Basic Behaviors Needed for This Skill Area: None. This is the most basic.

Pinpoint the Target Behavior for This Teaching Program: (A1)   Spontaneous Eye Contact.

Define the Target Behavior as Movements: Every time Jimmy looks me in the eye without being asked, even if he looks for only an instant.

How Is the Target Behavior to Be Changed? Increase the number of times it happens.

How Will the Target Behavior Be Shaped (by what small steps will it be changed?) It is already on the simplest step. ("Shaping" will be talked about in Chapter 6.)

When and Where Will the Target Behavior Be Taught? All day, wherever the target behavior happens when I am around.

How Will You Signal the Target Behavior? No signal. I will wait for eye contact.

How Will the Target Behavior Be Prompted? If needed, I will hold a bite of candy up to my eye for a few seconds when Jimmy is looking my way. ("Prompts" will be talked about in Chapter 6.)

What Will Be the Rewarding Consequences and Reward Schedule for the Target Behavior? Behavior will be rewarded every time (Continuous Schedule) with praise, bites of candy, and activities which naturally follow eye contact.

What Other "Good" Behavior Will Be Rewarded? Sitting at the table, coming when called, smiling.

When Will the Target Behavior Be Measured? Between 1:00 and 3:00 P.M. each day (120 minutes).

What Teaching Behavior Will Be Measured? The number of candy rewards for spontaneous eye contact.

What Will You Count With? Two wrist counters, one for eye contact and one for the number of candy rewards. An aide will help take *reliability checks*.

Below is the table Mrs. Oaks used to write down the *behavior count* for each day.

So, during the teaching program, Mrs. Oakes rewarded Jimmy with praise, activities, and a piece of candy every time he made eye contact during the whole day. But she *counted* the number of his eye contacts and her rewards only between 1:00 and 3:00 P.M. Notice the "Baseline Period." Before she started her teaching program, Mrs. Oaks watched and counted Jimmy's eye contacts between 1:00 and 3:00 P.M. (just as she was going to watch and count during her teaching program), but she did

Day:	Baseline Period Before Program				During Teaching Program				
	Mon.	Tues.	Wed.	Thurs.	Fri.	Mon.	Tues.	Wed.	Thurs.
Number of Minutes Watched	120	120	120	120	120	120	120	120	120
Number of Eye Contacts by Child	4	5	4	9	21	28	37	44	49
Number of Candy Rewards by Teacher	0	0	0	9	21	28	37	44	49
Reliability		Eye Contact 100%		Rewards 90%				Eye Contact 95%	

not reward his eye contacts during the baseline. Rewarding eye contact was going to be the teaching program for Jimmy.

In other words, before she started her teaching program (rewarding spontaneous eye contact), Mrs. Oaks took a *baseline* of 3 days, watching and counting spontaneous eye contact, but not rewarding it. Once she started the teaching program, she could use the baseline counts of spontaneous eye contact to tell her how well her teaching program was working. If, after a week of the teaching program, the number of eye contacts each day was not much more than it was during the baseline, Mrs. Oaks would know that the teaching program was not working.

Look at the number of spontaneous eye contacts Jimmy made and the number of times he was rewarded for eye contact. Notice that during the *baseline period*, when he was not rewarded for eye contact, the number of times he made eye contact between 1:00 and 3:00 P.M. was only about four. But when Mrs. Oaks began to reward spontaneous eye contact every time (continuous schedule) during the teaching program, the number of eye contacts between 1:00 and 3:00 P.M. increased very fast to forty-nine in 6 days.

Also notice that Mrs. Oaks took a *reliability check* every few days and wrote the behavior and the percentage of agreement in the boxes for those days.

Here is another *behavior count* for a teaching program run by a parent. First the *teaching program plan* is given.

"Teaching Program Plan for Increasing How Much Time Child Plays"

Name of Child: Jimmy Smith

Name of Teacher: Mr. Smith

Skill Area for This Teaching Program: Looking, Listening, and Moving (B).

Basic Behaviors Needed for This Skill Area: Spontaneous Eye Contact (A1), Eye Contact on Request (A2), Cooperation with Simple Spoken Requests (A4), Sitting to Work at Some Task (A5).

Pinpoint the Target Behavior for This Teaching Program: Working Simple Puzzles (B18).

Define the Target Behavior as Movements: Jimmy is working puzzles in a constructive way, sitting at the table and looking at what he is doing. Just pushing puzzle pieces around does not count.

How Is the Target Behavior to Be Changed? Increase the number of minutes Jimmy plays with simple puzzles on his own.

How Will the Target Behavior Be Shaped (by what small steps will it be changed)? Jimmy has already learned how to work puzzles during teaching sessions. Now we want to increase how long he does them on his own outside of sessions. So we will not shape this behavior. It has already been shaped. ("Shaping" will be talked about in Chapter 6.)

When and Where Will the Target Behavior Be Taught? Between 6:00 and 8:00 P.M. each evening after I get home from work.

How Will You Signal the Target Behavior? At 6:00 P.M. I will bring out certain puzzles, put them on the coffee table, and tell Jimmy, "Okay, here are some puzzles for you to play with."

How Will the Target Behavior Be Prompted? No prompts will be used. Jimmy knows how to play with these toys. ("Prompts" will be talked about in Chapter 6.)

What Will Be the Rewarding Consequences and Reward Schedule for the Target Behavior? Jimmy will be praised and hugged while he plays. The number of minutes he must play to be rewarded will change after each reward (Changing Interval Schedule).

What Other "Good" Behaviors Will Be Rewarded? Talking about what he is doing, asking questions, and smiling.

When Will the Target Behavior Be Measured? Between 6:00 and 8:00 P.M., but the number of minutes I watch and count will *change each evening*. Hence I will have to find the *rate of playing* (the *percentage* of the time Jimmy played.

What Teaching Behaviors Will Be Measured? The number of times Jimmy is rewarded.

What Will You Count With? I will count how long I watch with a wall clock. I will count how many minutes Jimmy plays with a stopwatch. I will count how many times I reward him with pencil and paper. Mrs. Smith will help take *reliability checks.*

Below is the *behavior count table* made by Mr. Smith. Note that Mr. Smith *divided the number of minutes Jimmy played each evening by the number of minutes he watched and counted.* This told him how much Jimmy played *per minute* (the *rate*) or the *percentage of time* Jimmy played. Mr. Smith had to find the *rate* or *percent* because the number of minutes he watched and counted changed each evening.

In this program, Mr. Smith put out puzzles for Jimmy and counted how many minutes Jimmy played with them, how many times Jimmy was rewarded for playing, and how many minutes he was able to watch and count Jimmy's playing. Since he watched and counted for a different number of minutes each night, he had to find the *rate* of playing or the *percentage* of time Jimmy played.

During the *baseline period,* he did not reward playing, and the percentage of time Jimmy played was very low—around 8 percent. During the teaching program, he rewarded Jimmy with praise and hugs every so often (*Changing Interval Schedule*), and the percentage of time Jimmy spent in playing went up to 67 percent in 6 days. Also note that Mr. Smith took *reliability checks* every few days on the target behavior (playing) and the teaching behavior (rewards for playing).

GOOD JOB. REWARD YOURSELF.

9. CHARTING

The last thing to do when you are measuring a target behavior is to *chart* what you have counted. By making a chart and putting it where everyone can see it, you will be able to tell how much the child's behavior (and your behavior) is changing. It is a good idea to *draw a line* across the chart and to use the line as your *goal.* In other words, try to increase or decrease the target behavior *at least* to the *goal line.* If you have to find the *rate* of the behavior each day, then *chart the rate,* not the number of times or how long the behavior happened.

Figure 5-1 shows the charts of the behaviors counted each day in the two teaching programs with Jimmy Smith. The charts came from the

Day:	Baseline Period Before Program					During Teaching Program			
	Monday	Tuesday	Wednesday	Thursday	Friday	Saturday	Sunday	Monday	Tuesday
Number of Minutes Watched	60	50	120	120	50	60	50	60	120
Number of Minutes Child Played	5	2	10	20	10	20	20	40	80
Rate or Percent of Time Playing	$\frac{5}{60}=8\%$	$\frac{2}{50}=4\%$	$\frac{10}{120}=8\%$	$\frac{20}{120}=17\%$	$\frac{10}{50}=20\%$	$\frac{20}{60}=33\%$	$\frac{20}{50}=40\%$	$\frac{40}{60}=67\%$	$\frac{80}{120}=67\%$
Number of Times Child Was Rewarded	0	0	0	8	10	15	15	20	30
Reliability	Playing 100%		Rewards 100%	Rewards 100%				Playing 90%	

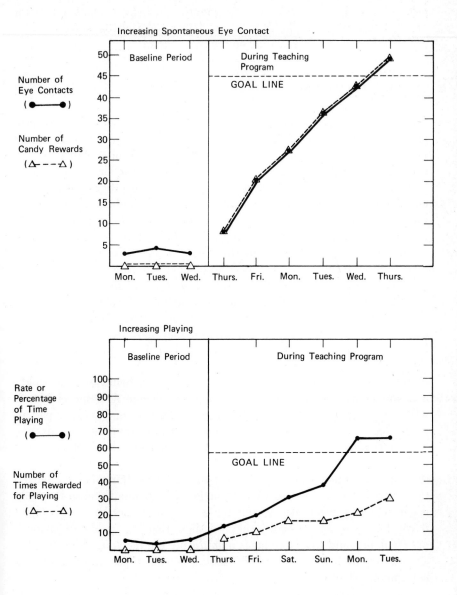

Increasing Spontaneous Eye Contact

Number of
Eye Contacts

(●——●)

Number of
Candy Rewards

(△ --- △)

Baseline Period

During Teaching
Program

GOAL LINE

Mon. Tues. Wed. Thurs. Fri. Mon. Tues. Wed. Thurs.

Increasing Playing

Rate or
Percentage
of Time
Playing

(●——●)

Number of
Times Rewarded
for Playing

(△ --- △)

Baseline Period

During Teaching Program

GOAL LINE

Mon. Tues. Wed. Thurs. Fri. Sat. Sun. Mon. Tues.

tables made by Mrs. Oaks and Mr. Smith. To help you get a feel for *charting*, compare the numbers in the boxes for each day in the tables with the dots made for each day on the two charts.

10. BASELINE PERIOD

We talked about *baseline periods* in the two examples of teaching programs for Jimmy Smith. The *baseline period* runs for a few days *just before you start a teaching program*. During the baseline, watch for and count the *same behaviors* you are going to watch for and count during the teaching program. But do not start the teaching program during the baseline; leave things *the way they usually are*—whether that means rewarding problem behaviors or not rewarding "good" behaviors.

There are three reasons for doing a baseline before you start a teaching program. First, after counting the target behavior for a few days, you may find that it does not really need to be changed after all. For instance, you may think that the child throws too many tantrums, so you take a baseline count of the number of tantrums each day, for 3 days or a week. You may find that the child throws only one or two tantrums a day—less than you thought. So taking a baseline may show you that a teaching program for a target behavior you picked is not needed as much as a program for other behaviors.

In fact, sometimes just watching and counting a behavior (the child's and yours) during the baseline is enough to change it. Some children's whining decreases when they see you standing around with a pad of paper, writing down each time they whine. Or, by counting rewards, you may find yourself rewarding a "good" behavior more than before.

The second reason for doing a baseline is that it gives you a way of showing that the teaching program (and not something else) changed the target behavior. Sometimes a behavior will change because the child is getting older or because of something else you do not know about. But if you take a baseline for a week and show that the child's behavior is *not changing*, and that it *changes only during the teaching program*, it is a good bet the behavior changed *because of* your teaching program and not something else.

Third, the baseline period gives you something to look back on, to see just how much progress the child has made. Even if the going is slow during a teaching program, you can see from the baseline that the child really has come along. This will be rewarding *for you!*

We want you to take a baseline before you start many of your teaching programs, especially the first few. Take a baseline in the same way you measure at any other time. After you *pinpoint* and *define* the important behaviors (of the child and yourself) in the teaching program, decide *when* and *how long* to watch and count them, decide what to count with, start watching and counting, and take *reliability checks. Write down (record)* what you have counted on a piece of paper, in a box for each day. Then *chart* what you have counted.

Usually, the baseline period lasts from 3 days to a week. The idea is to run the baseline until the target behavior of the child is fairly steady (does not change much from day to day). A week should be long enough for this. Besides, you want to get the teaching program started.

11. WHAT YOU HAVE LEARNED IN THIS CHAPTER

In this chapter you have learned the following things:

1. Measuring behavior has many good results. It lets you know how much the target behavior is changing. It lets you find out how well your teaching program is working. It helps you plan what to do next in the child's educational program. And it keeps you on the lookout for your own teaching behaviors.

2. To measure behavior, begin by *pinpointing a target behavior.* Be sure to clearly *define* the pinpointed behavior as *movements* which can be seen or heard.

3. After pinpointing a behavior to change, decide if you are going to count the *number of times* it happens or the number of seconds, minutes, or hours (the *amount of time*) it lasts. For target behaviors such as eye contact, cooperation with requests, correct motor and verbal imitations, and sounds, words, and sentences the child says, you can count the number of *times* the behavior happens. On the other hand, for target behaviors such as playing, working at a task, and paying attention, you can count the *amount* of time (number of minutes, hours) the behavior happens.

4. Next, choose a time to do your watching and counting. Count during sessions. Outside of sessions, if the behavior does not happen very much, watch and count a large part of the day. If it happens very much, watch and count it for an hour or two each day. If you cannot count for the same amount of time each day, find the *rate* of the behavior.

5. Next, choose something to count with. You can use a pencil and a piece of paper to mark down each time the behavior happens. Or you can use some kind of counter, clicking it each time the behavior happens. Or you can use a stopwatch, wristwatch, or wall clock to count the number of minutes or hours the behavior lasts.

6. Then write down or record what you have counted. On a piece of paper, write who the child is, who the teacher is, what target behavior is to be changed, how the target behavior is to be changed (increased, decreased), what consequence (or signal) will be used to change the behavior, when and how long the observations will be made, and how the counting will be done. Set aside one box on the paper for each day you watch and count. Then mark down what you have counted in that box.

7. Take *reliability checks* every few days.

8. Finally, *chart* what you have counted each day, either the numbers or the rate.

TAKE A BREAK!
Then go on to the assignment for this chapter.

ASSIGNMENT: TAKING A BASELINE ON TARGET BEHAVIOR

This assignment brings you one step closer to starting the first teaching program. It has two parts.

Part One.   In Part Four of your assignment for Chapter 4, you pinpointed the first *target behavior* to *increase* in your first teaching program. In the next chapter we will be planning that teaching program. But first take a *baseline* on the target behavior you pinpointed (Step 5 of the Table of Steps to Follow). This will help you to make sure that the target behavior really needs to be changed, and will give you something to look back on once you start the teaching program.

To help you plan the baseline, answer the questions in the spaces of Table 5-2. They are some of the same one you will answer when you write a *teaching program plan* in the next chapter. Make copies of the blank tables and chart on the next few pages so that you can use them to take baselines on other behaviors later on.

Now that you have answered these questions, you are ready to start the *baseline period.* For one week, watch and count the target behavior during the time you planned, and reward it only as often as it was rewarded before. In the box for each day in Table 5-3, write down the number of *times* or the number of *minutes* (or seconds, hours) the target behavior happened during the observation time each day. Also write

Table 5-2.   Planning a Baseline
1. Name of Child:
2. Name of Teacher or Parent:
3. What is the *skill area* for the target behavior?
4. What *basic behaviors* are needed for this skill Area? (List them from the Table of Basic Behaviors, Table 4-2.)

5. *Pinpoint* the target behavior (Write its number and name from the BET):

6. *Define* the target behavior as movements. (What does it look or sound like? Be specific.)

7. How is the target behavior to be changed? And what will you be *counting*? (Remember: pinpoint a behavior to *increase*. Write down *what* needs to be increased—the number of times or how long it happens.)

8. *When* and *where* will the target behavior be measured?
   a. When? from_____to_____each day (make it the *same* amount of time each day).
   b. Where?

9. What is the *rewarding consequence* the target behavior will be getting during the baseline, *if any*? (Remember: during the baseline the target behavior should earn the same reward it has usually gotten, and should be rewarded just as often or as little as before.)
10. What will you *count* with?

down the number of times the target behavior got the rewarding consequence, and fill in what day it is over each box. Do not forget *reliability checks*.

Each day, go back to your table and look at the numbers you wrote in the boxes for the target behavior and the rewarding consequence. Then make dots on the chart in Figure 5-2 for those numbers. For instance, if the target behavior happened ten times on Monday, put a dot on the chart *even with* the number 10 on the side and *over* "Monday" on the bottom. Do the same thing for the number of times the target behavior was rewarded each day. Then connect the dots. Of course, you have to

How Often
Target Behavior
Happened
(use dots)

(●———●)

Number of Times
Target Behavior
Was Rewarded
(use triangles)

(△– – –△)

___ day ___ day ___ day ___ day ___ day ___ day ___ day

Fig 5–2. Chart for baseline.

Table 5-3. Behavior Count Table for Baseline

Day:	__day	__day	__day	__day	__day	__day	__day
Number of Minutes (Hrs.) Watching and Counting							
How Often Target Behavior Happened (Number of Times, Minutes, Hours)							
Number of Times Target Behavior Was Rewarded							
Reliability							

put numbers up the side of the chart as your guide. Check back with the tables and charts on Jimmy Smith in Sections 8 and 9 to see how to do this.

Part Two. The second part of your assignment is to start reading the next chapter, Chapter 6, after you have run the baseline for about 3 or 4 days. Then you will be ready to plan the teaching program.

REFERENCES AND EXTRA READINGS

Baer, D. M., Wolf, M. M., and Risley, T. R. "Some current dimensions of applied behavior analysis." *Journal of Applied Behavior Analysis*, 1968, 1, 91-97.

Bijou, S. W., Peterson, R. F., and Ault, M. "A method to integrate descriptive and experimental field studies at the level of data and empirical concepts." *Journal of Applied Behavior Analysis*, 1968, 1, 175-191.

Gaasholt, M. "Precision techniques in the management of teacher and child behaviors." *Exceptional Children*, 1970, 37, 129-135.

Gelfand, D. M., and Hartmann, D. P. "Behavior therapy with children: A review and evaluation of research methodology." *Psychological Bulletin*, 1968, 70, 204-215.

Hall, R. V., Christler, C., Cranston, S., and Tucker, B. "Teachers and parents as researchers using multiple baseline designs." *Journal of Applied Behavior Analysis*, 1970, 3, 247-261.

Hall, R. V., Fox, R., Willard, D., Goldsmith, L., Emerson, M., Owen, M., Davis, F., and Porcia, E. "The teacher as observer and experimenter in the modification of disrupting and talking-out behaviors." *Journal of Applied Behavior Analysis*, 1971, **4**, 141-149.

Lindsley, O. R. "A reliable wrist counter for recording behavior rates." *Journal of Applied Behavior Analysis*, 1968, **1**, 77-78.

Sidman, M. *Tactics of Scientific Research*. New York: Basic Books, 1960.

CHAPTER SIX

How to PLAN
and RUN
the FIRST
TEACHING PROGRAM

1. GOOD TEACHING IS GOOD BUSINESS

This is the chapter you have been waiting for. It tells you how to plan and run the first teaching program in a child's education. Of course, you will also use the ideas here to plan and run "advanced" teaching programs for harder behaviors and skill areas later in the child's education. Chapter 8 is about advanced programs. This is a long chapter, but you will not be reading it all at once. In fact, you will be starting your first teaching program a few pages from now.

Teaching should be fun for you and the child, but it should also get good results. To get good results (change behaviors in a way that helps the child), you must teach in a *businesslike* way, which means carefully *planning* your educational and teaching programs with the Table of Steps to Follow (Table 4-3) in Chapter 4.

You have finished the first four steps of Table 4-3: (1) filled out the BES and BET; (2) picked the first skill area to work on; (3) pinpointed the first target behavior for a teaching program; and (4) found out how it needs to be changed. Now you should be doing Step 5—taking a *baseline* on the target behavior.

2. WHAT DID THE BASELINE (STEP 5) TELL YOU?

You pinpointed a behavior from the BET that you thought the child needed help with—a behavior to *increase*. The baseline tells you if you were right. *Does the chart you made during the baseline period say that the behavior still needs to be increased?* If the chart tells you the behavior *does not* need to be increased (because it happens *more* than you thought), *pinpoint another behavior from the same skill area* and run a baseline on it for a few days. Then go to Section 3.

3. READ PART OF THE CHAPTER ON HOW TO CHANGE THE TARGET BEHAVIOR (STEP 6)

If the baseline for a target behavior tells you the child *does* (or *may*) *need help*, it is time to *read part of the chapter that talks about the skill area and target behavior you pinpointed*. For example, if the target behavior you pinpointed is (A2) Eye Contact on Request, and the baseline tells you the child *does* (or *may*) *need help* with Eye Contact on Request, then read about *how* to change (teach) it in Chapter 9, "Learning Readiness Skills."

You do not have to read the whole chapter. Just read (1) the first section, which tells what the chapter is about; (2) the section on teaching the target behavior; and (3) maybe the section on the next target behavior to work on.

PLEASE READ HOW TO INCREASE THE TARGET BEHAVIOR NOW. IT WILL HELP YOU TO PLAN A TEACHING PROGRAM FOR THAT TARGET BEHAVIOR.

4. WHAT GOES INTO PLANNING AND RUNNING THE FIRST TEACHING PROGRAMS?

Skim over the *teaching program plans* written by Mrs. Oaks and Mr. Smith in Section 8 of Chapter 5. They are like the plans you will soon be writing.

Now let us talk about each part of a teaching program.

Skill Area for the Teaching Program

Chapter 4 told you how to pick the first skill area to work on in the child's education: (1) fill out his BES and BET; (2) pick an easy skill area from the Skill Sequence Table (Table 4-1) in Chapter 4; (3) look at the Table of Basic Behaviors (Table 4-2) in Chapter 4 to see which basic behaviors are needed for that skill area; (4) look at the child's BET to see if he is *ready* (has the basic behaviors) for that skill area; (5) if he *is* ready, start with that skill area; if *not,* pick an easier one. Always write the name of the skill area at the top of your program plan.

Basic Behaviors Needed for the Skill Area

Also list the basic behaviors needed before the child can work in the skill area. Then, if he has a hard time learning the target behavior, you will know he may need help with some of the basic behaviors, and you should work on them.

Pinpoint the Target Behavior for the First Teaching Program

For the first teaching program, Chapter 4 tells you to pinpoint an *easy* target behavior from the skill area—near the *top* of the list on the BET. Target behaviors in later programs will be farther down the list. Write the name and the number of the target behavior on your program plan.

Define the Target Behavior as Movements

Make sure to *describe* the target behavior as *movements,* so clearly that you and anyone else can tell just what it looks and sounds like. The better you describe it, the easier it is to see. If you have a hard time defining the target behavior, check back with Chapter 5, Section 7.

How Is the Target Behavior to Be Changed? And What Will You Be Counting?

For your first teaching program, pinpoint a behavior to *increase.* In later teaching programs you will work on behaviors that need to be done with more skill, done at the right time and place, or replaced and decreased.

You can count either *how many times* or *how long* (minutes, hours) the target behavior happens each day. One or the other is best to measure about the behavior. Pick one and count it during the teaching program. If you have any trouble, Sections 8 and 11 of Chapter 5 will help you to decide whether to count the number of *times* or *how long*.

How Will the Target Behavior Be "Shaped"?

You may have read about *shaping* in the chapter on the target behavior. *Shaping* has to do with *giving the child more skill* at a behavior. Rewarding a behavior every time (Continuous Schedule) will get it started (on the *increase*), but this does not mean that the child can do the behavior any *better* or with more skill. He just does it more often or for a longer time. How do we teach him to do it better? The most important method is shaping.

HOW DO I SHAPE BEHAVIOR?

Shaping will be part of most teaching programs, no matter how big or small the behavior. Remember the idea that *people learn best in small steps? Shaping* means

TEACHING A BEHAVIOR IN SMALL STEPS.

Most behaviors can (and should) be taught in small steps (*shaped*). For instance, a target behavior might be working simple puzzles (Looking, Listening, and Moving skills). If the child does not even know how to put in one piece, you have to *reward him for something simpler— like moving a puzzle piece near the right hole.* But as he gets better at moving the puzzle pieces *near* the holes, you *hold off and reward him only for putting in a piece.* In other words, you teach him the target behavior (working puzzles) in small steps (from moving puzzle pieces, to fitting one piece at a time, to putting in all the pieces by himself). You can shape a whole skill area too. For example, you start with easy target behaviors in a skill area and move to harder ones.

But to *shape* a behavior (teach it step by step) you must know what the steps will be. This means that, *before you start a teaching program, you break down the target behavior into smaller and easier steps.* Once you have a *list of small steps,* teach the behavior by following the steps. *Start with the easier steps and work up to the harder ones as the child gets more skill..*

Let us use speech as an example. Suppose that you want to teach the child to say "eat" to ask for food. If he does not know *how* to say "eat," you could not just stop giving him food until he says it well! You would have to teach him to say "eat" in *small steps.* You would start by rewarding him for saying something easier.

First break down the word "eat" into small steps, and write the list in your teaching program plan. Your list of steps might look like this:

1. Child *opens* his mouth when I say, "What do you want to do?"
2. Child opens his mouth and makes *any* sound when I say, "What do you want to do?"
3. Child says, *"Eee"* when I say, "What do you want to do?"
4. Child says something *close* to "eat" when I say, "What do you want to do?" (For instance, he says *"Eeeddd"* or *"Eeth."*)
5. Child says "Eat" when I say, "What do you want to do?"

Do you see that each step is a little harder, and that they all lead to the behavior you wanted to teach ("eat")?

After you have made your list of small steps, begin with the first step. Help (prompt) the child to open his mouth (Step 1) after you say, "What do you want to do?" and *reward* him for opening his mouth. It may take a few days until he learns to open his mouth by himself when you say, "What do you want to do?"

When he is doing the first step by himself, start working on the second step in line. But do not reward him for just opening his mouth (Step 1) *any more. In other words, do not reward him for behavior that is on a lower step.* And, as before, when he is doing the second step by himself, move to the next harder step.

WHAT DO I DO IF THE CHILD DOES NOT GET BETTER AT A STEP?

This is very important. If the child does not seem to be getting much better at a step, *maybe you moved ahead too fast. Back up to an easier (lower) step for a while to make sure he can do the behavior on that step. Then go ahead again.*

For example, if the target behavior is kicking a ball, you might break it down into the following steps:

1. *Lifting* leg.
2. Lifting and *swinging* leg back and forth.
3. Lifting leg and swinging it *at* a ball on the ground.
4. Lifting leg and swinging it at a ball until the foot *kicks* the ball.

If the child gets to Step 4 and stops making progress, you should back up to Step 3 for a while, to make sure he has Step 3 down pat. Then go ahead again to Step 4.

Table 6-1 tells you how to *shape* a behavior.

When and Where Will the Target Behavior Be Changed?

It is important to plan when and where to teach the child. For many behaviors, it is good to start with *short teaching sessions*, at the same place and time each day. In that way, the child gets much practice on the target behavior and learns to do it with more skill. Also, as often as you can during the day, *prompt* the child or give him *many chances* to do the target behavior in more *natural settings*, and reward him for doing it. For example, during sessions you might be rewarding eye contact with food on a Continuous Schedule. At other times of the day, too, you should prompt him to make eye contact before you give him natural rewards,

Table 6-1.   How to Shape a Behavior

---

1.   First *break down* the target behavior into *small steps*, from *easy* to *hard*. Make sure that each step is just a *little harder* than the one before.

2.   Make a *list* of steps you will follow later. Write the list on your teaching program plan.

3.   *Start* teaching the behavior on the *first* step.

4.   Help (*prompt*) the child to do the behavior and *reward* him for trying.

5.   Always reward him if he happens to do a behavior on a *harder* step, even if you are *not* there yet. For example, if you are teaching him to say "*Eee*" and he happens to say "Eat," *reward him!*

6.   When the child does the behavior at a step over and over without *any help*, move up to the *next* harder step on the list.

7.   At the *start of* a new step, use a *Continuous* Schedule of rewards. Then go to an *Intermittent* schedule when he gets better.

8.   *Do not* reward the child any more for behaviors that are on *lower* steps. For example, if you are teaching him to kick a ball, and he already knows how to aim his foot at the ball, do not reward him if he just swings his leg.

9.   If the child does not get much better at a step, *go back to an earlier, easier step* to make sure he knows it. Then go ahead again.

10.   If the child still does not get much better, look in *Chapter 7* for problems in the teaching program that may need to be fixed.

---

such as letting him go outside. Also, as a behavior increases, have *other people* prompt the child to make eye contact with them and reward him.

WHEN SHOULD I RUN SESSIONS?

At first, run sessions at the *same* time of day, for about *20 minutes* (*less* if the child is not ready to work that long). For some children, the best time for sessions, at the *start,* is mealtime, when they can be rewarded with bites of food as they learn. For others, a good time is just *before* a favorite activity, for example, a television program, the arrival of the ice cream man, or a ride. In that way, good sessions can be followed by a reward (the activity), and sessions will become more fun for the child.

As the child's work habits improve, the sessions can be made longer and held at different times and places. Be sure to write on your program plan when you will have sessions each day and how long they will last.

WHERE SHOULD I RUN SESSIONS?

Run most sessions in a place where the child will not be *too* distracted. But do not strip the room. If he gets used to working in a bare room, it will be harder for him to learn to pay attention in more natural (noisier) places. So, in the beginning, have sessions in a place where the two of you can be alone, but not an empty room. If, after a week or so, you find that some noise or object keeps the child from paying attention, remove it. Then as his attention increases, start bringing back more normal sights and sounds.

SEATING

Often, to learn a target behavior, the child must watch your face and body movements and be close enough for you to physically prompt him. A good way to sit is *facing each other,* either across or around the corner of a table. Of course, on some tasks you want to *fade* yourself *out* and let the child work more on his own. So you might begin to stand next to him or *behind* him as he works. For example, when the child is learning Small Motor skills, you might have to sit next to him or in front of him at first, to prompt him to work puzzles, stack blocks, or color with crayons. As his skill and attention improve, and as he needs less help, you can slowly move behind him so that he can work on his own.

How Will You Signal the Target Behavior?

Signals start and stop behaviors. Since most teaching programs are to increase behaviors, we will talk only about signals to start behaviors.

Chapters 2 and 5 talked about signals. Some examples are (1) directions or requests, such as "Look at me," or "Put the red block on top of the blue block"; (2) Grandma's Law, such as telling the child, "As soon as we finish our work, we can wrestle"; (3) questions, such as, "What is your name?"; (4) modeling or showing a child a movement (model) he is to imitate or repeat; and (5) ringing a bell or timer to start an activity or lesson.

During the child's education, you will use most of these signals to start a target behavior. The chapter you read on the target behavior told you which signals to use and how to use them. For now, a few simple rules are as follows:

1. If you want to start a behavior, use a *direction* or *request* that tells the child what you want him to do. *Do not* start behaviors with questions like, *"Can you* tell me what this is?" or *"Do you* want to get to work?" or *"Will you* put in this puzzle piece?" When you want the child to do something, do not ask him *if* he will do it. He might just say "No." Then what would you do?
2. *Grandma's Law* is a good way to start a teaching session or activity because it tells the child what *Activity Reward* is at the end of the session or at the end of his hard work. He knows what he is working for. Always use Grandma's Law in a *positive way*. Tell the child what he *will get if* he does something, not what he will miss if he does not. Say, "As soon as you finish your lesson, you can watch television," not, "If you don't finish your lesson, you can't watch television." If you tell him what he cannot do, you are begging for a fight.
3. *Bells* and *timers* are easy and fast ways to get certain behaviors going at the right time and place. If the child finds out that, when the breakfast bell rings, he has 5 minutes to be at the table or his breakfast is over, hearing the bell will get him to the table on time. A bell can be used in the same way to start a child on his lessons; he learns that after the bell rings he has only 20 minutes to finish his work, and if he finishes in time, he gets a strong reward.

So, in your teaching program plan, write what kinds of signals you will use to get a behavior started. Will you use directions? Grandma's Law? A bell? And what will you say when you signal a behavior?

How Will the Target Behavior Be "Prompted"?

"Prompting" is another word you may have read in the chapter on the target behavior. Like shaping, *prompting* teaches the child to do a target behavior better or with *more skill*. What does "prompting" mean?

Prompting means helping 'the child to do a behavior that will be rewarded.

One way to prompt the child is by *moving* him with your own hands or putting him through the right motions. For example, you can help him improve at working puzzles by moving his hands for him, or you can help him get more skill at making sounds by moving his lips and chin so he makes the right sounds.

Another way to prompt a child is by giving him some kind of *coaching*. You can *point* to what you want him to do (for example, you can point to the place where a puzzle piece fits). You can also *tell* the child what to do or how to do it. For instance, you can coach him to dress himself by telling him, "Hold your sock with *both hands.*"

Remember! *As the child gets better and better at the behavior, help (prompt) him less and less.* The more he can do it by himself, the less help you should give him. *But, as you stop helping him, do it very slowly.* In other words, *fade out* your prompts. Hold his hands with less force each day. Or give him instructions less often and use a softer voice.

On your teaching program plan, write *how* you will prompt the target behavior, and which prompts will be used first, second, third, and so on. The following is the kind of list we mean. It is for prompting the child to work simple puzzles.

1. At first, *set up* the puzzle piece for him so it is easy for him to place it; *move* his hands through the motions; *point* to the right spot; and *tell* him how and where to move the puzzle piece.
2. Later, *point* to the right spot and *tell* him how and where to move the puzzle piece, but only give his hand a gentle push in the right direction.
3. Still later, only *point* to the right spot.

PROMPTING AND SHAPING GO TOGETHER

Each time you go to a harder step on the shaping list, you are moving to a behavior the child needs help with. So be ready to *prompt the child more*. And, as he gets better at the behavior in the new step, *slowly fade out* the prompts.

Also, when the child starts to do a behavior by himself (without prompting), give him a *big* reward, the same as if he did a behavior on a harder step on the shaping list.

The next two parts of your teaching program plan have to do with consequences (rewards) and reward schedules. TO REFRESH YOUR MEMORY, PLEASE GO BACK TO CHAPTER 3 AND READ SECTION 7 AGAIN. BUT, FIRST, MAKE YOURSELF A HAM ON RYE.

What Will Be the Consequence (Reward)?

The consequences you use to change the target behavior are the most important part of your teaching program. Since the first teaching program is to increase a behavior, let us stick to rewards.

FINDING A STRONG REWARD

As you know from Chapter 3, there are four kinds of rewards: Primary, Social, General, and Activity Rewards. *Finding and using effective rewards is a must.* The consequence has to be rewarding to the child, and not something adults think children "ought" to enjoy. The child's BES and BET, and the "Reward List" you made for him as Part One of the assignment for Chapter 3, will help you to pick *effective rewards.* Let us do that now.

Turn to the section on Learning Readiness skills in the child's BES and read items A7 and A8. They tell you whether being with others, getting hugged, and being praised are Social Rewards for the child. If they *are not,* you may have to use Primary Rewards during teaching sessions in your first programs, along with Activity Rewards (Grandma's Law) at other times of the day. Now turn back to Part One of your assignment for Chapter 3. In each of the boxes you should have listed things that are rewarding to the child. Again, if there are few Social or Activity Rewards for the child, and if he does not know what General (token) Rewards are all about, *it may be best to start with Primary Rewards (food).* If you must start with food, please follow these rules:

1. Use food the child really enjoys. If ice cream is his favorite, use it, even if sessions are during breakfast.
2. Rewards must be given *fast.* So either cut up the food into *very small bites,* or use foods that are bite-sized (cereals, nuts, M & M's, berries) or that can be spooned out fast (pudding, thick soup).
3. *Do not fight* over food. Keep it in a lunch box or bowl near you or on your lap, but too far away for the child to grab. If he snitches a bite of food, laugh it off (to yourself!) and keep it farther from his

reach. If he still tries to snitch food, end the session each time he starts or *time* him *out* each time, and reward the target behavior faster or more often.

4. Teach the child to enjoy Social Rewards by praising and hugging him *just before* you give him a bite of food. Over time, praise and hugs will become *learned rewards.*

Besides food, list *Activity Rewards* to be used at other times of the day for the target behavior and *other good behaviors.* For instance, pick *Activity Rewards* to use when the child follows Grandma's Law. Remember to praise or hug the child *just before* you give him an Activity Reward, too.

Of course, if you are *sure* that *Social Rewards are strong* rewards for the child, *try* them in your first teaching programs instead of food. It will not be the end of the world if it turns out that Social Rewards *by themselves* are not yet strong enough to increase the target behavior. After about a week, if your chart shows the target behavior is not increasing much, *try another reward.*

Finally, if the child *does* understand *General Rewards* (he uses money or will work for tokens, points, check marks, gold stars), you can try to start his teaching program with General Rewards, that is, a *token system.* If so, read Section 1 of Chapter 8. It tells you how to set up and run token systems.

To sum up, read items A7 and A8 in the child's BES to see if praise and hugs are Social Rewards for him. Then check the Reward List you made out for him at the end of Chapter 3.

USE THE STRONGEST AND SUREST REWARDS ON THE LIST IN YOUR FIRST TEACHING PROGRAMS AND WITH NEW TARGET BEHAVIORS.

We said "reward*s,*" not "reward." Switch between several kinds of rewards. If you use only one reward, the child will be sick of it in no time.

DO NOT WASTE REWARDS

If a person is full of (satiated on) the reward for a certain behavior, what happens to that behavior? If you think it will *decrease,* you are right. When a child (or anyone) has had his fill of ice cream, when he has had enough of being hugged or told how good he is, and when he has gone for enough rides, he will stop doing things (behaviors) to get them. In fact, if a child is *already full of* whatever reward you plan to use, that reward will not even start to increase his behaviors.

The point is this:

IF A CHILD GETS THE REWARDS FOR NOTHING, HE WILL DO NOTHING.

So, if you will be having teaching sessions during meals, with food rewards, do not let the child eat *anything* between meals. In the home and classroom, keep foods out of reach. And lay down the law:

"NO MORE GETTING INTO THE REFRIGERATOR OR CLIMBING ONTO COUNTERS FOR FOOD!"

If a child does not care about your rules and gets into food often, you may have to use *time out* (put him in his room or in a time out room for 5 or 10 minutes) every time he *starts* to get into food.

The same goes for Social Rewards. Do not hug and kiss the child all day, except for the target behavior or other good behaviors. If he gets hugged a great deal anyway, a few more hugs for the target behavior will not turn him on.

As for Activity Rewards, they too must be given *only* as a consequence for good behaviors. If you have been taking the child for rides, letting him watch TV, or giving him free time, either out of kindness or as a means to quiet him down, you must *start having him earn these Activity Rewards for good behaviors.* In fact, these are activities to use as rewards in Grandma's Law, for instance, "As soon as you finish your lesson, you can watch TV."

We are not saying that you should starve children of food, affection, or activities they enjoy. We are saying that the things they enjoy should be used *only* as rewarding consequences for the target behavior and for other good behaviors during the day. *This does not mean that the children will be getting fewer rewards. It means that they will be getting rewarded for different behaviors.* The rewards they are taking for granted, getting for nothing, or getting for whining, tantrums, yelling, and demanding—all these *rewards must be given only for good behaviors.* In fact, as good behaviors increase, the children will be getting rewarded *more often* than before.

In sum, when you plan which rewards to use, also plan how to *make sure that they are not given away or given accidentally for problem behaviors.* In a word, *no more "freebies."*

Does this sound too strict? One last point may show you that it is not! Some children with learning and behavior problems who are rewarded for nothing or for disruptive behaviors grow worse over the years. They either never learn the rules of give and take, or they learn to tease and torment to get what they want, because these behaviors work for them;

they are rewarded every time people "give in." All too often, such children "have to be sent away." The tragedy is that this might have been avoided if the right behaviors had been rewarded over the years.

We talked about *satiation* in Chapter 3. It means that the child has had enough of a reward; he is sick of it. And when this happens, the behavior decreases. To keep the child from becoming satiated, (1) *switch* from one reward to another during sessions and from day to day; (2) with food, use *small bites* and keep sessions *short;* (3) change the way you praise the child, so you will not sound like a broken record; (4) as for Activity Rewards, have a large stock of them to use, switch among them, and *stop* an activity *before* the child really wants to. Stop before he has had enough.

REWARD THE CHILD QUICKLY

To work best, a reward must be given *fast*—within 1 or 2 seconds after the target behavior. If it is given too slowly, the child may not know what he was rewarded for, or he may do something else in the meantime, and that is what will be rewarded. So

REWARD THE TARGET BEHAVIOR AS FAST AS YOU CAN.

What Will Be the Reward Schedule?
In your first teaching programs, and with just about any *new* target behavior, use the *strongest* rewards you can. And reward the behavior *every time* (Continuous Schedule). In other words, every time the target behavior happens, it is *followed* by a rewarding *consequence.* But this does not mean that the rewarding consequence has to be the *same* every time! (Remember the word "satiation"?) You can rotate rewards every few times the target behavior happens, as long as you are using strong rewards. For instance, the target behavior could be rewarded *every time,* but with a bite of food one time, a hug the second, a "good boy!" the third, and a bite of food again the fourth time.

What Other Good Behaviors Will Be Rewarded?

People learn best when they are learning more than one behavior at a time. In each teaching program there may be only one or two target behaviors, but the child does more good behaviors than that during the day. They should be rewarded too, for several reasons. First, if you do not reward other good behaviors, they may decrease. Second, rewarding them will keep the child and you from becoming bored. And, third, the other good behaviors may help the child to learn future target behaviors.

For example, if you are working on eye contact with a child who also does not sit when you ask him to, you may find that, as eye contact increases, the child starts sitting near you. By rewarding him for sitting near you, you will increase his sitting behavior. This will make it easier to work on behaviors for which good sitting is a *basic behavior,* for instance, Small Motor activities.

So, as part of your teaching program plan, write down any *other good* behaviors you can think of to reward and state how you will reward them.

When Will the Target Behavior Be Measured?

First of all, count behaviors *during* teaching sessions. As for the *rest* of the day, follow this rule:

THE *MORE* A BEHAVIOR HAPPENS, THE *LESS* TIME YOU NEED TO WATCH AND COUNT TO GET A GOOD IDEA OF HOW MUCH IT IS CHANGING.

If the target behavior happens many, many times a day, pick *1 hour each day* to watch and count. If it hardly ever happens, watch for it most of the day. Remember: try to watch and count for the *same* amount of time each day. If the amount of time *changes* each day, you must *divide the number of times the behavior happened by the number of minutes (or hours) you watch* to get the *rate.* Section 8 of Chapter 5 will help you to plan when and how much time to watch and count.

What Teaching Behavior Will Be Measured?

In every teaching program, one or more of your own behaviors (teaching behaviors) are most important in changing the target behavior. Write on your program plan which of your own behaviors you think is most important, and count it during the program. Usually, the kind of *reward* and the *reward schedule* are the most important teaching behaviors. So, during your first teaching program, *count how many times you reward the target behavior.* In later programs, you might count how many times you prompt the target behavior or use a certain signal.

What Will You Count With?

The last item of your program plan is what you will count with. Chapter 5 told you that you can make hash marks (/) on a page of a small pocket notebook each time a behavior happens. Or you can use a golf counter or grocery store counter. To count how long a behavior lasts, use a wristwatch, wall clock or stopwatch. You can also use a large calendar to record behaviors that happen only a few times a day.

Do not forget to take *reliability checks*. Section 8 of Chapter 5 tells you how. At the end of each day, write down on your table what you counted and chart it.

GET SOME EXERCISE.
Then go on to Section 5.

5. WRITING THE FIRST TEACHING PROGRAM PLAN AND RUNNING THE FIRST TEACHING PROGRAM (STEPS 7 AND 8 OF THE TABLE OF STEPS TO FOLLOW, TABLE 4-3, CHAPTER 4)

Now let us write the first teaching program plan and run it.

Writing the Teaching Program Plan to Increase a Behavior

In the last section of this chapter is a blank *General Teaching Program Plan* (Table 6-2). From now on, *every time* you plan a *new, advanced,* or *revised* teaching program for behaviors that need to be increased, done with more skill, or done at the right time and place, please fill out a fresh General Teaching Program Plan. *Make copies* of the blank Table 6-2 for future teaching programs. A teaching program plan for replacing and decreasing problem behaviors, on the other hand, is given at the end of Chapter 15.

Please fill out Table 6-2 now. Question 11 does not apply to your first program. It has to do with *advanced* programs, when you are working on both new and old target behaviors. After you fill out the program plan, come back to the next section, on how to run and measure the teaching program.

Running and Measuring the Teaching Program

For the next week, do not read any more. Just run the teaching program. All you have to do is the following:

1. *Use strong rewards.*
2. *Reward the target behavior (and any other good behaviors) as often as you can, wherever and whenever they happen (Continuous Schedule).*
3. *Count the target behavior each day (number of times or how long).*
4. *Count how many times you reward the target behavior.*
5. *Write your behavior counts (the numbers) on the Behavior Count Table* (Table 6-3) *and chart the numbers or rate* (on Figure 6-2).
6. *Reward yourself for good teaching.*

COUNTING AND CHARTING DURING THE TEACHING PROGRAM

At the end of this chapter are *Behavior Count Tables* (Table 6-3) and *Behavior Charts* (Figure 6-2) for you to fill out each day. They are like the one in Chapter 5 for Jimmy Smith. First, fill out the blanks at the top of the Behavior Count Table and Behavior Chart. Write the days on the top of the table and the bottom of the chart. Then draw a line across the chart as your *goal line.* Try to increase the target behavior at least as high as the line, and to keep it up there.

"How do I know where to draw the goal line?" The section you read in a later chapter on how to teach the target behavior gave you an idea of how much you want the target behavior to increase. For instance, the goal for spontaneous eye contact is about 40 in 20-minute sessions. So the goal line on the chart for sessions should be near 40.

Each day, write what you counted on your golf counter, note pad, or watch in the boxes for the target behavior and teaching behavior. The Behavior Count Table has a few extra rows for the number of times a target behavior was *signaled* and the number of times a target behavior was *prompted.* Do not fill in the signal and prompt rows in your first teaching program. Maybe you will in later programs. Just count the target behavior and the number of times it was rewarded.

Look at the rows for (1) the number of minutes in the session, (2) the number of minutes you watched and counted outside of sessions, and (3) the rate. If sessions are for the *same* number of minutes each day, or if you watch and count outside of sessions for the same amount of time each day, forget about the row for *rate.* But if the number of minutes in sessions changes each day, or if you watch and count outside of sessions for different amounts of time each day, you must find the rate of the target behavior.

Section 8 of Chapter 5 tells you how to find the rate. Just *divide the number of times (or amount of time) the behavior happened by the number of minutes (or hours) you watched and counted each day.* This gives you the number of times (or how long) the target behavior happened *per minute* (or *hour*). For example, if you counted eight times that the behavior happened, and you watched and counted for 2 hours, the RATE is 8/2, or four per hour.

At the end of the day, *chart* what you counted and wrote on the table. Sections 8 and 9 in Chapter 5 will help if you have any trouble. Also, *make copies* of the blank tables and chart for future weeks.

RELIABILITY

Remember to take *reliability checks every few days* in your first teaching program, and about once a week after that. Have another person watch and count the same behavior, at the same time. Then *divide the larger number counted into the smaller number*. This gives you the percentage of *agreement*. For instance, if one person says that the behavior happened eight times and the other says ten times, the PERCENTAGE OF AGREEMENT is 8/10, or 80 percent.

In the box for that day, write which behavior you took a reliability check on and what the percentage of agreement was.

NOW START YOUR FIRST TEACHING PROGRAM. WHEN THE TABLE AND CHART ARE FILLED OUT (1 WEEK), GO TO THE NEXT SECTION, SECTION 6.
HAVE A NICE WEEK.

6.   HOW WELL IS MY TEACHING PROGRAM WORKING, AND WHAT DO I DO NEXT?
(STEP 9 OF TABLE OF STEPS TO FOLLOW, TABLE 4-3, CHAPTER 4)

Your first teaching program has been running for about a week. Take a good, hard look at it. Is it going well enough or not? If it *is* going well, *keep on* with the *same* program until the child is ready to work on the *next* target behavior or skill area. If it *is not* going very well, read Chapter 7 to find out what is wrong, and *revise* the program plan. Now let us find out how well the program is going.

How to Find Out If the Teaching Program Is Going Well Enough

You have been *counting* and *charting* the target behavior all week. The *chart* tells you how fast and how much the target behavior is changing. It can go only one of three ways: increase, stay the same, or decrease. Take a close look at your chart. Here is what to look for:

FOR THE FIRST FEW DAYS, THE TARGET BEHAVIOR *MAY NOT INCREASE* VERY MUCH. BUT THEN, IF YOU HAVE A GOOD PRO-GRAM PLAN AND ARE FOLLOWING IT, THE TARGET BEHAVIOR SHOULD *START* TO INCREASE. AFTER 2 OR MORE WEEKS (WITH SOME UPS AND DOWNS), THE TARGET BEHAVIOR SHOULD START TO *LEVEL OFF*.

So at this time you want the target behavior to be *starting* to *increase. If it is, the teaching program is going well enough, and you can keep on with it.* The three charts in Figure 6-1 show what we mean. They are for three children and the same target behavior—(A1) Spontaneous Eye Contact.

Study the three charts. The chart for Child B stayed about the same (no change); the chart for Child C decreased; and only the chart for Child A shows the target behavior on the increase. *So, the teaching program for Child A is going well enough. But something is wrong with the programs for Children B and C.* The next two sections tell you what to do in both cases.

What to Do If the Chart Shows That the Program Is Not Going Well Enough During the First Week

If your chart is like the one for Child B or C, something may be wrong with the program plan or with the way the program is being run. Maybe

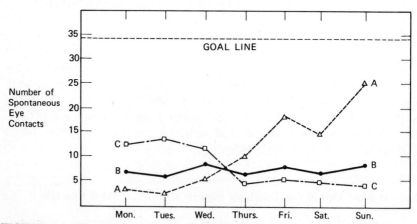

FIGURE 6-1 How the chart for the first week might look. Number of Spontaneous Eye Contacts for three children (A, B, C). All sessions were 20 minutes long. A Continuous Schedule of rewards was used.

the reward is not strong enough, or the target behavior is not being rewarded often enough or fast enough, or perhaps a problem behavior is getting in the way of the target behavior, and you need to decrease the problem behavior (Step 10).

You must find out what is wrong, *revise* the program plan, and *try again*. So, if your chart is like that for Child B or C, *go now to Chapter 7!!* It tells you how to find common problems and revise the program plan. After you revise the plan, run and measure the program for *another week*. If the revised program is going well, come back here and start to read the next section. If the revised program still is not going well, get more help from Chapter 7 and *try, try again*.

DON'T WORRY!
IT OFTEN TAKES A FEW TRIES BEFORE THE FIRST TEACHING
PROGRAM GETS OFF THE GROUND.
When the teaching program is finally going well, start the next section.

What to Do If the Chart Shows That the Program Is Going Well Enough During the First Week

On the other hand, if your chart is like the one for Child A (the target behavior is starting to increase), *keep on with the same program for a second week*. During that time, try to increase the target behavior up to or above the *goal line* you drew across the chart. It may have ups and downs, but should increase overall. If it increases fast enough, it may level off near the end of the second week.

Of course, keep counting and charting. (Remember to make blank copies of Table 6-3 and Figure 6-2). If the chart tells you that the behavior is no longer increasing fast enough or has been decreasing for more than a few days, *go right to Chapter 7*, find out what is wrong, and *revise* the program plan.

Two weeks of running the first teaching program, revising when needed, should increase the target behavior enough so that the child is ready to start on a new target behavior. So, when the 2 weeks are up, read Chapter 8, on *advanced* teaching programs.

Table 6-2.   General Teaching Program Plan: For First, Revised, and
Advanced Programs

Name of Child: _____ Name of Teacher: _____
Week of: _____ to _____

1.   What is the *skill area* for the target behavior?

2.   What *basic behaviors* are needed for this skill area? (List them from
     Table 4-2, Chapter 4.)

3.   *Pinpoint* the target behavior for this teaching program. (Give name and
     number from BET.)

4.   *Define* the target behavior as *movements*. (Describe it as well as you can.)

5.   *How* is the target behavior to be changed? And what will you be *count-
     ing*? (Underline in *a* and *b* below.)

     a.   Increased; done with more skill; done at the right time and place.
     b.   Number of times it happens or how long it happens each day.
6.   How is the target behavior to be *shaped*? (List the small steps by which
     you will teach the behavior. See Table 6-1.)

     a.

     b.

     c.

     d.

     e.

Table 6-2 (*continued*)

Other steps:

7. *When* and *where* will the target behavior be taught? During meals? Before a favorite activity?

   a. When will TEACHING SESSIONS be held?
       From _____ to _____ each day. Number of minutes: _____ or
       hours: _____.
   b. Where will *teaching sessions* be held?

   c. How will you *spread around* the target behavior? (List *places* and
       times outside of teaching sessions when you will work on the target
       behavior. *Who* else will help?)

8. How will you *signal* the target behavior? (List the ways you will start
   teaching sessions and get the target behavior going during sessions and in
   other places.)

9. How will the target behavior be *prompted*? (List the kinds of prompts you
   might use, in the order you might use them, from giving the child the
   most help to the least help.)

   a. (Most help)

   b.

   c.

   d.

   e. (Least help)

10. What will be the *reward schedule* for the *new* target behavior in this
    teaching program? (Continuous or Intermittent? If Intermittent, what
    kind of Intermittent Schedule? Number or Interval? Fixed or Changing?)

Table 6-2 (*continued*)

And what will be the *rewarding consequences* for the new target behavior? (Food? Social? General? Activities? What kinds of food, Social Rewards, back-up rewards, and activities?)

Remember: use a *continuous schedule* and *strong rewards* for a *new* target behavior. If you have any problems, see Section 7 of Chapter 3 and Section 4 of Chapter 6.

Below, list the *reward schedule* for the new target behavior and the *rewards* you will use in that schedule.

Reward Schedule	Rewards
	a.
	b.
	c.
	d.

11. If this is an *advanced* teaching program, which *old* target behaviors from *earlier* teaching programs need to be kept going? What will be the *reward schedules* for the *old* target behaviors? (Continuous or Intermittent? If Intermittent, what kind of Intermittent Schedule? Number or Interval? Fixed or Changing?) And what will be the *rewarding consequences* for the *old* target behaviors? (Food? Social? General? Activities? What kinds of foods, Social Rewards, back-up rewards, and activities?) Remember: after a target behavior has increased, keep it going with a more *natural schedule* (Changing Number or Changing Interval may be best for most behaviors) and more *natural rewards* (Social, General, and Activity Rewards). If you have any problems, see Sections 8 and 9 of Chapter 3. Also see Chapter 8.

Below, list the *old* target behaviors to keep going in this program, the reward *schedule* for *each* behavior, and the *rewards* you will use in each schedule.

Old Target Behaviors	Reward Schedule	Rewards
a.	a.	a.
b.	b.	b.
c.	c.	c.
d.	d.	d.

12. What *other good behaviors* might be rewarded? (List any other good behaviors to reward and the kinds of rewards you might use.)

   a.

   b.

   c.

   d.

13. When will target behaviors be measured? (List times you will measure behaviors, both during teaching sessions and outside of sessions. If you have any problem, see Section 8 of Chapter 5 and Section 4 of Chapter 6.)
   a. Teaching sessions: From _____ to _____ (Copy from number 7*a* above.)
   b. Outside of teaching sessions: From _____ to _____.
   Number of minutes: _____ or hours: _____.

14. What *teaching behavior* will be measured? (Which of your own behaviors will be measured? Usually, you measure the kind of reward and the number of times you reward the target behavior. You can also count the number of times a behavior had to be signaled or the number of times it had to be prompted.)

   a.

   b.

   c.

15. What will you *count* with? _____

PLEASE MAKE COPIES OF THIS TABLE.

Table 6-3.　Behavior Count Tables for Teaching Programs

Name of Child: _____ Name of Teacher: _____
Skill Area: _____ Target Behavior: _____
Week of: _____ to _____

BEHAVIOR COUNTS DURING TEACHING SESSIONS

Day of Session	__ day	__ day	__ day	__ day	__ day	__ day	__ day
Number of Minutes in Session[a]							
How Often Target Behavior Happened (Number of Times, Minutes, Hours)							
Rate of Target Behavior[a]							
Number of Times Target Behavior Was Rewarded							
Number of Times Target Behavior Was Signaled							
Number of Times Target Behavior Was Prompted							
Reliability[b]							

BEHAVIOR COUNTS MADE DURING THE DAY OUTSIDE OF
TEACHING SESSIONS

Day of Session	__ day	__ day	__ day	__ day	__ day	__ day	__ day
Number of Minutes Watched Outside of Session[a]							
How Often Target Behavior Happened (Number of Times, Minutes, Hours)							
Rate of Target Behavior[a]							
Number of Times Target Behavior Was Rewarded							
Number of Times Target Behavior Was Signaled							
Number of Times Target Behavior Was Prompted							
Reliability[b]							

[a] Remember: if the amount of time you watch and count is different each day, you have to find out the *rate* of the behavior. *Divide the number of times the behavior happened by the number of minutes (or hours) you watched.* This gives you the number of times the behavior happened per minute (or hour).

[b] Take a reliability check every few days. In the box for that day, write the behavior you reliability-checked and the percentage of agreement.

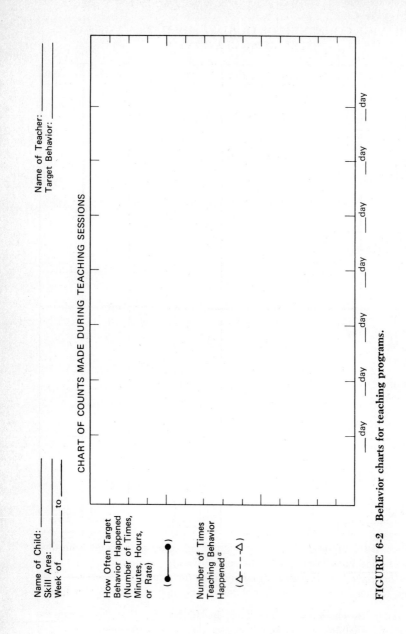

FIGURE 6-2 Behavior charts for teaching programs.

152

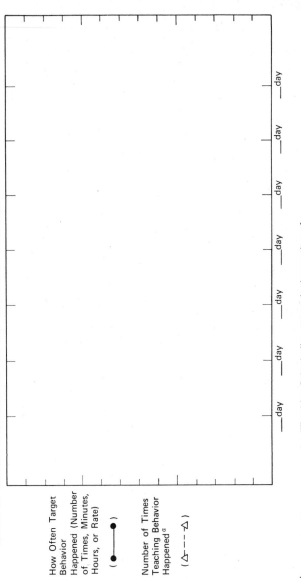

CHART OF COUNTS MADE DURING THE DAY OUTSIDE OF TEACHING SESSIONS

How Often Target
Behavior
Happened (Number
of Times, Minutes,
Hours, or Rate)

(●——●)

Number of Times
Teaching Behavior
Happened[a]

(△ — — △)

___day ___day ___day ___day ___day ___day ___day ___day

[a] In most teaching programs, the "Teaching Behavior" to count is the number of times the target behavior was rewarded.

DON'T FORGET TO DRAW A GOAL LINE ACROSS THE CHART.

FIGURE 6-2 (continued).

REFERENCES AND EXTRA READINGS

Bijou, S. W., and Sturges, P. S. "Positive reinforcers for experimental studies with children—Consumables and manipulatables." *Child Development*, 1959, **30**, 151-170.

Bugelski, B. R. *The Psychology of Learning Applied to Teaching*. Indianapolis: Bobbs-Merrill, 1964.

Galloway, C., and Galloway, K. C. "Parent classes in precise behavior management." *Teaching Exceptional Children*, 1971, Spring, 120-128.

Holland, C. J., "An interview guide for behavioral counseling with parents." *Behaviour Therapy*, 1970, 1, 70-79.

Lindsley, O. R. "Direct measurement and prosthesis of retarded behavior." *Journal of Education*, 1964, **147**, 62-81.

Madsen, C. H., Jr., Becker, W. C., and Thomas, D. R. "Rules, praise, and ignoring: Elements of elementary classroom control." *Journal of Applied Behavior Analysis*, 1968, 1, 139-150.

Mager, R. F. *Preparing Instructional Objectives*. Belmont, Calif.: Fearon Publishers, 1962.

Meacham, M. L., and Wiesen, A. E. *Changing Classroom Behavior: A Manual for Precision Teaching*. Scranton, Pa.: International Textbook Co., 1969.

Michael, J. "Principles of effective usage." In R. Ulrich, T. Stachnick, and J. Mabry (Eds.), *Control of Human Behavior*, Vol. II: *From Cure to Prevention*. Glenview, Ill.: Scott, Foresman, 1970. Pp. 28-35.

Pipe, P. *Practical Programming*. New York: Holt, Rinehart and Winston, 1966.

CHAPTER SEVEN

Handling
Common PROBLEMS
of TEACHING

Sometimes all your hard work to increase a target behavior does not seem to pay off. If a target behavior in your teaching program is staying the same or is decreasing—if it is like the charts for Children B and C in Figure 6-1, Chapter 6—then this chapter will help. There are many simple problems that can keep a teaching program from working right. We want you to know how to spot those problems, remove them from your program, and prevent them from happening again.

1. WHAT ARE SOME OF THE COMMON PROBLEMS?

1. Measurement Is Not Correct

Chapter 5 told you how important it is to measure the target behavior you are trying to change, to see if your teaching program seems to be working. What if the *chart* shows that the target behavior *is not changing* as it should? For example, you may have worked for a week to increase the number of times the child makes eye contact, and the chart shows that he is making eye contact no more often than when you started. Do you drop the teaching program?

No! The first thing to do is check your measurements to see if they are correct. Maybe you did not chart the behavior right. Maybe you made a mistake in your adding. Also, make sure you have *pinpointed* and *defined* the target behavior correctly. For instance, maybe your pro-

155

gram is to increase the number of times the child makes Spontaneous Eye Contact (A1) but you are really counting *only* the number of times he makes Eye Contact on Request (A2). Spontaneous eye contact may be increasing, but your chart will not show it because you are counting and charting a different behavior. Have someone take some *reliability checks* with you to see if your measurements are correct.

2. Consequences Are Not Effective

This is probably the most common problem. The target behavior may not be increasing because the consequence you are following the behavior with is *not really a reward*. There is only one way to find out if a certain thing (*consequence*) is a reward, and that is to follow the behavior with that consequence over and over. If the behavior does not increase, that consequence is simply not a reward *and you must try something else.*

Whenever you plan a teaching program, as you did in Chapter 6, you are only *guessing* that the consequence is a reward for that behavior. *But it may not be!* It is a good bet that food will be a reward (to a hungry child), but *praise* ("Good boy"), a hug, a gold star, or a *token* may not be rewarding at first. *Do not keep on trying to "reward" a behavior with something that is not really a reward. Try something else.*

3. Child Is Getting the Rewards for Free

If a child already gets whatever you are going to reward him with, it will not really be a reward. What do you think will happen if Billy's mother lets him snack all day, and then at 4 o'clock in the afternoon tries to reward him with more snacks for working at puzzles? Do you think he will work very hard? Probably not! His belly is already full. *The same goes for attention.* If the child gets attention from you all day long—hugs, praise, or talking to him—these will not be rewarding to him during the few minutes or hours you are trying to teach him. Why should he *do* anything for your attention, and how can your attention "turn him on," when he gets attention no matter what he does? Why should he do anything to get food, music, attention, toys, or roughhousing when he has been getting them all day and has learned that he will get them regardless of his behavior—at least tomorrow. You know the answer as well as we do.

IF HE GETS THESE THINGS ALL THE TIME ANYWAY, YOU CANNOT USE THEM AS REWARDS.

The key is to make sure that you *save* the things you are going to use as rewards, and make sure the child *earns* them for doing the target behavior and other good behaviors. If you are going to use food as a reward, you must not let the child snack all day; you must not let him eat before a teaching session; and you must not let him eat so much at meals that he is stuffed for hours afterwards. If you are going to use praise or other kinds of attention, you have to make sure he is not already getting too much extra attention, *except* for the behaviors you are going to reward with attention.

This does not mean starving the child of food and attention. It simply means that these are used *only* to reward behaviors you are trying to increase. In fact, if your program is working right, he will be getting more rewards than ever before, because the rewarded behavior will increase.

4. Consequences Are Not Given Often Enough

At the start of any program to increase a behavior, *it is very, very important that the behavior be rewarded just about every time it happens,* that is, on a *Continuous Schedule.* In other words, the rewards are always there when the behavior happens.

The reason it is important to reward a *new* behavior every time (on a Continuous Schedule) is that, each time the behavior happens but is *not* rewarded, it is as if the behavior is being *ignored*—and you know what happens when a behavior is no longer rewarded or is ignored. It decreases, So, if you do not reward a new behavior just about every time in the beginning, you will be working against yourself. You will be increasing the behavior each time you reward it and decreasing it each time you do not reward it.

So, at the start of a new teaching program, *reward the behavior on a Continuous Schedule or as many times as you can.*

The next problem is like this one, but has to do with *advanced* teaching programs.

5. Shift from Continuous Schedule to Intermittent Schedule Was Made Too Fast

At first, a new behavior should be rewarded every time (*on a Continuout Schedule*). But the more it is rewarded, the faster the child will get sick of the reward (*satiated*). Besides, it is just plain impossible to keep on rewarding every good behavior that happens. So, after a target behavior has increased and leveled off, begin to *reward it less and less*.

For example, when the child is first starting to work hard puzzles, you must reward him every time he puts a piece in right (*a Continuous Schedule*). But, once he is working many puzzles a day, he does not have to be rewarded every time. He can be rewarded every three, four, or five times (*an Intermittent Schedule*).

But when you start to reward him less, *you must do it very slowly*. What would happen if for a week you rewarded the child every time he correctly named pictures and objects, and the next day you rewarded him only one out of ten times? He would get very upset, throw a tantrum, and *stop talking*.

Therefore you must *wean* the child from a Continuous Schedule very slowly. For example, instead of rewarding the target behavior every time, reward it four out of five times, then two out of three, and so on. In this way, the child will hardly notice that he is being rewarded less often. In fact, you may increase the target behavior even more if you move to an Intermittent Schedule slowly enough.

6. Consequences Are Not Given Fast Enough

At the start of any program to increase a behavior, *it is very important that the rewarding consequence follow the behavior immediately—within 1 or 2 seconds*. If you wait too long to tell the child what he did right or to reward him, how will he ever learn what he did right or what behavior you are praising him for? The answer is that he might not learn, and the behavior might not increase very much.

Another reason to reward a behavior immediately is that *whatever behavior came just before the reward is the one that was rewarded and is the one that will increase*. If you wait too long to reward the behavior, the child will have already done something else, and so the *wrong behavior* will have been rewarded. For example, if the child makes eye contact with you and you reward him 3 seconds later, he may have looked at the ceiling in the meantime, and that is the behavior that will increase.

"But what if I am too far away to reward the child immediately?" If the reward is food or a token and you are too far away to give the reward immediately, at least *give him some signal that the reward is on its way*, for instance, by saying, "Hey, that's *good working!*" while you quickly walk to him with the reward. In this way, the words "good working" will become learned rewards too.

7. Consequences Are Given Too Many Times

Reread the first sentence of number 3 above. How do you like it when someone says "Hello" to you in the *same way* every day? How would you like to eat the same thing for lunch every day or watch the same movie every night? How long do you think the same kind of food, attention, or activity would be rewarding to a child if he got them over and over again, minute after minute and day after day? The answer is that they would stop being rewards. They would no longer increase the behaviors they follow.

The word we use when a person has gotten the same rewarding consequence so many times that it is not a reward any more is "satiation." The person is just plain full of food or sick of hearing someone say, "Good boy." He is *satiated*. And he will stop doing the behaviors which are followed by the rewards he is sick of. You stop laying your money on the counter (behavior) when you are full of beer (satiated).

So one thing to do is to *switch between many different kinds of rewards, from day to day and even during the same short teaching session*. Reward the child with a big hug (if this is a reward) one time, with a bite of food the next, and with some roughhousing the third time. *Keep him on his toes*. Make things exciting by not letting him know just what the reward will be each time. Use a *different tone of voice* and *different words* when you praise him. Switch between different kinds of food rewards if, at first, you must use food.

Also, *stop an activity before the child has had enough*. Turn off the music or stop free time while the child is still enjoying it. In that way, he will want the activity again later and will work to earn it. *Rotate* the different Activity Rewards you can use. Every few days, take some of the toys away and bring back others.

Above all, *once a child is satiated on (full of) a reward, do not use it for a long time*. You cannot push it on him. He will just stop paying attention, start whining, or fight you off.

8. Child Does Not Have the Basic Behaviors

Sometimes a target behavior does not increase because the child is not really *ready* to work in that skill area. He does not have the *basics*. Always list the basic behaviors needed for a skill area on your teaching program plan. Table 4-2 in Chapter 4 tells you which ones they are. Then if a target behavior does not increase very much, make a simple *test* to see if the child has the basics.

For instance, if you are working on a Small Motor activity (Looking, Listening, and Moving skills) and the child does not seem to be learning it, test him to see if he has the basic behaviors needed before he can work in that skilled area. During the teaching session, *watch* to see if he (1) makes a good deal of spontaneous eye contact; (2) makes eye contact on request with no trouble; (3) has good sitting behavior; and (4) cooperates with simple spoken requests. If you find he needs help with any of these, *begin to work on them and put the target behavior* (the Small Motor activity) *on the back burner for a while. Do not stop* working on the Small Motor activity; just work on it less and reward the basic behaviors more. When the child is in good shape on all the basics, go back to your program plan for the target behavior.

The next problem is like this one but has to do with *shaping* a target behavior.

9.   Target Behavior Is Not Being Taught in Small Enough Steps

We have said many times that people learn best in small steps. This means teaching a target behavior by breaking it down, starting with the easiest step, and moving to harder steps as the child becomes skilled at the easier ones. Now the reason the child learns the harder steps is that you *hold off* on rewards for the easier ones. In other words, when he has mastered Step 1, you do not reward him for it any more—he is rewarded only for harder steps. In this way, if you *prompt* him, he will stop doing Step 1 and *try* Step 2. As you reward him for trying, he gets better and better at Step 2.

But what if you hold out for behavior on a step that is just too hard? Or what if you wait for a behavior that is "perfect"? Chances are the child will not be getting rewarded even for trying, because he cannot do that behavior yet. If he is not rewarded for trying, will he keep on trying? No, he will not! In fact, when you *push* a child in this way, his other good behaviors, such as making eye contact, sitting, and cooperating, will not be rewarded either, *and they will decrease.* After a while, the child will start whining, crying, looking away, and not doing anything you ask, because while you were waiting to reward a "perfect" or too hard behavior, you *ignored* all of the other good behaviors he was doing. And you decreased them all. Once that happens, you are in

trouble because you have to go back and increase the other good behaviors.

The key is to *start with a step easy enough that the child has a good
chance of being rewarded often.* And, when you move to a harder step,

HOLD OUT FOR A BEHAVIOR THAT IS JUST A *LITTLE BIT* BETTER;
PROMPT (HELP) THE CHILD TO DO THE BEHAVIOR AT FIRST;

and

USE *BIGGER REWARDS* AND GIVE THEM FASTER FOR GOOD TRIES.

In this way, the child will keep getting rewarded, he will stay interested,
and you will have behavior to build on.

So, if your chart shows you that the target behavior is not increasing
or is decreasing, *you might need to back up to an easier step or break
down the next harder step even more.* Then *slowly work up to harder
steps.*

For example, if the child is not getting any better at saying "Water,"
do not keep pushing him to say it. Instead, back up to rewarding him
for saying "Wa-er," and once he has that down pat, go ahead again to
"water."

10. Wrong Behavior Is Being Rewarded

Of course, if you reward the wrong behavior, the target behavior you are
measuring will not increase. It is very easy to reward the wrong behavior, even if you know exactly what the target behavior is. If you
wait too long to reward the behavior, the child will have done something
else in the meantime, and that is what you will have rewarded. (Reread
number 6 above.)

Sometimes you may reward the wrong behavior by accident. A good
example of this is trying to stop some kind of problem behavior by telling the child to stop. In fact, you may be accidentally rewarding the
problem behavior with your attention. With some children, just about
anything you do to stop a problem behavior really rewards that behavior,
and it will increase. The best thing to do then is to *ignore the behavior,
as if it were not even happening.* But *do not make a show of ignoring!*
If you turn your head away or cover your eyes, you *may* still be rewarding the child, because he has gotten you to do something; he is still
controlling you. *Ignoring behavior means not reacting to it at all.*

The next item will help if a problem behavior keeps happening even
if you are not rewarding it.

11.   Problem Behavior Is Getting in the Way of the Target Behavior

Even if everything else in your teaching program is perfect—you are rewarding fast enough and often enough, using an effective reward, and working on an easy enough step—the target behavior may still not increase *because the child keeps doing some problem behavior instead*. He is not finding out that he will be rewarded for other, "good" behaviors because he is too busy with the problem behaviors, such as whining, walking around the room, making strange hand movements, or throwing tantrums.

If that is the case, you must *replace and decrease the problem behavior in a more direct way*. You need to write a program plan for replacing and decreasing it. Go to Chapter 15, on "Replacing Problem Behaviors," if this difficulty applies to your teaching program.

12.   Child Is Given a Signal When He Is Not Looking

What are the chances that the child will imitate some movement of yours if he is not looking at you when you show him? What are the chances that he will learn how to say "Mama" if he does not look at your mouth when you say it for him? Very slim!

But the problem is even worse than that. Every time you give the child a *signal* (for instance, when you say, "Look at me" or when you show him a movement to imitate) and he *does not* do what he was signaled to do because he was not looking, your signal loses its power to *direct* or guide his behavior. Every time you run a red light, it gets easier to do so. The red light loses its control over your stopping behavior. Every time someone asks you to do something and you do not do it, it is easier to ignore them when they ask you the next time.

So, when you are trying to increase a behavior, *it is very important that the child look at you when you give him a signal*. This increases the chances that he will do what the signal says. Of course, if the child's attention behavior is weak—for example, he does not make spontaneous eye contact or eye contact on request very often, he does not look at your face or at things you point to, he does not look at what he is doing—you must work on these behaviors during sessions.

13.   Child Is Asked Questions Instead of Being Given Directions

Answering questions (such as "What is your name?" or "What color is the horse?") is important behavior. It is one of the kinds of Functional

Speech. But we often ask people questions when we want more than just an answer. For instance, we ask, *"Will you* do this for me?" or *"Can you* take out the trash?" We really do not want just a "Yes" or "No" answer; we want the person to *do* what we asked. In other words, we are not saying what we mean, which is all right since the person "understands" that we want him to do something.

But, when you ask a child questions like this, when you really want to signal him to do something, he will not always do it, either because he does not understand what you *really* want, or because he is giving you a straight answer ("Can you say 'Mama'?" . . . "No."). So, if you want to start a behavior, give the child a direction ("Say 'Mama!'"), not a "Can you" question. If your chart shows that the target behavior is not increasing, check yourself to see if you are asking "Can you" or "Will you" questions.

The next problem has to do with another wrong way to use *signals*.

14. Same Signal Is Given Over and Over

It is easy to get in the habit of using the same signal over and over when the child does not cooperate with it. For example, if you hold up a picture and ask, "What is this called?" and the child does not answer, you may repeat the question over and over, until either the child answers or you give up. Or, if the child is outside and you want him to come back in, you may say, "Billy, time to come in." If he does not come in, you may say, "I said, it's time to come in," and still later, "Come in this minute!" Finally, you get so angry that you drag him in. And, when you do, you have rewarded him for not cooperating with *all* of the signals.

The point is this: Each time you repeat a signal, you are rewarding the child for not cooperating with the one before, by paying attention to him. As a result, not cooperating with signals increases, until you feel you are wasting your breath. At that point, the child looks as if he "is out of it" or "has poor attention" or "does not understand." But he has really *learned not to listen to you or to do what you say.*

The cure?

GIVE THE CHILD A SIGNAL ONLY WHEN HE IS PAYING
ATTENTION TO YOU
and
GIVE A SIGNAL ONLY ONCE.

If the child does not cooperate with the signal, *do not* repeat the same signal over and over. Instead, *wait* 5 or 10 seconds. Then, either (1) let him find out that the consequence of not cooperating is *missing a reward;* or (2) *give the signal again* and *prompt* him through the motions of cooperating with the signal. For instance, if you hold up a picture, and ask, "What is this called?" and the child gives the wrong answer or does not answer at all, put the picture down, wait about 5 seconds, hold up a *different* picture, and try again. In this way, the child gets no attention for not answering and he misses rewards he would have gotten if he had answered correctly. Of course, if the child does not *know* the answer, you would *prompt* him at first by telling him the answer.

On the other hand, if you give the child a direction or a request to do something ("Jimmy, hang up your coat, please"), and he ignores you or starts to do the behavior the wrong way, *do not* keep telling him to hang up his coat. Instead, wait a few seconds, give the signal again, and *put him through the right motions* of hanging up his coat.

So, if your chart shows the target behavior is not increasing (or shows that it is decreasing), check yourself to see if you are repeating the same signal even though the child is not cooperating with it. If you are, learn to ignore the fact that the child has not cooperated, wait a short time, and either give a different signal or put him through the right motions the next time. Also, set things up so that not cooperating with signals is followed by *nothing rewarding* and may result in *missing* a chance to earn a reward.

15. Threats Are Used as Signals

Use signals in a *positive* way. Avoid telling the child what he will not get if he does not do something, or what bad thing will happen to him if he does something you do not like. Threats will only start fights and make the child less likely to cooperate.

16. Child Is Not Being Helped (Prompted) Enough

When you are trying to increase a behavior, you want the child to do it many times so that you can reward him for it. Often, he will need help doing the behavior, for instance, imitating movements, working puzzles, or doing a chore. When you help the child by moving his hands for him, by putting him through the motions, or by telling him how to do something, we call this "prompting." *Prompting* increases the child's chances of doing the behavior well enough to be rewarded.

If you do not prompt the child so that he does the behavior well enough to be rewarded, he is not being rewarded for *trying*. After a while, he will stop trying. *So, at the start, it is important to prompt the child so that he does the behavior well enough to be rewarded.*

17.   Child Is Being Helped (Prompted) Too Much

Sometimes a behavior does not increase or get done with more skill because the child is being prompted too much, when he no longer really needs so much help. If you keep on *prompting* the child, he will get so used to your prompts that he will hardly try to do the behavior unless you prompt him. He will wait for your prompts. In other words, he has learned to be *dependent* upon your *prompts.*

You will know that this has happened when you try to stop helping (*prompting*) the child and he does not even try to do the behavior by himself. In that case, go back to a simpler behavior that the child did learn to do by himself, and then work up again to the new behavior, but this time use less prompting.

The best thing is to avoid this problem, by (1) using as *few prompts as you can* from the start; and (2) *slowly* helping (*prompting*) the child less and less as he gets more and more skill. When you slowly help him less and less, we call this "fading the prompt." For example, at first you might have to prompt the child to say "Mama" by moving his lips and jaw. But once he *starts* to move them the right way by himself, let go of his lips and jaw just *before* the right sounds come out. As time goes by, let go of his lips and jaw earlier and use less pressure (*fade the prompts*), Finally, he will be saying "Mama" by himself.

18.   Child Has Been Working Too Long at the Same Thing

Please read number 7 again. Just as the child can get sick of the same reward (*satiation*), so he can get sick of the same task (*boredom*). Variety is the spice of life—and learning. *Do not work on the same behavior for too long at one time or for too many days in a row.* Once you find out how long it takes before the child *starts* to get a little restless (squirming in his seat, looking away, not trying very hard), you must run your teaching sessions so that they *end before he becomes bored.* Otherwise you will have a hard time ever getting him back to another session.

If the target behavior is not increasing because the child is bored, *switch to a new activity for a few days.* To keep this from happening again, *switch often between the behaviors the child has learned and the behaviors you are teaching him. Do not spend too much time on one behavior. Work on many behaviors during the same teaching session.*

19. Child Is Making Too Many Errors in a Row

If you ask the child to point to the picture of the red ball (*signal*) and he points to the picture of the house (*error*), are you going to say, "Good boy"? If you clap your hands (*signal to imitate*) and he stamps his feet, are you going to say, "Right, that was very good"? Of course not. You are not going to reward errors, or else you will be increasing them.

Every time the child makes an error two things happen. First, the signal that you used gets *weaker,* because the child did not do what the signal told him to do. (See number 14.) Also, if his behavior was not correct enough but was partly correct, and he was not rewarded, you have ignored the fact that he made some attempt—he tried. This will decrease his trying.

So you can imagine what will happen if the child makes the same error over and over, many times in a row. *The signal you are using will lose all its power. And, if the child is not rewarded because he was making errors, even though he was partly correct, he will stop trying.* After a while, the child will stop looking at you and listening to you; he will walk away, and you will have a hard time getting him back. The solution is to *stop working on a behavior if the child makes more than a few errors in a row. Go on to a different behavior and come back to the first one later. Or go back to a simpler behavior and make sure that the child can do it before you move ahead to the one he was having trouble with.*

For example, if you ask the child to look at you two or three times and he does not, stop asking him and start rewarding him for something even easier, like looking at you on his own. Or, if he is not imitating you correctly when you clap your hands, either help (*prompt*) him or go back to a movement he can imitate. These two methods—prompting and backing up—will ensure that the child is rewarded for at least trying.

20. Child Is Not Being Rewarded for Other Good Behaviors

One of the biggest mistakes is to reward only the behavior you are trying to increase—the target behavior. But isn't the child doing many good things besides the target behavior? Of course he is. The target behavior may be correct word imitations, but the child may also be looking at you, sitting in his chair, and following instructions. What will happen if he is never rewarded for these behaviors any more? You know what will happen. They will decrease, and all you will have left is a child who does only the target behavior.

Therefore *it is most important to reward the child every so often for behaviors he used to be rewarded for.* This will keep them happening at a high level. For example, when you are working on speech and are way past working on eye contact, reward him for eye contact once in a while anyway. *But do not overdo it!* You want him to keep learning harder behaviors. If you reward easy behaviors too much, he will stop trying the hard ones. The key words are "once in a while."

Also, *stay on the lookout for any good behaviors to reward, especially at the start of a program.* The reason is that the more the child is rewarded, the more he will enjoy working with you, and the more those behaviors will increase. So *take every chance to reward good behaviors.*

21.   Child Is Not Being Told What He Is Doing Well

It is a good idea to *tell the child what behavior he is being rewarded for.* In this way, he learns what that behavior is *called* and you can use the name for it in a signal. For example, if you are trying to increase eye contact, tell the child when he makes eye contact, "Good boy for looking at me." Once he learns that he is *looking* at you, you can begin to signal eye contact by saying, "*Look* at me." Also, it is good to tell the child what he is doing well, or why he is being rewarded, when you cannot reward him immediately. At least you will be filling in the gap and calling his attention to what he did.

2.   WHAT DO I DO WHEN THE TARGET BEHAVIOR IS NOT INCREASING?

When your chart shows that the target behavior is not increasing as it should, look at the Checklist of Common Problems of Teaching (Table 7-1). Then ask yourself if any of the problems on it are keeping your teaching programs from increasing the target behavior. Here are some guidelines to follow.

If your program is just getting started, and the target behavior is not increasing, it is a good bet that the problem has something to do with the rewarding consequence. For example, the consequence may not be effective (item 2), the child may be getting rewards free (item 3), the consequence may not be given often enough (item 4) or fast enough (item 6), or you may be rewarding the wrong behavior (item 10). On the other hand, the child may not have the basics for that behavior (item 8), it may be too hard for him (item 9), or a problem behavior may be getting in the way (item 11).

If the target behavior was increasing but now is decreasing, maybe the shift to Intermittent Schedules was too fast (item 5), the consequences are given too many times (item 7), the child is given signals when he is not looking (item 12), he is asked questions instead of told what to do (item 13), the same signal is used over and over (item 14), the child is threatened (item 15), he has worked too long at the same thing (item 18), he is making too many errors (item 19), he is not rewarded for other good behaviors (item 20), or he is not told what he is doing well (item 21).

When you think you have spotted the problem, change or *revise* your *teaching program plan*. Try to use the ideas given in this chapter in the section for that problem. For example, if you have been using Social Rewards (praise), and the target behavior is not increasing, maybe Social Rewards are *not effective* yet (item 2). Try a stronger reward, such as food. Above all,

TRY, TRY AGAIN.

Most of the time, the solution to a teaching problem is simple and can be found in this chapter.

TAKE A BREAK.
When you come back, do the assignment, which is to REVISE your
TEACHING PROGRAM PLAN.

ASSIGNMENT: REVISING THE TEACHING PROGRAM PLAN

The assignment is to spot the problem or problems that might have hurt your teaching program and to *revise* the program. First answer the following questions:

1. *Which* problems from the checklist (Table 7-1) do you think hurt your teaching program? (Use the name and number from the checklist.)

2. *How* did each problem hurt the program?

3. *What* will you do about each problem, that is, how will you take care of it or *revise* the program plan?

Table 7-1. Checklist of Common Problems of Teaching

1. *Measurement* is not correct.

2. Consequences are not *effective*.

3. Child is getting the rewards for *free*.

4. Consequences are not given *often enough*.

5. Shift from Continuous Schedule to Interm'ttent Schedule was made *too fast*.

6. Consequences are not given *fast enough*.

7. Consequences are given *too many times*.

8. Child does not have necessary *basic behaviors*.

9. Target behavior is not being taught in *small enough steps*.

10. *Wrong behavior* is being rewarded.

11. A problem behavior is *getting in the way* of the target behavior.

12. Child is given signal when he is *not looking*.

13. Child is asked questions instead of being given *directions* to signal his behaviors.

14. Same signal is given *over and over*.

15. *Threats* are used as a signal.

16. Child is not being helped (*prompted*) enough.

17. Child is being helped (*prompted*) too much.

18. Child has been *working too long* at the same thing.

19. Child is making *too many errors* in a row.

20. Child is not being rewarded for *other good behaviors*.

21. Child is not being told *what he is doing well*.

Now, please rewrite the teaching program plan for the target behavior you have been working on. Use a copy of Table 6-2 (General Teaching Program Plan) at the end of Chapter 6. Then run the program according to the revised plan. Count and chart behaviors, using Table 6-3 and the chart in Figure 6-2 at the end of Chapter 6. If there are any more problems, come back to this chapter and *try again*. If the revised program goes well during the first week, go to Section 6 of Chapter 6 and find out what to do next.

CHAPTER EIGHT

How to PLAN
and RUN
ADVANCED
TEACHING PROGRAMS

When the first target behavior has been increasing (with some ups and downs) for about 2 weeks, it is time to start an *advanced* teaching program.

1. WHAT GOES INTO AN ADVANCED TEACHING PROGRAM?

To plan and run an advanced teaching program, follow the same steps as in the first teaching program.

Pick the Next Target Behavior or Skill Area

First take a look at the Table of Steps to Follow (Table 4-3, Chapter 4). To pinpoint a new target behavior in the *same* skill area,

PINPOINT THE NEXT HARDER BEHAVIOR THE CHILD NEEDS HELP WITH DOWN THE LIST ON THE BET.

Or, if the child has already learned most of the basic behaviors in the first skill area, he may be ready to start on a *new skill* area. If so, (1) look at the Skill Sequence Table (Table 4-1, Chapter 4) to see which skill area comes next; (2) check the Table of Basic Behaviors (Table 4-2, Chapter 4) to see which ones are needed before the child can work

171

in that skill area; and (3) check his BET to see if he has learned the basic behaviors (is ready). When you have picked the next skill area, pinpoint the first target behavior to work on. Pinpoint (and work on) the *easiest* one the child needs help with on the list for that skill area on the BET.

Run a Baseline

After you have pinpointed a new target behavior, run a *baseline* on it for a few days (Step 5). If the baseline chart says that the behavior needs to be changed, *read* how to change it in the chapter for that skill area (Step 6).

Of course, the next step (Step 7) is to *plan* and *write* the advanced teaching program. Here are some "extras" to keep in mind when you do that.

Rewards and Reward Schedules to Use with the New Target Behavior and the Old Target Behavior

There are two tasks in an advanced program:

KEEPING THE FIRST (OLD) TARGET BEHAVIOR (OR BEHAVIORS)
GOING STRONG,
and
INCREASING THE NEW TARGET BEHAVIOR.

HOW DO I KEEP THE OLD TARGET BEHAVIORS GOING?

That's a good question. To find out, please read Section 8 of Chapter 3 again *now*, on using more *natural rewards, reward schedules, and chains.*

REWARD YOURSELF FOR GOOD READING BEHAVIOR.

As you just read, when a target behavior has increased and started to level off, it is time to *keep it going*—time to put it on the "back burner" —while you work mostly on a new target behavior. To keep the first target behavior going, (1) *slowly* put it on an *intermittent schedule* (a *Changing Number Schedule may be best*); (2) *slowly* use *Social, General,* and *Activity* Rewards *more* and *Primary* Rewards *less;* and (3) *chain* the older (stronger) target behavior to the new (weaker) target behavior, so that the reward for the new behavior will also reward the old one.

To help you remember to reward the old target behavior, draw a *goal line* on your chart for it and try to keep the behavior *above* the goal line.

HOW DO I INCREASE THE NEW TARGET BEHAVIOR?

You know the answer to this. *At the start,* increase the new target behavior in the same way you did the first one. Be sure to (1) use *strong* rewards, and (2) reward the new target behavior *every time (Continuous Schedule).* And, most important,

WHEN THE *NEW* TARGET BEHAVIOR HAS INCREASED AND STARTED TO LEVEL OFF, USE MORE NATURAL REWARDS AND REWARD SCHEDULES WITH IT, TOO.

Jimmy Smith's program shows which rewards and reward schedules to use with the new and old target behaviors. The target behavior in Jimmy's first teaching program with Mrs. Oaks (Chapter 5) was (A1) Spontaneous Eye Contact, and it was rewarded with candy (Primary Reward) and praise on a Continuous Schedule. After 1 week, the number of spontaneous eye contacts increased enough so that Mrs. Oaks started an advanced teaching program. She kept working in the Learning Readiness skill area and pinpointed (A4) Cooperation with Simple Spoken Requests as the new target behavior.

Mrs. Oaks had to do two things: (1) increase the new target behavior (cooperation); and (2) keep the first target behavior (spontaneous eye contact) *going.* So, with the new target behavior (cooperation), she *started* with a Continuous Schedule, using candy, praise, and activities as rewards. At the same time, Mrs. Oaks *slowly* changed the rewards and reward schedules for spontaneous eye contact (the older and stronger target behavior). For example, she did the following:

1. Used candy (Primary Reward) less and less (*Intermittent Schedule*) and praise and hugs (Social Rewards) more and more.
2. Used Activity Rewards when eye contact happened at the right time and place. For instance, if Jimmy walked over to Mrs. Oaks, who was standing by a locked door, and looked her in the eye, she opened the

door for him. Of course, she had to *hold out* on many Activity Rewards *until* Jimmy made eye contact.

3. *Chained* eye contact and cooperation together. For example, *before* she gave Jimmy a chance to cooperate (before she gave him a simple request), he *first* had to make eye contact. Then, by rewarding him for cooperating, she also rewarded the eye contact.

As long as her charts told her that

SPONTANEOUS EYE CONTACT WAS STILL GOING STRONG
and
COOPERATION WAS INCREASING,

Mrs. Oaks *kept on with the same program plan.* But, if either of the two behaviors had decreased, she would have gone to Chapter 7 to find out what was wrong and how to *revise* her program.

After about 2 weeks of the advanced program, cooperation increased and started to level off. What do you think Mrs. Oaks did then? If you think that she used more natural rewards and schedules with the target behavior, you are right! She used praise, hugs, and Activity Rewards (Grandma's Law) more and more, *and candy rewards less and less.* She also started a teaching program for a third behavior.

The charts in Figure 8-1 show how the two target behaviors (spontaneous eye contact and cooperation) were rewarded, how they changed, and how Mrs. Oaks counted and charted them.

You see that Mrs. Oaks counted and charted *both* target behaviors each day. She also *overlapped* the programs for the two behaviors. She *did not work on the new one (cooperation) and forget about the old one (eye contact).* Instead, when she started the program for the new target behavior (cooperation), she kept working on the old one (spontaneous eye contact). But she began using *different rewards* and *reward schedules* for spontaneous eye contact. She used *more natural* rewards and reward schedules. Finally, when the new target behavior (cooperation) had increased enough and leveled off, Mrs. Oaks started to use more natural reward schedules to keep cooperation going strong. So now she is ready to start a teaching program for a third target behavior.

SWITCH REWARDS OFTEN

It is very important to

SWITCH REWARDS OFTEN, BEFORE THE CHILD
BECOMES SATIATED.

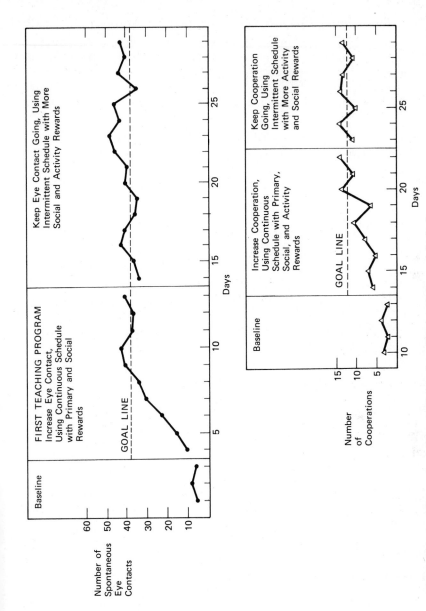

FIGURE 8-1 How a chart for an advanced teaching program might look.

For example, during the day, Mrs. Oaks would reward eye contact with candy one time, a hug the next, an activity the third time, and so on. She did the same for cooperation. In that way, each reward would "turn Jimmy on."

TAKE A BREAK.
When you come back, we will talk about using GENERAL REWARDS (TOKEN SYSTEMS).

How to Run a Token System

Some children may be ready to earn General (token) Rewards. Token rewards are good in three ways: (1) you can use them to wean a child off Primary Rewards; (2) since tokens can be used to "buy" many other rewards, the child is not likely to become satiated with them; and (3) learning to use tokens teaches the child other good behaviors (earning, waiting, choosing, spending). Before you go on, please read about General Rewards in Section 4 of Chapter 3.

General Rewards (tokens, money) are rewards *only* because of what they can buy. In other words, tokens and money are *followed by back-up rewards.* General Rewards are used like any other reward; they are given as a *consequence* for a target behavior. We get money for working. A child can be given tokens for learning a skill or working at his lessons. When we have *earned enough* tokens or money, we can *exchange* them for a *back-up reward.*

SETTING UP A TOKEN (POINT OR CHECK MARK) SYSTEM

Here is how to set up a token system.

1. *Pinpoint target behaviors to reward with the tokens, points, or check marks.* For example, you might reward the child for working at Small Motor activities or at his lessons, doing chores, answering questions, getting dressed, or almost any behavior. Be sure to list these behaviors in your program plan.

2. *Make a list of strong back-up rewards.* The child must get things he

enjoys *in exchange* for his tokens, points, or check marks. You can use the rewards you wrote in the boxes for Primary, Social, and Activity Rewards in the Reward List at the end of Chapter 3. Also, be on the lookout for anything that turns the child on (makes him smile) and activities he does a great deal (*high* behaviors). And learn how to use a "reward menu" to find out what is rewarding to the child.

3. *List the back-up rewards in the order of how much the child enjoys them.* Put those he likes most at the *top* of the list. The list tells you *how much* each back-up reward should *cost.* Here is a good rule to follow: *The more the child enjoys a certain back-up reward, the more tokens (points, check marks) it should cost.* For example, if the child will do almost anything for chocolate ice cream, it should be on the top of the list and cost the most.

Then *decide how many tokens (points or check marks) each back-up reward on the list will cost.* Write the cost next to each back-up reward on the list. Change the order of rewards on the list as you find new back-up rewards and as the child's tastes change. You should also change the *cost* of the back-up rewards. For example, as the child gets better at earning tokens, *increase prices.* Or, if you want him to start buying a certain back-up reward because it will be good for his education (for instance, an educational toy), *decrease* the price of that item.

4. *Pick the kind of general reward to use.* You can use *tokens* (small plastic chips, like poker chips), *points* (for instance, three points for finishing a lesson and one point for answering a question), *check marks* on his lesson papers, or even *pegs* the child is given while working (which he puts in his pegboard). These are the things the child gets as the immediate consequence of his behavior.

It does not matter much what you use. Tokens or pegs may be the easiest for a child to understand, but they can get lost, stolen, or put in the mouth. Check marks and points cannot.

5. Now that you know which target behaviors to reward, what to use as a General Reward, which back-up rewards to use, and how much each back-up reward will cost, *decide how many tokens the child will get for doing each target behavior.* Write the number of tokens he will earn next to each target behavior on the list. Here is a good rule to follow: *The weaker a target behavior is* (the *less often it happens or the more help the child needs*), *the more tokens he should earn for it.*

6. *Finally, decide where and how often you will exchange the back-up rewards on the list.* The rule is: *The weaker the target behavior is, the more often you should have an exchange.* If you are rewarding the child with tokens during a teaching session, it is a good idea (when the behavior is weak) to have several exchanges *during* the session and one ex-

change right after the session. As the behavior increases, you can slowly cut out the exchanges during the session. For other behaviors, such as doing chores or self-help tasks or playing during the day, you can have the exchange at the end of the day. You might even have one behavior (such as cleaning his room) that the child can do each day, and at the end of the week he gets to exchange his tokens, if he has enough of them, for one big reward. And, in a classroom, you can have *store time* a few times a day after hard lessons.

Table 8-1 shows how a token system might be set up.

Study Table 8-1. The child can earn twenty tokens a day if he (1) cooperates with about six requests; (2) cleans his room; (3) clears the supper table; (4) brushes his teeth after every meal; and (5) finishes his workbook lesson. And, if he spends his tokens on ice cream, TV, and a ride each day, he can save seven tokens a day. With these, he can buy cartoons every Saturday and go to a ball game every few weeks.

STARTING A TOKEN SYSTEM

The easiest way to start a token system is to *explain it*. With many children this is enough, and you just run the system as planned. A fast way to start the system with a child who does not understand is to start with the *last* step in the token exchange—exchanging one token for a back-up reward. This teaches him that a token has *value*; it gets him something he likes. With such a child do the following:

1. *Show* him the back-up rewards (for instance, hold up some toys or foods).
2. *Show* him a token and *tell* him he needs one to buy the back-up rewards.
3. When he asks for the token (or makes eye contact if he does not talk yet), *praise him* and *give him the token*.
4. Then *hold out* your hand and *ask* for the token back. If necessary, *prompt* the child to put it in your hand.
5. When he does, *praise* him and give him the back-up reward or let him choose one.

Repeat these steps many times. Then, during teaching sessions, have the child *earn* tokens by doing things he has already learned. For example, reward him with praise and tokens as he works puzzles. Make sure to exchange back-up rewards for the tokens very *often* at first. As time goes on, have him earn more and more tokens before he can buy a back-up reward, and have him do the target behavior better and

Table 8-1. Set up for a Token System

Target Behaviors and Numbers of Tokens They Will Earn	Back-Up Rewards to Buy and Numbers of Tokens They Cost	Where and How Often to Exchange Tokens for Back-Up Rewards
1. Cooperating with requests (Each cooperation earns one token.)	1. Going to ball game (Costs forty tokens.)	1. Child is told a week ahead that there is a ball game on Saturday. Saturday morning he exchanges tokens.
2. Cleaning room (Earns two tokens.)	2. Watching Saturday morning cartoons (Costs twenty tokens.)	2. Exchange tokens for Saturday morning cartoons just before they start each week.
3. Clearing supper table (Earns one token.)	3. Ice cream (Costs six tokens.)	3. Exchange tokens for ice cream snack right after lesson in afternoon.
4. Brushing teeth after meals (Earns two tokens each time.)	4. Watching TV after supper (Costs four tokens.)	4. Exchange tokens for TV right after supper.
5. Finishing lesson in workbook (Earns five tokens.)	5. Going for a ride in the car (Costs three tokens.)	5. Exchange tokens for ride in the car after lunch.

179

better before he earns a token. If a Primary Reward has been used up to now, use it as one of the back-up rewards.

Once the token system is working well during teaching sessions, you can begin to use it at other times of the day. For example, instead of exchanging tokens for back-up rewards during sessions, you can exchange tokens earned during sessions only when the session is over. And you can have the child start *earning Activity Rewards* he has been getting around the home or classroom, such as free time, TV, playing outside, or roughhousing. Instead of getting them for nothing, he must *buy* them with tokens earned during sessions or for doing simple chores and tasks or cooperating.

Here are rules to help you run token systems.

1. When you move away from Primary and Activity Rewards to the token system, move *slowly*. Use a great many Social Rewards when you start the token system, because the child does not yet know what tokens are all about. And use the rewards he has been getting (for instance, food or activities) as back-up rewards in the token system.

2. When you start a new and harder task, give the child *more tokens for doing the task or for trying*.

3. *Switch* some of the back-up rewards each day, so that the child will not become satiated.

4. Teach the child to keep his tokens in a certain place, for instance, his pants pocket, an apron, a token bank, a token jar, or a pegboard.

5. If he *loses* his tokens, it is *too bad*. Give him extra chances to earn more, but do not reward him for being careless by replacing his tokens.

6. If a child steals tokens or fights with another child to get them, either *fine* him a certain number of tokens or use *time out*.

7. If a child is saving too many tokens, *increase* the *costs* of the back-up rewards, use more enjoyable back-up rewards, or reward target behaviors with fewer tokens. To decide what to do, you must find out why he has so many. Are tasks too easy? Is he sick of the back-up rewards?

Note: if you plan to run a token system, make a table like Table 8-1 that you can follow.

Spread Behaviors Around to Other Times, Places, and People

It does not help the child much if he does his new behaviors only with you, and only at the time and place where he first learned them. If you are not careful, this is just what will happen. He will make eye contact or talk with almost no one else and only during sessions. So you must help him learn to *spread around* his new behaviors.

As a target behavior increases, and as the child learns to do it with more skill, *change* the time of the teaching sessions, little by little, run some of them in new places (add the new places slowly), and have new people work with him (at first, with you there). For example, as Jimmy's spontaneous eye contact increased with Mrs. Oaks, she started running a short extra session at another place and time, and she had Jimmy's brother begin rewarding Jimmy for making eye contact with him. As time went on, Mrs. Oaks had more new people reward Jimmy for making eye contact with them in different places.

The same goes for a skill area as advanced as Functional Speech. When the child learns to ask for a few things he wants during sessions (for example, "Give me cookie," "Want soda pop"), begin teaching him to ask for these (and new things) in other places, at other times, and with other people (for example, at the lunch counter, in the dime store, with his brother, sister, or neighbor). Remember: *as soon as a target behavior increases and the chlid is becoming more skilled at it (it is a stronger behavior), spread it around to more natural settings.*

In your advanced teaching program plan, write how, when, where, and with whom you will spread around the target behaviors.

Prompting

Remember: when you start an advanced program, prompt the new target behavior if the child needs it. As he gets better, *fade out* your prompts and reward him for doing the behavior more on his own.

Modeling

Prompting and shaping are two ways to give a child more skill at a behavior. *Modeling* is another way. It means *showing* the child how to do the behavior. Once the child has learned to watch you and to look at things you point to, you can begin to use modeling. Chapter 11, "Motor Imitation," tells you how to do this.

Switching Tasks

In an advanced program you may be working on many target behaviors during the day: eye contact, Small Motor skills, Large Motor skills, Verbal Imitation, cooperation, and Functional Speech. It is a good idea to

SWITCH BETWEEN THE DIFFERENT BEHAVIORS
YOU ARE WORKING ON.

Spend a little time on one and then go to another *before* the child gets bored. You can switch off *during* a teaching session, at different times of the day, and even from day to day. In other words, take a break from working on a certain behavior for a few days. You and the child will feel refreshed when you come back to it.

Handling Problem Behaviors

Sometimes, even though you are rewarding good behaviors, a strong problem behavior gets in the way of the target behavior. For example, the child may throw so many tantrums that he never learns he will get more rewards for working at simple, enjoyable activities. If this happens in an advanced teaching program, read Chapter 15 and run a program for replacing and decreasing the problem behavior.

Keeping an Eye Out for Changes in Other Behaviors

In your advanced programs, remember to reward any and all good behaviors, not just the target behaviors. Also, be on the lookout for changes in other behaviors on the child's BES. If you find any, change your answer to that item on the BES. In other words, *update the BES as the child's education goes along.*

2.   WRITING THE ADVANCED TEACHING PROGRAM PLAN

Now write your *advanced teaching program plan* on a copy of Table 6-2 at the end of Chapter 6, in the same way you wrote your first teaching program plan. If you want to run a *token system,* make a table just like Table 8-1, and use it along with questions 10 and 11 of the *program plan* (on rewards and reward schedules) to help you plan the token system.

   When you have written the advanced program plan, go on to the next section, Section 3.

3. RUNNING AND MEASURING THE ADVANCED TEACHING PROGRAM

Now that the advanced program plan is written, run the program just as you did the first one. In other words:

1. *Slowly* use more *natural* rewards and reward schedules with the old target behaviors. Start with strong rewards and a Continuous Schedule with the *new* target behavior, and, as it increases, slowly switch to more natural schedules and rewards.
2. *Count* and *chart* the *new* and *old target behaviors*, as well as the *teaching behavior*. Use one copy of the Behavior Count Table (Table 6-3) and the Behavior Chart (Figure 6-2) at the end of Chapter 6 for *each* behavior—new or old.
3. *Spread around* both the new and old target behaviors.
4. As long as the old target behavior keeps going and the new one is increasing, *keep on with the same advanced program plan.* If one or both starts to decrease, or if the new target behavior does not increase very much, get help from Chapter 7 and *revise* the program plan.
5. When the new target behavior has increased and is starting to level off, *pinpoint* another one and plan a program for it by repeating the steps listed in Section 4 and the Table of Steps to Follow (Table 4-3) in Chapter 4. When the child has learned most of the *basic behaviors* in a skill area, pick a new one and read the chapter on it.
6. During your advanced teaching programs, fill out copies of Tables 8-2 and 8-3. They will help you to keep track of the child's progress.

Table 8-2.   Using Grandma's Law

Use Grandma's Law as much as you can from now on. Just set things up so that the child does a *little* of a *low behavior* to get a *great deal* of a *high behavior* (an *Activity Reward*). Signal Grandma's Law by saying something like, "As soon as you . . . (*low behavior*), you can . . . (*high behavior*)." Quickly praise the child and let him have the Activity Reward when he co-operates with Grandma's Law. You have already made a list of Activity Rewards to use (assignment for Chapter 3). Now have the child *do something* to get them.

Each week, fill out a copy of the table below on how much you use Grandma's Law and how well it works.

IT WORKED FOR GRANDMA. IT WILL WORK FOR YOU!

Low Behaviors Child Must Do	High Behaviors (Activity Rewards) He Will Get

Table 8-3.   Changes In Other Behaviors

No matter what target behaviors you are working on, you are bound to get changes in other behaviors too. Sometimes other "good" behaviors will increase (or decrease), and sometimes problem behaviors will decrease (or increase). It is important to keep track of these changes. It will help you to pinpoint behaviors you may need to work on. So make copies of this table, and each week write down changes you have seen in behaviors that are not in your teaching programs. If any of them are also on the BET, update the child's BET.

Other Behaviors That Have Changed	*How Have They Changed?*

REFERENCES AND EXTRA READINGS

Axelrol, S. "Token reinforcement programs in special classes." *Exceptional Children,* 1971, **37**, 371-379.

Ayllon, T., and Azrin, N. *The Token Economy: A Motivational System for Therapy and Rehabilitation.* New York: Appleton-Century-Crofts, 1968.

Birnbrauer, J. S., Wolf, M. M., Kidder, J. D., and Tague, C. "Classroom behavior of retarded pupils with token reinforcement." *Journal of Experimental Child Psychology,* 1965, **2**, 219-235.

Ferster, C. B. "Arbitrary and natural reinforcement." *Psychological Review,* 1967, **17**, 341-347.

Homme, L. E., DeBaca, P., Devine, J. V., Steinhorst, R., and Rickert, E. J. "Use of the Premack principle in controlling the behavior of nursery school children." *Journal of the Experimental Analysis of Behavior,* 1963, **6**, 544.

Kuypers, D. S., Becker, W. C., and O'Leary, K. D. "How to make a token system fail." *Exceptional Children,* 1968, **35**, 101-109.

Piper, T. J. "Effects of delay of reinforcement on retarded children's learning." *Exceptional Children,* 1971, **38**, 139-145.

Scott, P. M., Burton, R. V., and Yarrow, M. R. "Social reinforcement under natural conditions." *Child Development,* 1967, **38**, 53-63.

CHAPTER NINE

Learning
READINESS SKILLS

1. WHAT THIS SKILL AREA IS ABOUT

This is the first skill area on the Skill Sequence Table (Table 4-1) in Chapter 4. It is very important in two ways. First, a child *must* learn the four *basic behaviors* in it *before* he can learn much in any other skill area. Second, working in this skill area gives you a chance to start his education on the right foot. Let us talk about this a little more.

Two "Kinds" of Children

There are two "kinds" of children. No, we are not going back to labels! We are still talking about behaviors. But some behaviors make a big difference in a child's education. We all know of children who are easy to work with. They may need lots of help, but once hard behaviors are broken down into small steps and they are rewarded for learning, they make progress. They may tease a bit at first, throw tantrums sometimes, and backslide for a week or so, but, overall, they *cooperate* and seem to enjoy learning.

In other words, there is already a good deal of give and take between such a child and his parents and teachers. He does things others like, and in return they do things for him that he likes. The child follows the *signals* given by his parents and teachers. Their signals are able to start and stop his behaviors. And the child is *rewarded* by the things that are often rewards for children, such as praise. So, from the start of his education, or after a short period of "testing" and getting used to each other, the parent or teacher is able to *guide* the child's education. And both the child and his parents or teachers are rewarded as he learns new behaviors.

On the other hand, we all know children who are called "negative" or "noncompliant." Some people call them "brats." They do not cooperate when you try to teach them. Instead, they tease and play games. When asked to do a simple task, they run or sneak away, or pretend that they do not hear or understand (unless you say, "Billy, do you want some ice cream?"). They have tantrums or whine when they are not given their way. In fact, a big reward for them is making people angry.

There is very little give and take between the "negative" child and his parents and teachers. It is mostly "take." The child gets rewards for nothing or for behavior no one can stand. In other words, his problem behaviors *are not* under the *control* of his parents and teachers. Instead, parents and teachers are under the control of *his* problem behaviors, especially tantrums, whining, pulling, and getting into things. Such a child knows how to make people leave him alone. He knows how to yell and have tantrums so long and loud that he gets what he wants. Living with him and teaching him are constant battles that no one wins, least of all the child. When many children like this get too big to handle or satisfy, their parents and teachers really give up on them.

For the first child, the Learning Readiness area gets his education off to a flying start. As for the second child, the Learning Readiness area lets you *replace* some of the problem behaviors that might otherwise keep him from making any progress. Basically, he learns that there is a *new game in town*, that he will be rewarded *only* for *good behaviors*, and that unless he follows directions and cooperates with simple requests he will not get any of the rewards he has learned to take for granted.

The next sections talk about how to start a child's education on the right foot and how to teach the four *basic behaviors*.

2. STARTING ON THE RIGHT FOOT: REWARD ALL "GOOD" AND IGNORE ALL "BAD" BEHAVIORS

This is the first step in a child's educational program. If he already cooperates, this step will increase his good behaviors even more. If he does not cooperate yet, he soon will. There are three things to do. First, *make sure that the child earns his rewards*. This means no more snacks, no more TV, no more rides in the car, and as little "free" attention as possible, *except following "good" behaviors*. If the child already makes eye contact, cooperates, and knows how to ask for what he wants, keep making sure that he does these behaviors before he gets rewards around the home and school. If he does not make eye contact very often, play, or know how to talk, give him plenty of *chances* to do *simple tasks* you can reward.

Second, *reward "good" behaviors as much as you can.* If cooperation, eye contact, and playing are weak behaviors, reward the child whenever he does or *tries* to do these behaviors. In other words, *be on the lookout for behaviors to reward.* "What do I use as rewards?" Reward the child with the things you stopped letting him have for nothing.

And, third, *ignore "bad" behaviors as much as possible.* This means no going after the child, trying to find out why he is having a tantrum, and no cuddling him or giving him what he wants when he is crying or whining. This may make *you* feel better, but it just *increases* his bad behaviors. From now on, *you do not even see or hear these behaviors.* Just go about your business, or, better yet, pay attention to another child who is doing some good behavior. Show the whining child that only children who ask nicely get what they want. When a bad behavior stops for a few minutes and the child has started to do something else (just about *anything* else, as long as it is a good behavior), then reward him. Or give him a simple task to do, and reward him if he cooperates.

On the other hand, if you cannot ignore certain behaviors, such as wild tantrums, messing the room, or hitting, use *time out* immediately, every time, and without talking to the child about it. Chapter 15, "Replacing Problem Behaviors," tells you when and how to use time out.

Isn't This Too Strict?

Does this sound too strict? Well, it is not. If a child already cooperates, he will end up having more fun and being rewarded more often than ever. If he is very uncooperative, and if he is the kind of child whose problem behaviors have been making people jump for years, a few weeks of your making it *very clear* to him what he can and what he cannot do, what pleases you and what does not please you, will let you both get down to the business of teaching him.

All of us need and should be given love and affection, but not while we are doing things that are unlovable. There are no "ifs" about this. As we said before, children who keep getting rewarded for nothing or for bad behaviors either never learn anything or learn more bad behaviors. They learn the behaviors that are rewarded. This is not a matter of taste, either. At some point you must draw the line between behaviors that are good for the child (behaviors you want him to keep doing or to do more often) and behaviors that are bad for the child (behaviors you do not want him to do). You may as well draw the line at the start. You do not want to be still "fighting" with the child when you are working on a skill as important and hard as Verbal Imitation or Functional Speech.

So, do the three things we talked about above. They will give the child's education a boost and will help you to replace problem behaviors.

Plan and Run the Teaching Program

The next sections tell you how to teach the four *basic behaviors*. Here is a list of them.

(A1) Spontaneous Eye Contact: The child looks at people's eyes on his own.

(A2) Eye Contact on Request: The child looks at people's eyes when he is asked to.

(A4) Cooperation with Simple Spoken Requests: The child does easy tasks when asked.

(A5) Sits and Works at a Task Long Enough to be Rewarded: The child sits with a parent or teacher and works at easy tasks for 10 minutes or so.

Now please read again the section on Learning Readiness skills in the BES.

As you just read, there are other behaviors in this area besides the four *basic behaviors*, but these four are the ones the child *must have before he goes on to a harder skill area*. You circled behaviors on the child's BES and BET that he needs help with, and the BES tells you what kind of help he needs. Pinpoint the *easiest one* (closest to the *top* of the BET) as your first target behavior, and take a *baseline* for a few days. If the child still needs help with that behavior, *read* a later section of this chapter on how to teach it and *plan* a teaching program with the help of Chapter 6. Then write the program plan on the General Teaching Program Plan (Table 6-2) at the end of Chapter 6. Keep track of how well the program is working by using Table 6-3 and Figure 6-2, also at the end of Chapter 6. If the teaching programs are not going very well after a few days, go to Chapter 7 for help.

When the child has learned the first target behavior, pinpoint the next one he needs help with down the list on the BET as your second target behavior. Use Chapter 8 to write an *advanced* teaching program plan for the second and later target behaviors. When the child has learned *at least* the four *basic behaviors,* go on to the next area you think the child is ready for on the *Skill Sequence Table.*

3. SPONTANEOUS EYE CONTACT (A1)

A definition of this target behavior is as follows: the child looks you in the eye on his own. This is an important behavior. It is part of *paying attention* to others. Also, in everyday life, we use eye contact as a *signal.* For instance, we often signal people to talk to us or come over to us by making eye contact with them. So your goal is to teach the child to make eye contact on his own more often and to hold his gaze for a longer time. You want him to *use* eye contact to signal others, and to learn that when others make eye contact with him, it is *his* signal to do something, for example, follow a direction.

How to Increase Spontaneous Eye Contact

First of all, you are *not* asking the child to look at you, but just *waiting* for him to look at you on his own. At the start, use a *strong reward* and a *continuous schedule,* to show him that people will *react* very quickly to his good behaviors. If praise is not a reward for him yet, use small bites of his favorite foods. Then, each time he makes eye contact, no matter where you are with him, *praise him loudly and clearly* ("Good boy for LOOKING at me!") and quickly give him the bite of food. For some children, this means putting the bite in their mouth to make sure they are rewarded fast. In fact, if the child is across the room when he makes eye contact, praise him and *run* across the room to reward him. It is a good idea to wear an *apron* (for instance, a carpenter's apron) loaded with the small pieces of food rewards.

IN A NATURAL WAY

Work on eye contact in *natural* ways. Make it fun. For example, reward eye contact when you are roughhousing with the child, when he is taking a bath, or during free time. Besides praise and food, use *Activity Rewards* and *Grandma's Law.* When the child is trying to get out the the door, do not open it until he looks up at you. Wait until he makes eye contact before you toss him a ball or give him a piggy-back ride. Wait for eye contact before you get down a toy for him or turn on the TV. In other words, use food (if you have to) to get eye contact on the *increase;* use everyday activities to get eye contact under *natural control.*

Count and *chart* the number of eye contacts the child makes during the observation period each day.

If the child *avoids* looking your way, or if the number of eye contacts does not start increasing in a few days, *prompt* eye contact in one or more of the following ways:

1. *Hold* the bite of food in front of your face near your eyes to get his attention. You might move it back and forth.
2. Make a *loud noise*, such as slapping on the table.
3. *Peek* at him through a short cardboard tube.
4. *Gently* turn his head or chuck him under the chin, but try this only a few times and only if the other prompts do not work. You cannot *force* eye contact.

Of course, *slowly fade out* your prompts as soon as the child begins to make eye contact more often.

SIT-DOWN SESSIONS

Most work on eye contact should be done *away* from the table, but if the child will sit with you, run short teaching sessions during the day, for 10 or 20 minutes, either during snack times or mealtime. If the child can work at other tasks (puzzles, lessons) during these sit-down sessions, fine. Work on them and reward the child *both* for doing the tasks and for making eye contact.

If the child *will not* sit with you yet, reward eye contact outside of sessions for a few days and give *big* rewards whenever he comes near you when you are sitting down. When he comes near you, try to *prompt* him to sit down with you. If he does, reward him with praise and a bite of food every few minutes for good sitting ("Billy, you are sitting so well") and reward him also for eye contact. If possible, have simple tasks for him to work once you have him sitting.

SESSIONS FOR MEALS

For most children, rewarding spontaneous eye contact in natural places, whenever and wherever it happens, is enough to increase this behavior. For the very uncooperative child with many problem behaviors, however, it may not be. When he finds out that you want him to look at you, he stops doing it. For such a child, have sit-down sessions *during one meal a day.* If he still "refuses" to look at you, or if the number of eye contacts does not increase very much in a few days, run sessions at *every meal.* Mealtime sessions should last only a certain amount of time —say 20 minutes—and when the time is up, the session and the meal are over. Of course, *no food is given between meals.* Outside of meals you should still *require* eye contact *before* the child can have natural activity rewards.

If the child becomes very disruptive, either during sessions or when you are requiring eye contact before he gets a natural reward, you can do five things. Try using the methods in the order in which they are listed.

1. *Ignore* the behavior completely, and *wait* for the next eye contact.
2. Set a small kitchen timer for a few minutes. Put it near the child, pick up the food and all other task objects (for instance puzzles), and *Walk Out* of the room. Come back in and start again when the timer rings.
3. *Time out* the child in a time out room every time the disruptive behavior starts.
4. *Turn off the lights* in the teaching room when the disruptive behavior starts. To use this method, get a silent switch to work with your hand under the table, a switch that turns off all the lights so that it is pitch dark. Do not use this method, however, if the child is afraid of the dark. The idea is to teach him that he gets nothing for disruptive behavior, not to scare him to death. Turn the lights back on when the child is quiet.
5. *End the session* as soon as a disruptive behavior starts, and have the child wait until the next meal before he gets a chance to earn food rewards.

Remember: you want sessions to be enjoyable. *Prompt* the child to make eye contact so that he can be rewarded. And if he does not earn many rewards during a session, have the next one a little *earlier.* The idea is to increase spontaneous eye contact and cooperation, and replace some problem behaviors, not to starve the child! It should only take from a few days to a week of sessions for every meal (with *no food between sessions!*) to get spontaneous eye contact on the increase.

Count and *chart* the number of eye contacts each session. Try to keep sessions the same number of minutes each time.

Again, we know how this sounds. We are not saying that every child must earn all his food. But there are some children who have been so uncooperative for so long, and whose good behaviors are so few and far between, that unless a strict method is used from the beginning, their education gets nowhere. We have seen and worked with many children for whom no past method did any good, but those children settled down and started to learn good behaviors after a week of finding out that *no behaviors would be rewarded except the ones picked by their parents and teachers.*

INCREASING THE LENGTH OF TIME THE CHILD HOLDS HIS GAZE

Up to now, reward the child even if he makes eye contact for a second. This will increase the number of times he makes eye contact. But in later skill areas (Looking, Listening, and Moving, Motor Imitation, and Verbal Imitation) the child must make eye contact or look at you for a *longer* time. In other words, he must learn to *hold his gaze—to watch* you. So, when the number of eye contacts each day has increased, begin to *shape longer* eye contacts.

This is easy to do. Just reward the child when he *holds* his gaze with you for a little longer than usual. In other words, *hold out* on the reward until you get an eye contact that is a few seconds longer. For instance, if he looks away while the food is moving to his mouth, pull the food back and prompt him to make eye contact again by holding the food near your eye. When he makes eye contact again, *slowly* move the food toward his mouth and put it into his mouth only if he holds his gaze all the way down.

This does not mean that you should *always* hold out for longer eye contacts. There is not much point in the child's holding his gaze and staring at you unless you are having him look at things or watch what you are doing. So *keep on rewarding* short eye contacts, but hold out for *some* longer ones, until *you are able* to keep the child looking at your eyes for about 5 seconds.

SPREADING EYE CONTACT TO OTHER PEOPLE AND PLACES

After eye contact has been increasing for about a week, start having other people reward the child when he looks at them. Add new places and times to run sessions. And reward the child in new places (in the park, at the store) with praise, activities, and food (if still needed). For example, push the child on the swings or buy him a gum ball at the grocery store only after he makes eye contact.

Your goals are to (1) increase spontaneous eye contacts to about forty in 20-minute sit-down sessions, or a *rate* of about two per minute; (2) teach the child to hold his gaze on *some* eye contacts for at least 5 seconds; and (3) teach the child to make eye contact in other places and times for natural Activity Rewards.

When the child reaches these three goals, begin to do two things: (1) *slowly* put spontaneous eye contact on an *Intermittent Schedule*, using food less and less, praise and activities more and more; and (2) work on the *next* target behavior, which for many children will be eye contact on request.

Figures 9-1 and 9-2 show how spontaneous eye contact was increased in a home program run by a child's mother. The child was 4 years old. Figure 9-1 is for *any* spontaneous eye contact, no matter how short. After Day 14, these had increased enough, so the mother began having the child hold his gaze on some eye contacts for at least 5 seconds. Figure 9-2 is for the longer eye contacts. This was all done *outside* of sessions.

4. EYE CONTACT ON REQUEST (A2)

When the child is coming close to the goal of about forty spontaneous eye contacts in 20-minute sessions, or about two per minute, and some of them are at least 5 seconds long, begin working on Eye Contact on Request. A definition of this target behavior is as follows: the child

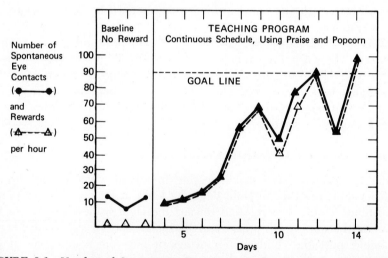

FIGURE 9-1   Number of Spontaneous Eye Contacts (A1) for Mark Kane. During the baseline, eye contact was not rewarded. During the teaching program, eye contact was rewarded on a Continuous Schedule with praise and small bites of popcorn. Eye contacts were rewarded all day but were counted only in the afternoon. The chart shows the number of eye contacts per hour. Virginia Hudson was the behavioral consultant for the family.

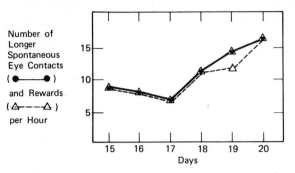

FIGURE 9-2   Number of longer spontaneous eye contacts for Mark Kane. During the teaching program, the mother held out on some rewards until the child made eye contact for at least 5 seconds. These longer eye contacts were rewarded on a Continuous Schedule with praise and popcorn. This was done all day, but eye contacts were counted only in the afternoon. The chart shows the number of longer (5-second) eye contacts per hour. Virginia Hudson served as consultant.

makes eye contact within a few seconds after you say something like, "Billy, look at me," or "Look at me." For most children, increasing Eye Contact on Request will be easy, because you have already increased Spontaneous Eye Contact.

Shaping is a painless way to increase this behavior. Begin by waiting until the child is *just about* to make eye contact on his own. Then beat him to the punch by saying, "Billy, LOOK AT ME," a split second *before* you think his eyes will meet yours. If he looks at you within 5 seconds after you ask him, praise him and give him a bite of food (if food is still needed to increase his behaviors).

Take this step nice and easy. Do not ask him to look at you twenty times in a row or all day long. Timing is important here. Spread out your requests ("LOOK at me") during the day, a few at a time, when he is about to look at you anyway. Then *slip in* the request. If he makes eye contact within 5 seconds, reward him.

Also, begin to request eye contact when the child *wants something*. For instance, stand in front of the refrigerator when you see him coming. Wait for him to start to look at you or for him to reach for the door. Then request eye contact: "LOOK at me" or "As soon as you LOOK at me, I will open the door." Hold out on the reward until he makes eye contact. Also, if he is working on simple tasks with you, request and get eye contact before you give him the next puzzle piece, block to stack, or question to answer.

As the number of eye contacts on request increases, begin to hold out for some that are at least 5 seconds long. Also, work on eye contact on request at other places and times and with other people.

Some children may *refuse* to make eye contact on request. When you say, "LOOK at me," they turn their heads the other way, wiggle their eyes around, leave their seats, or whine and throw a tantrum. If a child does this, *run sessions during mealtime*. Wait until he is sitting quietly. Then say, "LOOK at me." If he looks within 5 seconds, praise him loudly and clearly and give him a *bite of food*. If he does not look, *ignore* it and wait 5 seconds before you ask him again. Try *prompting* eye contact after you give the request. Run sessions in the same way we talked about running them for spontaneous eye contact. That means:

Every bite.
Every meal.
Nothing between meals.
Ignoring disruptive behavior, setting timer and leaving the room, using time out, or ending the sessions.
Prompting the child (if needed) after you give the request.
Requesting eye contact for natural rewards during the day.

During sessions and outside of sessions, *count* the number of times you *request* eye contact and the number of times the child *makes eye contact on request*. *Chart* both. You want the line for the number of eye contacts on request to rise to about forty in 20-minute sessions, or about two per minute, and for the line to get close to the line for the number of requests.

In other words, you want the lines to look something like those on the chart below. As you see, the number of eye contacts on request is increasing and getting closer to the number of requests each day.

Therefore your goals are to (1) increase the number of eye contacts

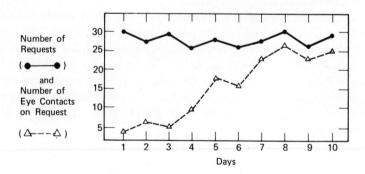

Number of Requests (●——●) and Number of Eye Contacts on Request (△---△)

Days

on request to about thirty or forty during 20-minute sessions, or about two per minute; (2) teach the child to make eye contact at least three out of four times that you request it (75 percent of the time); (3) teach him to hold some eye contacts on request for at least 5 seconds; and (4) teach the child to make eye contact on request with other people and at other times and places for natural rewards.

When the child reaches these goals, move to the next target behavior. Also, keep Spontaneous Eye Contact   (A1) and Eye Contact on Request (A2) going by having the child make eye contact before he gets *natural rewards* and by using food or praise on an *Intermittent Schedule*.

5.   COOPERATION WITH SIMPLE SPOKEN REQUESTS (A4)

A definition of this target behavior is that the child follows simple requests to do easy tasks around the home or classroom, for instance, to open the door, pick up his coat, put his plate on the table, put his cup in the sink, or push his chair under the table. By increasing eye contact on request, it is easier to teach this target behavior. The idea is to teach the child to cooperate more often and to get his cooperation under the control of natural rewards.

The method is simple. Begin by waiting until the child wants something or until he is about to do something. Then, before you give him what he wants, or before you let him start to do what he was going to do, slip in your request. You can state it as Grandma's Law. For example, give him his dessert dish and show him the ice cream. But before you put ice cream in his dish, tell him, "Here's the ice cream. As soon as you put your supper plate in the sink, you can have ice cream." Or just tell him to put his plate in the sink. If he cooperates with the request, praise him and give him the ice cream. Of course, if he tries to cooperate but does it wrong, *prompt* him by *pointing*, putting him through the *motions*, or *repeating* part of the request. For example, if he goes to put his plate on the counter instead of in the sink, point to the sink, take him by the hand, or repeat, "IN the SINK."

Set up *many* easy cooperation tasks during the day for *different* natural rewards. Start with tasks the child understands, for instance, hanging up his pants before you tuck him in bed, putting his dish in the sink before he can go outside, putting paper in the trash before he can watch TV, pulling his chair out from under the table, or helping to set his place at the table before he can eat.

Give the child lots of praise and hugs right after he cooperates and just before you give him the natural reward. For example,

"As soon as you bring me the book, I will read you a story."	→Child gets book	→"Thank you very much, Jimmy."	→Child listens to story
(*Request, Grandma's Law*)	(*Cooperates*)	(*Social Reward: Praise*)	(*Natural Activity Reward*)

If the child has been very uncooperative, or if the natural reward is not a strong one, also give him a token or a bite of food.

As the child gets used to following simple requests, add tasks which may be *new* to him and may not always be followed by strong natural rewards. Examples might be cleaning the blackboard, pulling the shade down, turning off the lights, and wiping the table. In other words, ask him to do tasks that a member of the family or class should learn to do. As a reward for cooperating with these kinds of tasks, use praise, activities, and (if needed) a token or a bite of food. Also, reward the child with a *special treat* for cooperating well during the day. For example, take him for a ride, go to the ice cream store, or let him pick something he likes. "You cooperated so well today, Mike. You wiped the table and took out the trash. Let's go to the park." Use food less and less, praise and activities more and more.

Have the child do a few of the *same* tasks each day and from day to day for practice (to increase his skill), but switch off every few days and add new ones so that he will not become bored. Slowly fade out your prompts until the child can do a task by just hearing the spoken request, with no prompts.

Also, begin to have other people request the child to do tasks he has learned, and work on tasks in new places. For instance, have the child help you in the grocery store, by pushing the shopping cart, getting items off the shelves, and unloading the cart at the check-out counter. Can you think of a good reward for helping out in the grocery store? Of course! A gum ball or a ride in the shopping cart when you leave will be fine.

Keep track of this behavior in two ways. First, *count* the number of *requests* you give the child during the day and the number of times he *cooperates* with those requests. *Chart* both of these behaviors (requests and cooperations). You want the number of cooperations to increase almost as high as the number of requests. Also, make a *list* of the tasks you ask the child to do. Next to each task, write down what day you started working on it, what kinds of prompts the child needs, where he does the tasks, and with whom he cooperates.

Your goals are to (1) teach the child to cooperate with requests for at least ten different simple tasks without prompts; (2) increase cooperation to the point where the child follows at least three out of four requests (he cooperates at least 75 percent of the time); and (3) teach the child to follow requests in other places and with other people.

When the child reaches these three goals, move on to the next target behavior he needs help with.

6.   SITTING AND WORKING AT A TASK LONG ENOUGH TO BE REWARDED (A5)

This is the last *basic behavior* in the Learning Readiness area. Here is a definition of the target behavior: the child sits with a parent or teacher and works at easy activities. The goals are to (1) increase how much time the child sits and works at simple tasks to about 10 minutes; and (2) teach the child to sit on request. If the child has already learned to Cooperate with Simple Spoken Requests (A4), it should be easy to get him sitting down. In fact, he may already have fairly good sitting behavior. But if you are dealing with a child that likes to tease and have tantrums, you may have to use one of the following methods to get him seated.

How to Shape Sitting

If the child already sits on request, all you have to do is increase how long he sits. Let us say that the child *does not* sit on request. When you tell him to sit with you, he grins and runs the other way or pretends he does not hear you. Or maybe he is always on the move and hardly ever sits. How do you get him to sit down? Here are a few methods.

First, make sure that you have a strong reward you can give quickly and many times. Food, praise, and tokens are examples. Pick an hour or two to shape sitting. Then watch the child. Quickly reward him for moving *toward* a chair or couch. If he turns away after the reward, ignore it. When he turns back to the chair or couch, reward him again. As the hour goes by, reward him only for *getting closer* and closer to the chair or couch. Still later, reward him when he *touches* the chair or couch. And, finally, reward him only when he is seated. If he gets up, ignore it and wait until he is seated again. Then sit next to him and reward him. If he stays seated, reward him *about* every 20 or 30 seconds.

Another way to *shape* sitting is for you to sit down and wait for the child to come over to you. If you have been rewarding him for some other behavior (like eye contact) and he sees you holding the reward, he is likely to come to you. When he is standing near you, praise him and give him the bite of food. Then ask him to sit down with you or in a chair next to you. If he does not, ignore it. But, next time, reward him only for standing closer to you than before. Later, reward him only when he is touching the chair or couch you want him to sit in. Finally, reward him only when he is sitting. Then reward him about every 30 seconds or so that he stays seated.

WHAT IF THESE TWO METHODS DO NOT WORK?

If these two methods do not get the child seated, because he runs away and teases when you ask him to sit down or after you reward him, just tell him he *is going* to sit, pick him up, put him in the chair, and *make him sit!* If he sits quietly then, reward him. If he fusses and tries to get up, *hold him.* Do not ease up until he relaxes in the seat. When he relaxes, give him a bite of food, stroke him, and *count* the seconds *out loud.* When he has been sitting quietly for a count of five or ten seconds tell him, "Okay, now you can (do something he wants to do)," and let him up. When he will sit quietly for ten seconds, slowly increase how long he must sit to earn the food reward and be allowed to get up. *But do not let him up until you say so, and only when he is quiet.*

Sitting on Request

If the child sits when you ask him, fine. If not, teach him to sit on request the same way you teach a child to make eye contact on request (see Section 4). *Wait until he is about to sit.* Then slip in the request ("Billy, sit down"). If he sits, give him lots of praise and a bite of food (if food is still needed). If he runs the other way, do not chase him. Ignore it and try again later. If he just stands there, *prompt* him to sit by pointing to or patting the place where you want him to sit, and reward him when he sits. Repeat the steps shown below:

Waiting until he is about to sit	Requesting him → to sit	Prompting him → to sit (if needed)	Rewarding him → for sitting

several times a day.

If this works, request him to sit when he is *further* away from the chair or couch. Ignore it if he runs away, prompt him if he needs it, and reward him when he cooperates with the request to sit.

After several days, if the child still refuses to sit when asked, tell him to sit down, put him in the chair, and make him sit by holding him until he relaxes. Then reward him for sitting quietly and count to ten *out loud*. Let him have an activity reward for sitting quietly. Slowly increase how long he is to sit quietly. Repeat this several times a day until he sits a *few minutes* without having to be prompted or held.

Increasing the Length of Time the Child Sits While Working at Some Task

So, what if the child is sitting? The only reason you want him to sit is that it is easier to learn some skills that way. Standing up gets tiring after a while. Therefore, when you have gotten the child to sit—either by shaping, requesting, or making him sit—give him something to do and reward him for doing it. Work on simple activities, such as puzzles, coloring, stacking blocks, reading him a story, pointing to pictures, or a lesson. Do this several times a day.

Reward him often with food, praise, or tokens for doing the task or activity well. *Also reward him for good sitting.* Use a Changing Interval Schedule. One time, you might reward him for good sitting after 30 seconds; the next time, after 2 minutes; the third time, after 1 minute; and the next time, after 4 minutes. In other words, keep the rewards coming for doing the task and for sitting, but do not let him figure out how long he must sit for a reward. What should you use as rewards? Use food (if needed) while he is sitting, and use *activity* rewards (by letting him get up) after he has sat and worked *a little while*. You can use a kitchen timer at the table to signal when he can get up and do *what he wants*.

Remember to keep eye contact going when you are working on tasks. Reward spontaneous eye contact a few times each session. Also use *chaining*. For example, wait for or request eye contact *before* you give the child the next puzzle piece, before you turn the page, or before you ask him to point to a picture.

If the child gets up during these little sessions, ignore it and wait for him to come back, but *reset* the timer when he is back. In fact, if someone else is sitting near you (husband or wife, another child, or teacher), start doing the task with him. Ham it up to get the child's attention. Show him that people who sit and work with others are rewarded. When he comes back, *do not reward him right away;* that will only teach him to leave and come back for a reward. Wait until he has been sitting and working for a minute or so.

Often, when a child's good sitting behavior falls apart—he will not stay seated any more or puts up a fuss—it has something to do with working at the tasks. Remember: at this time your goal is to get the child sitting and working for only 10 minutes. He should be *just beginning* to sit and work at tasks. In the next chapter ("Looking, Listening, and Moving") we will talk about sitting problems.

Figure 9–3 and 9–4 show how good sitting was increased in home teaching programs. Figure 9-3 shows the program run for 7-year-old Karen by her mother. For the first week, Karen's mother used shaping. She rewarded Karen when the child came over and sat down next to her. As sitting increased, Karen's mother began to request Karen to sit with her. Then they would work on simple tasks.

Figure 9-4 shows the program run by Patty's mother and father during breakfast and supper. Patty, a 6-year-old, used to get up from the table many times during a meal. So her parents set a time limit of 20 minutes on meals. They paid no attention to her when she left the table, but

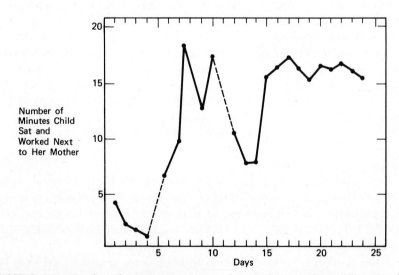

FIGURE 9-3 Number of minutes Karen sat and worked next to her mother. For the first week, sitting was shaped by rewarding Karen with praise and candy whenever she came over and sat by her mother on the couch. Her mother then worked with her on simple tasks. After the first week, the mother started requesting Karen to sit with her. She also rewarded Karen when Karen sat with her on her own. John Peters served as behavioral consultant.

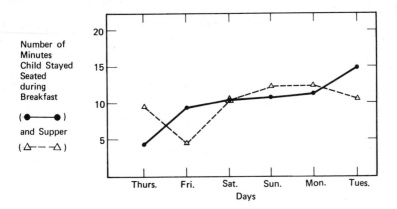

FIGURE 9-4 Number of minutes Patty stayed seated during breakfast and supper. Each meal was 20 minutes long. Patty was rewarded with praise and a marshmallow about every 2 minutes she was sitting and eating the food on her plate. Greg Hudson served as consultant.

rewarded her with marshmallows and attention every few minutes when she was sitting and eating.

As you see from the two charts, good sitting was increased in a short time in both children. In fact, Karen reached the goal of 10 minutes in one week.

When the child has learned to sit and work at tasks for about 10 minutes, and to sit on request, he is ready to go on to the next target behavior in this skill area or to the next skill area. Chapter 4 tells you how to pick the next target behavior or skill area. Chapters 6 and 8 tell you how to plan and write teaching programs for the new target behaviors.

REFERENCES AND EXTRA READINGS

Brown, R. A., Pace, Z. S., and Backer, W. C. "Treatment of extreme negativism and autistic behaviors in a 6 year old boy." *Exceptional Children,* 1969, 36, 115-122.

Cowan, P. H., Hoddinott, B. A., and Wright, B. A. "Compliance and resistance in the conditioning of autistic children." *Child Development,* 1965, 36, 912-923.

Davison, G. C. "A social learning therapy programme with an autistic child." *Behaviour Research and Therapy,* 1964, 2, 149-159.

Hutt, C., and Ounsted, C. "The biological significance of gaze aversion with particular reference to the syndrome of infantile autism." *Behavioral Science,* 1966, 11, 346-356.

Lovaas, O. I., Freitag, G., Kinder, M. I., Rubenstein, B. D., Schaeffer, B., and Simmons, J. Q. "Establishment of social reinforcers in two schizophrenic children on the basis of food." *Journal of Experimental Psychology,* 1966, 4, 109-125.

McConnell, O. L. "Control of eye contact in an autistic child." *Journal of Child Psychology and Psychiatry*, 1967, 8, 249-255.

O'Connor, N., and Hermelin, B. "The selective visual attention of psychotic children." *Journal of Child Psychology and Psychiatry*, 1967, 8, 167-179.

Robson, K. S. "The role of eye to eye contact in maternal infant attachment." *Journal of Child Psychology and Psychiatry*, 1967, 8, 13-25.

Silverman, J. "The problem of attention in research and theory in schizophrenia." *Psychological Review*, 1964, 71, 352-379.

CHAPTER TEN

LOOKING,
LISTENING,
and MOVING

1. WHAT THIS SKILL AREA IS ABOUT

This area covers many *Large* and *Small* Motor activities. Work on them during the child's whole education to help him (1) *replace* aimless behaviors (getting into things, staring out the window); and (2) learn the harder skills (Motor Imitation, Chores and Self-Help tasks).

Is the Child Ready for This Area?

Table 4-2 in Chapter 4 says which *basic behaviors* a child must have before he can work in this area. They are all from the Learning Readiness area—A1, A2, A4, and A5. If any of these are still circled on the child's BET, he is *not* ready. Use Chapter 9 to teach him whichever basic behaviors he needs help with. If none of the basic behaviors is circled, keep reading here.

What Behaviors Are in This Skill Area?

Skim over the section on Looking, Listening, and Moving in the BES or BET.

As you saw, there are three groups of behaviors: (1) *Large Motor* activities; (2) *Small Motor* activities; and (3) *Social Skills*. There are many behaviors to teach the child in each group. For instance, in the Large Motor group you can work on kicking a ball and pedaling a tricycle; in the Small Motor group you can work on puzzles and coloring; and in Social Skills you can teach the child to work and cooperate with others on the Large and Small Motor activities.

One or more *basic behaviors* is written in CAPITAL LETTERS for each group. Of course, you can work on any and all behaviors in a group, but the basic behaviors are *musts*.

Pinpoint a Target Behavior and Take a Baseline

Look at the child's BET in the column for this skill area. You circled all the behaviors you thought he needed help with. *Pinpoint* the easiest one of these as your first target behavior. If possible, take a *baseline* on it for a few days. Section 10 of Chapter 5 tells you how. Of course, it is hard (and really not necessary) to take a baseline on behaviors such as kicking a ball, hopping, or stacking blocks. But you can count how much *time* the child spends on these activities during the day. And you can at least write down *how well* he does them. After you take a baseline, come back and read the next section.

Where and When Do I Work on Looking, Listening, and Moving?

In the home and school, have one or two teaching sessions each day, for 10 or 20 minutes. These should be set up ahead of time, say 20 minutes in the morning and during or just before a snack in the afternoon or evening. Also work on these skills *all over* the house and in places where the child spends lots of time (on the couch, in his room) or where you want him to learn to play (at the table, on the floor). Follow the child's lead. If he sits down near his toys, picks up a book, or starts to play with a ball, praise him and get a little session going. "Hey, those are nice pictures. See the dog? I am POINTING to the dog. Now YOU POINT to the dog."

Tips on Teaching

Here are some tips that will make programs in this area go well.

1. *Count and Chart Behaviors.* Remember to *count* behaviors. For in-

stance, you can count how long the child plays during the day, how many minutes he pays attention, or how many puzzles he puts together during a session. Also count important teaching behaviors, such as the number of times you reward, signal, or prompt a target behavior. *Chart* what you count each day.

Also, *keep notes* on behaviors you are working on. For instance, write down *how well* the child is doing or what *problems* he may be having.

2. *Use an Effective Reward.* Give plenty of praise, loud and clear, to reward the child for finishing a task. Praise him and give him a soft pat now and then to keep him working on hard behaviors. If you must use food, praise and hug the child right before you give him a food reward.

Make sure he *earns* rewards during the day and does not get them for nothing. Use Grandma's Law: "As soon as you put in this puzzle piece, you can have the next one," or "As soon as you stack these blocks, you can work the puzzle."

If you think that the child is ready for a *token system,* read Section 1 of Chapter 8 to find out how to plan and run one. For example, the child might earn tokens during work sessions and whenever he plays well on his own during the day or during free time in class. After the session and at other times during the day, he exchanges his tokens for back-up rewards.

3. *Switch Tasks You Are Working On.* Work on a task for only a few minutes at a time. Then *switch* to another one. Add new ones every couple of days.

4. *Break Down Hard Behaviors into Easier Steps (Shaping).* Make a list of small steps by which you will teach a behavior. Reward the child at first for just trying. Later, hold out on rewards for a better job.

5. *Use a Continuous Schedule at the Start of a New Task.* As the child gets better, slowly move to an Intermittent Schedule.

6. *Keep Old Target Behaviors Going Strong.* Target behaviors you have worked on before, such as eye contact, good sitting, and cooperating with simple requests, should still be rewarded once in a while. *But do not overdo this.* If you are working on a harder task and you reward the child too much for easier behaviors, he will not try very hard to learn the new one.

One way to keep earlier behaviors going is by *chaining.* For example, have the child make eye contact *before* you hand him the next puzzle piece, and make sure he is sitting and looking at you before you give him a direction. You can also use more *natural rewards*—praise, a hug, a soft pat, or a token every now and then.

7. *Prompt the Child at the Start and Help Him Less (fade the Prompts) As He Grows More Skilled.* There are many prompts to use: *moving* him through the right motions, *pointing* to what you want him to do, or *telling*

him how. At first, try to prompt the child *before* he makes a wrong move. Later, let him do the task by himself and learn to correct his own mistakes.

8. *Use Positive Practice When the Child Makes the Same Mistake.* If the child makes the same mistake again and again, and goes on from there, he may never learn the right way to do the task. He may think the mistake is really part of the task. "Positive practice" means doing a task again until all its parts come out in the right order.

For example, if a stacking toy has eight rings of different sizes that fit over a stick, and the child keeps putting on the fourth ring at the wrong time, show him when to put on the fourth ring, but then have him *back up* and go through the task again. In other words, have him do some of the rings that lead up to the fourth one so that he will learn when it goes on.

Use positive practice on a task only a few times in a row, or else the child will get sick of the task. Work on it some more the next day.

9. *If the Child Becomes Disruptive or Stops Paying Attention, Look into Chapter 7.* Maybe you need to reward him more often, prompt him more, switch rewards, or go back to easier tasks for a few days. If none of these works, look into Chapter 15.

10. *Reward Any and All Good Behaviors.* Keep on the lookout for *other* good behaviors besides the activity the child is working on. For example, if you are telling him to stack blocks and he points to your mouth, reward him for this and say, "Right! That is MY mouth. Point to YOUR mouth." Then work on pointing for a little while. But do not carry this too far. Make sure the child comes back to the task.

11. *End Each Session on a Good Note.* End sessions *before* the child gets tired or stops paying attention. If you end sessions while he is fussing, he will learn that he can get out of sessions by not paying attention or by putting up a big enough fuss. Stop after the child has done a job well and has been rewarded—while he is still having fun.

12. *Keep Things the Way They Are.* You do not have to shut the windows, take down the pictures, or work in a barren room. If you find that the noise of other children, the TV, or some object keeps the child from paying attention, remove them during sessions until he learns good work habits.

Plan and Run the Teaching Program

Each of the following sections is about one of the three groups and the *basic behaviors* in it. *Now* read the section on how to teach the target behavior you pinpointed and took a baseline on. Write a teaching program plan on a blank copy of Table 6-2 at the end of Chapter 6. Start the teaching program. If there are any problems, see Chapter 7. If not, keep it up. When the child has learned the first target behavior, pinpoint the next easiest one he needs help with in this area and write an *advanced* teaching program for it with the help of Chapter 8. When the child has learned most of the *basic behaviors* in this area, work on the next skill area he is ready for. Chapter 4 tells you how to find out which skill areas the child is ready for.

2. LARGE MOTOR ACTIVITIES

Large Motor activities use larger parts of the body (arms, legs, back, chest). As the child gains skill at moving his body, he will be able to spend more time in constructive ways. It will also be easier for him to learn Motor Imitation skills and Chores and Self-Help tasks.

You circled behaviors on the BET he needs help with. Here are some more you can work on.

1. Bending and stretching one arm or leg.
2. Bending and stretching both arms and legs on one side of the body at a time (when the child is lying on the floor).
3. Rolling with arms at his sides.
4. "Freezing" in different positions.
5. Crawling forward and backward.
6. Crawling by putting the right arm and left leg forward and then the left arm and right leg forward.
7. Side-stepping.
8. Marching in place.
9. Walking with one foot placed right in front of the other (heel-to-toe walking).
10. Walking with each foot crossing in front of the body.
11. Hopping on both feet; hopping on one foot.
12. Running in a straight line.
13. Running in a circle.
14. Jumping over objects.
15. Catching a balloon in the air.
16. Throwing a ball with two hands; with one hand.
17. Bouncing a ball with two hands; with one hand.
18. Catching and throwing a bean bag.
19. Drawing a large circle on the board with one hand.

20. Drawing two circles, with chalk in each hand.
21. Walking on a line.
22. Walking on a raised beam.
23. Walking on two beams side by side.
24. Following a crooked line.
25. Following an "obstacle course" (go under the table, go over the footstool, go around the table, kick the ball, throw the bean bag, and come back again).

Of course, you can add others to this list. In fact, give the child some practice on the ones he really does not need help with.

Work on Large Motor activities at *any* time. Have a few short teaching sessions alone with the child or with other children each day. Start with easy ones and work up to the harder ones. You might play music during sessions to help the child learn to keep time. Here are some simple steps to follow.

1. *Wait* until the child is looking at you or request eye contact.

2. Then *tell* him what to do and *show* him how, for example, "Jimmy, STRETCH your arms UP like this," or "Sally, BOUNCE the ball, like me."

3. *Prompt* the child through the motions at first.

4. *Reward* him with plenty of spirit while you are prompting him and when he finishes.

5. *Reward* old target behaviors (eye contact, cooperation) once in a while, but not too often. Save most rewards for the new target behavior.

6. *Fade out* prompts as the child gets more skill. Use lots of praise when he does the behavior by himself.

7. Use *positive practice* to teach the right sequence of movements. For example, if the child makes a mistake near the end of the sequence, *back up* and have him do the sequence again until he gets it right. But do this only *a few* times and then switch to another activity.

8. Every few days, *practice* old movements and add new ones.

9. As the child gets more skilled, cooperates, and enjoys the activities, work on them *in new places* (in the park or yard) and *with other people*. Have a new person reward the child. When he is used to being rewarded by the new person, that person can also work with the child on the activity. Also, add a few children to make it a group.

Outside of sessions, reward the child for doing any of the activities on his own. If you see him start, praise him and join in. For instance, if you have been teaching him to play catch and he picks up a ball later that day, reward him and play catch. The idea is to increase skill and the amount of *time* he spends at these activities.

It may be hard to *count* some of the target behaviors in the Large

Motor group. If so, *take notes* on how well the child is doing. Use Table 10-1 at the end of this chapter. If you can count and chart a target behavior, do so. For instance, you can count and chart how many minutes or hours the child spends with these activities each day. You may also be able to count the number of times the target behavior happens. Figure 10-1 shows a chart made by Karen's parents (a chart on Karen's sitting behavior is in Chapter 9). They counted the number of times they tossed her a ball and the number of times she caught it. She was rewarded with praise and M & M's. You can see from Figure 10-1 that Karen got much better at catching, but only after her mother and father revised the teaching program so that she was prompted more.

The *goal* or *basic behavior* for Large Motor activities is that the child has Skill at *Many* Activities you have worked on and Spends *Much Time* at Them (B13) during the day. When the child (1) has learned to do about five of them without prompts; (2) cooperates and pays attention pretty well when you teach him; (3) is starting to work on these activities with others; and (4) spends about 30 minutes a day at them, he is ready to start on the next group—Small Motor activities.

3. SMALL MOTOR ACTIVITIES

ing together to do a task. Examples are working puzzles, stacking blocks, In Small Motor activities, a person's fingers, hands, and eyes are all work-

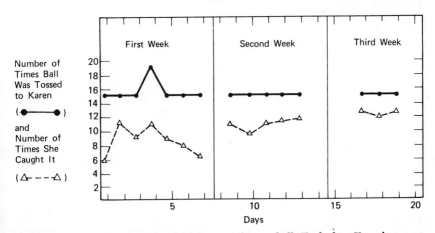

FIGURE 10-1   Increasing Karen's skill at catching a ball. Each day, Karen's parents had a session to teach her to catch a ball. They used praise and M & M's as rewards. The number of times she caught the ball during the first week did not increase, so during the second week they prompted her more by standing a little closer. John Peters served as behavioral consultant to the family.

and copying simple figures. Have sit-down sessions once or twice a day, starting with 5 minutes (or even less) and working up to 20 or more. Also, work on Small Motor activities wherever you can—on the floor, couch, or any place where it is natural for the child to play. Later, have others work with the child—brother or sister, grandparent, neighbor, another teacher, or child in his class. The more places he learns and the more people he learns with, the more likely he is to *play* outside of sessions.

The next section is about the first *basic behavior* (B14). Work on it if it is circled on the child's BET.

Looking at Objects, Parts of the Body, Face, and Mouth   (B14)

By now, the child should be making eye contact many times a day on his own and on request. But does he really look at things around him? Or does he mostly watch television, or stare out the window, at shiny objects, and at bits of string he is fiddling with? Looking at Objects, Parts of the Body, Face and Mouth (B14) is the first *basic behavior*. How can a child work hard puzzles or imitate words if he does not look carefully at objects or at what people are doing?

A definition of this target behavior is as follows: the child looks at objects and parts of his and your body, face, and mouth within 5 seconds after you point to them or tell him to look. Work on this at the table and other places. You need a picture book, a box full of everyday objects (comb, fork, knife, spoon, socks, ball, blocks, cup, and so forth) and a mirror large enough so that the child can see your *and* his face in it. During sit-down sessions, the child should be in front of you. When he is sitting quietly, *hold up* one of the objects from the box and *wait* for him to look right at it. If he looks at the object within 5 seconds, reward him and tell him the name of the object. For instance, "Yes, this is a SOCK." If he does not look at it on his own, prompt him by (1) telling him to look; (2) moving the object back and forth; (3) pointing to it; or (4) gently moving his head. Start with *bigger* objects, like a ball, and when he is looking many times at them, hold up smaller ones.

Each time he looks at an object, say its name, reward him, and move on to another object. Once he is looking at objects, have him *point* to them, too. For instance, when he looks at the cup you hold up, say, "Good, this is a CUP. Now POINT to the CUP." Show him how to point and prompt him if necessary. Try to get him to *say* the name of the object, but do not push this yet. You are not trying to teach him the difference between objects. At this time, the idea is just to get him to look at and point to things you hold up.

Also, have him look at and point to parts of his and your body (hair, ears, eyes, nose, chin, mouth, tummy, arms, legs). Wait until he is quiet. Then *point* to what you want him to look at and *tell* him what it is ("This is my MOUTH"). *Prompt* him to look at it and point to it. *Reward* him if he does.

Use a mirror to teach him the parts of his own body. First, point to and name the parts of his face while he is looking in the mirror. Then prompt him to do the same. Switch between pointing while looking at the mirror and pointing without the mirror. For example, tell him to look at the mirror and point to his chin. Then move the mirror away or cover it and have him point to his chin again.

Work on looking and pointing in other places. Take him for walks around the block, house, and classroom. Have him look at and point to the sidewalk, car, house, chair, table, wall, lamp, and floor.

To sum up, the goal is to teach the child to look at and point to objects and to parts of his and your face and body. You want him to look and point on his own and within 5 seconds after you tell him to look. Move to the next section when this behavior increases.

Increasing Skill and Amount of Time the Child Spends at Small Motor Activities   (B21)

This section tells you how to teach a *basic behavior* (B21) and many different Small Motor activities (B15 through B20).

INCREASING SKILL AT SMALL MOTOR ACTIVITIES

Run one or two sessions a day for 10 to 20 minutes, even less than 10 minutes if needed. A good time is just before a snack or favorite activity. Start with *easy* tasks, such as (1) simple puzzles that have three or four pieces that fit into different places; (2) stacking blocks, cups, rings; (3) Tinker Toys; (4) simple sorting toys with places to put different shapes or colors; or even (5) easy wind-up toys. These are tasks that need only a *few movements* and can be done *fast*.

Put the task object, for instance, a puzzle, in front of the child. Keep rewards (food, tokens) and everything else out of the way. Sit facing the child. Wait until he is sitting quietly and makes eye contact. Prompt or request eye contact if you have to. When he makes eye contact, reward him ("Oh, you are sitting so straight," or "Hi, Jimmy") and give him *one* puzzle piece. Tell him what to do with it—"PUT the (tell him the name of the piece) IN the puzzle." When he takes the piece, make sure he *looks at it* and help him to put it in the right place in the puzzle.

Either point to the right spot or help him to put it on the edge of the right spot and let him push it the rest of the way. Reward him with a soft touch or a few kind words *while* he is working ("You are working so well").

When he fits the piece in place, praise or hug him and give him a bite of food or a token (if you are using a token system). Tell him what he did and give him the *name* for the object ("Good job! You put the BEAR in the puzzle"). Every once in a while, reward older target behaviors, such as eye contact, good sitting, and cooperating. Follow the same steps with the rest of the pieces in the task. Reward the child for *every* correct movement. Make sure that he is sitting quietly and makes eye contact before you give him each piece.

At first, use only one puzzle piece or block at a time. Hold back all the pieces but the one he is to put in. As his skill and attention increase, give him a few pieces at once. You can even let him dump them out.

One problem that may come up is *wrong movements*. For instance, the child may keep trying to put a puzzle piece in the wrong spot. At first, prompt him so much that he does not make wrong moves. Later, let him learn to correct his mistakes. Of course, do not reward mistakes. If he keeps making the same wrong move, prompt him more and use *positive practice,* that is, have him back up a few steps in the task and go ahead again so that he does all of them in the right order.

Another method for teaching the right sequence of movements is called *back-chaining.* This means teaching the task by starting with the *last step.* For example, while the child is watching, *you* can put in all the puzzle pieces but the last one, which he puts in. Next time, you put in all but the last two pieces, and the child puts them in. In this way, by the time he is ready to start with the first step, he really knows the rest very well.

The better the child gets at any task, the less you should prompt him and the more specific you should be about which behaviors you reward. Instead of rewarding him for every correct movement (Continuous Schedule), reward him (1) for *finishing* a task (and later for finishing two, three, and four tasks); (2) for doing a task *by himself* (without prompting); and (3) for doing a task *better* than before (for instance, making a tower of six blocks instead of five, or working a harder puzzle). In other words, after working on a task for about a week, do not give him a bite of food or a token if he had to be prompted. Tell him, "Good try! Let's do it again." Save rewards for a better job.

In the beginning, spend only a few minutes at the same activity. Switch to others and add new ones every few days before the child gets bored. You can even take a break and work on Large Motor activities during sessions. When you add a new task, reward and prompt the child more, until he gets more skill.

Once the child can do *many* simple tasks, add *harder* ones, such as (1) puzzles with four or five pieces making a picture; (2) cutting and pasting; (3) copying figures (squares, circles); (4) coloring; and (5) working with Play-Doh. Remember to *break down hard tasks into easier steps (shaping)*. For example, cutting paper with a pair of scissors means holding the paper and scissors a certain way, squeezing the scissors, and moving them through the paper. So one way to teach a child to cut with scissors is to *teach him the easier steps first*. For example, make sure that he can hold the paper and scissors *before* you try to get him to cut.

When he is fairly good at doing the *parts* of a hard task, help him to put them together. Have him hold the paper in one hand and the scissors in the other. Then have him open the scissors and put the paper between the blades. Finally, prompt him to squeeze the scissors to cut the paper. At each small step in the chain, prompt him if needed, reward him, and tell him what he is doing: "That's right—SQUEEZE the scissors. It is CUTTING. Good job."

Again, you can use *back-chaining* by having the child learn the *last step first*. For instance, to teach him to draw a square, you could have him watch while *you* draw three sides. Then he draws the last side. When he has learned to draw the last side without prompting, you draw the first two sides and he draws the last two. Keep working backwards until he is starting with the first side.

Keep track of the child's skill at these tasks by (1) using Table 10-1 (at the end of this chapter) to take notes on how well he is doing or what problems he is having; and (2) counting and charting the number of correct movements he makes or the number of tasks he finishes during sessions. The chart in Figure 10-2 shows the number of correct task movements made by Michael, a 5-year-old boy, during teaching sessions. He was working on Small Motor activities. Each time he correctly put in a puzzle piece, stacked a block, or strung a bead, it was counted.

As you can see from the chart, at first Michael's correct task movements were rewarded on a Continuous Schedule with praise and bites of food. Working at tasks increased fast. When the behavior started to level off, an Intermittent Schedule was used, and Michael worked even faster.

INCREASING THE AMOUNT OF TIME THE CHILD SPENDS AT SMALL
MOTOR ACTIVITIES

As the child learns how to do many Small Motor activities, teach him to spend more *time* at them outside of sessions, as play activities. There are

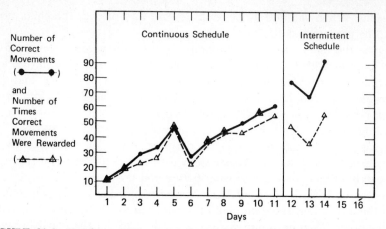

FIGURE 10-2 Teaching Michael Small Motor activities. Each day, Michael's mother ran a 20-minute session to teach him simple puzzles, stacking blocks, stringing beads, and other tasks. She used food and praise as rewards. A Continuous Schedule was used first. After Michael learned to work the tasks and did them faster, his mother used an Intermittent Schedule. Martin Kozloff served as behavioral consultant for the family.

three steps for doing this. First, teach him to work more by himself. Put one or two tasks that he can do well on the table. Get him started. Then slowly stand away from the table. Tell him that he is to keep working and that he is doing a good job. Give him a soft pat and slip him a bite of food or a token now and then while he is working hard. When he finishes the task, give him a big reward—a snack, a ride, or a bout of roughhousing. As the days go by, *fade* yourself out farther from the table and for a longer time. Tell him, "I'll be right back. You FINISH the puzzle." If he stops working when you stand away from the table, come back for just a minute and give him more rewards for working. Later, reward him only for working and finishing tasks by himself.

Second, use *Activity Rewards* more. During sessions, use Grandma's Law to get the child to do harder tasks: "As soon as you finish this puzzle (one he does not care for), you can play with the Tinker Toys (which he likes)." Also, have Activity Rewards come after sessions. When the child works for a certain number of minutes or finishes a certain number of tasks, he gets to go outside, watch TV, or have a snack. Slowly *increase* the number of minutes or tasks he works during sessions. You can use a kitchen timer with a bell to signal when he has worked enough. Use a *Changing Interval Schedule* (the interval between bells changes after each reward). Make sure that he is working when the bell rings.

Third, start the child playing during the day, fade yourself out, and give him an Activity Reward when he has played for a certain amount of time (a little longer each day). At first, you might use Grandma's Law to start him playing: "As soon as you color the square, we will play catch." Later, just set out play objects, praise him, and slip him a bite of food or a token while he is playing, and have an Activity Reward come after he plays. Switch the Activity Reward each day.

Remember: as the child learns to work at tasks, teach him to do them in new places and with other people.

Use a watch to keep track of how much time the child spends with Small Motor activities outside of sessions. Chart the number of minutes or hours each day. A goal to shoot for at this point is between a half hour and an hour. In later months, you can increase this much more.

The next section is about another *basic behavior* to work on at the same time.

Strengthening Good Work Habits, Such as Sitting, Listening, and Working   (B22)

While the child is getting more *skill* at Small Motor activities and is learning to spend more *time* at them outside of sessions, you should also be strengthening good work habits, such as sitting, listening to directions, and working for a longer time. Here are a few ways to strengthen good work habits.

1. *Keeping Old Target Behaviors Going.* The Learning Readiness area gives the child a head start on good work habits. There you can increase eye contact, good sitting, and cooperating. When you start on Small Motor activities, keep these old target behaviors going strong by rewarding them once in a while. For instance, when the child sits down at the table, give him a pat; reward him with a small bite of food (if you use it) for spontaneous eye contact; reward him when he cooperates with a simple request and when he is looking at what he is doing.

Also, use *natural chains.* Make sure that the child is sitting and that he is making eye contact *before* you hand him a task object or give him a direction. For instance, either hold up a task object and wait until he makes eye contact, or say, "Do you want another one?" Give him the object when he makes eye contact. But do not reward these old behaviors too often, or the child will do them instead of the newer and harder tasks.

2. *Teaching the Child to Work Longer.* Some children work on tasks

for only a few minutes at a time and then "drift" or run away. There are two ways to keep a child working. One way is to *let the rewards and reward schedules do their job. You* do not have to keep a child working. The rewards and reward schedules will do this *if you use them right*.

This does not mean that you should keep on with the same teaching program plan if the child stops working for more than a day or two. Something may be wrong, and Chapter 7 will help you to find out what it is. But, if you are using a *strong* reward, are rewarding the child often enough, are using a Changing Schedule (so that he does not know just when he will be rewarded), and are not rewarding him when he runs or "drifts" away, the schedule will finally take effect. The child will settle down and work. *Slowly* increase the length of time he must work before he is rewarded.

Second, when the child runs or drifts away, *ignore* it. He just loses the chance to earn rewards for working and misses the Activity Reward at the end of the session. Begin to work at the activity yourself or, better, with someone else. Make the activity seem like fun. This will often get the child's attention back. Then let him join in.

3. *Teaching the Child to Listen.* Up to now, you have been prompting the child or helping him through the right motions of a task until he can do it by himself. But are you sure he *listens* to your directions? You had better make sure before you go on to harder skill areas.

The method for teaching the child to listen is simple. Use it during sessions on Large and Small Motor activities and at other times. Begin with simple directions for him to do something, such as "Stand up" or "Give me the ball." In other words, start with movements he can *already* make. Prompt him if needed and reward him for following the direction. Once he is following simple directions, give him harder ones that ask him to do two or three things in a row, for example, "Pick up the BALL AND the BLOCK" or "THROW the ball to me AND SIT DOWN." Again, prompt him at first and reward him.

It is also very important to teach the child to follow signals that tell him to *stop* or *wait*. One way to teach the child to wait is to hold up an object (one that he has learned to point to). The idea is to have him point to the object, but *he must wait until you ask him to point*. Prompt him to wait until you give the direction. Reward him only when he waits for the direction and follows it.

Teach the child to *stop* in the same way. While he is working at a task, tell him, "STOP a second, please." When he does, give him a little hug or rub his head, and then let him go on with what he was doing. Or, when he is just about to open a door, tell him, "STOP. Pick up the ball FIRST, please." Reward him when he does and then let him go back to opening the door. Do this once or twice during sessions and a few times at other times of the day.

Keep track of the child's work habits. Use a stopwatch or wristwatch to count the number of minutes he sits, pays attention, and works during each session. Every few days, count the number of spontaneous eye contacts and the number of times the child cooperates with requests. Your goals are to teach the child to (1) sit, pay attention, and work for at least 15 minutes out of 20-minute sessions (or 75 percent of the time); (2) look at what he is doing most of the time; (3) listen to and follow most simple directions to start and stop behaviors, and follow directions to start a few harder behaviors; and (4) have good work habits with a few other people and in a few new places.

When the child is coming close to the goals for the first three *basic behaviors* in the Small Motor group (B14, B21, and B22), start working on the next basic behavior (B23).

Teaching the Child to Point to or Match Objects by Name   (B23)

By taking the child for walks, telling him the names of things, and having him point to them, you give him a head start on Functional Speech. This section tells you how to give him even more practice. The definition of the target behavior is that the child *points* to objects when you say the name, and *matches* (puts in the same place) objects with the same name, color, or shape.

MATCHING OBJECTS

This teaches the child to see how some objects are the *same* and some are *different*. Start by sitting down with him at a table with different objects on it. Take a box and divide it into two or three compartments, or use two or three shoe boxes. Paste a picture of a different object on each box or put a *sample* object in each box, for example, a spoon in one, a sock in the second, and a block in the third. Have extras of all of them.

When the child is sitting quietly, hold up one of the extra objects. When he looks at it, tell him what it is. Have him *point* to it. Then show him the one just like it (the sample) in the box or compartment. Give him the object you held up, and *quickly* prompt him to put it in the box or compartment with the one it matches. Try not to let him put it in the wrong box. Guide his hand to the right one. Slowly *fade out* your prompts (by waiting longer before you point to the right place and by guiding his arm less and less) and, later, reward him only when he does this matching right. Switch back and forth between the different kinds of objects. Add new ones every few days.

When the child is matching objects well, teach him to match *shapes* and *colors*. Have boxes with samples of differently colored objects (poker chips, paint samples) pasted on or in them. Then hold up one of the extras from your pile, tell the child the name of the color, and have him put it in the right box. Switch between the different colors. Do the same thing with simple shapes, such as squares and circles.

When you are working on matching, count and chart the number of times each session that you ask the child to match objects (the number of tries) and the number of times that he correctly does it without prompting. You want the line for the number of correct matches to get close to the number of tries.

POINTING TO OBJECTS BY NAME

Matching means that the child sees how objects are the same or different. You should also teach him the names for objects. If the child points to an object when you give the name, it is a good bet he has learned its name. You need pictures of many common objects (foods, furniture, toys, clothes), which you can buy or cut out of magazines, and a box of small objects (sock, ball, spoon, pencil, and so on).

First make sure that the child knows how to *point to* or *pick up* objects. Put *one* object or picture on the table in front of him. Wait for him to look at you or at the object. Then tell him, "This is a DOG. Point to the DOG." Prompt him to point if necessary, and reward him when he does. Move to the next step when he can and does pick up an object or picture when you tell him to.

Now teach the child the names for the objects, one at a time. Wait until he is looking at you. Then hold up an object or picture. When he looks at it, tell him the name and prompt him to point to it. "This is an APPLE. POINT to the APPLE. . . . Good, APPLE." Repeat this a few times. Then go on to the next object or picture and do the same thing— tell him the name and have him point to it. Then put *both* on the table. When the child is looking at them, point to each and tell him the name. "Here is the DOG, and here is the APPLE." Then tell him to point to one of them. "Okay, now POINT to the APPLE." If he does this correctly within about 4 seconds, reward him. If not, *prompt* him by moving his hand to the right one or by pointing with your finger. Repeat this a few times, but move the pictures to different places on the table.

When the child correctly points to the first picture or object several times in a row, have him point to the second one. "Good. Now point to the DOG." Move the pictures around, and repeat a few times. Then switch back and forth between the two. One time ask him to point to the apple. Shuffle the pictures around and ask him to point to the dog. Slowly fade out any prompts. Be careful not to prompt him by leaning toward or looking at the right picture.

When the child correctly points to the first two even when they are at different places on the table, add a third picture or object. Teach him its name in the same way as you did the first two. Here are the steps again.

1. *Wait until he is sitting still and looking at you.*
2. *Hold up the picture or object.*
3. *When he looks at it, tell him its name and have him point to it.*
4. *If he can talk, ask him to repeat the name.*
5. *Put the picture on the table next to one or two other pictures.*
6. *Tell him to point to it.*
7. *Prompt him at first, if needed.*
8. *Move the pictures around each time and ask him to point to the same one. Later, have him point to a different one each time.*
9. *Later, reward him only when he correctly points without a prompt.*

As the days go by, add new objects or pictures. Work on them most, but practice on the old ones too. Still later, use objects and pictures that look a little different but have the same name, for instance, two or three houses, dogs, cars, chairs, and so on. Also, keep taking the child for walks, and have him point to objects by name.

As with matching, count and chart the number of times you ask the child to point to or pick up objects and pictures (the number of tries) and the number of times he does this correctly and without prompts. The goal at this early time is to teach him to point to or pick up about ten objects or pictures by name, without prompting, among others lying on the table. We will work on this more in the chapter on Functional Speech.

4. SOCIAL SKILLS

The last group in this area is Social Skills, which means teaching the child to use his Looking, Listening, and Moving skills with other people.

Teaching the Child to Use Eye Contact to Get Natural Rewards (B24)

The child should already make Spontaneous Eye Contact (A1) and Eye Contact on Request (A2) often. What is his eye contact getting him? It should be getting him praise, food once in a while, and the chance to do a task. It is time to teach him to *use* his eye contact to get many *natural* rewards around the home and school. We talked about this before. *From now on, be sure that the child makes eye contact before you give him what he wants.* There must be no going with him just because he pulls on your sleeve or takes you by the hand, no giving him a snack because he gets into the cupboard and takes out the pudding, no turning on music for him because he is whining for it.

Instead, make him back up and try again, but he has to *at least* make eye contact and, if he can talk, ask in the right way. For example, if he is pulling on your sleeve, just stand there and wait for him to make eye contact without pulling on you. If he is whining for music, send him out of the room. When you let him back in, tell him, "As soon as you ask me (or look at me), I will turn on music."

Do this as much as you can during the day. If the child learns to make eye contact to get natural rewards, it will be easier for him to learn to use speech to get natural rewards. Measure this behavior by counting the number of times during an observation period that the child makes eye contact for a natural reward. Your goal is for the child to make eye contact (if he cannot talk) for just about everything he wants.

Teaching the Child to Play with Others   (B25),
Cooperate on a Task   (B26), and Take His Turn   (B27)

These three behaviors are important. The Large and Small Motor activities the child is learning will not do him much good if he does them only with you. The three behaviors can be taught in small steps (*shaped*). So first let us get the child playing *near* other children.

PLAYING NEAR OTHER CHILDREN

Remember Nancy from Chapter 1? She knew how to play, but played only by herself or when she was with her parents or teachers. When other children came around, Nancy left and tried to get the teachers' attention. How do you teach a child to play near other children? The answer is simple: Each day, reward the child only when he or she is playing a little *closer* to the other children than before. This means that, when the child comes up to you and tries to get attention by whining or making a big fuss over a tiny scrape, ignore that behavior. Then, either prompt the child to get started on a more constructive activity or wait until he begins to play a little closer to the other children. Give the child lots of attention when he is nearer the others. As the days go by, stay on the lookout for times when the child is nearer the others; and reward him.

COOPERATING ON A TASK AND TAKING TURNS

When a child can work or play by himself and will do so near another child, teach him to cooperate or play with another child. Have two children sit next to each other. Start with simple tasks they both can do, for example, four-piece puzzles or blocks to stack. At first, give each child, in turn, *one* task object, prompt him to place it, and praise him when he does. When the whole task is done, reward both children with plenty of praise, food, or tokens (if you are using them). Repeat this with other simple tasks and add harder ones.

After a few weeks, give each child three or four objects at a time for the common task, for instance, puzzle pieces. Stand behind the children, prompt them to take turns ("Okay, Nancy, JIMMY put in the DOG. Now YOU put in the COW"), and reward them when the task is done. Slowly *fade out* your prompts for them to take turns. Give *big* rewards to both children only when the task is done.

Still later, teach them to cooperate on things that are more like play, for example, farm, house, and train sets. Stand behind the children and prompt them to move the pieces around and put the sets together. Talk to them about what they are doing. "Oh, that was very nice, Nancy. You are putting the COW in the BARN. Jimmy, do you see where Nancy put the COW? She put it in the BARN." If Jimmy points to the cow or barn, or imitates the word "cow" or "barn," reward him. Then, if necessary, prompt him to place one of the pieces and reward him when he does. If tokens were used during this activity, have a token exchange at the end of the session.

As a child learns to cooperate and take turns with one other child, have him work with new children. You can even slowly add enough other children that you have a small group activity.

Measure these three behaviors by counting and charting: (1) how many minutes a child plays near other children during a play period; (2) how many minutes a child sits and pays attention when he is supposed to be cooperating on a task; and (3) how many times a child takes his turn without prompting. Your goals are for the child to spend over half the time playing near other children, sit and pay attention for at least 15 minutes out of 20-minute cooperation sessions, and take his turn most of the time without prompting.

Table 10-1.   Progress in Looking, Listening, and Moving
This table will help you to keep track of a child's progress with Looking, Listening, and Moving activities. Make copies of this blank table. Each week that you work on an activity, write it on the table for that week. Take notes on how well the child is doing the activity. (How many of the movements in it can the child do? Does he do the movements in the right order? What kinds of prompts does he need? How much prompting does he need? What problems is he having?). When the child has learned an activity—he can do it well and without prompts—*underline it* on the table for that week and *update* the child's BES and BET to show that he has learned the activity. At the bottom of the table, write down *any other changes* you have noticed in the child's behaviors, whether or not you worked on them.

Name of Child: _____ Name of Teacher: _____

Date: Week of _____ to _____.

Large Motor Activities (Which ones? How well? What prompts? What problems?)

Small Motor Activities (Which ones? How well? What prompts? What problems?)

Social Skill (Which ones? How well? What prompts? What problems?)

Other Changes Noticed in the Child's Behaviors

REFERENCES AND EXTRA READINGS

Barsch, R. D. *Achieving Perceptual-Motor Efficiency.* Seattle: Special Child Publications, 1967.

Bortner, M. *Evaluation and Education of Children with Brain Damage.* Springfield, Ill.: Charles C Thomas, 1968.

Doland, D. J., and Andelberg, K. "The learning of sharing behavior." *Child Development,* 1967, 38, 695-700.

Frostig, M., and Horne, D. *The Frostig Program for the Development of Visual Perception.* Chicago: Follett, 1964.

Frostig, M., Lefever, W., and Whittlesee, J. *Marianne Frostig Developmental Test of Visual Perception.* Palo Alto, Calif.: Consulting Psychologists Press, 1966.

Golick, M. "Strictly for parents: A parents' guide to learning problems." *Journal of Learning Disabilities,* 1968, 1, 366-377.

Hart, B. M., Reynolds, N., Baer, D. M., Brawley, E., and Harris, F. R. "Effect of contingent and noncontingent social reinforcement on the cooperative play of a preschool child." *Journal of Applied Behavior Analysis,* 1968, 1, 73-76.

Martin, G. L., and Powers, R. B. "Attention span: An operant conditioning analysis." *Exceptional Children,* 1967, 33, 565-570.

O'Brien, F., Azrin, N. H., and Bugle, C. "Training profoundly retarded children to stop crawling." *Journal of Applied Behavior Analysis,* 1972, 5, 131-137.

Robins, F., and Robins, J. *Educational Rhythmics for Mentally and Physically Handicapped Children.* New York: Association Press, 1967.

CHAPTER ELEVEN

MOTOR
IMITATION

1. WHAT THIS SKILL AREA IS ABOUT

Right now, you might want the children you are working with to talk and do things for themselves. You are right to want children to learn these skills. They are very important. But wait a minute! What does it take to learn these skills? And what is the fastest way to teach them?

Let us look at how people usually learn hard skills. What do you think would be the fastest way to learn to drive a car: If you got behind the wheel and tried to learn by yourself (*trial and error*)? If someone *told* you all the things you had to do? Or if someone *showed you how*? If you think the fastest way would be for someone to show you how, you are right! If you tried to learn in the other two ways, you would make so many mistakes or errors that you would give up. In fact, you might never learn how to drive a car unless someone showed you.

The same goes for children. Many of the things children know how to do were learned because they *watched* what their parents and teachers were doing and then *repeated* or *imitated* what they saw or heard. For example, a child learns how to talk by *watching* the way his parents move their mouths and by *listening* to the sounds his parents make when they talk. Then the child *repeats* or *imitates* what he saw (mouth movements) and heard (sounds). And if his parents *reward* him when he imitates them, the child will imitate and talk more and more.

So, by just *watching* and then *imitating* what their parents do, children learn many behavior skills. And they learn *very fast*.

What Does This Have to Do with the Children I Am Working With?

If you try to teach children all the behavior skills they need to learn by breaking down each one into small steps, telling them how to do the step, prompting, and rewarding as they get better, *it will take you a very long time just to teach a handful of simple skills.* In fact, the children might *never* learn hard skills like *speech.* They need to learn a simple and fast way to learn other skills. And that way is *imitation. Imitation is the key to a child's education.* Once he learns how to imitate you, it will be much easier to teach him the hard Large and Small Motor activities, Verbal Imitation, Functional Speech, and Chores and Self-Help skills.

Is the Child Ready for This Area?

Before you read any more, take a look at the Table of Basic Behaviors (Table 4-2) in Chapter 4. Table 4-2 tells you that before a child works on Motor Imitation he should have learned the following *basic behaviors* from other skill areas:

(A1)   Spontaneous Eye Contact.
(A2)   Eye Contact on Request.
(A4)   Cooperates with Simple Spoken Requests.
(B13)   Skill at Many Large Motor Activities.
(B14)   Looks at Objects, Parts of the Body, Face, Mouth.
(B21)   Skill at Many Small Motor Activities.
(B22)   Good Work Habits, Such as Sitting, Listening, and Working at a Task.
(B24)   Uses Eye Contact to Get Natural Rewards.

If any of these are circled on the child's BET, he is not ready for this skill area. Instead, teach him the *basic behaviors* he still needs help with. When he has learned them all, come back here and read on.

What Behaviors Are in This Skill Area?

Skim over the section on Motor Imitation in the BES or BET.

As you see, there are ten behaviors you can work on in this area. Six of them are *basic behaviors.* Teach the child any and all of the behaviors he needs help with (that are circled on his BET), but make sure he learns the *basic behaviors*. He will need them before he can work in the Verbal Imitation, Functional Speech, and Chores and Self-Help areas.

Plan and Write a Teaching Program

Plan and write teaching programs for this area in the same way you did for other areas. *Pinpoint* the easiest behavior the child needs help with in the column for Motor Imitation on the BET. This is your first target behavior. Take a *baseline* for a few days to make sure the child really needs help on it. If he does, *read* the section in this chapter that tells you how to teach it. *Plan* a teaching program for the target behavior with the help of Chapter 6. Also plan how to keep older target behaviors (eye contact, good sitting, cooperation) going with the help of Chapter 8. Then write the teaching program plan on Table 6-2 at the end of Chapter 6. Keep track of how well the child is learning the target behavior, and how well you are keeping older behaviors going, by counting and charting them on Table 6-3 and Figure 6-2 at the end of Chapter 6.

When the child has learned the first target behavior, pinpoint the next easiest one he needs help with on the BET as the second target behavior. Plan, write, and run a new teaching program with the help of Chapter 8. When the child has learned most of the *basic behaviors* in this skill area, pick the next skill area with the help of Chapter 4, especially the Skill Sequence Table (Table 4-1).

2. HOW DO I TEACH MOTOR IMITATION?

The method for teaching Motor Imitation is easy. The idea is to teach the child to *move* his body in the *same way* you do, *right after* you do. At first, you may have to help or *prompt* him to imitate your *movements* by saying, "Do this," by telling him what to imitate ("PAT the table"), or by putting him through the motions. But, after a while, you want him to imitate your movements (*models*) without any prompts.

You can work on Motor Imitation standing up or sitting down, but be *across* from the child and *close enough* that you can *prompt* him and reward him fast. It might be a good idea to start by using *food* or *tokens* and lots of *strong praise*. If you find that certain things keep the child from paying attention (like the television or other children), remove these things during teaching sessions.

As with Large and Small Motor skills, work on Motor Imitation during teaching sessions at a time you set aside for it, like 5, 10, or 15 minutes in the morning and afternoon, before a favorite activity. You *should* also work on Motor Imitation at *other* times. For example, when you are working on puzzles and other Small Motor or Large Motor activities, you can throw in a few minutes of Motor Imitation. Make a game of it in the car, in the bath, on the floor, in the yard. Have the child imitate scrubbing his face, sweeping the floor, and other movements that are *natural* to where you are.

To teach Motor Imitation, *first pinpoint a movement you want the child to imitate.* Start with *easy* movements he can already do. For example, you could start with Large and Small Motor movements you have already worked on, like patting the table or raising the arms over the head. Then wait until the child is looking at you, or tell him to look at you. *As soon as he is looking at you, show him the model* (you pat the table) *and say,* "DO THIS" or "BILLY, PAT THE TABLE." *Only show him the model when he is looking.* Wait about two seconds. *If he does not imitate your model (or do what you told him to do), prompt him through the motions.* At first, you should reward him even if you had to prompt him.

Slowly, but surely, *fade out your prompts.* Do this by showing the model when the child is looking, but *waiting a little longer each time* before you *tell* the child what to do. For example, the first time you show the model, tell the child what to do at the *same time* you are showing it. The next time you show the model, *wait one second* before you tell the child what to do. The next time you show the model, wait two seconds; the next time three seconds; and after that, wait four seconds before you tell the child what to do (Touchette, 1971). The method looks like this:

First Try: Child looks; say, "DO THIS," show model *and tell* him what to do ("PAT THE TABLE"); Prompt through the motions if needed; Reward.

Second Try: Child looks; say, "DO THIS" and show model; *wait one second* and then *tell him* what to do ("PAT THE TABLE"); Prompt through the motions if needed; Reward.

Third Try: Child looks; say, "DO THIS" and show model; *wait two seconds* and then *tell* him what to do ("PAT THE TABLE"); Prompt through the motions if needed; Reward.

Fourth Try: Child looks; say, "DO THIS" and show model; *wait three seconds* and then *tell* him what to do ("PAT THE

	TABLE"); Prompt through the motions if needed; Reward.
Fifth and Later Tries:	Child looks; say "DO THIS" and show model; *wait four seconds* and then *tell* him what to do ("PAT THE TABLE"); Prompt through the motions if needed; Reward.

The idea is for the child to start imitating the model *before* you get a chance to tell him what to do.

When he starts trying to imitate the model before you tell him what to do, begin to give him *less help*. That is, put him through the motions less and less. Also, when he gets more skilled at imitating a certain model, *make sure that you reward him only for better and better imitations*. For example, if you are teaching him to imitate hand-clapping (the *model*), and you have gotten him to the point where he will raise his hands and *almost* bring them together, do not reward him any more for *just* raising his hands. Praise him and tell him, "That's pretty good. Let's try again." The next time you show him the model, reward him if he does better than just raising his hands. But, if he does not do any better the next time, *go back to prompting him some more* and then try to *fade out your prompts again*. You should also be rewarding him only when he imitates or tries to imitate *right after* you show him the model— say, within 5 seconds.

Once he can imitate the model (the movement) (1) without prompts (by himself) and (2) right after you show him the model, start to fade out telling him, "DO THIS." Just wait until he is looking, show him the model very clearly, and reward him for closer and closer imitations.

Work on the same model *only a few times in a row* during a session; then switch to another one. *Make sure the other one you switch to is very different from the first one,* so that the child can easily see the difference. So, during a session, switch between different models. Each day, go back to the same ones for practice, until the child gets better at imitating them. Once he can imitate two or three different models all by himself and just about every time, add a few new ones. Even when he can imitate a model perfectly, give him practice on it every few days, *and reward him with plenty of praise and, once in a while* (if you are using it) *with food or a token.* Exchange tokens for a back-up reward at the end of the session.

3. WHAT MODELS OR MOTOR IMITATIONS DO I WORK ON?

There are *four* groups of models: Large Motor models (moving larger parts of the body—arms and legs), Small Motor models (using the fingers, hands, and eyes together), Mouth Positions, and Object Placements. Table 11-1 lists some of the different models you can work on in each group. Can you think of others?

Learning to imitate about five models in *each* group very well (five times in a row without prompting and without a mistake) is a *basic behavior*.

What to Do If the Child Does Not Imitate You or If You Are Just Starting on This Group

The best models to start with are Large Motor models, because they are easiest to see, and Small Motor models in which a noise is also made (patting table, clapping hands). Begin with movements the child can *already* do by himself. For example, if you have already taught the child how to bend down and touch the floor or how to stretch his arms over his head, use these when you start on Motor Imitation—only now have him *imitate you* when *you* bend over and touch the floor or stretch *your* arms over your head.

THE WHOLE IDEA IS FOR YOUR BEHAVIOR TO BECOME A *SIGNAL* FOR HIM TO *REPEAT* (IMITATE) YOUR BEHAVIOR.

It may take a few days or even a week before the child learns to imitate two or three Large Motor models *very well* and *without prompts*. When he does learn to imitate two or three very well, start teaching him to imitate a few Small Motor models that you have picked from the list or that you think of. Then switch between Large and Small Motor models during sessions. Also work on them outside of sessions for fun.

Once the child is imitating about five models from the Large and Small Motor groups *very well, with few, if any, errors* and *without prompts*, move to the next section.

What to Do When the Child Can Imitate Some Large and Small Motor Models Very Well

After the child has learned to imitate about five models from the Large and Small Motor groups very well, *add a few* Object Placement and Mouth Position models to your sessions. Later, run a short session each day on Object Placements or Mouth Positions.

Table 11-1. Movements or Models to Imitate

Large Motor Models   (C1)

Stretch arm over head
Stand up
Bend over
Shake head
Pat head
Raise arms over head
Swing arms
Jump over objects
Stamp foot
Swing leg
March in place
Run
Touch foot
Roll
Crawl
Hop
Walk on a line
Walk on a raised beam
Follow an obstacle course

Object Placement Models   (C3)

Move objects from one hand to another
Pick up blocks
Stack blocks
Draw lines (straight line, circle, triangle, square)
Ring bell
Hit tambourine
Do simple puzzles (child puts in the same pieces you did)
Fold paper
Throw ball
String beads (in the same way you do)
Put plate on table (on counter, in sink)
Move toothbrush on teeth
Pick up toys
Wash and dry dishes
Hang up jacket, pants, hat

Small Motor Models   (C2)

Clap hands
Wave "bye-bye"
Pat table
Blink eyes
Wiggle nose
Touch or point with finger to nose, eyes, ears, tummy
Touch forefinger and thumb together

Mouth Position Models   (C4)

Open mouth
Shut mouth
Chew
Stick out tongue
Put tongue on upper lip
Put lips together (as in *P* or *M* sound)
"Purse" lips (as in *Uuuu* sound)
Pucker up and blow
Pull lower jaw down with finger (This is one way to prompt the *Ah* sound)
Put index finger over both lips (this is one way to prompt the *P* sound)
Pinch lips together (prompt for *M* or *B* sounds)
Put tongue on edge of upper teeth (position for *TH* sound)
Put tip of tongue just behind upper teeth (position for *T* or *D* sound)
Put tongue on roof of mouth (position for *L* sound)
Put upper teeth on lower lip or "bite" lower lip (position for *F* or *V* sound)
Close teeth together (position for *S*)
Open mouth wide with tongue pushed way back (for *GAh* or *KAh* sound)
Smile

IMITIATING OBJECT PLACEMENTS (C3)

This will help the child to learn harder Small Motor activities, as well as Chores and Self-Help tasks. Examples are imitating the way *you* stack one block on top of another, the way *you* draw a line, the way *you* fluff the pillows, and the way *you* brush your teeth.

As with Large and Small Motor imitations, wait until the child is looking at you and then show him a model (for instance, fluffing up the pillows). Then prompt him to do the *same* thing. Reward him for closer and closer tries. When he can imitate one Object Placement very well, start on another but continue to give him practice on the first one often.

The secret of teaching the child to imitate an Object Placement that has many parts (for instance, stacking four blocks) is to give him a way to *prompt himself* by telling himself *what he is doing*. For instance, when showing the child how to stack four blocks, make sure he is watching you while you slowly stack each block, saying, "One . . . two . . . three . . . four." When the child is imitating your model, prompt him by moving him through the motions if necessary, *and* by saying, "ONE . . . TWO . . . THREE . . . FOUR" *while he* is stacking them. Slowly fade out counting with him until you are just whispering and, later, not prompting him at all.

The same goes for other kinds of object placements, such as picking up objects in the same order as you do. Let us say that there are three objects on the table—a ball, a toy dog, and a block. The model may be to pick up all three: first the ball, then the dog, and then the block. As you show the model, *say* what you are doing: "Ball . . . dog . . . block." When it is the child's turn to imitate this, prompt him by hand *and* by saying, "BALL . . . DOG . . . BLOCK," while he is picking them up. If he can talk, prompt him to prompt himself by saying, "Ball . . . dog . . . block" while he is picking them up, and reward him for prompting himself in this way.

Please take a look at the Skill Sequence Table (Table 4-1) in Chapter 4. It shows that Chores and Self-Help skills comes after Motor Imitation. When the child is learning to imitate Object Placements very well and does not need much help with this *basic behavior* any more, you can start working on Chores and Self-Help Skills, too.

IMITATING MOUTH MOVEMENTS AND POSITIONS (C4)

When the child has learned to imitate some Large and Small Motor models very well, you should also start teaching him to imitate *mouth movements and positions*. This will help him when it comes time to work on Verbal Imitation.

Start off your sessions by working on puzzles or by practicing a few of the Large and Small Motor models the child can already imitate. Then slip in an *easy* Mouth Position model. When he is *looking at your face or mouth,* show him the model (such as opening his mouth wide or sticking out his tongue). You may have to prompt him to open his mouth wide by pulling his lower jaw down. Other lip and tongue positions can be prompted with a tongue depressor, as well as with your fingers. You can prompt a child to stick out his tongue by "teasing" it out with a lollipop. And you can prompt him to pucker up and blow by molding his lips with your fingers while you push in on his tummy. Of course, reward him for imitating mouth positions better and without prompts.

If the child makes a good *sound* while he is imitating a mouth position model, reward him. Then try to have him imitate that mouth position *and* sound again. For example, if you are teaching the child to open his mouth wide, and he says "*Ah,*" reward him: "*Ah,* very good." The next time, open *your* mouth wide and say "*Ah.*" Prompt him, if needed, to imitate "*Ah*" and reward him if he tries. If you find that the child *does* try to imitate a few sounds at this time, he may be ready for Verbal Imitation, and you should check the Table of Basic Behaviors (Table 4-2) in Chapter 4 to see if he has all the *basics* for Verbal Imitation.

4.   WHAT PROBLEMS MAY COME UP? AND WHAT DO I DO?

Whenever problems happen, look over Chapter 7, "Handling Common Problems of Teaching," to see if you can spot what is causing the problem and how you can handle it.

One problem may be that the child just does not get much better on a certain model. It may be that he is bored, or that the model is too hard, or that he is not being rewarded enough. First *stop working on that model for a few days.* If he still has trouble when you come back to it, maybe it is too hard. *Break it down into easier steps and reward him for imitating them.* For example, if the child is having trouble learning to imitate stamping his foot, back up to teaching him to imitate just raising his foot. Once he has that down solidly, go back to teaching him to stamp his foot. Also, make sure to give him *more* rewards or *stronger* rewards. Reward him for *trying* and praise him with *vigor.* Be careful, though! Reward and prompt the child more for a few days. After that, *hold off on rewards except for slightly better imitations that he does with less help.*

Another problem may be that the child *stops paying attention.* This may happen because he is bored with imitation in general. You may have been working on it for too long or too fast. In that case, *switch to another skill area for a few days to a week,* for instance, Small and Large Motor skills. This will give both you and the child a break. If this does not increase his attention, *run sessions during mealtime.* Praise and snacks may not be strong enough rewards, and so you may have to work with him during meals, when food is sure to be a strong reward.

A general rule to follow is this:

ALWAYS MAKE THE TEACHING SESSIONS AS ATTRACTIVE AS YOU CAN, BY REWARDING MORE TIMES, USING STRONGER REWARDS, BACKING UP TO EASIER TASKS, AND SWITCHING TO DIFFERENT TASKS.

5. GENERALIZED IMITATION, OR MAKING SURE IMITATION STAYS STRONG AND NATURAL (C7 THROUGH C10)

In Chapter 3 we talked about what "normal" means. The imitation behaviors of two children, Billy and Johnny, may look the same. But Johnny will imitate most people, just about anywhere, and his imitations are rewarded by praise and natural consequences. He "likes" to do what Daddy does. Billy, on the other hand, will imitate only in class with his teacher, and his imitations are rewarded and kept going by food. *Billy's imitation behavior is not normal.* It is *not controlled* by *natural signals* (he imitates his teacher only in class). And it is not controlled by *natural rewards* (he imitates only as long as he is rewarded with food).

Teaching a child to (1) Imitate Some Models Even if He Is Not Rewarded (C7); (2) Move His Body or Do Chores as Others Do on His Own (C8 and C9); and (3) Imitate Motor Models of Many People (C10) is very important. In fact, C7 and C10 are *basic behaviors.* The child must Imitate Some Models Even if He Is Not Rewarded (C7) before he will do very well in the Verbal Imitation and Functional Speech areas.

Teaching the Child to Imitate Some Models Even if Not Rewarded (C7)

This is mostly a matter of time and of rewards and reward schedules you use. As the child gets better at imitating, *slowly* move from a Continuous to an Intermittent Schedule—a *Changing Number schedule*—so that he does not know just which imitations will be rewarded. Of course, when he does *perfect* imitations, reward them. Second, wean the child off food or token rewards and use more Social Rewards (praise, hugs) and natural Activity Rewards (during and at the end of sessions). At other times of the day too, follow correct imitations more and more with natural rewards. For instance, when the child imitates getting a glass from the shelf, fill it with soda pop; when he imitates jumping up and down, have a bout of roughhousing with him; and when he imitates licking a lollipop, give him one.

Keep track of how well the child imitates models that are not rewarded by testing him every week or so. During your session that day, set aside a few models that you will not reward, for example, clapping hands and opening his mouth wide. Run the session as usual, and reward him for correctly imitating models, except the few you picked to test him on. If he imitates them right, just go on to the next model.

Count how many times he correctly imitates the rewarded models and the models that were not rewarded. Your goal is to teach him to imitate unrewarded models about as much as rewarded models.

Teaching the Child to Move his Body and Do Chores as Others Do on His Own   (C8 and C9)

Little children often move their bodies like other people. For example, when a child sees his mother brush her hair, he may do the same thing with his hand; when he hears someone cough, he coughs too; and when he sees his father hammer a nail, he picks up a stick and pretends to hammer. This is great, because it means imitation is strong. The child "enjoys" doing "like Daddy and Mommy do." And he will learn many behaviors in this way.

When you are teaching a child to imitate, it is important to teach him to imitate outside of sessions in the "normal" way children do. Whenever you see the child imitating what you (or someone else) are doing, quickly reward him for it and tell him what he is doing ("Good boy. You are CROSSING YOUR LEGS like me").

Teaching the Child to Imitate Models of Many People   (C10)

If you are the only person who works with a child on Motor Imitation, he may not imitate anyone else. And, if you work with him only in one place, he may not imitate anywhere else. So, *once a child has learned to imitate five to ten models very well, you should have other people work with him and in other places.*

First, slowly *change* the teaching session by having another person come in (brother, sister, another teacher, or neighbor)—someone the child has had contact with before. Have this person sit *next* to you while you are showing the child models to imitate (ones that he already knows well). After a few minutes, have the other person reward the child for imitating *your* model (*you* are still showing the models). If the child does poorly with the new person around, go back and reward him yourself. When he improves again with you, have the other person try giving the rewards again.

Next, have the other person show models *and* reward the child for correct imitations. You may have to *coach* or *prompt* the other person so that he or she rewards the child fast and prompts him if he needs it. Slowly let the other person work with the child for longer and longer periods. When this is working, you can bring in a third person—a visitor, for example.

Third, when the child is imitating models with other people, work on imitation in *different places*. When you go on field trips, to people's homes, or to the grocery, have the child imitate models that are natural to those places, for instance, picking up a leaf, pushing a chair up to the table, taking a can off the shelf.

6. WHAT DO I MEASURE?

Keep track of how well the child is doing on Motor Imitation. This will help you to decide when he is ready to work on another skill area, such as Verbal Imitation.

During sessions when you are working *mostly* on Motor Imitation, count two things:

1. the number of times *you show models* during each session; and
2. the number of times the *child correctly imitates* the models you show, without any help.

At the beginning, you may get mostly *close tries* and very few *perfect* imitations, but you should count only the *perfect ones*. Write the number of times you show models and the number of perfect imitations each session on a copy of Table 6-3, and chart the numbers each day on a copy of Figure 6-2 at the end of Chapter 6. Or you can find the *percentage* of correct imitations by dividing the number of models you show each session *into* the number of correct imitations. For example, if you show models twelve times and the child imitates correctly six times, you have 6/12 or 50 percent correct imitations. Chart the percentage of correct imitations for each day.

Each week, you should also fill out a progress sheet on Motor Imitation. Make copies of the blank Table 11-2 at the end of this chapter. Write down which models you are working on, how much the child needs to be prompted, which models he will imitate even if he is not rewarded, where and who else he will imitate, and what movements or chores of other people the child has imitated on his own. When the child can imitate a model perfectly with no prompts, day after day, *underline it* on the progress sheet for that week. Do not forget to give him practice on it every few days.

An Example of Progress on Motor Imitation

Figures 11-1 and 11-2 are charts showing how Karen (7 years old) learned to imitate Large Motor, Small Motor, and Mouth Position models. Her mother and father worked on Large and Small Motor activities for a few weeks (see Figure 10-1 in Chapter 10). When Karen became more skilled at these activities, they began *adding* some Large Motor models for her to imitate during sessions, for example, stretching hands above head, touching toes, and hopping on one foot. They worked on Large Motor models for 27 days. On the twenty-eighth day they started adding *both* Small Motor models (drawing lines, finger movements) and Mouth Position models (kiss, blow, open and close mouth, stick out tongue) to sessions. In other words, they worked on the different Motor Imitation groups along with Large and Small Motor activities (puzzles, playing catch).

Karen's correct imitations were rewarded with praise, bites of food (once in a while), and Activity Rewards. For example, when she imitated a model right, she could have the next piece of a puzzle to work. Her parents counted the number of times they showed models and the number of times she imitated them correctly. The chart shows the *percentage* of models that she imitated correctly. In other words, the number of times models were shown was divided *into* the number of correct imitations. If twenty models were shown and Karen imitated fifteen correctly, the percentage of correct imitations was 15/20 or 75 percent. *Reliability checks* were made by *both* parents counting the number of correct imitations during a session. The *percentage of agreement* is shown by a triangle ($\triangle$) on the charts.

The two charts are very interesting. Do you see that Karen did *not* get much better at Large Motor imitations? She imitated Large Motor models correctly about 75 percent of the time, which is pretty good. But she did get much better at imitating Small Motor and Mouth Position models.

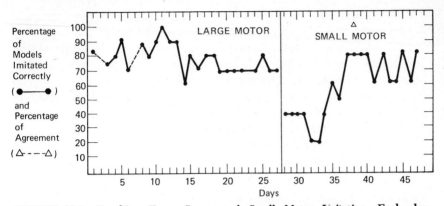

FIGURE 11-1 Teaching Karen Large and Small Motor Imitation. Each day, Karen's mother and father ran a teaching session on Large and Small Motor activities. During those sessions, they added Large Motor models for her to imitate. A few weeks later, they added Small Motor models. Karen was rewarded on a Continuous Schedule with praise, food (once in a while), and Activity Rewards. The chart shows the percentage of her mother's models that Karen imitated correctly. John Peters served as behavioral consultant.

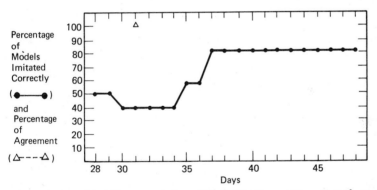

FIGURE 11-2 Teaching Karen to imitate Mouth Positions. When Karen's parents started teaching her to imitate Small Motor models, they also started teaching her to imitate Mouth Position models. The chart shows the percentage of her mother's Mouth Position models that Karen correctly imitated. John Peters served as behavioral consultant.

Why did she need work on them and not on the Large Motor models? The answer might be that the Large Motor models are easier to see. But something else seems to be happening, too. When Karen's parents filled out her BES, they said that she needed a great deal of help on Motor Imitation, *including* the imitation of Large Motor models. They also said that she did not cooperate when they tried to teach her Motor Imitation. Between the time they first filled out Karen's BES and the time they started working on Motor Imitation, Karen's parents worked on the Learning Readiness skills, including Cooperation with Simple Spoken Requests (A4). And Karen's cooperation behavior improved. That may be the reason why she *no longer* seemed to need help on the imitation of Large Motor models. Not only are they *easier* to see, but Karen had become *more cooperative* in the mean time. So you can see how working on *basic behaviors* in the Learning Readiness skills area helps the child in harder skill areas as well.

Table 11-2.   Progress in Motor Imitation
Make copies of this table and fill one out each week. When the child has learned to imitate a model perfectly and without any help, and he can do this about five times in a row, *underline* it.

Date: Week of _____ to _____

Large Motor Models (Which ones? How well? What prompts? What problems?)

Small Motor Models (Which ones? How well? What prompts? What problems?)

Object Placement Models (Which ones? How well? What prompts? What problems?)

Mouth Position Models (Which ones? How well? What prompts? What Problems?)

Which Models Does the Child Consistently Imitate Even If He Is Not Rewarded?

Where Else and Who Else Will the Child Imitate?

What Movements or Chores Has the Child Imitated on his Own?

REFERENCES AND EXTRA READINGS

Baer, D. M., and Sherman, J. A. "Reinforcement control of generalized imitation in young children." *Journal of Experimental Child Psychology*, 1964, **1**, 37-49.

Baer, D. M., Peterson, R. F., and Sherman, J. A. "The development of imitation by reinforcing behavioral similarity to a model." *Journal of the Experimental Analysis of Behavior*, 1967, **10**, 405-416.

Baer, D. M. "Some remedial uses of the reinforcement contingency." In J. M. Schlien (Ed.), *Research in Psychotherapy*, Vol. III. Washington, D.C.: American Psychological Association, 1968. Pp. 3-21.

DeMyer, M. K., Alpern, G. D., Barton, S., DeMyer, W., Churchill, D. W., Hingtgen, J., Bryson, C. Q., Pontius, W., and Kimberlin, C. "Imitation in autistic, early schizophrenic, and non-psychotic subnormal children." *Journal of Autism and Childhood Schizophrenia*, 1972, **2**, 264-287.

Lovaas, O. I., Freitas, L., Nelson, K., and Whalen, C. "The establishment of imitation and its use for the development of complex behavior in schizophrenic children." *Behaviour Research and Therapy*, 1967, **5**, 171-181.

Lovaas, O. I. "Some studies on the treatment of childhood schizophrenia." In J. M. Schlien (Ed.), *Research in Psychotherapy*, Vol. III. Washington, D.C.: American Psychological Association, 1968. Pp. 103-122.

Metz, J. R. "Conditioning generalized imitation in autistic children." *Journal of Experimental Child Psychology*, 1965, **2**, 389-399.

Peterson, R. F. "Some experiments on the organization of a class of imitative behaviors." *Journal of Applied Behavior Analysis*, 1968, **1**, 225-235.

Steinman, W. M. "The social control of generalized imitation." *Journal of Applied Behavior Analysis*, 1970, **3**, 159-167.

Touchette, P. E. "Transfer of stimulus control: Measuring the moment of transfer." *Journal of the Experimental Analysis of Behavior*, 1971, **15**, 347-354.

CHAPTER TWELVE

VERBAL IMITATION:
Teaching a Child to Imitate Sounds, Words, Phrases, and Sentences

1. WHAT THIS SKILL AREA IS ABOUT

There are two sides to speech or *verbal behavior*. One side is learning *how* to say sounds, words, phrases, and sentences by moving the lips, tongue, jaws, vocal chords, and breathing muscles together in different ways. The other side is learning what words, phrases, and sentences *mean* and when to *use* them in daily life. This chapter is about Verbal Imitation, the first side of verbal behavior—teaching the child *how* to say sounds, words, phrases, and sentences. The next chapter, Chapter Thirteen, is about Functional Speech—teaching the child the *meaning* of words, phrases, and sentences and the right time to *use* them.

What is Verbal Imitation?

We were not born with words in our heads. We *learned* to talk. But how? No one sat down and taught us every word. Instead, we learned by (1) *listening* to our parents talk; (2) *watching* the ways they moved their lips, tongue, and jaws while they were talking; and (3) *trying* to *repeat* or *imitate* what we heard and saw. Most important, people *reacted* when we tried to talk. They smiled, praised us, and gave us things we wanted. In other words, we were rewarded as we learned to imitate. And the more we were rewarded, the harder and *more often* we tried, and the *better* we became. So *Verbal Imitation* is the way children usually learn *how* to say sounds, words, phrases, and sentences.

Tips on Using This Chapter

First of all, remember that *people often learn best in small steps.* You are not trying for the big "breakthrough," but for a little progress each week. Every sound or word the child learns makes it easier for him to learn the harder ones. And rather soon they will add up. In other words, the breakthrough will take care of itself.

How We Will Teach Verbal Imitation in Small Steps. For some children, Verbal Imitation is a big jump from what they have been learning, so we have to move carefully. First, we must make sure the child has all the *basic behaviors* he needs (Section 2). Then we will spend a week or so *easing* the child into Verbal Imitation (Section 3). After that, we will really get down to business. In Section 4 we will talk about how to teach Verbal Imitation. In Section 5 we will talk about how to teach *basic sounds* (*M, Ee, Ah*). In Section 6 we will teach the child to *hook up* or *chain* basic sounds into *syllables* (*MAh, BU, LAh, DEe*). Section 7 talks about how to *chain* sounds and syllables into *words* ("mama," "baby," "eat," "more"). And Section 8 is about teaching the child to imitate *phrases* and *simple sentences* ("Want to eat," "Go out," "That's a ball").

What the child learns in one section helps him in the next. But keep one rule in mind, no matter what section or step you are working on:

AS SOON AS THE CHILD CAN SAY OR IMITATE *ANY* SPEECH SOUND, WORD, OR PHRASE, TEACH HIM TO *USE* IT TO GET THINGS HE WANTS. MAKE IT FUNCTIONAL.

In other words, at the *same time* he is learning *how* to say sounds and words, apply Grandma's Law to teach him to *use* them, *even if he does not say them just right yet.* For example, "You want me to OPEN the door? ASK me. Say 'OPEN.'" The more chances the child gets to *use* what he can say, the faster he will learn to talk.

Where Do I Start?

Here are a few ideas to help you figure out where to start in this chapter.

1. First, read Section 2, "Planning Teaching Programs in This Area,"

and Section 3, "Easing the Child into Verbal Imitation." Read and follow these two sections even if the child already imitates a few words or phrases. Then read Section 4, "How to Teach Verbal Imitation."

2. Work on *basic sounds* if the child does not talk or says only a few words. Go to the next step (*syllables*) when he imitates some basic sounds well.

3. Also work on *basic sounds* if the child says or tries to say a few words, but has trouble with many of the sounds in the words (for example, if he says "ow" instead of "out"). Give him more practice on basic sounds before you hook up sounds into syllables or words.

4. If the child says or imitates *many* words, but has trouble with some of the basic sounds, you can skip the sections on basic sounds and syllables and work on *words*. But pinpoint which sounds he has trouble saying and use the section on basic sounds to help him with those sounds. Then teach him to say words with those sounds in them.

Do not be afraid to go back to an earlier step. If the child is having a hard time with the *T* sound in the word "eat," go back to Section 5 on basic sounds to teach him how to say *T*. Or, if the child is having trouble with the word "pick" in the phrase "Pick me up," go back to Section 7 on *words* and teach him to say "pick" better. Then go ahead to the phrase "Pick me up."

Can I Do the Job?

If you have gotten a child this far, it proves that *you have been a good teacher*. It is also a good sign that the child *will learn Verbal Imitation, too!* But let us be honest: learning to talk is not easy. The child must put together many of the skills he has been learning. And teaching him to talk means putting *demands* on him to do *hard* things. So *he will need as much real praise as you can give him while he learns*, to keep him *trying*. And he will need *lots of prompting* to help him imitate.

But sometimes, no matter how hard you try to make the work in this skill area enjoyable, the child may go into a "slump," may stop paying attention, may leave the table, whine, or throw a tantrum. When this happens, go to the end of this chapter and to Chapter 7 to find out what may be wrong and how to correct it. Maybe the child really does not have all the *basic behaviors;* maybe the sound or word is too hard, and you should back up to an easier step; maybe he is not being rewarded or prompted enough; or maybe you both need a break.

Finally, since it is going to be pretty hard work for you, make sure to *reward yourself*. Set things up so that you do something you like after a session. If you are working in the home, share chores with your spouse, praise each other, and surprise each other with a treat now and then. Besides, you deserve it.

No matter how much speech the child has now, READ THE NEXT TWO SECTIONS. SPEND 1 WEEK WORKING ON EACH ONE.

2. PLANNING TEACHING PROGRAMS IN THIS AREA

Is the Child Ready for This Area?

Look at the Table of Basic Behaviors (Table 4-2). To work in this area a child must first learn the following *basic behaviors* from other skill areas:

(A1)   Spontaneous Eye Contact.
(A2)   Eye Contact on Request.
(A4)   Cooperates with Simple Spoken Requests.
(B14) Looks at Objects, Parts of the Body, Face, Mouth.
(B22) Good Work Habits, Such as Sitting, Listening, and Working at a Task.
(B24) Uses Eye Contact to Get Natural Rewards.
(C4)   Imitates Mouth Movements and Positions.
(C7)   Imitates some Models Even if Not Rewarded.

If any of these are still circled on the child's BET, do not go on until he has learned them.

Even if the child has learned all the *basic behaviors,* now is the time to make sure that they are *still strong.* Follow the directions for *all* the behaviors below for about a week.

SPONTANEOUS EYE CONTACT   (A1) AND EYE CONTACT ON REQUEST   (A2)

Reward spontaneous eye contact on an Intermittent Schedule while you are running sessions on another skill area (such as Looking, Listening, and Moving or Motor Imitation). Reward spontaneous eye contact about five times an hour at other times. Request eye contact when it is natural, for example, before you ask the child to do something. Count both behaviors during sessions and for about an hour at other times in the way Chapter 9, "Learning Readiness Skills," tells you. If these behaviors are not high enough, increase them again by rewarding them more often.

COOPERATION WITH SIMPLE REQUESTS   (A4)

Is the child still cooperating with most requests? Keep track of his cooperation for a few days. If it is still high, great! If it has slacked off, you *must* increase it again. Section 5 of Chapter 9 tells you how—mostly by using Grandma's Law.

LOOKS AT OBJECTS, PARTS OF THE BODY, FACE, MOUTH   (B14)

The child will not learn to imitate speech if he does not listen to and *look* at the speech models. Run sessions on Small Motor activities for a week or so. During those sessions and at other times of the day, have the child look at and point to your mouth and his mouth. Section 3 of Chapter 10 tells you how. Also do the following:

1. Reward the child whenever he looks at your mouth while you are talking.
2. Repeat sounds he makes. Reward him if he looks at your mouth when you are repeating his sounds.
3. If he makes a sound and looks at your mouth at the same time, reward him.

GOOD WORK HABITS, SUCH AS SITTING, LISTENING, AND WORKING   (B22)

To learn Verbal Imitation well, the child has to sit, pay attention, and listen. During sessions on Small Motor activities, keep track of how much time the child is really working or paying attention and how well he listens to what you say. Before you work on Verbal Imitation, the child should be (1) sitting and paying attention for at least 15 minutes out of 20-minute sessions; (2) looking at his work most of the time; and (3) listening to and following simple directions ("Pick up the block," "Okay, put this puzzle together"). Section 3 of Chapter 10 tells you how to increase these behaviors.

USES EYE CONTACT TO GET NATURAL REWARDS   (B24)

By this time, you want eye contact to be a "habit" for the child. He should be making eye contact when he comes to you and wants you to do something for him. He should turn and look at you when you talk to him. If the child has slipped back on this behavior, strengthen it again with the help of Section 4, Chapter 10.

IMITATES MOUTH MOVEMENTS AND POSITIONS   (C4)

It is much easier for the child to learn Verbal Imitation (repeating sounds, words, and phrases) if he already imitates some of the mouth movements and positions used to make different sounds. During sessions and at other times of the day, give him extra practice on Motor Imitation for about ten minutes to keep it strong. Practice Large and Small Motor models. Also make sure that the child still imitates some of the basic Mouth Position models (open mouth, shut mouth, stick out tongue).

When the child learns to imitate some Mouth Position models well, work on more of them, such as breathing and moving his jaws, lips, and tongue, before you start on the imitation of sounds or words. This will help him get *control* over the mouth movements he must make when talking.

Teach him the different mouth movements in the same way you taught him Motor Imitation:

1. Make sure that he is *looking* at your mouth.
2. When he is looking, say, "Billy, do this," or "Billy, OPEN YOUR MOUTH." Then quickly show him the mouth movement.
3. Keep showing him the mouth movement or position *while* you *prompt* him to do it.
4. Then give him lots of *praise* and maybe a bite of *food*.
5. Slowly *fade out* the prompts when he gets better at doing the movements, but keep on giving him praise with punch to it.
6. If you can, *teach him to prompt himself with his fingers.*
7. Show him what the model looks like in a *mirror*.
8. Work on one movement a few times and then switch to another. Every few days, add two or three more mouth movements and practice the old ones.
9. *Be sure to reward the child if he makes a sound when his mouth is in the correct position.*

A list of the different mouth movements to practice is given below. Practice on *yourself* before you try them with the child. While you are reading, make a checkmark next to the ones you are going to start working on right away.

1. **Breathing.** If the child has never done these kinds of movements before, it may take a while for him to get used to doing them. So do not

force him. Go slowly, prompt him, and reward him. Here are some breathing movements to work on.

> Breathing *in* and *out* through the *mouth*
> Breathing *in* and *out* through the *nose*
> Breathing *in* through the *mouth* and *out* through the *nose*
> Breathing *in* through the *nose* and *out* through the *mouth*
> Taking short, fast breaths (panting)

You can prompt these movements by (1) pushing *in* and *up* on the child's tummy; (2) hanging a strip of tissue paper in front of his and your mouth or nose to show him the air coming out; and (3) *gently* holding his mouth or nose shut to help the air come out the other one. Remember to tell him what movement you want him to do each time, and later try to teach him to *imitate* the movements.

2. Blowing. Blowing might be a little easier than the breathing movements. Some blowing movements to practice are:

> Blowing a strip of tissue paper hanging in front of the child's mouth
> Blowing candles
> Blowing a soap bubble pipe
> Blowing a toy pinwheel
> Blowing bubbles through a straw in a glass of water

Remember to show the child how to do these movements (model them) before you ask him to try them. Pushing *in* and *up* on his tummy is a good prompt for blowing.

3. Jaw Movements. Jaw movements are fairly easy to see and do, but it may take a few days for the child to get used to doing them. Take it slowly, and use lots of praise.

Here are some jaw movements to practice.

Opening the mouth *wide*. (This will help with the *Ah* sound.) When he opens his mouth wide, *reward him for any sound that comes out.*

Opening the mouth wide and closing it.

Moving the jaw right and left. (Prompt this by gently holding his lower jaw and moving it while you show him how.)

Closing the mouth so that the front teeth are edge to edge. (Prompt this by spreading his lips at the corners and moving his jaw so that the front teeth come together on edge. This position looks like a grin.)

4. Lip Movements. Many sounds require little movements of the lips, for example, *M, Buh, Puh, F, V, U,* and *Wh.* For this reason it is important to give the child practice on the lip movements listed below.

Making the lips *round*. (This is for the *Oh* and *U* sounds. Prompt this position by putting your thumb and forefinger at the corners of his mouth and pushing the lips slightly toward the center. After a few days' practice, try to get him to imitate "*U*" when his lips are in the rounded position. Reward any sound that comes out.)

Sticking out the lips *together*, like pouting. (Prompt this by putting your thumbs and forefingers near the corners of his mouth and gently squeezing his lips together and out.)

Sticking out the *lower lip*. (Prompt this by gently pulling or "teasing" the lower lip down and out.)

Sticking out the *upper* lip. (Prompt this by gently pulling or "teasing" the upper lip up and out.)

Spreading the lips *wide* apart with the teeth closed, like a big grin. (Prompt this by spreading his lips wide at the corners with your thumb and forefinger and moving his jaw with your other hand so that his teeth are shut.)

Flapping the lips fast (sounds like a motor boat—"B-B-B-B"). (Prompt this by having him blow. Then wiggle his lips up and down with your finger.)

Closing the lips and blowing through them. (Prompt this by gently closing his lips while pushing *in* and *up* on his tummy.)

5. Tongue Movements. The tongue helps make many sounds, like *T, Th, S, Sh, L, GUh, KUh, D,* and *N.* Make sure that the child gets practice on the tongue movements listed below.

Hold a lollipop or spoonful of his favorite dessert in front of his mouth and have him *reach* for it with his tongue. First teach him to stick his tongue *out*. Then teach him to move his tongue to the *left* and *right, up* and *down*.

Dry his tongue with a tissue and hold it with your fingers. Then move it from side to side. Do not force him. Later, try to have him *imitate* these movements without the prompt.

Teach him to put his tongue way *back* into his mouth by touching the tip of his tongue with your finger or with an ice cube. This will help him with the *GUh* and *KUh* sounds. After you do this for a few days, try to prompt him to say or imitate "*GUh*" or "*KUh*."

Teach him to hold his tongue still and *flat* in his mouth by gently pushing it down with your finger or a tongue depressor (or a Popsicle stick).

Teach him to *lift* the *tip* of his tongue by holding his lower jaw open, and when it is open, touch his upper lip with a lollipop or lift up his tongue with a tongue depressor. Prompt him to touch the *edge* of his upper teeth (for the *Th* sound) and to touch just *behind* his upper teeth (for the *L* and *T* sounds). When he can do this pretty well, prompt him to say "*Th*," "*T*" or "*L*" when his tongue is in the right place.

Have him learn to chew, lick, and suck on large lollipops and pretzel sticks for practice on lip, jaw, and tongue movements.

IMITATES SOME MODELS EVEN IF NOT REWARDED   (C7)

You want the child's motor imitation to be so strong that he will keep imitating even if he is not always rewarded for it. The reason is that you cannot always reward him when you are working on Verbal Imitation. And if his imitation behavior is weak, he will soon stop trying. We cannot say it often enough: *Get Motor Imitation Good and strong before you start on Verbal Imitation!* You may be eager to start on speech and feel that working on Small Motor activities and Motor Imitation is a waste of time. It isn't! Spending a week to get all the *basic behaviors* strong will save months when you start on Verbal Imitation. In fact, without the basics, the child may get nowhere.

When the *basic behaviors* are good and strong, start the next section.

What Behaviors Are in This Skill Area?

Skim over the section on Verbal Imitation in the BES.

There are eleven behaviors you can work on. Seven are *basic behaviors* for this skill area, and they are the ones you are shooting for. Read items D3 and D6 carefully in the BES. These two are *musts* before you try to teach the child to Imitate Basic Sounds   (D7), Syllables   (D8), Simple Words   (D9), and Phrases and Simple Sentences   (D10).

Plan and Write a Teaching Program

Pinpoint the first behavior the child needs help with on the list for Verbal Imitation in the BET. This is your first target behavior. If possible, take a *baseline* on it for a few days. For example, if you pinpoint item D3, *count how often* the child makes sounds on his own and *how many* different sounds he makes during an observation period. Or, if you pinpointed item D7, give the child a short "test" on how well he imitates basic sounds, by running through a list of sounds you think he might be able to imitate. Write down how often he correctly imitates each *sound model* without a prompt. Of course, reward the child if he makes correct imitations or if he *tries* at all. Do not push this too far. You want the child to start on the right foot—enjoying the sessions.

Next, *read* Section 4 and a later section in this chapter on how to teach the target behavior you pinpointed. Then *plan* and *write* the teaching program with the help of Chapters 6 and 8. Remember: if problems come up, turn to the end of this chapter and to Chapter 7 for help. *Revise* the program if necessary and *try again*. When the first target behavior has increased, pinpoint the next one and write an *advanced* teaching program with the help of Chapter 8. You have to go back and forth between this chapter and Chapter 13 on Functional Speech. For example, as the child learns to imitate a few words, teach him what they *mean* and how to *use* them with the help of Chapter 13.

No matter what target behavior you have pinpointed, READ AND FOLLOW THE DIRECTIONS IN THE NEXT SECTION, SECTION 3, FOR ANOTHER WEEK.

3.   EASING THE CHILD INTO VERBAL IMITATION (D1 THROUGH D6)

By the time you read this section, the child should have all the *basic behaviors* needed for this area. And you should have pinpointed the first target behavior, taken a baseline on it, and written a teaching program. So it is time to *ease* the child into Verbal Imitation. Here are step-by-step methods for doing it. Use them for about a week before you start on any target behaviors after D6.

Teaching the Child to Pay Attention to the Speech of Others   (D1)

The child must learn to look at people when they are talking, or he will not learn how to talk in the normal way. One way to teach a child to pay attention to the speech of others is to *talk to yourself (self-talk) in his presence.* When you are talking to *other* people, it may be very hard for the child to really see and hear the sounds and words you are saying, because people often talk fast and at the same time. So, when the child is near you, *talk about what you are doing. Use very simple words and short phrases.* For example, when you are in the kitchen, you might say things like:

> CUP . . . WASH CUP . . . PUT CUP HERE . . . GLASS . . . PICK UP GLASS . . . WATER . . . WATER IN GLASS . . . DRINK WATER . . . WIPE GLASS . . . GLASS DOWN . . . CHAIR . . . MOVE CHAIR . . . CHAIR UNDER TABLE . . . WIPE TABLE.

This may seem a little silly. But if you have other children you probably did the same thing when they were learning to talk. That is one of the ways they learned *how* to say simple words and *when* to use them.

If the child *looks* at you when you are *self-talking,* if he *makes a sound,* or if he *imitates* your movements, be sure to *praise* him and give him a hug or a soft touch. The idea is *not* to push him to talk at this point. It is to give him many chances to hear *simple* talk about everyday things and to be *rewarded* for paying attention to what you say and do. Have *other people* self-talk when they are with the child, too.

You should keep on with self-talking even after you start working on the imitation of sounds, words, and phrases. In that way, the child will pick up new words and learn when to use them.

Teaching the Child to Make Sounds on His Own   (D2 through D5)

If the child does not imitate sounds, syllables, or words as yet, teaching him to make sounds on his own is a must before you start on Verbal Imitation. The goal is to teach the child to Make Many Different Sounds on His Own, Often   (D3). Below are methods for doing this. *Use them for a few days to a week before you start on Verbal Imitation* (imitation of sounds, syllables, or words).

WHAT SOUNDS DOES THE CHILD MAKE ON HIS OWN, AND HOW OFTEN DOES HE
MAKE THEM   (D2)?

First, take a *baseline* on the sounds the child makes on his own. Set aside
an hour each day for 3 days. Each time the child makes a *speech sound*
on his own (not clicking with his tongue, whining, or other noises) write
it down on a note pad and put a hash mark (/) next to it. To write what
you heard. Section 5, "Teaching Basic Sounds," shows you how to write
sounds. Every time the child *repeats* a sound you wrote down on the
pad, put another hash mark (/) next to it. When he makes a *new* sound
that is not yet on the pad, write it down.

At the end of the 3-day baseline, here is what your note pad may look
like.

Baseline Day 1 3:00 to 4:00 P.M.		*Baseline Day 2* 3:00 to 4:00 P.M.		*Baseline Day 3* 3:00 to 4:00 P.M.	
Ee:	////	*Ee:*	////	*BAh-BAh:*	////
Ee-Ah:	///	*Uh:*	/////	*GAh:*	////
BAh:	////	*BAh:*	///	*DUh-DUh:*	//
BAh-BAh:	///	*MAh-MAh:*	////	*MAh-MAh-MAh:*	///
Ah-Ee:	//	*GAh:*	///	*Ee-Ah:*	/////
MAh-MAh:	////				

How many *times* did the child makes sounds—*any* sounds—on Day 1?
To find out, just count the number of hash marks. He made sounds
twenty times. How many times did he make sounds on Day 2? Again,
just count the hash marks.

And which *different basic sounds* did the child make? Let us take
them one day at a time. On Day 1 he used *Ee, Ah, B,* and *M.* Do you see
that everything he "said" was "made out of" those four *basic sounds?*
Did he use any *other basic sounds* on Day 2 or Day 3? Yes, he did. On
Day 2 he also used the *Uh* and *G* sounds, and on Day 3 he also used the *D*
sound. So what is the list of *different basic sounds* the child used during
the baseline? They are underlined in the little table above. The answer
is: *Ee, Ah, B, M, Uh, G,* and *D.* Everything he said over the 3 days came
from these seven basic sounds.

Now take a baseline for 3 days and keep track of the child's sounds
as we did above. Then come back here.

By now, you have a good idea of which *different basic sounds* the child uses and *how often* he makes sounds on his own. It is time to make a new list of the basic sounds he uses to update the one you made for item D2 in the BES. Turn to the Speech Table for Verbal Imitation and Functional Speech (Table 12-1) at the end of this chapter. It will help you to keep track of the child's progress all through the Verbal Imitation and Functional Speech areas.

The Speech Table is divided into weeks, and each week is divided into basic sounds, words, phrases, and sentences. On the far *right*-hand side is a column to write the sounds, words, phrases, or sentences that need the most work. Since the Speech Table covers only 3 weeks, make copies of it.

Use the column on the far *left* to write the list of basic sounds the child made during the baseline days. Just write down all the *different basic sounds* he said on his own. For example, if the child used *Ee, Ah, B*, and *M* during the first day of the baseline, also used *G* the second day, and also used *F* the third day, your baseline list on the Speech Table would be *Ee, Ah, B, M, G*, and *F*. Please write the child's baseline list of sounds on the Speech Table now.

You also know *how often* the child made sounds during each baseline session. You made a hash mark each time he did. If the child made sounds only once in a while, you need to *increase* the number of times he makes sounds. Even if he made sounds often during the baseline, he needs to learn that making sounds has an *effect* on the scene around him. In other words, he needs to learn that making sounds will be rewarded.

So there are two things to do now: (1) teach the child to make sounds on his own *often;* and (2) teach him to make *different* sounds.

HOW TO TEACH THE CHILD TO MAKE DIFFERENT SOUNDS ON HIS OWN, OFTEN   (D3)

This is item D3 on the BES and BET. It is impotrant to increase the number of sounds the child makes and the number of times he makes them *before* you start on Verbal Imitation. In that way, he will be more likely to say *something* when you give him a sound or word model to imitate. Here is the method to use:

FOR A FEW DAYS TO A WEEK BEFORE YOU START WORKING ON VERBAL IMITATION, REWARD THE CHILD EVERY TIME HE MAKES A SPEECH SOUND.

At first, use *strong rewards* that you can give *fast,* for example, bites of food. Even if you have to run across the room to reward the child, do it! And *repeat* the sound he just made, for example, *"Ee.* Good boy." If he tries to repeat the sound after you, reward him again.

Do this *as much as you can* during the day and during sessions. The idea is to teach the child that making sounds has nice *consequences;* it gets rewards. During sessions, you might be working on Small Motor activities or Motor Imitation (especially Mouth Positions). Every time the child makes a speech sound during these sessions, repeat the sound and reward him.

If the child hardly ever makes sounds on his own, get him started by bouncing him on your knee, poking his tummy, talking, reading, or singing to him, playing music, or just about anything that will get a sound out of him. Reward him fast when he makes a sound. When he starts making sounds more often, fade out these prompts.

Does this sound easy? It is. It is the same method used for increasing spontaneous eye contact (Chapter 9, "Learning Readiness Skills"). *But there is one catch.* Some children will start making the *same sound over and over.* For example, if you reward them when they say *"Dah,"* they just repeat *"Dah"* again and again. And the more you reward them for saying *"Dah,"* the more they say it and the less they say any *other* sounds. If you are not careful, by the time you start teaching them to imitate sounds, they will be using only a few different sounds on their own. And that is not what you want! What can you do to make sure that a child will say *different sounds*—maybe even a few *new* ones—and not just repeat one or two? Take a few minutes to see if you can figure it out.

The answer is this:

1. As soon as a child begins to make sounds more often (in a few days), switch to an *Intermittent Schedule—a Changing Number Schedule* —so that he is rewarded after about two, three, or four sounds.

2. Keep an ear open for *any new sounds* he may say, and reward them.

3. If he keeps repeating the same sounds, and uses other sounds less and less, *stop* rewarding him for saying the same sounds and *wait* for him to say *something else.* Then reward him.

During sessions and for 1 hour a day, write on a note pad the sounds the child is making and put a hash mark next to each sound, just as you did during the baseline. Use the second column in the Speech Table

(Table 12-1) to list the sounds he is using this week. Your goals are to
(1) increase *how often* he makes sounds on his own to about *two per minute* (less outside of sessions); and (2) increase the number of *different basic sounds* he says often to at least five *before you start on Verbal Imitation* (imitation of sounds, syllables, words, phrases, and sentences).

Figure 12-1 shows how fast you can increase the number of times a child makes sounds on his own. The chart was made by Freddy's mother. She ran three sessions a day for 20 minutes and rewarded him with praise or a small bite of candy every time he made a speech sound. She also rewarded him during the day with praise, candy, and Activity Rewards (going outside) every time he made a speech sound. The chart is for sounds Freddy made outside of sessions. His mother counted the number of times he made sounds for 1 hour each day.

BABBLING   (D4)

Item D4 on the BES asks you how the child makes sounds. Does he make short "bursts" of sound like "*Eeee-Ahhh*"? Or does he put many sounds together, as if he liked to hear himself or were "talking" but without using words, for example, "*GAh-GAh-MAh-DAh-BEe-BEe*"? When you are rewarding the child for making sounds, try to get him to make *long* streams of sounds (*babbling*). You want him to enjoy hearing and making sounds. The more he babbles, the more practice he gets at using his mouth and voice.

There are two ways to do this. First, when he makes a sound, keep him doing it by repeating his sounds back to him, picking him up, or

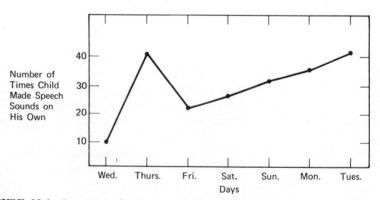

FIGURE 12-1   Increasing the number of times Freddy made speech sounds on his own outside of sessions. His mother rewarded him with praise, a bite of chocolate, or an activity every time he made a speech sound on his own during the day. She counted for 1 hour each day. Greg Hudson served as behavioral consultant.

bouncing him on your knee. Second, you can increase the number of sounds a child makes one after the other by rewarding him *only after he has put more and more sounds together*. For example, at first you would reward him even if all he said was *"Ee"* or *"BUh."* The more you reward him for these "short" sounds, the more sounds he is going to make. And some of them are going to be close together. So, after a few days, reward only sounds that he says *close together*. Slowly, hold out for longer and longer streams of sounds.

IMITATING HIS SOUNDS   (D5)

All the while you are rewarding the child for making sounds, you should be *repeating* back to him what he says. *Make sure to reward him if he repeats what you said*. This is one way to ease a child into Verbal Imitation. If he starts imitating or trying to imitate what you repeat back to him, it will be easy to teach him to imitate other sounds. Remember to *underline* on the Speech Table any sound the child is imitating.

TEACHING THE CHILD TO MAKE EYE CONTACT AND A SOUND AT THE SAME TIME TO GET THINGS HE WANTS   (D6)

The child should already make eye contact to get natural rewards. During this week his sounds should be increasing. So now it is time to help him to *chain up* his eye contact and sounds.

In daily life, we do not walk around staring at people and making sounds. We *use* eye contact and sounds (talking) to get things we want. Even if the child cannot talk yet, teach him to use eye contact and sounds in the normal way, *just as if he could talk*.

The method for *hooking* up or *chaining* eye contact and sounds is easy. First of all, make sure you reward the child whenever he looks at you and makes a sound at the same time. Second, and more important, *wait until he makes eye contact and makes a sound before you give him things he wants*. For example, when he wants an apple, wait until he makes eye contact, and then wait a few more seconds for him to "ask" by making a sound. If he holds his gaze and makes a sound, *repeat* the sound back to him, praise him, and give him the apple.

If he makes eye contact but does not say a sound to go with it, *prompt* him by saying, "Tell me what you want," "Ask me for it," or, "Say 'APPLE.'" If he holds his gaze and says *any* sound, reward him.

At first, reward him for holding his gaze and saying *any* sound to "ask" for what he wants, even if the sound is not close to the right word. For example, at first it is all right if he uses *"Ah"* to ask to go outside. But once he learns to make eye contact plus a sound to get what he wants, *hold out* for a sound that is *a little closer* to the right word. Instead of letting him go outside when he looks at you and says "Ah," tell him, "Good try, but say 'OUT.' " If he tries to say "Out" or anything like it, let him go outside.

So, as much as you can during the week before you start on Verbal Imitation, have the child make eye contact and a sound to get things he wants. Do not "push" him to make the right sounds yet. We will worry about that later. Start with the sounds you listed for item D6 on the BES.

Figure 12-2 shows how 4-year-old Mark Kane was taught to make eye contact and a sound at the same time by his mother. During afternoon sessions, they worked on Small Motor activities. Mark was given puzzle pieces only when he made eye contact and a sound to "ask for" the puzzle pieces. When he was working at the activities, if he happened to make eye contact with his mother and make a sound, he was also praised and given a small bite of food. Sessions were about an hour long, ranging from 45 to 60 minutes. Therefore Figure 12-2 shows the *rate* of Mark's behavior (the number of times he made eye contact and a sound at the same time, divided by the number of minutes in the session). Actually, he made eye contact and a sound at the same time 63 times the first day and 117 times the last day.

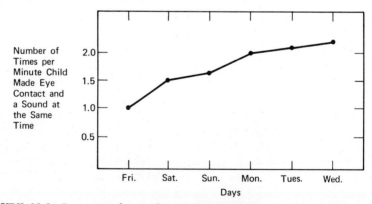

FIGURE 12-2 Increasing the number of times Mark Kane made eye contact and a sound at the same time. During afternoon sessions about 1 hour long, when they were working on Small Motor activities, Mark's mother rewarded him with praise and food every time he made eye contact and a sound at the same time. He also had to "ask" for puzzle pieces by making eye contact and a sound. Virginia Hudson served as behavioral consultant for the family.

Chaining Motor Imitation and Verbal Imitation

One last way to *ease* the child into Verbal Imitation is to hook it up to Motor Imitation. When you are working on Motor Imitation, have the child "warm up" with a few Small Motor and Mouth Position models. Then add a *sound* for him to imitate. The sound model should be for a sound the child already says often on his own.

For example, have him imitate some motor models one at a time and then have him imitate a sound model.

Parent or Teacher	Child
1. "Do this" (raises arm)	Raises arm
2. "Do this" (claps hands)	Claps hands
3. "Do this" (opens mouth wide)	Opens mouth wide
4. While child's mouth is still open, says *"Ah"*	Repeats *"Ah"*

Go back and forth this way between *motor* and *sound* models.

Another method is to show the child a short chain of models that has one sound model in it. For example:

Parent or Teacher	Child
Says, "Do this" Stands up Says "Ah" Sits down again	Stands up, says *"Ah,"* and sits down

Go through chains of models like this a few times during sessions and at other times of the day.

Summary of Ways to Ease the Child into Verbal Imitation

For about a week or so before you start on Verbal Imitation, here is what you should do:

1. When the child is near you, *talk to yourself* about what you are doing and reward him for looking at you or imitating you.

2. Take a *baseline* on how often the child makes sounds on his own and which different basic sounds he says. Then *reward him as much as you can for making sounds on his own*. Be careful to *reward him for different sounds*. Write down the sounds he used during the baseline in

the left-hand column of the Speech Table (Table 12-1). Write down the sounds he used the week you rewarded him for making sounds in the second column of the Speech Table.

3. As the days go by, *reward the child for saying more and more sounds close together*. Instead of rewarding him for saying "*Ee*" or "*BAh*," hold out for longer streams of sounds like "*Ee-Ah-BAh-BAh*."

4. *Repeat* the child's sounds back to him. Reward him if he imitates the sounds you just repeated.

5. Have the child make *eye contact and a sound at the same time* before he gets natural rewards.

6. Work on *Motor Imitation* and *slip in a sound model*.

Begin the next sections when the child (1) starts to pay attention when you and others *self-talk;* (2) makes at least five different sounds often; (3) says some sounds close together in longer streams; (4) imitates some of the sounds you repeat back to him; (5) makes eye contact and a sound at the same time to get many things he wants during the day; and (6) starts to imitate a few of the sound models during Motor Imitation sessions.

If the child does not talk yet or needs help with many sounds, work on *basic sounds*. If he can say many words but needs help with some of them, start with the section on *words*, but use the section on *basic sounds* to teach him the ones he has trouble with.

4. HOW TO TEACH VERBAL IMITATION

Some children will start their work on Verbal Imitation with *sounds* (*M, BUh, Ah, Ee, F*). Others will start with *words* ("mama," "eat," "ball"). The best method for teaching Verbal Imitation is the same in both cases.

How to Run Sessions

Run sessions on Verbal Imitation in the same way you ran sessions on Small Motor activities and Motor Imitation. Do *some* of your teaching at the table. Sit *close* enough to prompt and reward the child, and sit *across* from him so that he can see your face. Start with 10- or 15-minute sessions and work up to longer ones as the child gets used to them.

Remember: sit-down sessions are just to give the child a great deal of practice in a short time. They do not teach him when and where to *use* what he is learning to say. So *most* of your work should be *outside* of sit-down sessions, during more natural activities, for example, while you are playing with the child or reading to him, during meals, and when he wants things. Use Grandma's Law as much as you can outside of sessions ("As soon as you say 'TURN,' I will TURN the page").

For children who do not say words yet, it is best to start working on Verbal Imitation during sessions on *other* skills, for example, Large and Small Motor activities and Motor Imitation. In other words, throw in a few verbal models during these first sessions and, as the days go by, add more and more.

Use *strong* rewards during sessions. Your praise must have *punch* to it. If the child does not say words yet or if he has a hard time imitating, it may be best to use *food* (and praise). The best time to use food is during meals and snack time. Bites of food should be small, so the child will not be filled too quickly. And the food should be his favorite. Do not use the same food day after day; switch often. Also, rewards have to be given *very fast*. You must be very quick to praise the child or give him a bite of food, or else you are sure to reward the wrong sound or mouth movement.

Since you and the child will need a break once in a while, work on a few different skills during sessions. Go back and forth between Motor Imitation, Small and Large Motor activities, and Verbal Imitation. If you take a break from working on Verbal Imitation at the table for a few days, make sure you *still use Grandma's Law many times during the day for different words or sounds.*

The Method for Teaching Verbal Imitation

Before each session, make a short list of *sounds* (if you are working on sounds) or *words* (if you are working on words). Start with sounds or words that (1) the child can *already* say; (2) are easy to *prompt;* and (3) are easy for him to *see*. Sounds like *Ah, M, BUh, U, PUh,* and *F* are good to start with. Easy words are "mama," "eat," "more," "out," "bye," "bee," "cup," "hat," "cookie," "meat," "no," "me," "eye," and "go." Also, start with words the child can *use* in daily life, for example, names for foods, activities, parts of his body, and people. *Practice the models in front of a mirror before you work with the child.*

Sit *across* from him at the table. *Wait* until he is *quiet* and is *looking* at your mouth. Or *prompt* him to look at your mouth by *telling* him to look, chucking him under the chin, or holding a small bite of food right next to your lips. When he is looking at your mouth, *give the model* (sound or word) you want him to imitate.

You can tell the child, "Say this . . . *Ah*," or "Now say 'EAT.'" Make sure you give the model SLOWLY ("*AAhhhh*," "EEEAT") and *clearly*. Open your mouth *wide*, pull your *lips* back to show your teeth, and maybe even *point* to your tongue or lips so that he can *see how* to make the sound or word.

Wait about 4 seconds. If the child *makes any sound, reward him as fast as you can.* If he does not make any sound, *repeat the model and prompt him* by gently moving his jaw, lips, or tongue, and by pushing *in* and *up* on his tummy to make the breath come out of his mouth. If this gets a sound out of him, *reward him fast*.

Wait until he is done chewing and is sitting quietly again. When he is looking at your mouth, *show him the model again*. If he *tries* to imitate the model, reward him. If he does not try, *repeat the model and prompt him*. Go through this a few more times, and then *switch* to another sound or word on your list. Then go back and forth between the two.

After a few days, the child should be *trying* to imitate some of the sound or word models. Sometimes he will imitate a model *better* than at other times. And sometimes he will need *more prompting* than at other times. So, after you have worked on a certain model for a few days and he is starting to get better at imitating it, *reward him with food only for very close tries or for perfect imitations of the model, and reward him with praise for pretty good tries. But do not reward him for a poor imitation if he has done better.* Instead, shake your head or say, "Pretty good. Try it again. Say 'EAT.'" And give him more chances to imitate the model. Then reward him if he imitates the model *any better*. (Please read this paragraph again.)

If he keeps on having trouble with a sound or word model, switch to another one for a few days. When you come back to the first one, *prompt him more and make sure to give him big rewards for imitating it a little better*.

As he gets better and better at imitating sounds or words from your list, *add a few new ones*. Imitations of the *new* models should get the *biggest rewards*. Good imitations of the old models should get *plenty of praise and, once in a while, a bite of food*. In other words, when the child is fairly good at imitating simple sounds or words, you do not have to reward *every* good imitation with food. But you *do* have to give him as much *praise, hugging*, and *stroking* as you can. Keep practicing a few of the old models each session.

Other People and Places

The more people the child imitates and the more places in which he imitates, the better. As soon as the child imitates a few of *your* sound or word models very well, start having him imitate the *same* ones in new places. Also, have another person *join* you in sessions. When the child is used to the other person, have that person work with him on easy models for a few minutes. If the child stops imitating, you start working with him again. Then *slowly* have the new person join your sessions again.

When the child is working well with the new person, let that person begin teaching him *new* sounds or words. Remember that all your work to spread Verbal Imitation to new people and places should be done *slowly*. If the child becomes fussy, stops imitating, or cries, go back to a more comfortable one-to-one session for a few days. Make sure that the child is rewarded often in a new place and by a new person.

Section 5 is on *teaching basic sounds*. If the child does not say or imitate words yet, or if he needs help with *many* sounds, start working through Section 5. But if he does say or imitate *many words*, and *only* needs help on some of the hard sounds, you can start working on Section 6 (syllables) or Section 7 (words). Remember to come back to Sections 5 and 6 to find out how to teach those hard sounds and syllables.

5. TEACHING BASIC SOUNDS (D7)

How to Teach Basic Sounds to the Child If He Does Not Say Words Yet

If the child does not say or imitate words yet, you must teach him some of the *basic sounds* so that he can put them together into *syllables* and then *words*. Start with sounds that (1) he can *already say* (check your answer to item D2 on the BES and the list of sounds you made during the week you were "easing" into Verbal Imitation—Section 3); (2) are *easy* to see and say (like *M, Ah, PUh, T, BUh, F, U, Oh,* and *Ee*); and (3) he can *use in many words* (like "eat," "out," "more").

As we said in Section 4, *wait until the child is looking at your mouth.* Then present the sound model for him to imitate: "*Ah*" or "Do this . . . *Ah*," or "Say '*Ah*.'" If he makes *any* sound at all, *reward him* with praise and a bite of food (if you are using food). If he does not make a sound in about 4 seconds, *prompt* him by moving his mouth into the right position and then present the sound model again. (Please read the last two sentences again.)

Do this about five times, and then work on a second sound. Make sure *that the second sound you work on is very different from the first.* This will help the child to see and hear the differences between the two. For example, if the first sound is *Ah*, the second one might be *BUh* or *M*, but not *Ee* or *Oh*. Work on the second sound about five times, and then go back to the first for a little while. In other words, switch back and forth during the session. Later you can add a third sound that is very different from the other two.

It may take a few days or even a week before the child is imitating the first sound correctly and on his own most of the time. Then you can use *praise* (often) and *food* (once in a while) to reward him for correctly imitating that sound. Once he learns his first two or three sounds, he will learn the others faster.

How to Make Sure the Child Has Success

There are a couple of things you can do to make sure the child has success at learning to imitate his first sounds.

1. If he makes a few errors in a row, *do not just ignore him, get angry, or go on to another sound.* Instead, shake your head and teii him he made a pretty good try. Then show him the correct way again. You might even imitate what he said and then say the sound again the right way. ("You said 'Ah.' Say 'Ee'.") and *prompt him by hand* the next time, so that he has a better chance of imitating in the right way.

2. It is a good idea to hold up *objects* or *pictures* with the same sounds in them that you are teaching him to imitate. Hold up a picture of a cup when you are working on the *KUh* sound, a picture of a glass of water when you are working on the *W* sound, or a fork when you are working on the *F* sound. For example, "This is a FFFork. You say 'FFF.'"

3. *Use Grandma's Law to teach him to use certain sounds to get things he wants.* Once he can imitate "*Ee*" pretty well, use Grandma's Law to have him say "*Ee*" before he gets something to eat. Or, once he can imitate "*WAw*," have him say "*WAw*" before you give him a glass of water or take him for a walk or wash his face. In other words, *get him to use sounds at the right time and place.* This is very, very important!

5. Many children who do not use words as yet try to get people to do things for them by pointing, tugging, and using other kinds of *gestures*.

Once the child can imitate a few sounds very well, you should *stop giving in to his gestures.* Instead, say, "Yes, you want to EAT. Say *'Ee.'*" If he tries to imitate the sound, give him what he wants. *But do not force the issue.* Start by doing this only a few times a day for sounds he can imitate *very well.* If it works and he starts to imitate sounds to get what he wants, then do it a little more during the day.

The next part of this section tells you how to *prompt* the different sounds so the child can learn to imitate them correctly. It is for children who do not say words yet *and* for children who can say words but have a hard time with some sounds.

How to Prompt the Basic Sounds

There are about forty sounds in the English language. Some are called *consonants,* and others are called *vowels.* Let us talk about the consonants first.

CONSONANT SOUNDS

Consonant sounds are made with the *lips, tongue,* and *teeth.* When you read the list of consonants below, notice how you move your lips, tongue, and teeth to make the sounds. Also, keep in mind that consonants are *sounds, not letters* in the alphabet.

Examples of consonants are:

H	(*H*elp, a*H*ead)	*K*	(*K*ey, nic*K*le, as*K*)
P	(*P*ill, sto*PP*ing, dro*P*)	*G*	(*G*ood, ci*G*ar, ba*G*)
B	(*B*oo, ro*BB*er, mo*B*)	*NG*	(si*NG*er, ha*NG*)
M	(*M*e, ha*MM*er, cla*M*)	*Y*	(*Y*es, be*Y*ond)
WH	(*WH*at)	*L*	(*L*ip, mi*L*k, ba*LL*)
W	(*W*e, s*W*im)	*R*	(*R*un, a*RR*ow, ca*R*)
F	(*F*un, a*F*ter, i*F*)	*S*	(*S*ee, me*SS*y, bu*S*)
V	(*V*an, ne*V*er, li*V*e)	*Z*	(*Z*oo, fu*ZZ*y, fi*ZZ*)
TH	(*TH*ree, bir*TH*)	*SH*	(*SH*e, bu*SH*el, di*SH*)
T	(*T*wo, but*TT*er, ba*T*)	*ZH*	(as in "measure")
D	(*D*og, mu*DD*y, woo*D*)	*CH*	(*CH*air, tea*CH*)
N	(*N*o, mo*N*ey, ma*N*)	*J*	(*J*ump, and as in "fudge")

In the next few pages we will talk about how to prompt each of the consonants. *Don't panic* because there are so many. You will be working on only a few sounds at a time. Practice the prompts on yourself in front of a mirror before you try them with the child. Notice that there are two or more ways to prompt each sound. If one does not work well, try another.

**H (*He*).
1. One way to prompt the *H* sound is to have the child *breathe out* with his mouth *wide open*. Let him see and feel the air coming out by holding a strip of tissue paper in front of his mouth or by having him feel the breath on the back of his hand.
2. You can also prompt the *H* sound by having him imitate "*Ha-Ha, Ho-Ho, He-He.*" Use a tongue depressor to hold his tongue *flat* in his mouth.

**P (*Pie*). First of all, make sure that the child really *sees how* you move your lips for the *P* sound.
1. Have him watch when you puff the *P* sound on his hand or on a strip of tissue paper.
2. "Pluck" his upper lip with your finger or a tongue depressor to make a *P-P-P-P* sound.
3. Or have him make the *H* sound. Then *quickly* close his lips and *pop* them open again.
4. Or push his lower lip up against his upper lip with your thumb and forefinger. Then quickly bring his lower lip back down to make a puff of air come out.

**B (*Boy*). Show the child the difference between the *P* and *B* sounds by going "*PUh-BUh-PUh-BUh*" *slowly*. Then do the following:
1. *Flap* his lips gently to make the *BUh-BUh-BUh* sound.
2. Close his lips lightly with your thumb and forefinger. Then open his lips fast.
3. Or have him babble "*BUh-BUh-BUh*" at the same time that you flap his lips up and down.

**M (*Me*). Show the child how you close your lips to make the *M* sound. Put your thumb and forefinger *under* his lower lip, and gently push his lips together. At the same time you are holding his lips, say "*Mmmmmmm*" and let him feel the sound coming out of your nose.

**WH (*WH*at). Have the child watch you blow onto a strip of tissue paper while you say "*WH-WH-WH.*" Put your thumb and forefinger at the *corners* of his mouth and push his lips into a *round* position. With your other hand push *in* and *up* on his tummy to make the air come out.

**W (*We*). Try to get the child to imitate "*Ah-WAh*" or "*U-Ee.*" This way he will slide the *W* sound right in.

**F (*F*ood). Have the child watch you when you "bite" your lower lip with your upper teeth for the *F* sound.

1. You can push his lip in place with your finger, or have him push his own lip into position.

2. Or tell him to "bite" his lower lip. Then prompt him to blow out by pushing *in* on his tummy.

**V (*V*an). The *F* and *V* sounds are almost the same. In the *V* sound the child puts his lips just as for the *F*, but he uses his *voice*. Have him put his lips and teeth in the *F* position and put your finger under his lower lip. Then flap his lip gently to make *V-V-V-V* sound. Show him the difference between *F* and *V* by saying "*F-V-F-V*."

**TH (*TH*in). Show the child how you put your tongue on your upper teeth to make the *TH* sound. Use a tongue depressor or your finger to push his tongue up and out until it is on the upper teeth. When his mouth is in this position, say "*TH*" and prompt him to push the air out.

**T (*T*op).

1. Show the child how you put the tip of your tongue on the *ridge* just behind your upper teeth to make the *T* sound. Letting him hear a watch ticking may help.

2. Use a tongue depressor to put the tip of his tongue in the right place behind his upper teeth. Do this *quickly* and let it go quickly to make the *T* sound.

3. Or, sometimes, just tapping his upper teeth or tapping just above his upper lip will prompt the *T* sound. Then have him make sounds like *T-T-T-T-T* or *TUh-TUh-TUh*.

**D (*D*ad). The *D* sound is made about the same way as the *T* sound. The difference is that the *T* sound is made by touching the tongue quickly against the roof of the mouth, while the *D* sound is made with a *slow* movement. (Try it yourself.) Prompt the *D* sound like the *T* sound, but keep the tongue in place a little longer with the tongue depressor. Let the child hear the difference by saying "*TUh-TUh-DUh-DUh-TUh-TUh*" or "*TEe-TEe-DEe-DEe*" slowly.

**N (*N*o).

1. Open your mouth wide, and have the child watch you put your tongue up and behind your upper teeth.

2. You can also have him put his finger next to your nose to feel the little noise the *N* sound makes.

3. Or you can use a tongue depressor to push his tongue up behind his upper teeth. Put your other hand on his chin. Then say "*NUh-NUh-*

NUh" and at the same time move his jaw and tongue up and down. Do not let his lips come together.

**K (Key).

1. Play a "coughing" game with the child to get him to say "KUh-KUh-KUh." Let him see how far back your tongue goes for the K sound.

2. Put a tongue depressor on the tip of his tongue, and push his tongue so that the *back* of it moves *back* and *up* and touches the top of his throat. Then prompt him to *whisper* "KUh."

3. Or put your thumb *under* his throat and push *up* quickly while you whisper "KUh." Teach him to prompt himself in the same way.

**G (Go).   The G sound is close to the K sound. Prompt it in the same way with a tongue depressor or by pushing up under the child's throat. *Hold* your thumb up under his throat while you say "GUh." *Let go* as soon as he starts the G sound. This will make it come out as GUh. Prompt him to say "GUh-GUh-GUh." Let him hear the difference between G and K by saying "GUh-KUh-GUh-KUh" slowly.

**NG (siNG).   This may be a hard sound. Let the child watch you say "NG-NG-NG." Prompt it with a tongue depressor, just like the K sound, by pushing the tip of his tongue so that the *back* of it goes way back. When his tongue is in this position, say "NG-NG-NG" and move his tongue *back and forth quickly* by pushing on the tongue depressor.

**Y (Yes).

1. The easiest way to teach the Y sound is to have the child say "Ah-YAh" or "Ee-U" over and over. In this way, he will slide right into the Y sound.

2. A tongue depressor may be used to push his tongue down a little flatter in his mouth while you have him imitate the model "YAh" or "Ee-U."

3. Or have him make the Ee sound and *pull his jaw down* while he is saying "Ee." This will make the Ee-Ah sound.

**L (Lip).

1. Give the child practice at lifting his tongue up to the right place. Have him watch you put the tip of your tongue on the ridge just behind your upper teeth. And have him watch and listen to you say "LAy-LAy-LEe-LEe-LOw-LOw" slowly.

2. Or say "Ah," and very slowly move your tongue to the L position while he is watching. This will make you say "Ah-LAh."

3. Or use a tongue depressor to prompt him to put the tip of his tongue on the ridge behind his upper teeth. Then have him imitate "LAh-LAh-LAh."

**R (*R*un).

1. Have the child watch while you slowly move your mouth to the *R* position and make the *R* sound.

2. Put your thumb and forefinger across his lower jaw and hold the corners of his mouth in an *open* position. Do not let him purse his lips into the *W* position. Prompt him to imitate "*R*" with his mouth in the open position.

3. Or you can gently lift the tip of his tongue with a tongue depressor until it *almost* touches the roof of his mouth. Then prompt him to imitate the *R* sound and pull his jaw *down* a little at the same time.

**S (See).

1. Have the child stick his tongue out in the *TH* position. When his tongue is in this position, quickly push it in with a tongue depressor or toothpick. This will make the S sound.

2. Or have him open his mouth and put the tip of his tongue on the roof of his mouth. Then use the tongue depressor to move the tongue back *along* the roof of the mouth. Have him make a hiss or SSSSS sound.

3. Sometimes you can help a child to make this sound by gently pressing his cheeks against his teeth.

**Z (Zoo). The Z sound is made in almost the same way as the S sound, but the Z sound has some *voice* in it.

1. Prompt it in the same way as the S sound, but press the child's cheek harder against his teeth.

2. Or have him make a V sound (with his lower teeth on his upper lip), and then prompt him to move to the Z position by pushing his lower lip down and away from his upper teeth.

3. Have him imitate "*BZZZ-BZZZ.*"

**SH (*SH*e). Prompt the SH sound by putting your thumb and forefinger on the child's cheek. Then squeeze his lips to an *almost round* position. At the same time, use a tongue depressor or a toothpick to push his tongue *up* and *back* near the roof of his mouth.

**ZH (mea*S*ure). Prompt this sound in the same way as for the *SH* sound, but press harder on the child's cheek. Let him hear and see the difference by saying "SH-ZH-SH-ZH." Tell him to make the sound of an airplane—ZHZHZHZH.

**CH (*CH*in). Have the child start to say the *SH* sound by squeezing in on his cheeks and pushing his tongue *up* and *back* a little with a tongue depressor. When the *SH* sound starts to come, *quickly* pull down his jaw. This will make the *CH* sound. Do this while you say the *CH* sound to him.

**J (*Jump*). Prompt this sound in the same way as the *SH, CH,* and *ZH* sounds by squeezing the child's cheeks rather hard against his teeth and by pushing his tongue *up* and *back* with a tongue depressor. When he starts to make the *ZH* sound, *slowly* pull his jaw down.

Remember to practice these prompts on yourself first.

VOWEL SOUNDS

Vowel sounds are the other kind of sounds that the child may need help with. Vowels are made without using the teeth or lips very much. The main difference between the vowel sounds is how much the mouth is open and how the tongue is moved.

Examples of vowel sounds are:

Ee	(s*Ee*)	*Oo*	(b*Oo*k)
Ih	(f*i*t)	*Oh*	(n*O*te)
Ay	(d*Ay*)	*Aw*	(s*Aw*)
E	(m*E*t)	*Ah*	(f*a*ther)
A	(c*A*t)	*Uh*	(*u*p)
U	(t*U*ne)	*Iy*	(b*i*te)

The next few pages show you ways to prompt the different vowel sounds. Practice the prompts on yourself in front of a mirror.

**Ee (*eat*).

1. Show the child the position for the *Ee* sound, with your mouth open a little and your lips *wide* at the corners.

2. Use your thumb and forefinger to spread his lips *wide,* and press the corners of his mouth *in* against his *upper* teeth. Present the model for the *Ee* sound.

3. It may help to flatten his tongue with a tongue depressor at the same time.

**Ih (*fit*).

1. Show the child the position for the *Ih* sound.

2. Open his mouth a little more than for the *Ee* sound, and pull his lips apart slightly at the corners. Present the model for the *Ih* sound while you push *down* on the *tip* of his tongue or his lower lip with a tongue depressor.

**Ay (d*Ay*). To prompt the *Ay* sound, put your thumb and forefinger on the child's *lower* jaw just under the corners of his mouth.

Press against the lower jaw and bring it *down* a little. Then present the model for *Ay,* and at the same time quickly move the lower jaw *up.*

**E (mEt).

1. One way to prompt the *E* sound is by moving the jaw *down* just a little. Present the model for *E* and then *press* with your forefinger under the lower lip, right in the *middle.*

2. Another way is to lower the jaw a little and push the front of the tongue down behind the lower front teeth while you are presenting the *E* sound.

**A (cAt).

1. One way to prompt the *A* sound is to lower the child's jaw a little. Then put your thumb and forefinger under the lower lip near the middle. Then present the *A* sound, and flatten the lower lip against the lower front teeth and out toward the cheeks.

2. Another way is to keep your fingers in the same place and to push the tongue down behind the front teeth with a tongue depressor while you present the model for *A.*

**U (tUne).

1. Show the child that his lips have to be *very rounded and tight* for the *U* sound.

2. Put your thumb and forefinger at the corners of his mouth. Present the *U* sound, and quickly purse his lips by moving them to the *middle* so that there is just a *very small opening* for air.

**Oo (bOok).

1. Let the child see how the lips are *rounded* for the *Oo* sound.

2. Prompt this sound with both hands. Put the thumb and finger of one hand *over the upper lip* by the corners, and put the thumb and forefinger of the other hand *under the lower lip* at the corners. Then present the model for the *Oo* sound and *scoop* your fingers toward the *middle* all at once. When you are scooping your fingers together, *press* with the fingers holding the lower jaw.

**Oh (nOte).

1. Show the child that he has to drop his lower jaw *a lot* for this sound.

2. Move his lower jaw down rather far. Put the thumb and forefinger of one hand *over the upper lip* by the corners, and the thumb and forefinger of the other hand *under the lower lip* at the corners. Present the model for the *Oh* sound. Lift the jaw up at the same time that you *scoop* your fingers together. This is the same as for the *Oo* sound, but the jaw is lower.

**Aw (tall). Drop the child's jaw rather far down. Put your thumb and forefinger at the corners of his mouth. Present the model for *Aw,* and push the corners of his mouth *outward* and *against* his jaw. It will help to also use the *edge* of a tongue depressor to *press* down the middle of the tongue.

**Ah (father). Prompt the *Ah* sound by dropping the child's lower jaw about as much as for the *Aw* sound. Put your thumb and forefingers under his lower lip near the corners. Present the model for *Ah. Press inward* and pull the jaw down. At the same time, use your other hand to move the *upper lips outward.*

**Uh (up). This sound is easy to prompt. All you have to do is take hold of the lower jaw near the chin. Present the model for *Uh,* and pull the jaw down a little.

**Iy (bite). Start by pulling the child's jaw *down* with your thumb and forefinger at the corners of his mouth. Present the model for *Iy,* and when he starts to imitate the sound, move his *jaw up* and *his lips out toward the corners.*

A Few Helpful Hints on Teaching The Basic Sounds

Below is a list of hints to keep sessions running smoothly and to help the child learn to say the basic sounds correctly.

1. *Show him the correct mouth position and the sound it makes* before you prompt him with your hand or tongue depressor.

2. When you have prompted his mouth into the correct position, *present the sound model you want him to imitate.* Then, when he starts to make a sound, *say it along with him.* This is called "chorusing." In other words, *chorus* along with the child while he is making the sound you have prompted.

3. Have the child *look at himself in a mirror while you prompt his mouth into the correct position.* You do not have to use a mirror all the time, but it may be helpful to do so *when you start on a new sound* and once in a while *for practice.*

4. Just because you have prompted the child's mouth into the right position, this does not mean that he will imitate the sound model correctly every time afterward. You may have to prompt him many, many times. *At first, reward him for any sound he makes after you present the sound model.* For example, if you have just started on the *U* sound, and the first time you present the model ("Say '*U*'") he says "*Ah,*" reward

him. If the *next* model you present is *P, reward him only if he says some-thing different from what he said to the first model.* If he says "*M*" after you give the model for *P*, reward him, because at least it is different from *Ah*. In other words, although he is not imitating the two models correctly, at least he is making a different sound after each model.

Later, use *shaping* to teach him to imitate each model better and bet-ter. For example, after a few days, *do not* reward him for saying "*Ah*" when you give the model for *U*. Instead, *reward him only for coming a little closer to imitating the model.*

5. Sometimes, instead of imitating the model, the child will "run through'" all the sounds he can say until he hits the right one. For ex-ample, if the model were "*Ee*," he might say, "*Ah . . . Uh . . . Oo . . . Oo . . . Ee*." If you reward him when he finally says the right sound, *you will be teaching him to make errors.* He will not be learning to listen and then repeat what he hears.

Therefore do not reward the child if he runs through many of his sounds until he hits the right one. Instead, *turn your head* the other way or *look down* at the table for about 5 seconds while he is rambling off a string of sounds. And, most important, the next time you present the model, *prompt him before* he has a chance to say the wrong sound.

6. If the child keeps having trouble with a sound, try a different way of prompting it, have him practice imitating the mouth position for it, or imitate the way *he* is saying it and then show him the right way, for example, "Pretty close. You said '*PUh*.' Now say '*BUh*.'" Then prompt him to say the sound right.

7. If the child does not like to be physically prompted, get him used to it by stroking his face when you reward him, and prompt him on sounds he can already imitate pretty well. When he is more used to having his face touched, move to harder sounds that need prompting.

8. If the child wiggles and waves his arms while you are showing the model, he is not likely to imitate it right. So settle him down first, either by *waiting* until he is quiet or by *gently* putting his hands at his sides or on the table. Praise him for sitting quietly and present the model.

9. As the child gets better at imitating basic sounds, start having other people work with him (a little at a time) and work in new places.

Keeping Track of (Measuring) the Child's Progress on Basic Sounds

There are two ways to keep track of the child's progress:

1. Day by day with a note pad.

2. Week by week with the Speech Table (Table 12-1) at the end of this chapter.

If possible, count the child's imitation of sound models each session. Make a list on a note pad of the sounds you are working on during a session. Each sound should have a *row* on the page. *Each* time you give the child a sound model to imitate, either you or a second person should write, in the row for that sound, how well he imitates the sound. When the child imitates a sound model correctly and without a prompt, write a "C" (for correct). When he imitates a sound model with a prompt, write a "P" (for prompted). And when he is way off or does not imitate at all, write an "I" (for incorrect). Here is what the page for one session might look like.

	Session 5										
B:	P	P	C	C	I	I	I	I	P	P	P
Ee:	I	I	I	P	P	P	P	C	P	P	P
F:	I	I	I	P	P	P	P	I	I	I	P
M:	C	C	C	C	C	I	P	P	C	C	C
Ah:	C	C	C	C	C	C	C	C	I	C	C

This tells you that the child has "learned" to imitate the *Ah* sound, because he is doing it correctly and without a prompt about 90 percent of the time. So, from now on, he should get a little practice on the *Ah* sound each session to keep it strong. On the other hand, you can see that the child still needs a great deal of work on the *B, Ee,* and *F* sounds.

Make sure to keep track of the child's progress week by week with the Speech Table at the end of this chapter. Use one column for each week. Write down all the sounds you are working on in the column for that week, even if you worked on them in past weeks. Write in the column called "Basic Sounds, Words, Phrases, and Sentences to Work On" any sounds the child is having trouble with, for example, the *B, Ee,* and *F* sounds in the above example.

When the child finally learns to imitate a sound correctly and without a prompt about 90 percent of the time, underline it in the column for that week. For instance, the *Ah* sound would be underlined on the Speech Table for the child in the above example. Then, as you look over the weeks on the child's Speech Table, *count the number of sounds that are underlined (sounds he has learned to imitate) and chart them.* The sample Speech Table below shows what we mean.

Week 1	Week 2	Week 3	Week 4
B	B	B (for practice)	B (for practice)
Ah	Ah (for practice)	(Ah) (for practice)	Ah (for practice)
F	F	F	F (for practice)
		Uh	(Uh)

You can see that the first week the child learned to imitate the *Ah* sound; the second week, the *B* sound; the third week, the *F* sound; and the fourth week, the *Uh* sound. He learned one new sound each week; that is what we would chart.

Figures 12-3 and 12-4 show the progress of two children (4-year-old Mark Kane and 8-year-old Jimmy Lawrence) in imitating basic sounds, words, phrases, and sentences. Their parents ran sessions on Verbal Imitation each day, using food (at first), praise, and activities as rewards. The rest of the day the children had to *use* the sounds they were learning to imitate to get things they wanted.

Both families worked on Learning Readiness, Looking, Listening, and Moving, and Motor Imitation skills for a month or so before they started on Verbal Imitation. The dots for the baseline show how many sounds, words, phrases, and sentences the children could say by the time their Verbal Imitation programs started. Follow the line for "Sounds" on each chart and see that there was steady progress, with the boys learning about two new sounds each week.

By the end of 9 weeks Jimmy had learned to imitate thirteen new sounds, and by the end of 6 weeks Mark had learned to imitate twelve new sounds. This may not sound like much, but keep two things in mind. First, before their programs started these boys did not talk much at all. Mark could *say* many sounds, but he did not *repeat* them after someone else (imitate). And Jimmy said only about nine sounds on his own. Second, their parents did not spend much time in teaching them to imitate new sounds. Instead, once the boys could imitate a few sounds, their parents spent most of their time teaching the boys to imitate *syllables, words, phrases,* and *sentences* and to *use* their words, phrases, and sentences around the house. If you look at the line for "Words," you will see that the boys were also learning to hook up sounds into many words.

So the message is this. After the child learns to imitate a sound, give him a little practice each session. But most important, *have him imitate it before he gets things he wants.* For instance, when he learns to imitate "*Ah*," have him say "*Ah*" before he gets to go outside; have him imitate

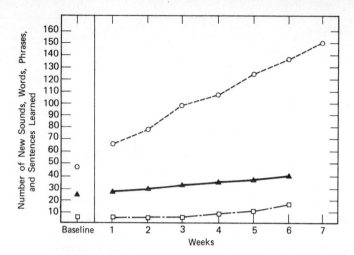

FIGURE 12-3 Number of sounds, words, phrases, and sentences Mark Kane learned by imitation in a home program. Each day, Mark's parents ran sessions with him on Verbal Imitation, using praise and, at first, food as rewards. The rest of the day they used natural Activity Rewards to reward good imitations. The dots for the baseline week show how many sounds, words, and phrases Mark could say by the time the Verbal Imitation program started. Each week after that, the number of new ones he learned to imitate was added on. Sounds (▲——▲), words (○——○), phrases (□—·—□). Virginia Hudson served as behavioral consultant.

or say *"Ee"* before he can eat; and have him say *"Uh"* before you pick him up. "You want me to pick up UP? Ask me. Say *'UhhhP.'* "

At first, reward him if he says *anything* when you tell him to ask. Later, as he gets better at imitating the sound during sessions, reward him only when he comes *closer* to saying the *word*. When he learns to *use* a sound in a *functional* way (to ask for or name things without a prompt), *circle it* in the column for that week. Notice that *Ah* and *Uh* are circled on the sample Speech Table above.

As soon as the child can imitate about five *consonant* sounds and about three *vowel* sounds, start thinking about teaching him to put his sounds together into *syllables* (like *MAh, BEe, LU, Uh, WAw*) and short *words* (like "baby," "mama," "me," "eat," "food," "go."). If the child does not say *words* yet or has trouble saying *many sounds,* you should start working on Section 6 (*syllables*). If the child can say *many words,* you should go to Section 7 (*words*). But no matter what section you go to next, it is very, *very important* that you get him *to use sounds, syllables, words,*

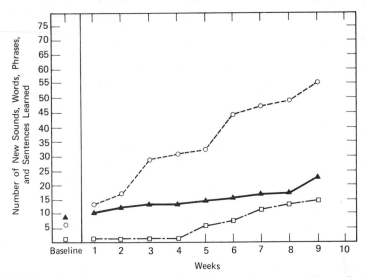

FIGURE 12-4   Number of sounds, words, phrases, and sentences Jimmy Lawrence learned by imitation in a home program. Each day, Jimmy's parents ran sessions with him on Verbal Imitation, using praise and, at first, food as rewards. The rest of the day they used natural Activity Rewards to reward good imitations. The dots for the baseline weeks show how many sounds, words, and phrases Jimmy could say by the time the Verbal Imitation program started. Each week after that, the number of new ones he learned to imitate was added on. Sounds (▲——▲), words (○——○), phrases (□—•—□). Greg Hudson served as behavioral consultant for the family.

phrases, and sentences functionally as fast as you can, even if he does not say them perfectly.

If you spend too much time just having the child imitate syllables, it will be hard to get him to put words together into phrases and sentences. So, *as soon as he can imitate syllables that are close to words* (like *Ee* or *WAw*), *have him use those syllables to name and ask for things* ("eat," "water"). And, *as soon as he can say* a few words ("eat," "wanna," "I"), *teach him to hook up those words and use them in phrases* ("Go out," "Big ball") and *sentences* ("I wanna cookie").

6.   TEACHING THE CHILD TO IMITATE SYLLABLES   (D8)

Syllables are just *basic sounds* hooked up into a little chain. For example, the syllable *MAh* is made from the basic sounds *M* and *Ah*. But *just because a child can say some basic sounds very well, this does not mean that it will be easy for him to hook up those sounds into syllables or words.* For example, he might be able to say the basic sounds *B, L,* and *U.* But he might not be able to put them together into the syllable *BLU* ("blue"). The reason is that *the way you say each sound in a syllable has to do with what sounds are next to it.* The *L* sound in *LUh* is not made the same way as the *L* sound in *BLU* ("blue") or the *L* sound in *BAwl* ("ball" or "bawl").

Say these three syllables slowly to yourself: "*LUh,*" "*BLU,*" and "*BAwL.*" Do you see that when you say "*LUh*" you *start* with your tongue in the *L* position? But when you say the *L* sound in *BLU* ("blue"), your mouth starts in the *B* position and then moves fast into the *L* position. And when you say the *L* in *BAwL,* your tongue is pushed down for the *Aw* sound and then moves up to the *L* position.

So, if the child has not said many sounds or words up to now, it may be pretty hard for him to put sounds together into syllables. And he may need some practice using basic sounds in *different places* in syllables. A good way to give him practice is teaching him to imitate *nonsense syllables.*

What Are Nonsense Syllables?

Nonsense syllables are syllables that do not mean anything. They are not really words all by themselves, but they are PART of many words. Examples of nonsense syllables are *LAh, BU, Ah-BAh, GAh-GAh, KAh-KAh.* There are three kinds of nonsense syllables. One kind *has a consonant first,* like *BU, LUh, MEe.* Another kind has a *consonant at the end,* like *OhK* ("oak"), *EF,* or *UhP.* And the last kind has a *consonant in the middle,* like *Ah-BAh, KAh-KAh,* or *U-LU.* It is very important to give a child practice with all three kinds of nonsense syllables so that he will learn to say syllables and words with the same basic consonant sounds in the first, middle, and end positions.

How to Work on Nonsense Syllables

Teach the child to imitate nonsense syllables in the same way you taught him to imitate basic sounds. In other words, wait until he is looking at your mouth and then *slowly* and *clearly* say the nonsense syllable model you want him to imitate. If he comes pretty close to imitating the model, give him lots of praise and food (if you are using food). If he does not try to imitate the model, or if he does not even come close, prompt him the next time by moving his mouth into the right position. *After* you have prompted him many times, you can start to *fade out* your prompts until you hardly have to touch his mouth at all.

The easiest nonsense syllables are the ones that have a *consonant first,* like *BUh* or *LU.* Start with nonsense syllables having basic sounds the child can *already say* or *imitate.* For example, if he can already imitate "B," "Ah," "M," and "Ee," work on nonsense syllables like *BAh, MAh, BEe, BEe-BAh, MEe-MEe, BAh-BAh-BAh,* and *MAh-MEe.*

To prompt him to imitate the nonsense syllable correctly, *put his mouth into the correct position for the first sound—the consonant—and then say the model.* This will help him to imitate the first part of the model. *Then quickly move his mouth into the position for the second sound—the vowel.* For instance, if you are teaching him to imitate "*MAh,*" prompt him to close his lips in the *M* position. Then present the model—"*MMMAhhh*"— and as soon as the *M* sound starts to come out of him, *pull his jaw down* for the *Ah* sound. Then reward him. Practice the same model three or four times, and then switch to another one. (Please read this paragraph again.)

After a while, the child may not need to be prompted so much. Let him try to imitate the model on his own, and prompt him only with the sound he is having trouble with. *Make up easy nonsense syllables out of all of the basic sounds he can say.* Give him practice on them until he can imitate several of them very well. Then go on to the next kind of nonsense syllable.

When the child can imitate nonsense syllables with a consonant *first,* teach him to imitate nonsense syllables with the *same sounds but with the consonant at the end.* For example, if you have worked on *MAh, BAh, MEe,* and *BEe,* teach him to *AhM, EeM, EeB,* and *AhB.*

If he needs help with the whole syllable, just put his mouth into the position for the first sound in the syllable—the vowel—before you present the model. Then present the model slowly. *As soon as the first sound starts to come out of his mouth, move his mouth into position for the next sound—the consonant.* For example, if you are teaching him to imitate "*EeB,*" move his mouth into the *Ee* position and then present the model—"*EeeBBB*"—and as soon as he starts to say "*Ee,*" close his mouth into the *B* position. (Please read this paragraph again.)

When he can imitate nonsense syllables that have the consonant *first* and at the *end*, start teaching him nonsense syllables that have the same consonant in the *middle*.

NONSENSE SYLLABLES WITH THE CONSONANT IN THE MIDDLE

To teach a child to imitate nonsense syllables with the consonant in the *middle, start with consonant and vowel sounds he can already say in the other two positions (first and last).* All you have to do now is to teach him to say a vowel first, then a consonant, and then a vowel, for example, *Ah-BAh, U-LU*, or *Ee-MEe.*

Prompt him to imitate this kind of nonsense syllable by moving his mouth into the position for the first sound *before* you present the model. Then present the model. As soon as he starts to say the first sound in the syllable, quickly prompt his mouth into position for the next sound, and when he is saying the next sound, prompt his mouth into the next position.

For example, if you are trying to teach him to imitate "*Ah-BAh,*" first prompt his mouth into the *Ah* position, and when he starts to say "*Ah,*" close his mouth into the *B* position. As soon as he says the *B* sound, prompt his mouth open again into the *Ah* position and reward him.

If he does not need help with all of the sounds in the syllable, prompt only the ones he has trouble with. For instance, in the syllable *Ah-BAh*, if he can start the syllable with the right vowel but has trouble with the consonant in the middle (*B*), wait until he says "*Ah*" and quickly prompt the *B* sound.

New Sounds and New Nonsense Syllables

Sometimes, practicing nonsense syllables will help the child to imitate new *basic sounds*. In fact, you should be helping him to learn new sounds anyway. Each time he learns to say a new sound, hook it up into new nonsense syllables with other sounds he can already say. Also, make sure to underline on the Speech Table any new sounds he learns to imitate.

How Long to Work on Nonsense Syllables

You should *not* spend too much time on nonsense syllables; that will make it harder for the child to learn to imitate and say *longer* words and phrases. *The idea is to give him practice in making the same basic sounds in different positions in syllables—sometimes first, sometimes in the middle, and sometimes at the end.* So work on nonsense syllables until

the child can say a few of them, like *BAh-BAh-BAh, LU-LU, Ah-KAh,*
and *MAh-MAh.*

And remember: as soon as he can say syllables that are pretty close to
being words (like *WAw* for "water" or *MOh* for "more"), prompt him
to *use* those syllables to ask for things everywhere this is natural. Do not
wait until he can say a word perfectly. Have him use it the way he can
say it now!

7. IMITATING WORDS   (D9)

This section is about *word imitation.* It tells you how to teach the child
to hook up basic sounds and syllables into words. Keep in mind that
imitating words is not as important as using words. As soon as a child
learns to imitate a word well enough that you know what he is saying,
have him *use it, even if he does not say it perfectly.* The more he uses
the word to get things that he wants, the more practice he will have and
the faster he will learn new words. Little by little you can prompt him
to say the words better and better and can hold back on the reward
until he does.

Also, as soon as he can say two or three words, start teaching him to
hook up those words into *phrases* and *sentences.* If you spend too much
time on words, it will be harder to teach him to imitate phrases and
sentences. So, when the child can say a few words ("eat," "food," "go,"
"out," "wanna," "I"), teach him to hook them up into phrases and sentences ("Go out," "Eat food," "Wanna eat," "Wanna go out," "I wanna
eat"). Do not worry that he is not saying phrases and sentences perfectly.
What is important is that he *try* to hook up different words into phrases
and simple sentences and *use* them.

Where Do I Work on Word Imitation?

You should work on word imitation during regular sessions at the table
so that you can give the child plenty of practice. Also, prompt him to
imitate and use words during the day at the right time and place. In
other words, *Use Grandma's Law as much as you can.* Prompt him to
say or imitate *"Out"* before he goes outside; have him say *"Eat"* before
you give him something from the refrigerator; have him imitate *"water"*
before you give him a glass of water; and require *"Ride"* before you take
him for a ride. It is all right if he does not say or imitate the words perfectly. He is learning to say something pretty close to the right word at
the right time and place.

What Words Do I Start With?

Start with words that

THE CHILD ALREADY TRIES TO SAY OR IS CLOSE TO SAYING;
HAVE SOUNDS AND SYLLABLES IN THEM THAT HE CAN AL-
READY SAY;
HAVE SOUNDS IN THEM THAT ARE EASY TO SAY AND SEE,
AND ARE EASY FOR YOU TO PROMPT;
and
ARE SHORT.

Good words to start with might be "baby," "bee," "big," "boy," "come,"
"cookie," "cup," "eat," "egg," "eye," "go," "gum," "hat," "home," "hot,"
"key," "kitty," "man," "mama," "me," "meat," "moo," "no," and "walk."
The best ones are those he can *use* in the home, school, and public places
to ask for things, like words for eating ("eat," "egg," "meat," "more")
and other activities he likes ("go," "come," "out," "up," "see," "walk").

Words that start with the consonants *M, B, P, W* and the vowels *Ee, E,
Ah* are the easiest. Words that start with consonants like *Y* ("you"), *R*
("run"), *L* ("lip"), *J* ("jump"), *SH* ("shoe"), *CH* ("chew"), and *Z*
("zoo") are much harder. Words that have *double consonants*, like *BL*
("blue"), *GL* ("glue), *FR* ("Frank"), *DR* ("drink"), *ST* ("stay," "must"),
SHR ("shrub"), and *NGL* ("jungle"), are also much harder. Save the
hard ones for later.

How Do I Run Sessions?

Before you start each session, make a *list* of words to work on. Also
write those words in the column for that week on the Speech Table.
*When the child learns to imitate a word correctly and without a
prompt about 90 percent of the time, underline it in the column for that
week.* Each week, *chart* the number of new words he has learned to
imitate.

"How do I know if he is imitating a word correctly 90 percent of the
time?" All you have to do is *count imitations* during sessions in the same
way you did with sounds. Use a page of your note pad each session,
and have a row for each word you work on. Write a "C" next to the
word when the child imitates it correctly and without a prompt; a "P"
when he says it with a prompt; and an "I" when he does not say anything or is way off. A page for one session might look like this.

Session 12

EAT:	P	P	P	P	I	I	I	P	P	C	P	C	C	C	C	P	C	C
GO:	P	C	C	C	C	C	C	C	C	C	C	C	P	C	C	C	C	C
MORE:	P	P	P	I	I	I	I	I	P	P	P	P	P	P	C	C	P	C
UP:	C	C	C	C	C	C	C	P	P	C	C	C	C	C	C	C	C	C

As you see, the child is imitating the words "go" and "up" correctly and without a prompt (C) about 90 percent of the time. So these two words can be *underlined on his speech table* (Table 12-1).

Most important, Grandma's Law should now be used as often as possible during the day to get the child to use these words in a functional way. For example, he should be prompted to say (or imitate) something close to "Go" before he is pushed on the swings, and something close to "Up" before he is picked up. *When the child starts using a word functionally, circle it in the column for that week on the speech table.*

Write the words he is having the most trouble with in the column called "Basic Sounds, Words, Phrases, and Sentences to Work On," and work on them the most. Maybe the child needs help with the *basic sounds* or *syllables* in them.

When you first start, work on three or four words during a session of about 20 minutes. Work on each one for a few minutes, and then switch to another. The one you switch to should look and sound very different from the first. For example, switch from "eat" to "mama," not from "eat" to "eye."

Once he learns to imitate a word pretty well, you can "put it on the back burner." In other words, you do not have to work on it as much as the others. But give the child some practice on it each session and use Grandma's Law during the day. Then add a few new words.

Give the biggest rewards when the child gets a little better at imitating words he used to have the hardest time with. Use *strong praise* and *food* (if you use it) when you start on a new word. As he gets better and better at a word, fade out the food rewards slowly for that word and use *strong praise* and *Activity Rewards* instead.

Methods for Hooking Up Basic Sounds and Syllables into Words

There are three methods for teaching words. Start with the first method. If that does not work in a few days, try the second method. And if that does not help in a few days, try the third method. One of the three methods will work. Again, do not look for the big "breakthrough." It may take a few weeks or more for the child to imitate the first few words.

TEACHING THE WHOLE WORD

This is the easiest way. First, make sure the child can imitate *all* the sounds or syllables in the word. For example, if you are going to teach him to imitate the word *"eat"* (*EeT*), first have him imitate the *Ee* and *T* sounds a few times to make sure that he can. Then, when he is looking at your mouth, slowly and clearly present the *word model*—"EAT" or "Say 'EAT.' " If he comes close at all, reward him, quickly. If he does not say the *first* sound in the word (the *Ee* sound), prompt his mouth into the *Ee* postion before you present the model the next time. Or, if he does not imitate the last sound in the model (the *T* sound), present the model ("EAT"), and after he says *"Ee,"* quickly prompt his mouth into the *T* position. Then reward him—because if you prompted him correctly, the right sound should come out pretty well. (Read this paragraph again, please.)

Keep practicing the word over and over, prompting any sounds that need it. As soon as he starts to make a sound by himself, slowly fade out your prompt.

Here is what the method looks like.

Parent or Teacher	*Child*	*Parent or Teacher*
"Say '*Ee.*' "	"*Ee*"	Rewards. (Repeat this a few times for practice.)
"Say '*T.*' "	"*T*"	Rewards. (Repeat this a few times for practice.)
"Say 'EAT.' "	"*T*"	"Pretty good. Let's try again." Next time, parent prompts child to open his mouth in the *Ee* position *before* parent presents model—"EAT." (Repeat this a few times.)
"Say 'EAT.' "	"*Eat*"	Rewards. (Repeat this a few times, and then go on to another word that looks and sounds different from "Eat.")

So, in this method, practice each sound in the word a few times. Then present the *whole* word as a model. Prompt whichever sound does not come out right. If the child still does not put the sounds together in the word, try the next method.

BREAKING UP THE WORD INTO SYLLABLES AND PUTTING IT BACK TOGETHER

Sometimes the child can imitate each sound or syllable in the word, but has a hard time putting them all together. Remember why? The way you say a sound in a word has to do with the sounds that are *next* to it in the word.

For example, you might be trying to teach the child to imitate "MAMA," and every time you present the model—"MAMA"—he says "MA." When you *prompt* him to say the second "Ma," he says it, but when you stop prompting him, all he says is "Ma." Or, you might be trying to teach him to imitate "EAT," and as long as you prompt his mouth into the *T* position he says "Eat," but when you stop prompting him, all he says is "*Ee.*" Or, you might be trying to teach him to imitate "WATER," and as long as you prompt his mouth into the *WAw* position he will say "Water," but when you stop prompting him, all he says is "Ter."

If the child *leaves off* some of the sounds or syllables in the word you want him to imitate, *break up the word into smaller sounds or syllables and put them back together a little at a time.*

One way to do this is the *forward* way. For example, if you are teaching the child to imitate "GO" (*Goh*) and he keeps leaving off the *G* sound, break up the word into *G* and *Oh.* Have him imitate *each one* a few times to make sure that he can. Then present the model for the *first* sound—"*G*" and reward him if he imitates. *Quickly* present the model for the *next* sound in the word—"*Oh*"—and reward him if he imitates. Practice the two sounds in the *right order* a few times—first *G* and then *Oh.* Next present the *whole word,* just as in the first method. But say the *G* sound in the model—"*GOh*"—with *stress.* Prompt the child by moving his mouth if he still needs it.

Here is what it looks like when you put the word "go" (*GOh*) back together in the *forward* way.

Parent or Teacher	Child	Parent or Teacher
"Say '*GOh.*'"	"*Oh*"	"Pretty good." (Child left off the *G* sound, so parent breaks down the word and works on *each part.*)
"Say '*G.*'"	"*G*"	Rewards. (Then *quickly* go on to the next sound in the word.)
"Say '*Oh.*'"	"*Oh*"	Rewards. (Then go *back* to the *G* sound and then to the *Oh* sound a few times for practice.)
"Say '*GOh.*'"	"*GOh*"	Big reward. (Repeat the *whole word a few times.*)

The idea is to *have the child imitate each sound or syllable of the word in the right order, over and over,* to give him the idea of which sound comes first and which sound comes next. Then present the *whole* word model with *stress* on the sound he was leaving off, and *prompt* him to say that sound if he still needs help.

Another way to break up a word and put it back together is the *backward* way. This may work if the child imitates the *first* sound in the word but *leaves off* the *last* sound. For example, when you present the word model "CAT" (*KAT*), he imitates the *KA* syllable but not the *T* sound at the end.

All you have to do is *have him imitate the last sound or syllable over and over.* For example, in the model "*KAT*" you would have him imitate the *T* sound over and over, until you are pretty sure he will imitate the *T* sound again the next time. Then, the next time present the *whole* word, and *really stress the last sound (T) that he has been leaving off.*

The idea is to *give the child practice in imitating the sound or syllable he has not been imitating.* Then have him imitate the whole word again.

The *backward* way looks like this.

Parent or Teacher	Child	Parent or Teacher
"Say '*KAT*.'"	"*KA*"	"Pretty good." (Child did not imitate *last T* sound, so parent breaks down the word and works on each part, starting with the *last* one.)
"Say '*T*.'"	"*T*"	Rewards. (Repeat this over and over, until child imitates the *T* sound very well.)
"Say '*KAT*.'"	"*KAT*"	Big reward. (Repeat the whole word over and over, and prompt some more if child still needs it.)

So, *if the child keeps leaving off one of the sounds in a word, first have him practice that sound all by itself, over and over. Then present the whole word model again, but when you do, make sure to stress the sound he has been leaving off.* If he leaves out the *T* sound in "eat," practice the *T* sound a few times and then present the word model "EAT" (*EeT*) again, with *stress* on the *T* sound. Or, if he leaves off the *K* sound in "cat," practice the *K* sound a few times and then present the word model "CAT" (*KAT*) again, with *stress* on the *K* sound. Prompt his mouth if he still needs it.

If these two methods do not work very well on a word or sound, try the next method.

SHAPING ONE WORD INTO ANOTHER

Sometimes there are sounds or syllables that you just cannot prompt very well and that are very hard for the child to imitate, like *Y* ("you"), *BL* ("blue"), *GL* ("glue"), or *R* ("run"). One way to help him to imitate words that have hard sounds or syllables in them is to *start with a word that is close to the one you want to teach him but has easier sounds. Then slowly shape him into saying the word you were after.*

A good example of this is the word "blue" (*BLU*). For many children, the *BL* sound is very hard. So *instead of working* on *BLU, work* on *BUh-LU*, which sounds a lot like *BLU,* but is easier to say. Try it yourself! Once the child can imitate "*BUh-LU,*" start *shaping him from saying "BUh-LU" to saying "BLU."* This means that you now have to get him to *stop saying the Uh sound in the middle.*

One way to get rid of the extra *Uh* sound is to *present the word model without* the *Uh* sound in it. In other words, do not use "*BUh-LU*" as a model anymore; just say "*BLU*" slowly. Give the child big rewards every time he comes close to imitating "*BLU*" without the *Uh* in it. Another way to get rid of the extra *Uh* sound is to *chorus along with him.* For example, present the model (*BLU*), and when he starts to say "*B,*" jump in and start imitating the model *along with him* so that he hears the model (*BLU*) without the *Uh* in it. A third way is to quickly *prompt* him to say the *LU* sound in *BLU* before he gets a chance to say "*BUh-LU.*" In other words, after he says the *B* sound, you quickly prompt the next sound—the *LU*.

You can do the same thing with words like "apple," "bring," "climb," or "bye." If the child has a hard time saying the *PL* sound in "apple" (*APL*), teach him to say "*A-POoL*" (as in "b*Oo*k"). Or instead of "bring" (*BREeNG*), teach him to say "*BUh-REeNG.*" And if he has a hard time saying "Bye" (*BIY*), teach him to say "*BAh-Ee.*" Once he can say these easier words with the *extra* sounds in them, *slowly* teach him to say the words correctly without the extra sounds by (1) presenting the word model as it should be *without* the extra sound; (2) *chorusing* the word along with him; and (3) *prompting* him to say the word without the extra sound.

There are a few other ways to *shape hard words from easier ones.* For example, if the child cannot say a certain vowel sound very well, *put in a different vowel that he can say.* Later, you can put in the right vowel sound. For instance, if he cannot say the *Oh* sound in the word "go" (*GOh*), you may be able to teach him to say "*GU*" instead. This will give him practice in moving his mouth from the *G* position to a vowel position that is close to the one you want. Once he can imitate "*GU,*" shape the *GU* into *GOh* ("go") by giving him more prompting on the mouth position for the *Oh* sound and by holding back on the rewards until he says something closer to *GOh*.

Another example is the word "you" (*YU*). Many children have a hard time saying the *Y* sound when it is at the beginning of a word. So, instead of working on *YU*, teach the child to say "*Ee-YU*," because the mouth position for the *Ee* sound is very *close* to the mouth position for the *Y* sound. Say "*Ee-YU*" to yourself slowly. Notice how the *YU* flows right from the *Ee* position. Once the child can imitate "*Ee-YU*," start to fade out the extra *Ee* sound.

Summary of Methods for Hooking Up Basic Sounds and Syllables into Words

1. Start with easy words that have sounds in them the child can already say. They should also be words he can put to use in many places.

2. Make sure that he can imitate all of the sounds and syllables in the word rather well. Give him practice in imitating the sounds and syllables before you put them together into a word. For example, before you work on "Water" (*WAwTR*), have him imitate "*WAw*" and "*TR*" a few times.

3. Start by teaching him to imitate the *whole* word, for instance, "water." If he has trouble imitating any sound in the word, *prompt* that sound the next time you present the model—"WATER."

4. If he keeps on having trouble imitating a sound or syllable in the word, have him *practice* that sound or syllable over and over by itself. Then present the model for the whole word again, *stressing* the sound or syllable he was having trouble with. Also, *prompt* that sound or syllable. For example, if he leaves out the *W* sound in "water," have him practice imitating "*W*" over and over. Then present the model—"WATER"— with *stress* on the *W* sound. Prompt his mouth into the *W* position first if you have to.

5. If he still has trouble imitating a hard sound or syllable in a word, teach him to imitate an *easier* word that is *close* to the one you want. For instance, if he cannot imitate the *BL* sound in "blue" (*BLU*), teach him to imitate "*BUh-LU*" instead. Once he can imitate the easier word, *shape* him to say the harder one. In other words, teach him to say "*BLU*" without the extra *Uh* sound by presenting only the correct model (*BLU*, not *BUh-LU*), by *chorusing the correct model* (*BLU*) along with him; and by *prompting* him to leave out the *Uh* sound.

Figures 12-3 and 12-4 in Section 5 show you how two boys learned to imitate many new words in home programs. During Verbal Imitation sessions, their parents taught them how to say basic sounds and to hook up sounds into words. The rest of the day, their parents taught them to *use* sounds and words in a *functional way* to name and ask for what they wanted. Look at the lines for "Sounds" and "Words." You can see that the boys were learning to hook up new sounds into many words, so that by the end of 7 weeks Mark had learned to imitate 106 new words, and by the end of 9 weeks Jimmy had learned to imitate 50 new words.

Some Ways to Make Sure That the Child Has Success

There are many "tricks" you can use to help the child learn to imitate words and to help you handle the little problems that may come up.

1. *Stressing the Sound or Syllable He Is Having Trouble With.* Sometimes the child will *leave off* the first sound or syllable. For instance, he will imitate *"AT"* instead of *"KAT"* ("CAT"). And sometimes he will leave off the last sound or syllable. For instance, he will imitate *"Ee"* instead of *"EeT"* ("EAT"). So, when you present the word model, put *stress* on the sound or syllable he has been leaving off. And reward him if he imitates that sound even a little bit better.

2. *Showing Him How to Make the Right Sound.* When the child has a hard time imitating a certain sound or syllable in a word, not only should you *stress* that sound or syllable, give him *practice,* and *prompt* it, but also you should *show* him how to say the correct sound or syllable by opening your mouth wide, showing him how to move his tongue or lips. Do this while you are presenting the model. For instance, if he is having trouble with the *L* sound in "blue," open your mouth wide and show him how to make the *L* sound when you are saying the model "BLUE." Use a *mirror* to show him what his tongue and lips look like when he makes the different sounds.

3. *Chorusing.* Chorusing is a good method for handling many little problems. It means that, when the child starts to imitate a model, you chorus it along with him. Use chorusing to help a child say the sound or syllable he keeps leaving out, or to help him leave out an extra sound he keeps putting in. The idea is that, just at the time he is saying the word in the wrong way, you are showing him the right way. For example, just when he is leaving out a sound, or when he is just about to leave out a sound, he is hearing and seeing you say it.

4. *Positive Practice.* We talked about *positive practice* in Chapter 10, "Looking, Listening, and Moving." Positive practice means going over

a chain of behaviors to make sure that the child has them down in the right order. Saying a word is often a chain of small behaviors—mouth movements. If the child leaves out a certain sound in a word or says it wrong, work on that sound a few times, *but also have him say the whole word again so that he learns where each sound goes in the word.*

For example, if you are working on the word "cookie," and the child leaves out the *K* sound (he says "Coo-ie"), give him practice on the *K* sound by itself a few times, *but then have him imitate "cookie" again before you go on to another word.*

5. *Fading Out Extra Sounds.* Sometimes the child will put in an extra sound all by himself. This often happens at the *end* of a word. Instead of imitating the word model, "CAT" (*KAT*), he says "*KAT-Uh*"; or instead of imitating "EGG" (*EG*), he imitates "*EG-Uh.*" This can happen if *you* have put stress on the *end* of the word to help him imitate the last sound or syllable. In other words, the child is imitating *your* stress.

This is not a very hard problem to correct. Usually, all you need to do is *whisper* the last sound in the word model. And you can *prompt* the child to close his mouth at the end of the word *before* he has a chance to add the extra sound.

6. *Teaching Him to Make Sounds Without the Voice.* Sounds like *GUh* and *BUh* have a little bit of voice in them. Sounds like *KUh* and *PUh* have the same mouth movements as *GUh* and *BUh*, but no voice. Say "*GUh*" and "*KUh*" to yourself to see how *GUh* uses the voice but *KUh* does not.

Sometimes a child may use his voice for sounds that should not have any voice in them. For example, he says "*GUhM*" ("gum") instead of "*KUhM*" ("come"), or he says "*BIy*" instead of "*PIy*" ("pie"). An easy way to teach him not to put in the voice is to *whisper* the sound that is not supposed to have voice in it. For example, when you present the model for "*PIy*" ("pie"), you say "*P*(whispered)*Iy.*"

Another way is to make sure to reward him every time he correctly leaves out the voice, even if he leaves it out only a little bit.

7. *Teaching Him to Leave Out a Stop.* Sometimes a child will add a *stop* between two sounds or syllables. Instead of saying "*BEe,*" he says "*B/Ee*"; or instead of saying "*KAT*" ("*CAT*"), he says "*K/AT.*" What is happening is that he is closing his throat for a second between the two sounds. This can happen when you have been teaching him to imitate a word one sound at a time, as in "*B-Ee*" or "*BUh-Ee.*" After awhile, the child starts to take a short break in between the *B* and *Ee* sounds.

This is not a very hard problem to correct, but it may take time. Sometimes, all you have to do is *chorus* along with the child *while* he is imitating the word, and to keep *dragging out* the sound that comes *right before* the little stop he has been putting in. For example, if the child says "*K/AT*" instead of "*KAT*" ("cat"), the next time you present the model (*KAT*), wait for him to start to imitate the *K* sound and then jump in and *chorus* "*KAAAAAT*," so that he really hears and sees that there is no stop or break between the *K* and *AT*—it is just one stream of sounds. Also reward him whenever he says the word with less of a stop in it.

8. *Self-Talk.* It will be much easier for the child to learn to say and use words if he hears people using those words during the day. When he is near you, use simple words to talk about what you are doing and about what he is doing. We talked about this before in Section 3. It will be important to use the same words you are teaching him to imitate. For example, if you are teaching him food words, use those words when you are in the kitchen with him. And reward him if he ever imitates what you say.

9. *Other People and Places.* As the child learns to imitate words, spread them to other places and people. Have other people slowly get involved in sessions. Coach the child's brothers and sisters, neighbors, and relatives to get him to imitate certain words at the right time and place.

Making Words Functional

As soon as the child is starting to imitate a word fairly well, use the next chapter, Chapter 13, to teach him to *use* the word *functionally* to *ask for* and *name* things he wants. The idea is to apply Grandma's Law. For instance, if the child is learning to imitate "EAT," have him say "Eat" before you give him his snack.

At first it is fine if he just *imitates* the word "EAT" before you let him eat. Do not hold out until he says the word perfectly. *Accept a little less.* It is more important for him to *use* a word at the right time and place than for him to say it perfectly all the time. Later, you can hold out for better imitations and prompt him to say "Eat" more on his own.

Once the child can imitate enough words to make even a simple *phrase* (for example, "More food," "Go bye-bye," or "Pick up"), start teaching him to hook up those words into a *phrase* or *simple sentence*. The next section, Section 8, tells you how to do this.

8. IMITATING PHRASES AND SIMPLE SENTENCES   (D10)

Teach the child to hook up words into *phrases* and *sentences* in the same way you taught him to hook up sounds and syllables into *words*. Here are some steps to follow.

1. Start with words he can already imitate very well. Use short words: "wanna," "eat," "I," "more," "out," and "go." Also, start with phrases he can use in many places, like "Go out," "Wanna eat," "Eat more."

Make a list of simple phrases and sentences to start working on. Write them in the column for that week on the Speech Table. When the child can imitate or say a phrase or sentence very well and about 90 percent of the time, *underline it*. *Chart* the number of new phrases and sentences he learns to imitate each week. And when you teach him to *use* a phrase or sentence to answer a question ("Where are you going?" . . . "Go out") or to ask for something ("What do you want?" . . . "Want eat"), *circle it*.

2. Before you present the whole phrase or sentence model ("I WANNA EAT"), give him practice on imitating each word ("I," "WANNA," "EAT") a few times. Reward him for correct imitations.

3. Then have him imitate each word model on the *right order*: first "I," then "WANNA," then "EAT." Repeat this a few times. At first, you might reward him after he imitates each word. Later, you can have him imitate "I," then "WANNA," and "EAT," and reward him only after he imitates all three words. Going over the whole phrase like this should teach him the right order of the words in the phrase.

After doing this for a few sessions, present the whole phrase or sentence model ("I WANNA EAT"), to see how much of it he will imitate. If he leaves out a certain word, repeat the whole model and prompt him to say the word he left out before. For example, if he repeats "I WA" instead of "I WANNA EAT," prompt him to say the *N* sound when it is time for it in the phrase. You should also *chorus* the phrase or sentence along with him when he starts to imitate it.

4. If he still leaves out some of the words, *break down* the phrase or sentence into words and put it back together a little at a time. For instance, if he keeps leaving out "eat," work on "I wanna" over and over, and on "eat" over and over. Then present the "I WANNA" part of the model and, if he imitates correctly, the "EAT" part of the model. Repeat this many times.

It should look something like this.

Parent or Teacher	Child	Parent or Teacher
"I WANNA EAT"	"I wanna"	"Pretty good." (Child left out the last word ("EAT"), so parent breaks down the phrase.)
"I WANNA"	"I wanna"	Rewards.
"EAT"	"Eat"	Rewards. (Repeats this over and over. Later, parent rewards child only after he has imitated "I WANNA" and "EAT.")

| "I WANNA EAT" | "I wanna . . ." | "Pretty good." (And parent prompts the "EAT" word next time.) |
| "I WANNA EAT" | "I wanna (prompt) eat" | Reward. |

If the child keeps leaving out the word "I," and just imitates "WANNA EAT" instead of "I WANNA EAT," have him imitate "I" over and over. Then present the whole model phrase, "I WANNA EAT." Prompt him to say the word "I" first.

5. *Chorusing* will be a big help. Present the whole model phrase, "I WANNA EAT." As soon as he starts to imitate, start chorusing the phrase along with him. Put *stress* on the word he has been leaving out. Chorusing a phrase with a child who leaves out the last word ("eat") looks like this.

Child Says: "I wanna. . . . . .eat."

Parent or Teacher
Presents Model: "I WANNA EAT."

Parent Says: "I WANNA *EEEEEEAT.*"

Keep on chorusing the phrase with him until you can slowly *fade* yourself out of the chorus.

6. As soon as the child even comes close to imitating the phrase, use Grandma's Law to get him to use it around the house or school. At first, it is enough if he just imitates the phrase to get what he wants. For example:

Parent or Teacher	Child	Parent or Teacher
"What do you want? . . . Say, 'WANNA EAT.' "	"Wanna eat"	Rewards. (Later, parent fades out the prompt, "WANNA EAT.")
"What do you want? . . . Say, 'WWWAAA . . .' "	"Wanna eat"	Rewards.

7. Each time the child learns to imitate a phrase or sentence, add a new one to your list to work on, but give him practice on the old ones a few times each session and during the day.

8. Remember to have other people work with the child on phrases and sentences as he gets better at imitating them.

Figures 12-3 and 12-4, on the progress of Mark and Jimmy, show how they learned to hook up words into phrases and simple sentences. Before his Verbal Imitation program started, Mark said only two phrases or sentences: "Come on in" and "Hi, Judy." At the end of 6 weeks, Mark had learned sixteen more phrases or sentences. Before Jimmy's Verbal Imitation program started, he did not say any phrases or sentences, but after 9 weeks he was saying fourteen (such as "'I love you," "Go see Grammy," and "I want to go out"). Of course, as soon as the boys were pretty good at imitating a phrase or sentence, their parents taught them to *use* it at the right time and place.

The last section, Section 9, tells you how to handle certain problems that may come up, no matter whether you are working on basic sounds, syllables, words, phrases, or sentences.

9. HANDLING SPECIAL PROBLEMS

Whenever the child stops paying attention, keeps making the same error, starts leaving the table, or begins throwing tantrums, you should look to Chapter 7, "Handling Common Problems of Teaching." This means that you might first try to reward the child more often, switch to sessions on a different skill area for a few days, or reward easier behaviors during sessions. If the child keeps being inattentive, leaving the table, and so forth, you can try one or all of the following methods.

A Change of Scenery

One thing you can do is stop having sit-down sessions for a few weeks. Instead, work on Verbal Imitation in a more natural way around the house and school, and in public places. For example, have the child imitate words like "UP," "DOWN," and "GO" while you are roughhousing with him; have him imitate food words ("EAT," "MORE," "FRENCH FRIES") when you go out to eat; and have him imitate words that describe things around him when you go for a drive or a walk ("CAR," "STREET," "SKY," "TREE"). Often, taking a break from sit-down sessions is all that is needed to get the child back to paying attention. In fact, if he learns just as fast away from the table, spend less time working at the table and more time working in natural places.

Modeling

People learn a great deal by watching others and then doing what they saw. People really learn fast this way if they see the other person being *rewarded.* You can use this method (*modeling*) to help a child if he keeps making errors or if he stops imitating you.

Just have another person that *can imitate,* maybe another child, sit with him at the table or wherever you want him to imitate you. Present the model sound, word, phrase, or sentence to the child. *If he does not imitate or if he imitates incorrectly, quickly turn to the other child and present the same model. Give the other child a big reward for imitating you.* Then turn back to the first *child and present the model again. Reward him if he imitates this time.* This will not work all at once. You may have to run a few sessions before the child finds out that he really is not going to be rewarded if he does not imitate, and that he and the other child will be rewarded when they do imitate. Make sure you give the child *big* rewards when he imitates.

Meals

Of course you do not want to be always using food as a reward. You want to be able to reward a child's speech with Social Rewards and Activity Rewards. But sometimes it takes a *strong* reward like food to get his speech started. Later, if the child keeps being disruptive during sessions (even though you are prompting him), you might start using bites of his food during meals to reward correct imitations.

But, if he leaves the table or throws tantrums during the whole meal, that is the end of the meal. He just has to wait for the next meal before he gets another chance. If he misses a meal because he was very disruptive or did not pay attention, have his next meal a few hours later. In other words, give him plenty of chances to work for his meals during the day, and make sure that you are prompting and rewarding him enough.

Some children make you think that this will go on and on. *But it will not.* As long as the food you are using is a strong reward, and as long as the speech models are *easy* enough for him to imitate, it will take only a few days to a week before the disruptive behavior slows down during sessions. Then you can go back to your usual work sessions.

We put this method last for a good reason. If you are working on easy enough models, prompting good enough imitations, and rewarding them, you should not have to go back to using meals. If problem behaviors start up, there is usually something wrong with the teaching program or the way it is being run. Look closely at how you are teaching. *Make sure that you are doing everything you can to make it easy for the child to make correct imitations and be rewarded.* Only then should you think about going back to using meals for a week or so.

Table 12-1. Speech Table for Verbal Imitation And Functional Speech

Week of ___ to ___			Week of ___ to ___			Week of ___ to ___			Basic Sounds, Words, Phrases, and Sentences to Work On
Basic Sounds	Words	Phrases and Sentences	Basic Sounds	Words	Phrases and Sentences	Basic Sounds	Words	Phrases and Sentences	

Use one column for each week. Write the dates at the top of each column. In each column, as the week goes on, write the basic sounds, words, phrases, or sentences you are working on, even if you worked on them in earlier weeks. When the child learns to *imitate* a basic sound, word, phrase, or sentence, underline it in the column for that week, for example, "EAT." When he learns to *use* a basic sound, word, phrase, or sentence in a functional way (to ask for things or answer questions), put a circle around it in the column for that week, for instance, ⟨EAT⟩ Write down any basic sounds, words, phrases, or sentences the child is having trouble with in the column headed "Basic Sounds, Words, Phrases, and Sentences to Work On." Make copies of this blank table.

REFERENCES AND EXTRA READINGS

Blake, J. N. "A therapeutic construct for two seven year old nonverbal boys." *Journal of Speech and Hearing Disorders*, 1969, **33**, 363-369.

Fudala, J. B., England, G., and Ganoung, L. "Utilization of parents in a speech correction program." *Exceptional Children*, 1972, **38**, 407-412.

Goldstein, S. B., and Lanyan, R. I. "Parent-clinicians in the language training of an autistic child." *Journal of Speech and Hearing Disorders*, 1971, **36**, 552-560.

Hewett, F. M. "Teaching speech to an autistic child through operant conditioning." *American Journal of Orthopsychiatry*, 1965, **35**, 927-936.

Hingtgen, J. N., Coulter, S. K., and Churchill, D. W. "Intensive reinforcement of imitative behavior in mute autistic children." *Archives of General Psychiatry*, 1967, **17**, 36-43.

Horowitz, F. D. "I. Partial and continuous reinforcement of vocal responses using candy, vocal, and smiling reinforcers among retardates." *Journal of Speech and Hearing Disorders*, 1963, Monograph Supplement 10 (January), 55-69.

Jacobson, T. A. "Speech preparatory exercises." St. Louis: The Jewish Hospital of St. Louis (unpublished paper), 1969.

Lovaas, O. I., Berberich, J. P., Perloff, B. F., and Schaeffer, B. "Acquisition of imitative speech by psychotic children." *Science*, 1966, **151**, 705-707.

Mowrer, D. E. "Evaluating speech therapy through precision recording." *Journal of Speech and Hearing Disorders*, 1969, **34**, 239-244.

Nemoy, E. M., and Davis, S. F. *The Correction of Defective Consonant Sounds* (Twelfth Printing). Magnolia, Mass.: Expression Co., 1970.

Peterson, R. F. "Imitation: A basic behavioral mechanism." In H. N. Sloane, Jr., and B. D. MacAulay (Eds.), *Operant Procedures in Remedial Speech and Language Training*. Boston: Houghton-Mifflin, 1968. Pp. 61-74.

Risley, T. R., and Reynolds, N. J. "Emphasis as a prompt for verbal imitation." *Journal of Applied Behavior Analysis*, 1970, **3**, 185-190.

Sherman, J. A. "Use of reinforcement and imitation to reinstate verbal behavior in mute psychotics." In H. N. Sloane, Jr., and B. D. MacAulay (Eds.), *Operant Procedures in Remedial Speech and Language Training*. Boston: Houghton-Mifflin, 1968. Pp. 219-241.

Sloane, H. N., Jr., Johnston, M. K., and Harris, F. L. "Remedial procedures for teaching verbal behavior to speech deficient or defective young children." In H. N. Sloane, Jr., and B. D. MacAulay (Eds.), *Operant Procedures in Remedial Speech and Language Training*. Boston: Houghton-Mifflin, 1968. Pp. 77-101.

Stark, J., Giddan, J. J., and Meisal, J. "Increasing verbal behavior in an autistic child." *Journal of Speech and Hearing Disorders*, 1968, **33**, 42-48.

Van Riper, C. *Speech Correction: Principles and Methods* (Fourth Edition). Englewood Cliffs, N.J.: Prentice-Hall, 1963.

Young, E. H., and Hawk, S. S. *Motor-Kinesthetic Speech Training*. Stanford, Calif.: Stanford University Press, 1965.

CHAPTER THIRTEEN

FUNCTIONAL SPEECH

1. WHAT THIS CHAPTER IS ABOUT

Chapter 12, "Verbal Imitation," gave you ways to teach a child *how to* say basic sounds, syllables, words, phrases, and sentences. But that is not enough. He must learn what words and phrases *mean* and when to *use* them to ask for and name things, answer questions, and make conversation. In other words, the child must learn *Functional Speech*. "When do I start working on Functional Speech?" The answer is simple. *When the child can say (imitate) a sound, word, phrase, or sentence fairly well, start teaching him to use it right away.*

What Is Functional Speech?

By now, the child you are working with should be imitating some basic sounds, words, and maybe even a few phrases. *But just imitating words and phrases is not natural speech.* Parrots can "imitate." *Functional Speech* means that the words and phrases a child says are under the *control* of *natural signals* and *natural consequences*. Let us talk about *natural control* for a minute.

When a child imitates the word "APPLE," what is the *signal* that gets him to say "Apple?" It is the word model "APPLE," or the request "Say 'APPLE'" that you give him. In other words, he is just repeating or imitating your signal, "APPLE." When you are working on Verbal Imitation, the *signals* that *control* the child's speech are the speech models (sounds, words, or phrases) that you say to him. After you show him the signal (model) he imitates the signal. All he does is *imitate the signal.*

And when the child imitates the word "CAT," "UP," "BOOK," or "MAMA," what does he get? What are the *consequences* for him? Most likely, the consequences for him when he imitates your signals (models) are praise ("Good boy") and maybe a small bite of candy. And these *consequences* are very important. Without them the child might never have learned to say or imitate anything! So, by rewarding him when he imitates your speech signals (models), you teach him to imitate your speech better and better.

But are these rewarding consequences (praise and food) really *natural* consequences? Is a piece of candy a *natural* reward for saying "Up?" No! There is *nothing natural* about rewarding a child with "Good boy" or with food for saying "Up," "Book," or "Cat." In everyday life, people *do not* reward us by saying "Good boy" or by giving us food when we say words or phrases. Instead, our talking is *controlled* by more natural consequences. In everyday life, talking brings us into *contact* with other people who *naturally* reward our talking by doing things we like. For example, *we get things we ask for;* people *answer our questions;* and people *keep talking to us.* These are *natural* (everyday) *rewards* for speech.

Think of a *natural consequence* to reward a child for saying "Up." Of course, picking him up would be a natural consequence (as long as he enjoys being picked up).

What are *natural signals?* In daily life, we do more than just *imitate* what other people say. Someone asks, "How was your day?" and we say "Fine." Or someone says, "Boy, I'm tired" and we say, "Me, too." Or someone asks, "Where are you going tonight?" and we answer, "To the movies." We do not just repeat or imitate the things (signals) people say to us. They ask us a question (signal), and we give them an answer. Or they make a statement (a signal like "Boy, it's cold"), and we make another statement ("It sure is").

In other words, *functional speech* is more than imitating signals. It is answering questions, asking for things, and making statements that follow from what others say or do. And the consequence for us when we talk is not usually a reward like "Good boy" or a bite of food. Instead, our speech is rewarded by natural consequences, like getting what we want and having other people talk to us.

The two examples below show what we mean. The first one is Verbal Imitation. The second one is Functional Speech. Look at the difference between the signals and consequences in the two examples.

Verbal Imitation

Parent or Teacher	Child	Parent or Teacher
Gives a *model* or signal. For example, parent says, "Say 'OUT.'"	*Imitates* or repeats the signal.	Says, "Very good," and gives the child a piece of candy.

Functional Speech

Parent or Teacher	Child	Parent or Teacher
Asks a *question*. For example, parent stands by the door and says, "Where do you want to go?"	*Answers* the question. For example, child says "Out."	Says "Okay," and opens the door for the child.

You see that in Verbal Imitation the child just repeats the signal. And the rewarding consequence is not a natural one. He might get a piece of candy for saying "Out." But in Functional Speech the consequence is a natural one. The child asks to go out, and he gets to go out.

To sum up, if the only speech a child has is imitating what people say, it is not *Functional Speech*, because his speech is not controlled by natural *signals*, like questions, statements, and everyday objects and events. All he is doing is imitating signals or models. And his speech is not controlled by natural *consequences*. He is being rewarded by praise and food, and not by the kinds of things people usually get for talking. So we have to get a child's words and phrases under the control of *natural signals* and *natural consequences*.

2. PLANNING TEACHING PROGRAMS IN THIS AREA

Is the Child Ready for This Area?

As always, first check the Table of Basic Behaviors (Table 4–2) in Chapter 4 to see if the child is ready for this area. Before he starts in this area, the child must learn the following *basic behaviors*.

(A1)   Spontaneous Eye Contact.
(A2)   Eye Contact on Request.
(A4)   Cooperates with Simple Spoken Requests.
(B14) Looks at Objects, Parts of the Body, Face, Mouth.
(B22) Good Work Habits, Such as Sitting, Listening, and Working at a Task.
(B23) Points or Matches by Name.

(B24) Uses Eye Contact to Get Natural Rewards.
(C4)   Imitates Mouth Movements and Positions.
(C7)   Imitates Some Models Even If Not Rewarded.
(D3)   Makes Many Different Sounds on His Own, Often.
(D6)   Makes Eye Contact and a Sound at the Same Time to Get Things.
(D7)   Imitates Basic Sounds.
(D8)   Imitates Syllables.
(D9)   Imitates Simple Words.

If any of the above are still circled on the child's BET, work on them before you go on. Even if you have already worked on them, make sure these behaviors are good and strong before you start in this area. Keep running sessions at the table and at other places on Small and Large Motor activities, Motor Imitation, and Verbal Imitation. If any of the Basic Behaviors are a little weak, work on them some more (the chapters on each skill area tell you how).

What Kinds of Functional Speech Are There?

There are *many* kinds of Functional Speech, and the older we get the more we learn. So this chapter cannot tell you how to teach a child all the kinds of Functional Speech there are. It will tell you how to teach the *basic* and most important kinds. Here is a list of them.

(E1) NAMING
This means learning the *names* for different objects. For example, you hold up a cup and the child says "Cup." Of course, naming and asking go together. Teach the child the name of a thing so that he can use the name to ask for it.

(E2) ASKING
This means using words to *get* things. For example, you say, "What do you want?" and the child says "Cookie." Or he comes up to you on his own and says "Up," and you pick him up.

(E3) IDENTIFYING AND DESCRIBING
Identifying and describing go together. Identifying means that the child can pick up, point to, or choose between different objects or pictures by name. For example, you put red, yellow, and blue blocks on the table and say, "Give me the RED block," and he picks up the red block. Or you show him a picture of a cat and a picture of a cap and say, "Point to the CAT," and he does.

Describing, on the other hand, means using words to talk about objects, pictures, and activities. For example, you hold up a red block and ask, "What COLOR is this?" and the child answers, "Red." Or you hold up a picture of a horse jumping over a fence and say, "What is the horse DOING?" and the child answers, "Jumping."

In other words, *identifying* (picking up or pointing to something by its name) means that the child "understands" the name. *Describing* means that the child can *use* words to talk about things.

(E4) ANSWERING SIMPLE QUESTIONS
This means that the child tells his name or his age when asked.

(E5) SAYING "HELLO" AND "GOODBYE"
Of course, this means that the child says "Hello" or "Hi" to people when he sees them and says "Goodbye" or "Bye" when he leaves or they do.

(E6) USING PHRASES AND SIMPLE SENTENCES
This means answering questions, naming, asking for things, and describing things with phrases or sentences, not just one word. For example, the child says, "That's a ball," instead of just "Ball"; he says, "I see a ball and a block and a car," instead of just "Ball . . . block . . . car."

(E7) IDENTIFYING ONE AND MORE THAN ONE
The *ending* of a word usually tells us if we are talking about one thing (cup) or more than one thing (cups). The section on this behavior tells you how to teach the child to identify one object or more than one object by the ending of the word you use, and to describe what he sees by using the right ending.

(E8) USING PREPOSITIONS
Prepositions tell us *where* things are, for instance, "on," "under," "in," or "next to." The idea is to teach the child to use prepositions to describe where things are ("ON the table") and to move things where you tell him according to the preposition you use ("Put the book UNDER the table").

(E9) USING PRONOUNS
Pronouns are words like "I," "you," "me," "he," "she," "us." The idea is to teach the child to USE pronouns to describe what he sees ("HE is running").

(E10) USING OPPOSITES
This means teaching the child that some things are very different from other things, for instance, teaching him that Daddy is a "MAN" and Mommy is a "WOMAN."

(E11) USING WORDS ABOUT TIME ("BEFORE"/"AFTER")

This means teaching the child to use words having to do with *time,* for example, teaching him to answer questions like "What did you pick up AFTER you picked up the block?" or "What did we do BEFORE we went for a ride?"

As we said, there are many more kinds of Functional Speech. Although this chapter does not talk about all of them, you can use the methods in this chapter to teach other kinds of Functional Speech.

Which One Do I Start With?

The kinds of Functional Speech above are listed from easier to harder. So it is best to start with the first ones that are circled on the child's BET. For children who are just beginning to learn to talk, start with items E1 and E2—Naming and Asking. This teaches them how *useful* speech is. Then move to item E3, Identifying and Describing. This teaches them more about the world around them. Later, go to the harder kinds of Functional Speech.

When you move on to the next harder kind of Functional Speech, *keep working* on the earlier kinds. For instance, when you start teaching the child to Answer Simple Questions (E4), keep working on items E1, E2, and E3, so that he will learn to name, ask for, describe, and identify new objects and activities. Also, just because you are working on Functional Speech, this does not mean you should forget about the other skill areas. Spend time playing with the child and giving him practice on Large and Small Motor activities. Work on harder kinds of Motor Imitation, such as Object Placements. And, most important, go back to Verbal Imitation to teach the child *how* to say new sounds, words, phrases, and sentences. Then use this chapter to teach him to understand and use those words, phrases, and sentences.

The Basic Method for Teaching Functional Speech

When you teach a child Functional Speech, you are teaching him to say "Apple" or "I want an apple" after you ask, "What do you want?" You are teaching him to say "Dog" or "That's a dog" when you ask, "What is this?" or when you hold up a picture of a dog. You are teaching him to say "Billy" when you ask, "What is your name?" and to answer, "I'm fine" when you ask, "How are you?" Or you are teaching him to say

"Out" or "I wanna go out" when he wants to go outside, and "Milk" when he wants a glass of milk. In other words, you are teaching him to *use* the words and phrases he can say in order to *name* and *ask* for things, *answer* questions, and *make conversation*.

This may seem like a big order, but the truth is that you already know many of the methods to teach Functional Speech. And if you ever used Grandma's Law to get a child to say a sound or word before you gave him what he wanted, you have already started working on Functional Speech.

The basic method is simple. First, you give the child some *signal*, for example, ask him a question. Then *prompt* him to say the correct answer by *telling* him the answer. The idea is to have him *imitate* the answer (the prompt). After you go over it several times, slowly *fade out* the answer (prompt) until he gives you the answer all by himself.

The method looks like this.

Signal⟶	Prompt⟶	Behavior⟶	Consequence
Teacher or parent holds up a picture of a dog and asks, "What is this?"	Teacher or parent waits a few seconds and then gives *prompt* ("DOG").	Child *imitates* the prompt ("Dog")	Teacher or parent *rewards* child for imitating prompt. *Repeats* many times. Slowly *fades out* prompt ("DOG") until child answers, "Dog" when teacher or parent just holds up picture of dog and asks, "What is this?"

Where and When Should I Work on Functional Speech?

Work on Functional Speech during regular sessions, just as you have been working on Small Motor tasks, Motor Imitation, and Verbal Imitation. Start by adding a few minutes of work on Functional Speech to your regular sessions on Verbal Imitation or some other skill area. Slowly spend more and more time on Functional Speech, and start having short sessions on it at other times of the day. Work up to sessions that are 20 or 30 minutes long. Also, *it is very, very important to work on*

Functional Speech whenever else you can. A child's Functional Speech will not help him at all if he uses it only with you at the table. He must learn to ask for things and to answer questions whenever and wherever it is *natural* to do so. So apply Grandma's Law and *prompt* the child to *use* functional speech in the car, at the store, on the playground, in the kitchen, at friends' houses, at times when he wants something in class, in the yard, and in any other place where he can and should be talking. *As soon as he can imitate a word or phrase, prompt and require him to use it (or try) whenever it is natural or right for him to do so.* And you should have him use his speech with *other people,* too, or else he will learn to talk *only* with you.

Teaching Materials

Part of Functional Speech is learning to *name, identify,* and *describe* things. So you will need the following materials: (1) a *box* of common *objects* from around the house or classroom, for example, cups, saucers, knives, forks, spoons, pencils, paper, sock, shoe, ball, colored pegs or blocks, toy animals, toy cars and so forth; (2) a set of *pictures,* for example, picture cards of foods, animals, furniture, people, and clothing (you can buy sets of pictures at department stores or educational supply companies or cut them out of magazines and paste them onto cardboard); (3) *picture books* that have many large and real-looking objects in them that the child can point to and name, and simple stories that you can talk about; (4) *anything* around the house, school, or outside that the child can name or describe, like furniture, foods, walls, rugs, door, ceiling, floor, sidewalk, street, mailbox, and many, many others.

Plan and Write a Teaching Program

First, *pinpoint* the kind of Functional Speech you will start with. As we said, many children should start with Naming (E1) and Asking (E2). Read the item you pinpointed on the child's BES to see just what kind of help he needs. Does he need to do the behavior better? More often? With more people?

Next, *read* the section below on how to teach the target behavior you pinpointed. Use Chapters 6 and 8 to help you *plan* the teaching program. *Write* your teaching program plan on a copy of Table 6–2 at the end of Chapter 6. If problems come up, see Chapter 7 and the end of this chapter for help. *Revise* and *rewrite* the teaching program plan whenever you need to. When the child is making steady progress on the first target behavior you pinpointed, begin to plan a teaching program for the next harder one he needs help with. *Remember:* (1) *keep working on the first target behavior;* and (2) *go back to Verbal Imitation to teach the child how to say new sounds, words, phrases, and sentences.*

Keeping Track of the Child's Progress on Functional Speech

Keeping track of the child's progress on Functional Speech is easy. First of all, use copies of the Speech Table (Table 12–1) at the end of Chapter 12. Write the words, phrases, or sentences you are working on in the column for that week. Keep the list handy; it will help you to remember what to work on during sessions and the rest of the day. If you work on the same thing (for example, the word "eat") for 4 weeks, write it down in the column for *each* of those weeks.

When the child learns to use a word, phrase, or sentence very well (for instance, to *name, ask for,* or *describe something), circle it in the column for that week.* But make sure that he has *really* learned it. In other words, he has to be using it *without a prompt* from you. And he has to be using it *correctly most of the time,* not just once or twice. So, before you circle a word, phrase, or sentence, give the child practice for a few more days to see if he really knows it. If he does, then you can circle it. After that, give him practice every few days during sessions, and use Grandma's Law as much as you can to keep the behavior strong.

Use blank copies of the behavior charts (Figure 6–2) at the end of Chapter 6, to *chart* the number of *new* functional words, phrases, or sentences the child has learned. Turn to the end of Section 4, "Asking for Things," to see how to do this.

Finally, for a certain amount of time each day (say 1 or 2 hours), *count how often the child uses Functional Speech* either (1) on his own, or (2) with prompting. For example, if you are working on Asking (E2), you should count how often the child correctly asks for things during the day and during sessions. Or, if you are working on Naming (E1), you should count the number of times the child correctly names things during sessions and during the day. You can use copies of the Behavior Count Tables (Table 6–3) at the end of Chapter 6 to write down how often the target behavior happened (how often the child used speech) and the chart in Figure 6–2, also at the end of Chapter 6, to chart what you counted each day. The end of Section 4 in this chapter will give you examples.

START WORKING ON THE SECTION FOR THE TARGET BE-
HAVIOR YOU PINPOINTED AFTER YOU WRITE A TEACHING
PROGRAM PLAN FOR IT.

3. NAMING THINGS (E1)

The method for teaching this kind of Functional Speech is just about the same method used for teaching all the other kinds. So read this section slowly and practice the method before you try it with a child. Remember that you should have some *objects* and *pictures* on hand that you are going to teach the child to name. *Write* the names in the column for that week on a copy of the Speech Table. When the child learns to name an object correctly and to do so without a prompt almost every time, a few days in a row, *circle it* on the Speech Table in the column for that week. Each week, *chart* the number of new names the child has learned to use. Also, spend an hour or so each day counting *how often* the child uses his words to name things.

Please turn to the end of the next section, Section 4, for examples showing you how to (1) *fill out the speech table;* (2) *chart the number of new words the child has learned; and* (3) *count and chart how often the child is using his words.*

What Are the Best Words to Start With?

It is a good idea to start with words the child can *already imitate* or *say* (or *tries to*) and that are *common*, like the names of furniture, kinds of foods, and parts of the body. Also, it is best to use *real* objects at first, instead of pictures.

Teaching Him to Name the Object by Imitation

When the child is sitting quietly, *hold up* one of the objects, for example, a cup. Make sure that he *looks at* the object. You might prompt him to look at it by saying, "Look at the CUP," or by having him *point to* it. If the child's looking behavior is not as strong as it should be, spend a few days just teaching him to look at and point to objects (or pictures) you hold up. Section 3 of Chapter 10 tells you how.

Once he has looked at and pointed to the cup, give him some practice in just *imitating* the word "cup." Do this three or four times. Then have him *look* at the cup again. When he is looking at it, ask, "What is this?" *Wait* 1 or 2 seconds. If he answers, "Cup," give him a *big reward*. If he does not answer, "Cup," *prompt* him by *telling* him the answer. In other words, you say, "What is this? CUP."

Since he already knows how to imitate the word "cup," he should imitate the prompt. If he does imitate the prompt ("CUP"), use any of the other ways of prompting verbal imitations, such as *moving* his mouth into the right position or saying the prompt *louder*. If he still does not imitate the prompt ("CUP"), have him just imitate the word "cup" a few more times and reward him for it. Then go on to holding up a cup and having him name it. Reward him if he imitates your prompt.

Repeat the whole sequence many times: (1) holding up the object; (2) waiting until the child is looking at it; (3) saying, "What is this? . . . CUP"; (4) prompting him to imitate "CUP"; and (5) rewarding him for imitating the prompt.

Once he will imitate the prompt almost every time, begin to *slowly fade out* the prompt, so that he answers the question by himself.

Fading Out the Prompt

You have been prompting the child to answer the question "What is this?" by telling him the answer ("CUP"). So all he is doing is imitating the answer or prompt. Now you want him to say the correct answer without a prompt. You want him to say "Cup" when you hold up the object and ask, "What is this?" There are several ways to fade out the prompt.

FADING THE PROMPT BY WAITING

One way is to *wait* a little longer on each try *before* you prompt him. In other words, on the first try, you say, "What is this? CUP." The next time, you say, "What is this? (1 second) CUP." The next time, "What is this? (2 seconds) CUP." The next time, wait 3 seconds. After that, wait 4 seconds—"what is this? (4 seconds) CUP." And, if the child says "Cup" *before you prompt him, give him an extra strong reward.*

FADING THE PROMPT BY SAYING LESS AND LESS

Another way to fade out the prompt is to say *less and less* of it. For example, once the child can imitate the prompt ("CUP") when you say, "What is this? . . . CUP," start to leave out *parts* of the prompt until the prompt is gone. At first:

Parent or Teacher Says	Child Says
"What is this? . . . CUP"	"Cup"

Later:

Parent or Teacher Says	Child Says
"What is this? . . . CCUUU"	"Cup"
"What is this? . . . CCUU"	"Cup"
"What is this? . . . CU"	"Cup"
"What is this? . . . C"	"Cup"
"What is this? . . ."	"Cup"

If the child WAITS for you to prompt him before he will say "Cup," *reward him only with praise.* Save food rewards for times when he says "Cup" with *less* prompting than before.

FADING THE PROMPT BY WHISPERING

Still another way to fade out the prompt is to say it *softer and softer.* At first you should give the prompt ("CUP") *loudly and clearly.* Once the child is imitating the prompt, say it more and more in a *whisper,* like this:

Parent or Teacher Says		Child Says
"What is this? . . . CUP!!"	(loud and clear)	"Cup"
"What is this? . . . CUP"	(regular voice)	"Cup"
"What is this? . . . Cup"	(almost a whisper)	"Cup"
"What is this? . . . cup"	(whisper)	"Cup"
"What is this? . . ."	(just the *mouth movement* for "CUP")	"Cup"

Make sure to use your strongest rewards when the child says "Cup" with less prompting than before.

When you are fading out the prompt ("CUP"), do not be afraid to back up and give the child *more* prompting if he needs it. For instance, you might have to say the prompt *loudly and clearly* a few more times; you might have to give the prompt *faster;* you might have to *move the child's mouth* some more; or you might have to give him the *whole* prompt again. Then, once he is back to imitating the prompt, start to fade it out again.

What to Do After the Child Learns to Name Something

Once the child learns to use a word to name an object, you should follow the next few steps.

ADDING NEW NAMES

When the child gives you the correct answer ("Cup") to the question, "What is this?" without any prompt, a few times in a row, start working on *new* names. The new names should *sound* different from the first one, and the objects or pictures should *look* different. In other words, do not move from "CUP" to "CAP"; they sound too much alike. Instead, move from "CUP" to "EGG," "WATER," or "COOKIE."

Once the child is naming two or three objects, go *back and forth* between all of them during sessions. In other words, make sure that the child really *knows the difference* between the different objects. For instance, have him name the cup, then the ball, then the cookie, then the ball again. If he makes a mistake in naming one of the objects, work on it a few times until he can name it correctly again. Then go on to another object. After a few minutes, go back to the one he had trouble with to see if he can still name it correctly. (Please read the last sentence again.)

SPREADING THE NAME AROUND

Not only should you teach the child new names, but you should teach him that there are *many objects* with the *same name*. Once he can name a certain object, show him *other* objects and pictures like it, and teach him to use the word "CUP" to name cups of different shapes, sizes, and colors.

You should also teach him to use the same word to answer *different* questions. So far, he has learned to say "Cup" when you ask, "What is this?" But he also needs to learn to answer questions like "This is a . . .," "The name of this is . . .," "This is called a . . .," or "That is a glass, and this is a. . . . " Give him practice by going back and forth between different questions ("What is this . . .?" "This is called a . . .," "The name of this is . . .") and different objects with the same name (blue and white, big and little cups).

Another way to *spread around* the name is to have the child use it in *other places* and with *other people*. Show him cups outside the house, for instance, in a store or restaurant. And have other people show him cups and ask him, "What is this?"

A final way to spread words around and teach the child *new* ones is to spend time *reading* to him and *self-talking*. Sit down with him and have him look at and point to the pictures. Then have him *name* some of the pictures. You should also keep on with the *self-talking*, especially with the words you are working on. Section 3 of Chapter 12 tells you about *self-talking*.

Finally and most important, once the child learns to use a word to *name* an object, teach him to use the word to *ask* for the object. For example, when he has learned to say "Cookie" when you hold up a cookie and ask him "What is this?" start having him say "Cookie" before you give him one. The next section, Section 4, tells you how to teach the child to *ask* for things.

What to Do If the Child Imitates Too Much

A big problem for some children is too much imitation. Sometimes a child will imitate the prompt all right, but when you fade out the prompt, he does not say anything. For example, if you say, "What is this? . . . BALL" he will say "Ball"; and if you say, "What is this? . . . COOKIE" he will say "Cookie." But when you hold up a ball and say, "What is this . . .?" he does not answer.

The problem is that the child is *waiting* for your prompt. The way to handle this problem is to go back and have him imitate the word over and over again. Then say, "What is this . . .?" and give him only *part* of a prompt, for instance, whisper "ball" or say "B." Then *move his mouth* into the right position for the word. Reward him if he says "Ball." Slowly, give him less and less of the prompt and wait longer and longer before you give him the prompt. Reward him with food *only* when he says "Ball" without a prompt.

Sometimes the child's problem is that he imitates the *question.* For instance, you say, "What is this? . . . BALL" and he repeats, "What is this?" or "What is this? . . . BALL." *Never praise the child for doing this!* One way to handle this is to *ignore* it and wait about 10 seconds before you ask again. A better way is to *say the question very softly (almost a whisper) and say the prompt in a loud voice.* For example, say, "what is this? . . . BALL!!" And reward him if he imitates the prompt ("BALL"). Then, slowly increase the loudness of the question and decrease the loudness of the prompt until you are asking the question ("What is this?") and saying the prompt ("Ball") with the same power.

When the child can name an object, use the next section, Section 4, to teach him how to *ask.* Of course, at the same time, you should teach him new *names.*

4. ASKING FOR THINGS   (E2)

Getting what you asked for is a *natural* reward. So it is important to teach the child to use words, phrases, and sentences to *ask* for things he wants.

What Should the Child Learn to Ask For?

Start by teaching the child to ask for the things he is learning to name. For example, if he can correctly name a ball when you hold one up, it is time to have him start saying "Ball" before you give him one to play with. Second, teach him to ask for things that are in *many places*, or that *happen often*. For instance, teach him to say and use words like "eat," "out," "up," "play," "ride," "bath," "toys," "come," "TV," "food," "more," "kiss," "open," "look," and "go" to *ask*. And, third, if the child has been using sounds to "ask" for things (for instance, he says *"Ow"* for "Out" or *"Wa"* for "Water"), those are words to work on.

Meals and play sessions are good times to work on asking. During meals the child can learn to ask for all the foods he wants. During play sessions he can ask for different toys on the table (puzzle, block, boat, horse) or for different activities (roll, up, jump, wrestle). Also, the child should learn to ask for things he wants during the day. When he is standing by the door, teach him to say "Out" or "Open" before you open the door; teach him to say "Go" before you push him on the swings, "Up" before you pick him up, and "Music" before you turn on the records.

The Basic Method for Teaching a Child to Ask

First of all, make sure the child can *say* (*imitate*) a word *fairly well* before you try to have him use the word to ask. You cannot expect him to ask for a ball if he cannot say the word. He does not have to be able to say it perfectly. If he can say or imitate "Baw" for "Ball" or "Coo-ie" for "Cookie," that is close enough to start. At the same time, use the chapter on Verbal Imitation to help him say the word better when he asks, and as he gets better at saying it, reward him for closer tries.

Make sure the child is *looking at* the thing he is to ask for. When he is looking at it (the *natural reward*), say, "What do you want . . .?" or "Tell me what you want." If he comes close to saying the right word, quickly reward him with praise and by giving him what he asked for. If he does not say anything or does not even come close, *prompt* him by telling him the right word to say. If he *imitates* the prompt, reward him. For example:

Parent or Teacher	Child	Parent or Teacher
"What do you want?"	Does not say anything	Waits a few seconds.
"What do you want? . . . COOKIE"	"Cookie" or "Coo-ie"	Rewards with praise and a cookie.

Repeat this many times: (1) *waiting* until the child is *looking* or prompting him to look; (2) *asking* him what he wants; (3) *prompting* him with the right word; and (4) *rewarding* him if he imitates the prompt.

FADING OUT THE PROMPT

Once the child is imitating the prompt ("COOKIE"), start to *fade out the prompt.* Fade it out in the same way as you did when you were working on naming. For instance, *wait longer* before you give the prompt, say the prompt *softer*, or say *less* of the prompt.

Parent or Teacher	Child
"What do you want? . . . COOK . . ."	"Cookie"

When you are fading out the word prompt ("COOKIE"), you can use *other prompts* to help the child ask with the right word. For example, say, "What do you want?" and then start *waving* the cookie around or *point* to the cookie. If you want him to say "Eat," ask "What do you want to DO?" and then pretend you are putting food in your mouth. Or, if you want him to learn to say "Out," ask "Where do you want to GO?" and then point to the door or to the outside. Later, you should fade out these prompts, too. But go *slowly.*

Be sure to use Grandma's Law during the day wherever you can teach the child to ask for things. As soon as he can imitate the word, he should have to say it (or try) before he is given what he wants.

FADING OUT THE QUESTION

When the child has learned to ask for something when you say "What do you want?" it is time to teach him to ask more *on his own.* This means fading out the question. Instead of always asking him, "What do you want?" or saying, "Tell me what you want," *wait* until *he wants* something. Then give him just a *little prompt* by *pointing* to what he wants; by *holding* it up; by saying, "Speak up," "Tell me," or "Ask me"; or by *whispering* the question, "what do you want?"

If the child does not say anything, do not give him what he wants. Have him wait a little while and then give him another chance to ask more on his own. Use another child who already knows how to ask on his own as a *model*. Have this child come up and ask for what the first child wants. Reward the child who is the model. If the first child imitates the model, reward him by giving him what he wants.

Modeling works nicely during mealtime, too. Just have another child who can already ask on his own (the model) sit with you and the first child at the table. Give each child a chance to ask for something on the table. Go back and forth between the two children. Reward the child who is the model when he asks for something. Reward the other child if he imitates the model. Later, reward the other child only if he asks when it is his turn. If he misses his turn a few times because he did not ask on his own, *prompt* him by (1) quickly giving the model child a turn so that the other child can hear how to ask; (2) asking the other child what he wants or telling him to ask you ("It's your turn. What do you want?"); or (3) giving him the name of something to ask for ("SANDWICH"). Then fade out the prompts until he asks on his own when it is his turn.

Keeping Track of the Child's Progress on Naming   (E1), Asking   (E2), and Describing   (E3)

There are two things to keep track of: (1) *the number* of new words the child is learning to use to *ask for, name,* and *describe things;* and (2) *how often* the child is using words to ask for, name and describe things.

HOW MANY NEW WORDS IS THE CHILD LEARNING?

As we said in Section 1 of this chapter, *write* all the words you are working on in the column for that week on a copy of the Speech Table (Table 12-1) at the end of Chapter 12. When the child learns to *use* a word in a functional way—to name, ask for, or describe things—*circle* it in the column for that week.

Below is a copy of part of the Speech Table made by Jimmy Lawrence's parents. Each time Jimmy's parents worked on a word during the week, they wrote it down in the column for that week. You can see that they worked on the same words for a few weeks in a row. Whenever Jimmy learned to *imitate* or *say* a word, his parents *underlined* it. The words that are not underlined are words they worked on but that Jimmy could not imitate yet. When Jimmy learned to *use* a word to ask for, name, or describe things, his parents *circled* it. Notice that, even after a word

Baseline	Week 1	Week 2
EAT	(EAT)	EAT
OUT	(OUT)	OUT
WATER	WATER	(WATER)
(MEOW)		
(RUFF-RUFF)		
CA-CA		
	(MOO)	
	(NOSE)	NOSE
	(HAIR)	HAIR
	(MOUTH)	MOUTH
	(EAR)	EAR
	(EYES)	EYES
	RIDE	RIDE
	COME	(YO-YO)
	DRINK	(MAMA)
		(CAR)
		PAPA
		WANT

was underlined ("EAT") or circled ("NOSE"), his parents kept working on it to give Jimmy practice.

Count the words circled each week. You can see that during the baseline (before his parents started working on speech) Jimmy could say six words, but *used* only two of them ("MEOW" and "RUFF-RUFF") to answer questions ("What does a cat say?" and "What does a dog say?"). The first week he learned to use eight more words, and the second week four more.

Each week, Jimmy's parents *charted* the number of *new* words he learned to use in a *functional way* to ask for and name things. In other words, they charted the number of words they *circled* each week. Figure 13-1 is a chart of the new words Jimmy Lawrence and Mark Kane learned to use each week. As you can see from Figure 13-1, after 7 weeks Mark had learned to use forty-four words, and after 9 weeks Jimmy had learned to use thirty-five. This may not seem like much, but keep in mind that their parents had to spend a great deal of time in teaching the boys *how* to say (*imitate*) basic sounds, syllables, and words.

HOW OFTEN IS THE CHILD USING HIS WORDS TO COMMUNICATE?

Learning new words does not help much if the child does not use them to communicate. So it is important to *count how often the child uses his words to communicate each day.*

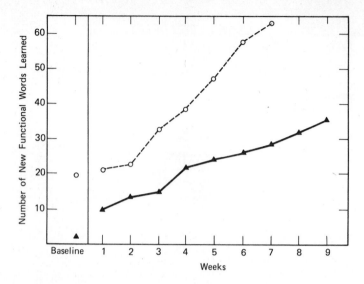

FIGURE 13-1 Number of words Jimmy Lawrence and Mark Kane learned to use to ask for and name things in home programs. Each day, the boys' parents ran sessions with them on Verbal Imitation and Functional Speech, using praise and, at first, food as rewards. The rest of the day, the boys had to use the words they had learned to say to get natural rewards. The dots for the baseline show how many words the boys used in a functional way (to name and ask) before their parents started working on speech. Each week after that, the number of new words they learned to use was added on. Mark Kane (O———O), Jimmy Lawrence (▲———▲). Greg Hudson and Virginia Hudson served as behavioral consultants for the families.

All you have to do is to wear a wrist counter and click the counter (or make a hash mark in your note pad) each time the child *uses* his words in a functional way during the day, to name, ask for, or describe things. You can either count *all day* or for a *certain amount of time* each day, say 1 or 2 hours. At the end of the day, *write down* the number of times the child used his words (the number of times he *communicated* with them) in the box for that day on a copy of the Behavior Count Table (Table 6-3) at the end of Chapter 6. Then *chart* the numbers you counted on a copy of the Behavior Chart (Figure 6-2), also at the end of Chapter 6.

The Behavior Chart in Figure 13-2 is for Jimmy Lawrence. Every day, his parents counted *how often* he used his new words to communicate. They used one wrist counter to count the number of times he named or asked for things on his own, and another wrist counter to count how many times he named or asked for things when they signaled him (for instance, by asking him, "What do you want?"). They counted almost all day. The chart is for Thursday of each week.

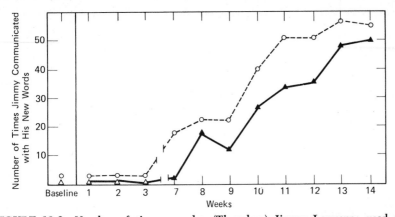

FIGURE 13-2 Number of times per day (Thursdays) Jimmy Lawrence used the words he had learned in a functional way, to ask for or name things. His parents counted the number of times he communicated on his own and the number of times he communicated with his new words after they signaled him, for example, by asking him a question ("What do you want?"). Number of times Jimmy communicated with his new words on his own (O——O); number of times he communicated with his new words after he was signaled by his parents (▲——▲). Jimmy's parents started working on Functional Speech on Week 7. During the gap between Week 3 and Week 7 they were working on other skill areas, such as Motor Imitation, and could not count how often Jimmy was communicating. Greg Hudson served as behavioral consultant.

You can see from Figure 13-2 that Jimmy's parents had good results in increasing the number of times Jimmy communicated with his new words. During the baseline, Jimmy used the words he could say only a few times a day. For the first 6 weeks of his educational program, his parents worked on Eye Contact (A1 and A2), Large and Small Motor skills, Motor Imitation, and teaching him to Make Many Sounds on His Own (D3) and to Make Sounds and Eye Contact to Get What He Wanted (D6).

During Week 7 they started working on Verbal Imitation and Functional Speech. By the end of Week 14, Jimmy was using his new words more than 100 times a day, over half the time on his own.

When the child can *name* about six objects and *ask* for most of them, start working on the next section, "Identifying and Describing." Remember to keep teaching the child how to say new words by using Chapter 12, "Verbal Imitation." Then teach him to *use* those words to name and ask for things.

5. IDENTIFYING AND DESCRIBING   (E3)

When the child has learned to name about six different objects and to ask for most of them by name, it is time to teach him to identify and describe. *Identifying* means that the child can pick out or choose between different objects by their names. It means that he *hears* the difference between the names and shows that he knows *which name* goes with *which object* (by pointing to or picking up objects when you name them). *Describing*, on the other hand, means that the child can *use* words to talk about the scene around him. He can tell you the *names* for things he sees; he can tell you their *color, shape,* and *size* (big/small); and he can tell you what they are *doing* (running, sitting).

To work on identifying and describing you will need (1) a box of common objects; (2) color chips or blocks of different colors; and (3) picture cards, books with large, real-looking pictures, and magazines. Work on identifying and describing during sessions (you can work on Verbal Imitation, naming, and asking at the same time) and at other times (for instance, during walks, in the store, or in the car).

Keep track of the child's progress in the same way as you did with naming and asking. Write down the words you are teaching him to identify and describe with in the column for that week on the Speech Table. When he learns to identify or describe with a word, *circle* it in the column for that week. Each week, *chart* the number of new words he learns to identify and describe with. Also, count and chart the number of times he *uses* words to describe things during the day. See the end of Section 4 above for examples of how to count and chart.

Identifying and Describing by the Whole Name

The idea here is to teach the child to pick out or talk about things by their whole names, no matter what the color, shape, or size. You will need pictures and a box of small objects to work on this.

Pick three or four objects to start with, for example, a dog, house, car, and apple. Use objects the child can *already name*. Spend a while making sure he can name them by (1) holding them up one at a time; (2) asking, "What is this?"; and (3) rewarding him for naming them correctly. Second, make sure the child knows how to *pick up* or *point to* objects. Put *one* of the objects or pictures on the table in front of him, and tell him, "Point to the dog," "Pick up the dog," or "Give me the dog." If needed, prompt him to point to it or pick it up. When he can pick up or point to *one* object when asked, start working on identifying.

IDENTIFYING BY THE WHOLE NAME

Put two or three objects the child can already name in front of him on the table. When he is looking at them, *you point* to each one and tell him the name. "This one is a DOG. This is a HOUSE. And this is a BOY." Then tell him to pick up or point to one of them: "POINT to the BOY." If he does this correctly by himself within about 5 seconds, give him a big reward. If he does not start to point in about 3 seconds, *prompt* him by gently *moving* his hand to the right one or by *pointing* to the right one. Also, try to catch him and move his hand in the right direction *before he makes a mistake.* Repeat this a few times with the *same* object or picture.

If the child makes many errors, prompt him by *pointing* to the correct object or picture *at the same time* as you are telling him which one to point to. On the next try, *wait 1 second* before you point. Each try, wait 1 second longer before you give the pointing prompt—up to 4 seconds (Touchette, 1971). You want him to start pointing *before* you have a chance to give the prompt.

Slowly fade out your prompts by (1) moving his hand only *part* of the way; or (2) pointing to the right picture or object for only a second. *Save the strong rewards for the times when he points correctly without a prompt or with less prompting than before.* If the child makes a few errors in a row after you start fading the prompt, go back to prompting him some more.

When the child can point to or pick up his first object or picture without a prompt (for instance, the boy), start on the second one of the set (for instance, the house). Do the same as before. Just put the same two or three objects or pictures on the table (including the first one he learned —the boy), and have him point to or pick up the house. Prompt him when needed. When he gets better at pointing to the second object or picture (the house), start *switching* back and forth between pointing to the first one (the boy) and the second one (the house).

Each time the child learns to point to or pick up an object or picture, add a new one. Give him the most practice on new ones, but spend some time practicing the ones he has already learned. Also, start moving the pictures around to different spots on the table, so that he learns to identify by name and not by place on the table. Later, start using pictures or objects that have the *same name*, but *look a little different.* For example, have two pictures of boys and two pictures of houses, and have him pick the boys from the houses. Or have two cups and two spoons on the table, and have him choose the cups from the spoons. Remember: when you add a new object for him to point to, teach him to *name* it as well.

DESCRIBING BY THE WHOLE NAME

When the child has learned to identify (point to or pick out) three or four different objects or pictures, start teaching him to describe scenes that have those objects or pictures in them. For example, lay out all the objects or pictures he has learned on the table. When he is looking at them, say, "Tell me what you see" or "What is on the table?" If he *names any* of the objects or pictures on the table, quickly give him a strong reward. If he does not name any of the objects or pictures within a few seconds, prompt him by *pointing* to one of them or by *telling* him *all* or *part of the name of one of them*. If he then names the one you prompted him on, reward him and repeat this a few more times.

Then say, "Tell me *what else* you see" or "*What else* is on the table?" Prompt him by pointing or telling him the name for a different one of the pictures or objects on the table. As the child learns to tell you the names for these objects, add a few new ones.

You can use the same methods to teach him to describe different scenes. For example, sit with him and hold up a picture book for him to see. As before, say, "What do you see?" or "What's in this picture?" Reward him if he names one of the objects in the picture on his own. If he does not, prompt him by pointing or by telling him. Reward him if he then names an object. Then have him name a different object in the picture.

It is very important to have him describe things in many places. For example, use the same methods to have him tell you what he sees (1) in the *store* (shelf, can, box); (2) on a *walk* (house, sidewalk, tree, car); (3) while he is going for a *ride* (car, street, house); (4) in the *house* or *classroom* (carpet, chair, TV, bed); and (5) in the *mirror* (face, shirt, arms, chest, mouth, hair).

After the child learns to identify and describe a few dozen objects by their whole names, move on to the next section.

Identifying and Describing What Is Different About Things

There are many ways in which things are different, for example, different colors, shapes, and sizes. Sometimes a *whole word* is used to show how things are different (*red* ball/*blue* ball; *big* dog/*small* dog). And, sometimes, just *part* of a word is used to show how things are different (big ball/big*ger* ball/big*gest* ball). When the child learns to identify and describe many objects by their whole names, start teaching him to identify and describe how objects are different.

COLORS

Do not work too long at one time on colors. Spread this out over a few months. Get yourself many small objects and pictures that have the same *shape* but *different colors*, for example, sets of dogs, horses, circles, and blocks of different colors. First teach the child to *imitate* four or five basic color words ("red," "blue," "yellow," "black").

Hold up *one* of the objects. (The child should be able to say or imitate the color name for the object.) Wait until he is looking at it. Then *tell* him the name of the color, for example, "RED. RED. This is RED. What color is this?" If he says "Red," give him a strong reward. If he does not say "Red," *prompt* him like this: "This is RED. What color is this? . . . RED," or "This is RED. What is this? . . . RED." Reward the child if he imitates all or part of the prompt ("RED").

Repeat this four or five times. When the child begins to answer by himself, or begins to quickly imitate the prompt, start *fading* the prompt. You can do this by (1) *saying less* of the prompt (What color is this? . . . RE . . ."); (2) saying the prompt in more of a *whisper*; and (3) *waiting longer* to give the prompt ("What is this? . . . . RED"). Start holding out on the rewards except when the child gives the answer with less prompting than before. But, if he makes more than a few mistakes in a row, go back to prompting him and then fade out the prompts more slowly.

When the child can describe (give the name for) one object or picture, show him *other objects with the same color*, so that he will learn to describe the color even if the objects are different. For example, once he can give the color for the red circle, have him name the color for the red block and the red dog.

When he has one color down very well, add a second one. As before, teach him to name one object or picture with the new color. When he can name an object with the new color, have him name other objects with that color, for instance, blue blocks, dogs, and horses.

Then *go back and forth between the different objects and the two colors*. Have the child give you the name for the red block, then the blue circle, then the blue block, and then the red dog. When you get to this point, you may have to use a little more prompting. After some prompting, start saving the biggest rewards for the times when he gives the color correctly without a prompt.

When the child can *describe* objects using a few color names, start having him *identify* objects and pictures by the color names. Use the same method we talked about for teaching the child to identify objects by their whole names. Just spread out three or four pictures or objects of different colors on the table in front of him. Tell him, "Point to the RED horse" or "Which one is the RED horse?" Prompt him by moving his hand or by pointing to the right one, and reward him for correctly pointing by himself. When he can point to the red horse, have him point to the red dog and the red block. When he can pick out red objects, start having him point to objects of a second color. When he is doing fairly well at pointing to objects of the second color, *switch* back and forth between objects of the two colors. Then work on a third color.

It is important to teach the child to identify different objects that have the *same color*. A good way to do this is to have the child point to or give you one object ("Give me a BLUE one"). When he does, reward him and then say, "Give me ANOTHER BLUE one" or "Give me SOMETHING ELSE that is BLUE" or "Find ANOTHER BLUE one." Prompt him if needed.

COMPARISONS

There are many ways to *compare* things: small/big, wide/narrow, short/long, near/far, small/smaller, big/biggest. To teach the child to compare objects, you need two and sometimes three objects or pictures of the same thing to compare, for example, three circles (one bigger than the next) or three lines (each wider than the next).

First teach the child to imitate or say the words—"small," "smaller," "big," "bigger," "wide," "narrow." Work on only a few sets at a time, though. Then hold up one of the objects or pictures in a set, for example, a picture of a small circle. Wait until the child is looking and tell him, "SMALL. SMALL. This is SMALL. What is this?" If the child says "Small," quickly reward him. Repeat this a few more times.

If the child does not answer "Small" the first time, *prompt* him by saying, "SMALL. This is SMALL. What is this? . . . SMALL." And reward him if he imitates the prompt. Then slowly *fade out* the prompt.

It is also a good idea to have the child point to the picture or object that you are having him describe. "SMALL. This one is SMALL. POINT to it. . . . That's right. SMALL. What is this?"

When the child is using the right word to describe the first object or picture in a set, add the second one in the *same set* to *compare* it with— a picture of a big circle. Teach it in the same way as the first one: (1) make sure he can say or imitate "Big"; (2) hold up the object or picture; (3) tell him what word to use to describe it ("BIG. This one is BIG") and ask him to describe it ("What is this?"); (4) reward him if he describes it by himself; (5) prompt him, if necessary, to use the right word ("What is this? . . . BIG"); and (6) fade out the prompt when he begins to answer more by himself.

When the child is describing the second object or picture in the set, start *switching* between the two. First hold up the big one, then the small one, and so on. Also have the child *point* to them. For example, put the two on the table and say, "Point to the BIG circle." Reward him if he does it right; prompt him by hand if he starts to do it wrong. Then move the pictures or objects around and have him point again. When he can point to one of the set, teach him to point to the other ("Point to the SMALL circle"). Then move the pictures around again.

Move on to another set (wide/narrow; short/long) when the child learns to describe and identify in the first (small/big) set. Remember to practice the first set a little each session. Also, have the child describe and point to big and small, wide and narrow things in *other places*, for instance, big and small chairs, balls, and windows; wide and narrow streets, belts, and pieces of paper.

When the child has learned a set of two (such as big/small), you can add words that end with "est" and "er." For example, you can teach him to compare the big circle he learned first with an even bigg*er* one, or to compare the narrow line he learned first with lines that are narrow*est*.

Use the same method you used above: (1) teach him to imitate the words; (2) show him a picture or object to be described; (3) tell him the word to use ("This one is BIG. And this one is BIGGEST"); (4) pull back one of them and have him describe the one that is left ("What is this?"); (5) reward him if he answers correctly and prompt him if he does not ("What is this? . . . BIGGEST"); and (6) slowly fade out the prompts. Have him go back and forth between describing and pointing to the two different objects or pictures.

Action Words (Identifying and Describing What Is Happening)

So far, we have talked about teaching the child to identify and describe things by name, color, shape, and size. We can also identify and describe what is happening around us. *Action words,* such as "running," "sitting," "jumping," and "raining," tell us what is happening.

You can teach action words in the same way as you teach other kinds of words. First make a list of action words to teach. Start with actions the child can see and hear *often,* for example, "sitting," "eating," "cooking," "banging," "washing," "sleeping," "ringing," "walking," "running," "crying," "jumping," "dressing," "laughing." Work on only a few action words at a time. Get pictures that show people and animals *doing* the actions you picked. It is best to have two or three pictures showing the same action. You can find many good pictures in children's books and magazines. Also use toys and other objects that make noises the child can learn to describe, for instance, the telephone, a bell, or a hammer.

Next, give the child practice in *imitating* or saying the few action words you picked. To teach him to identify and describe with an action word, hold up a picture, for example, a picture of a boy who is running. When the child is looking at the picture, say, "The boy is RUNNING. RUNNING. The boy is RUNNING. What is the boy DOING?" Wait 2 seconds. If the child says "Running," quickly reward him. If he does not say "Running," wait a few seconds and repeat the question, "The boy is RUNNING. What is the boy DOING?" Then *prompt* the child by giving all or part of the answer, for example, "What is the boy DOING? . . . RUNNING (or RUUUUUNN . . .)." Reward him if he imitates the prompt.

Repeat this a few more times. Slowly *fade out* the prompt until the child answers "Running" when you hold up the picture and ask, "What is the boy doing?" If he keeps having trouble answering without the prompt, have him just imitate the word "running" a few more times. Then go back to asking the question.

When the child gives the right answer to the first picture three times in a row without a prompt, start on the second picture. Make sure the second action picture looks very different from the first. When the child gives the right answer to the second picture three times in a row, start switching back and forth between the two pictures.

Next, teach the child to *identify* the right picture according to the action word you use. Hold up one of the pictures; tell him what it is ("The boy is RUNNING") or have him tell you what the boy is doing; and put it on the table in front of him. Then have him *point* to it: "Point to the boy who is RUNNING." Reward him for doing this correctly. Then hold up the second picture; tell him what the boy is doing ("The boy is SLEEPING") or have him tell you what the boy is doing; and lay it on the table next to the first one. Have him point to the second picture: "Point to the boy who is SLEEPING." Again reward correct pointing.

Have the child point to the *same* picture a few times in a row. Then switch between the two. *Prompt* him (if he needs it) by moving his hand to the right picture or by pointing to the right one. Have him point again (by himself) the next time after you prompt him. Occasionally move the pictures around on the table.

When the child can identify and describe pictures with two action words, add *other pictures* that show the *same actions,* for instance, pictures of girls running and jumping, dogs running and jumping. It is also very important to have the child describe and identify *real actions and sounds*. Have him point to other children who are jumping, and have him tell you what they are doing. Have him describe the sound of a hammer and a bell. Have him run and jump on request ("Billy, let's see you JUMP . . . VERY GOOD . . . Now let's see you RUN"). *Prompt* him to do the right action, and have him *tell* you what he just did ("What were you DOING?").

Then add a few *new* action words to work on. Be sure to give the child practice on the old ones. And use every chance you get to have him identify and describe what is going on around him with the action words. "What do you hear? . . . A BELL."

Remember to work on identifying and describing at other places besides the table. Take the child for walks around the house or school. Have him point to and name the different things he sees and hears. When he learns color names, have him point to and name objects of different colors. Have him point to big objects and small objects. And have him tell you what people are doing.

The next section has to do with another and very important kind of Functional Speech—answering simple questions.

6. ANSWERING SIMPLE QUESTIONS (E4)

So far, you have taught the child to answer questions like "What is this?", "What color is this?", or "What is the boy doing?" The reason that he could answer these questions was that he could *see* or *hear* the answer. For instance, he could see the picture you were holding up. Now it is time to teach him to answer other kinds of questions to which the answers are not so plain to see. For example, you want the child to learn answers to questions like:

What is your name?
How are you?
How old are you?

The same method is used as was used to teach the child *names*. First, give him practice in imitating or saying the words in the answer. Then, *tell him* the answer to the question you are going to ask, for instance, "Your NAME is MARK. MARK is your NAME. MARK. Your name is

MARK." *Point* to him and prompt him to point to himself while you are saying this. Then ask the question, "What is your NAME?" Wait about 5 seconds. If he answers "Mark" or comes close, give him a big reward. If he does not answer or gives the wrong answer (for instance, if he just repeats "NAME"), wait about 5 seconds and *repeat* the question. But this time, *prompt* him *before* he gets a chance to give the wrong answer. Prompt him by telling him all or part of the answer: "What is your NAME? . . . MARK (or MAARR)." If he imitates all or part of the prompt, reward him.

Ask the child the *same* question a few more times, and then go on to another task for a few minutes. Then come back and work on the same question a few more times. Slowly *fade out* the prompt by saying "Mark" *more* and *more softly,* by *waiting longer* before you give the prompt, or by *saying less* of the prompt. Give big rewards when he answers the question with less of a prompt.

When the child answers the first question a few times in a row without prompting, start on a second question, such as "How old are you?", "Where do you live?", or "How are you?" Work on the second question in the same way as the first. When he can answer the second question a few times in a row, take a break. When you come back, *switch* between the different questions. Later, give him practice a few times a day on old questions. Also, have other people ask him questions you have worked on.

The next section is on saying "Hello" and "Goodbye." You can work on these words at the same time you work on answering simple questions.

7. SAYING "HELLO" AND "GOODBYE"   (E5)

Saying "Hello" and "Goodbye" is important social behavior. When the child can imitate "Hello," "Goodbye," "Hi," or "Bye," teach him to use these words at the right time and place. These words are fairly easy to teach just using *natural consequences.*

Greeting People

One way to teach the child to *greet* people by saying "Hello" or "Hi" is for you to stand by the front door of the home or classroom before the child comes in. If he comes to the door and does not say anything, *you* greet him by saying, "Hello (or "Hi"), Jimmy." Wait a few seconds for him to *return* or *repeat* your greeting. If he does, praise him, tell him how glad you are to see him, and let him in the door.

If he does not return or repeat your greeting, *prompt* him by saying "I said 'HELLO.' Now YOU say 'HELLO.'" If he imitates all or part of the prompt, praise him and let him in the door. *If he can imitate or say "Hello" or "Hi" well, do not let him in the door until he tries to return or imitate your greeting.*

Repeat this routine whenever it is natural for the child to greet you. When he learns to return (or imitate) your greeting, teach him to greet you *on his own* (without a prompt). Just wait by the door as before. When he comes to the door, wait to see if he will greet you. If he does, praise him and let him in. If not, say, "What do you say?" If he does not answer by saying "Hello" or "Hi," prompt him by saying "HELLO" or "HI." Let him in when he imitates the prompt. As the days go by, fade the prompt ("What do you say? . . . HELLO") to a whisper, and still later, all the way out.

After about a week, use *positive practice*. If the child comes to the door and does not greet you on his own or return your greeting, have him *back up* about ten steps and come to the door again, so that his signal for greeting you is *seeing* you, and not your prompt.

Once the child is pretty regular about greeting you on his own, teach him to say "Hello" or "Hi" to *others* when he enters their house or room. While the child is coming to the door, coach him to say "Hello." For example, tell him, "When you see Mrs. Blake, say 'HELLO.'" As the child walks in the door, prompt him again, if he needs it, by telling him "What do you say?" or "Say 'HELLO.'" Reward the child if he says "Hello." If he does not say "Hello," have the other person in the room greet the child—"Hello, Billy." Prompt the child to repeat the greeting, and reward him when he does.

As the days go by, use *positive practice* to teach the child to greet others more on his own. Have him back up and come into the room again, until he greets the other person with less prompting from you.

Finally, teach the child to greet people who come into the room where he is. For instance, if he is sitting in a chair and someone comes into the room and walks over to him, prompt the child to say "Hello" or "Hi." At first, it is enough if he imitates your prompt. Slowly *fade out* the prompt by giving less and less of it ("HEL") and by whispering it.

Saying "Goodbye"

As the child gets better at saying "Hello," start teaching him to say "Goodbye" or "Bye-bye." When it is time to leave a place, prompt him to *say* "Goodbye" and to *wave* "Bye-bye." As soon as he imitates your prompt, let him out the door and reward him. After many tries, start fading out your prompts. Instead of telling him, "SAY 'GOODBYE,'" prompt him by saying "What do you say when you leave?" or by whispering "Goodbye." Start making sure he leaves the room *only* after he has said "Goodbye" a little more on his own.

Also teach him to say "Goodbye" when people are leaving the room he is in. Prompt him by saying, "What do you say when people leave? You say 'GOODBYE.'" Reward the child for imitating your prompt. Also reward him for imitating other people when they wave or tell him "Goodbye." Slowly fade out your prompts, and reward him when he says or waves "Goodbye" more on his own.

So far, the child has been using just one or two words to name, ask for, and describe things, to answer questions, and to say "Hello" and "Goodbye." The next section tells you how to expand his use of one word into phrases and sentences.

8. PHRASES AND SIMPLE SENTENCES (E6)

So far, we have talked about five different kinds of Functional Speech: naming, asking, identifying and describing, answering simple questions, and saying "Hello" and "Goodbye." In each of them, the child had to learn to say only one word. For example, he could answer the question "What is this?" by saying "Block." And he could ask for a cookie just by saying "Cookie." Sometimes, using just one word is enough. If a person asks how you feel, you can answer, "Fine." But sometimes one word does not tell the other person enough. If a child comes up to you and says "Car," you may not know what he means. Does he want to go for a ride in the car? Does he want to play with his toy car? Or is he telling you that he just saw or heard a car? About the only way the child can tell you what he means is by using more than one word. He needs to put his words together in a phrase or sentence: "See car" or "I see a car."

When the child has learned to use words in any of the five ways we have already talked about, teach him to put them into phrases and simple sentences. For example, when he has learned to name things with one word, start teaching him to name the same things (and new things) in a phrase or simple sentence. Instead of saying "Block," teach him to say, "That's a block." Instead of "Sandwich," teach him to say, "I want a

("Wanna") sandwich" or "Give me ("Gimme") a sandwich." And instead of "Dog," teach him to describe things by saying "I see a dog."

Notice that we used words like "wanna" and "gimme." These are not "good" English, but they are a start, and they are better than not talking at all. Besides, "Gimme" and "Wanna" are easier to say than "I want a" and "Give me." *Do not wait for the child to say a phrase or sentence perfectly.* Reward him for coming *close.* In fact, it is a good idea to teach him to say "I wanna" and "Gimme" at first. It is more important for the child to *use* what he can say to control the scene around him in a "normal" way (with speech), than for him to say everything perfectly. Later you can *shape* him to say his phrases and sentences better and better.

What Phrases and Sentences Should I Start With?

Start with phrases and simple sentences with words in them that the child already *uses* or can at least *imitate.* Also start with phrases and sentences the child can use *often.* These are good ones to start with:

I WANT _____ or I WANNA _____;
GIVE ME _____ or GIMME _____;
THAT'S A _____;
I SEE A _____; and
(<u>HOUSE</u>) AND A (<u>CAR</u>) AND A (<u>TREE</u>).

Basic Method for Teaching Phrases and Simple Sentences

First of all, make a *list* of the phrases and sentences you will start with. Pick one or two of the different kinds, for example, the "I want _____" or "I wanna _____" sentence and the "That's a _____" sentence. Also list *words* the child can use to *fill in* the sentences. Your list might look like this.

I WANNA (EAT, GO OUT, COOKIE, PLAY, RIDE).
THAT'S A (DOG, HORSE, COOKIE, CAR, TREE, CUP, BLOCK).

The first words to fill in the sentences should be words the child has already learned to use.

Next, make sure the child can *imitate* the phrase or sentence, or can at least imitate all the words in it. Section 8 of Chapter 12 tells you how to teach the child to imitate phrases and sentences. Use the phrase or sentence for a few days or a week during sessions to give the child practice in imitating the words in the phrases. For instance, give him practice saying the words by themselves: "eat," "ride," "that's," "wanna," "dog." Also give him some practice in putting the words together into phrases and sentences: "Wanna eat," "Wanna ride," "That's a dog."

As soon as the child can imitate a phrase or simple sentence fairly well, start teaching him to use it. Do not wait until he imitates it perfectly!

A good way to teach the child to say and use phrases and simple sentences is to *shape them backwards*. At first it is enough if he says just the *last word* in the sentence. Later, he must say the *last two words*. Still later, he must say the *last three,* and so on.

For example, at first it is enough if he answers the question, "What do you want?" by saying "Out." Slowly, *shape* him to answer by saying, "Go out," "Wanna go out," and "I wanna go out." Of course, this may take a few weeks. Reward the child for saying a little more of the phrase or sentence.

Here are ways to teach some of the basic phrases and simple sentences.

Asking for Things ("I want . . .," "I wanna . . .," or "Gimme a . . .")

When you are teaching the child a phrase or sentence to *ask* for something, make sure that he sees or is near what he is to ask for. When he is looking at it, tell him *how* to ask for it a few times. For example, say, "I WANNA COOKIE," and maybe eat the cookie yourself to show him that after you *ask* for a cookie you can *eat* one. Praise him and give him the cookie if he imitates all or *part* of "I WANNA COOKIE."

If he does not imitate you, say, "ASK me for it" or "TELL ME what you want," and then quickly *prompt* him by saying, "I WANNA COOKIE." Quickly reward him if he imitates all or most of the prompt.

Parent or Teacher	*Child*
"What do you want? . . . I WANNA COOKIE."	Imitates "Wanna cookie" or "I wanna cookie."

Do not reward the child if he just imitates "Cookie." He already knows how to ask with one word. He must at least say, "Wanna cookie." So if he just says "Cookie," tell him that he was pretty close, wait a few seconds, and tell him, "Say, 'WANNA COOKIE.'" If he imitates "Wanna cookie," reward him.

Every chance you get during the day, have the child ask for what he wants (eat, ride, out, play) by at least saying "Wanna _____." When he is pretty good at saying "Wanna _____," teach him to add the "I."

All you have to do is to have him imitate "I" a few times. Then, the next time he asks by saying, "Wanna (ride)," tell him, "That's good. Say, 'I WANNA (ride).'" Reward him if he comes close to adding "I" to the sentence. Repeat this as much as you can during the day. If possible, do this at meals or during snack time, when the child will get plenty of chances to use the phrase or sentence.

As he starts to imitate the prompt ("WANNA COOKIE" or "I WANNA COOKIE"), start fading out the prompt. Just say, "What do you want?" and wait longer until you give the prompt, say less of the prompt ("I WAAA"), and say the prompt in a whisper.

When the child is answering the question, "What do you want?" with the phrase or sentence "Wanna _____" "I wanna _____," start fading out the question. This is to teach him to ask with phrases or sentences on his own. Fade out the question by whispering it or by saying less of it ("What . . .?").

Use another child as a *model* for asking with phrases and sentences. Have the model child come up to you and the first child. Then have the model child use a phrase or sentence to ask for something the first child wants. Reward him. If the first child imitates what the model child said, reward him. Slowly fade out using the model child.. At first, reward the child if he only says "Wanna _____" on his own. Later, shape him to say "I wanna _____" on his own. Prompt him a little more if he needs it.

Naming and Describing ("I see . . ." or "That's a . . .")

When the child can use the "I wanna _____," "Gimme _____," or "I want a _____" sentences to ask for many things he wants, start teaching him to name and describe things with "That's a _____" and "I see _____" sentences.

Use the same method as with the "I wanna _____" sentences. Hold up an object. When the child is looking at it, *tell him* what it is called, for example, "That's a BALL." Then ask the question, "What is that?" Wait a few seconds. If he answers, "That's a ball" or "A ball," quickly reward him. If he does not answer or says only "Ball," *prompt* him again by saying, "THAT'S A ball," and reward him if he imitates *more* of the prompt.

Repeat this a few times with the same object. Slowly fade out the prompt ("THAT'S A ball") until he is answering the question "What is that?" with the sentence "That's a ball." Once he is using the basic sentence ("Thats' a _____"), have him use it with many other objects and in many places, for example, "That's a car," "That's a tree," "That's a dog."

If the child keeps having trouble saying the whole phrase or sentence, give him more *practice* in just *imitating* the words he is leaving out, such as "That's," "I," or "Want." Also, when he *starts* to say a phrase or sentence, *chorus* it along with him to help him say what he has been leaving out. You might prompt him by moving his mouth into the right position for the word he has been leaving out.

Using "And"

When the child can name or describe what he sees using a simple sentence ("I see a dog" or "That's a dog"), teach him to use the word "and" to name and describe more than one thing that he sees.

First, teach him to *imitate* "and" and "and a." Then put a few objects he can already name in front of him on the table. Have him *name each one while you point* to it. Go through this a few times, with the child naming the objects as you point to them. Next, prompt the child to say, "And a" between each two objects he names. For example, after *you* point to the dog and *he* says "Dog," prompt him to say, "And a." Then *you* point to the second object and have him name it. When he does, prompt him to say "And a" before you point to the third object.

At first, prompt the child to say "and a" between objects by having him *imitate* this. In other words, *you* say "AND A," and he imitates the words. Later, say less of the prompt ("AAN") and start whispering it. Keep moving the objects around and adding new ones.

The next step is to teach the child to use "and a" to describe things without your pointing to them. Show him the objects on the table, for instance, people, dogs, and furniture in a toy house, or pieces of a toy farm set. Say the name of each piece for him and have him repeat each name. Then tell him, "What is in the farm?" or "Tell me what you see." If he does not name any of the objects, *point* to one of them and name it for him. When he repeats the name, reward him and prompt him to say "And a" by whispering it. When he says "And a," *you* point to another object for him to name.

Here is what the method might look like.

TEACHER:	Says, "Tell me what you see." Prompts child to say, "I SEE. . . ."Points to one of the objects (dog).
CHILD:	Says, "I see (teacher points) dog."
TEACHER:	Says "Good" and whispers "And a. . . ."
CHILD:	Says "And a. . . ."
TEACHER:	Points to another object (house).
CHILD:	Says "House."

As the days go by, have the child say longer and longer strings of names, and fade out your prompts (pointing to the next object, whispering "And a").

Keeping Track of the Child's Progress on Phrases and Sentences

Write down any phrases or sentences you are working on in the column for that week on your Speech Table. When the child learns to *use* (not just imitate) a phrase or sentence without prompts, *circle* it. This means that he is using the phrase or sentence to name, ask for, or describe things. Each week, *chart* the number of phrases or sentences the child learned to use.

The next section is on teaching the child to identify and describe the difference between one and more than one object.

9. ONE AND MORE THAN ONE: PLURALS   (E7)

Usually, the end of a word tells us whether we are talking about one thing ("cup") or more than one thing ("cups"). But there are three different *endings*: (1) S ("cups"); (2) Z ("cubs"); and (3) EZ ("glasses"). All three *endings* (S, Z, and EZ) "mean" the same thing; they all mean "more than one."

How do you know which ending to tack onto a word? It depends on the sound at the end of the word. Here are some rules that apply most of the time. Check Section 5 of Chapter 12 to help you remember how the sounds are made.

IF A WORD ENDS WITH THE *P, T, K, F,* OR *TH* SOUND, TACK ON THE S SOUND TO MAKE THE WORD MEAN "MORE THAN ONE."

Examples are cup/cups, cat/cats, block/blocks, cliff/cliffs, faith/faiths.

IF A WORD ENDS WITH THE CONSONANT SOUND *B, D, G, V, M, N, NG, R, L, W, Y,* OR *H,* OR WITH ONE OF MANY OF THE VOWEL SOUNDS, LIKE *Ee, U, Iy, Uh, Oh, Ay,* OR *Aw,* TACK ON A Z SOUND TO MAKE IT MEAN "MORE THAN ONE."

Examples are tub/tubs (tubZ), bud/buds, dog/dogs, glove/gloves, ham/

hams, pan/pans, fang/fangs, ear/ears, bell/bells, cow/cows, high/highs, tree/trees, shoe/shoes, pie/pies, soda/sodas, saw/saws, tray/trays.

IF A WORD ENDS WITH THE S, Z, SH, ZH, CH, OR J SOUND, TACK ON AN EZ SOUND TO MAKE IT MEAN "MORE THAN ONE."

Examples are glass/glasses (glassEZ), nose/noses, flash/flashes, watch/watches, judge/judges.

When a child has learned to *name, ask for, describe,* and *identify* some *single* objects very well, it is time to teach him to understand and use *plural* words (words ending in S, Z, and EZ). The idea is to teach the child to use the right ending, depending on whether he is talking about one or more objects (cup/cups) and depending on the ending of the word (which tells him whether to add S, Z, or EZ). Also, the child must learn to *identify* whether *you* are talking about a single object or more than one object according to the endings *you* put on the words you say to him ("Point to the cup"/"Point to the cups"). Here are some steps to follow.

1. Make a list of words to use. Write down each word as it is used with single objects and with more than one object. Start with words the child already understands and uses to *name, ask for, identify,* and *describe* things. They should also be *common* words. Make sure to have words with the *three different endings* on your list. For example:

S Endings	Z Endings	EZ Endings
cup/cups	tub/tubs	face/faces
cap/caps	dog/dogs	nose/noses
cat/cats	pie/pies	rose/roses
hat/hats	bell/bells	match/matches
plate/plates	tree/trees	watch/watches
block/blocks	pan/pans	glass/glasses
sock/socks	can/cans	dish/dishes

Along with your list, you need pairs of objects and pictures (for example, a few cups, blocks, pictures of trees, faces, a few nails).

2. Give the child some practice in just *imitating* the names, *naming* the objects, and saying the S, Z, and EZ sounds. For instance, work on the S and Z sounds with him; have him imitate the words "shoe" and "shoes," "cat" and "cats"; and have him name the picture of a cat and of a shoe. Also make sure that the child still looks at and points to things on request. He does not have to *identify* the correct one—just point to something when you tell him to.

3. Start with one set of pictures or objects. Put a picture of a *single* object on one side of the table in front of the child and a picture of a *pair* of the *same* objects on the other side. For instance, put a picture of one cat on his left and a picture of a pair of the same two cats on his right. When the child is sitting quietly and looking at the pictures, *you point* to each one and *name* it for him. "This is a *CAT*. These are CATS." Then say, "Point to the CA*T*." If necessary, *prompt* him by *moving* his hand all or part of the way, or by *pointing* to the right picture. Reward him when he points to the right picture more on his own.

When the child has pointed to the single one (the cat) a few times in a row without prompting, tell him, "Now point to the CATS." and *stress* the S sound in "CATS." Again, prompt him if he needs it (*before* he points to the wrong one), and reward him for correctly pointing on his own.

When he has pointed to the picture of the pair of cats a few times in a row without a prompt, switch back and forth between the two pictures and move the pictures around the table. In this way, he learns to point by what he sees and by the name, and not by where the pictures are on the table.

When the child can go back and forth between the two pictures and point correctly without a prompt a few times in a row, it is time for the next step.

4. So far, the child is *identifying* pictures according to the *ending* you put on the word. He pointed to one of the pictures when you said "CAT," and to the other picture when you said "CATS." But can he *describe* the pictures? Teach the child to describe them in the same way as you taught him to name or describe anything else.

First, make sure that he can say the names ("CAT," "CATS"). Then hold up one of the pictures and ask, "What is this?" or "What do you see?" Wait a few seconds. If he answers correctly on his own, reward him. If he does not answer in a few seconds, prompt him by saying, "What do you see? (2 seconds) CATS." (*Stress* the S sound.) Reward him for imitating your prompt. Repeat this a few times, until he answers "Cats" without a prompt when you say, "What do you see?" Then start on the other picture. Just hold it up. When he is looking at it, ask him, "What do you see? . . . CAT." Reward him for imitating "Cat." Repeat this many times and fade out the prompt until he answers the question by himself.

When he learned to describe or name each picture, switch back and forth between the two and have him name them. Start on the next set (for example, plate/plates) when he can go back and forth between the first two and name them correctly many times without a prompt.

A very important point to remember is to *work on all three of the endings*. After you have worked on a few of the S endings (cat/cats, plate/plates), work on a few of the Z endings (dog/dogs, tree/trees) and then a few of the EZ endings (glass/glasses, nose/noses). Also, remember to go back and forth between having the child *identify* (point to) the pictures or objects and *name* or *describe* them. Finally, have the child name and identify one and more than one object in other places and with other people. Have him tell you when he sees one *car* and when he sees *cars;* have him point to one *rock* and to *rocks,* to one *boy* and to *boys.*

The next section is on prepositions. Make sure that the child is naming, describing, and identifying many things before you work very much on prepositions.

10. PREPOSITIONS (E8)

Prepositions are words like "on," "in," "under," "over," and "next to." The idea is to teach the child to use prepositions to *tell you where* objects are and to *move* objects in the way you tell him to ("Put the book UNDER the table"). For this you will need a few small objects, like coins, blocks, and a *box.*

When the child is looking, show him how to move the objects around. For instance, put the block *in* the box, *on* the box, and *next to* the box. And *tell him where* the block is each time: "See. The block is IN the box. IN. IN. IN the box." You should also prompt him to move the objects around, and *tell him* where he is moving them: "You put the block IN the box. Very good." If he imitates what you say, reward him.

Then pick one preposition, for instance "on." Put the block *on* the box a few more times, each time saying, "ON the box." Then hand the block to the child and tell him, "Put the block ON the box." Wait a few seconds. If he puts it on the box, reward him. If he does not, prompt him by taking his hand and putting the block *on* the box. Repeat this over and over. Slowly *fade out* your prompts until he can put the block on the box by himself when you tell him to.

Once he can do this correctly many times in a row, start on another preposition. It might be a good idea to *use different objects at first to teach different prepositions*. Instead of using the block and box to teach both "on" and "under," use a book and table to teach "under." Teach "under" in the same way you taught "on." Show the child what "under" means by putting the book under the table while he is watching, and say, "UNDER. The book is UNDER the table," as you put it under. Then tell him, "Put the book UNDER the table." Prompt him if needed and reward him for doing it more on his own.

When the child can *move* objects according to two prepositions, use different objects for the same two prepositions. For instance, have him put blocks, forks, paper, pencils, balls, and books *on* and *under* the table, boxes, chairs, bed, and so on. Then start working on a third preposition.

After he learns to *move* objects according to a few prepositions, teach him to *say* prepositions to *describe* where objects are. For example, have him put the block *in* the box. Then say, "The block is IN the box," several times. Reward him if he imitates "In."

Then say, "WHERE is the block?" Wait 2 seconds. If he says "In" or "In the box," quickly reward him. If he does not say "In" or "In the box," *prompt* him by saying, "IN the box." Reward him for imitating you. Do this over and over. Slowly *fade out* the prompt until he can answer "In" or "In the box" by himself.

Then start working on another preposition, using *different* objects. For example, have the child say, "NEXT TO the table," to describe where the book is. Each time he learns how to say a new preposition, start working on another one. Make sure to have him use prepositions to describe where many different kinds of things are, for example, "The car is IN the garage," "The chair is ON the floor," "The pillow is ON the bed."

The next skill to work on is using pronouns. Before you work on it, the child should be imitating and using a few simple phrases and sentences to *describe* things.

11. PRONOUNS (E9)

Pronouns are words like "I," "you," "he," "she," "we," and "it." You should teach the child to use pronouns to *answer questions* ("Who is Billy?" "I am" or "How are you?" "I am fine"). And you should teach him to use pronouns to *describe* things ("What is the dog doing?" "IT is running," or "What are WE doing?" "WE are sitting"). You can see that the child must already be able to use words and phrases to *describe* things—walking, running, sitting, pointing, and so on.

First of all, pick a few pronouns to teach the child, for example, "I" and "it." Then make a short list of sentences he can use those pronouns in, for instance, "I am eating, "I am sitting," "It is running." Use words that he can already say. Before you start, have him *imitate* the words you are going to have him use in a phrase or sentence. In other words, make sure he can imitate "I", and "it," as well as other words like "running," "eating" or "eat," and "sitting."

Then show the child objects or activities that he can describe by using the *pronouns*. For example, show him the picture of a dog and say, "The dog is running. IT is running. IT is running. What is the dog DOING?" Wait a few seconds. If he says, "It is running," reward him. If he says "Running," tell him, "Very good. IT is running," and have him imitate "IT" a few times. Then repeat the whole thing: "What is the dog DOING? . . . IT IS RUNNING." Prompt him to imitate the word "it." When he imitates "it," prompt him to finish the sentence "It is running." Then reward him.

Keep working on this sentence until he can answer "It is running" (or at least "It . . . running") without a prompt. Then teach him to use the "It is _____" sentence to describe *other* objects or activities, for example, "IT is sitting," "IT is eating," "IT is walking." Go back and forth between the different objects or activities to make sure he uses the correct word in the sentence ("eating," "sitting," "walking," "running").

When he uses one sentence ("It is _____") to describe a few different objects or activities, start on a new sentence, for example, "I am _____." To do this, have the child start some activity, like walking, sitting, or eating. Then tell him, "YOU are eating. What are YOU doing? Say, 'I am eating.'" Point to him when you say, "YOU are eating." Have him point to himself while you tell him to say, "I am eating."

Wait a few seconds. If he says "I am eating" or "I . . . eating," reward him. If all he says is "Eating," or if he does not say anything, ask him "What are you doing? Say, 'I am eating.'" Have him point to *himself* again. Then, if he imitates "I" or "I am eating," reward him.

If he still does not say "I" or "I am eating," prompt him to imitate "I" or "I am eating." Keep working on imitations of "I" and "I am eating." Then go back to the question, "What are you doing? . . . I AM EATING." And prompt him to say, "I am eating." Slowly fade out your prompt until he can answer, "I am eating," or, at least, "I . . . eating," by himself when you say, "What are you doing?"

When he can use the sentence "I am eating," teach him to use the "I am _____" sentence to describe other things he is doing, for example, "I am sitting," "I am pointing," "I am walking."

Then, when he can use both sentences ("I am _____" and "It is _____"), teach him to use them at different times. For instance, have him tell you what he is doing ("I am sitting") and what the sky is doing ("It is raining").

To teach the child to use the pronouns "he," "she," and "they," use pictures of people doing things. Use pictures of boys and men to teach him the pronoun "he," pictures of girls and women to teach him "she," and pictures of many people to teach him "they." Have him use the sentences "He is _____," "She is _____," and "They are _____" to describe what he sees in the pictures. Also, have him use those phrases to describe things happening in and outside of the house or school. Make sure that you go back and forth between pictures and activities for "he," "she," and "they." And keep giving him practice on "it" and "I."

One of the hardest pronouns to learn is "you," because when you ask the child the question "What am I doing?" his answer is "YOU are _____." At first, this will mix him up, so *prompt* him. For example, have him *point* to you and say "You" several times. Then have him point to himself while he says "I." Later, reverse this by pointing to yourself while saying "I," and pointing to him while saying "You."

Then point to yourself and say, "Who am I?" Quickly take *his* hand and point it to you. Prompt him to say, "YOU are (Daddy, Mommy, Mrs. Webster)." Repeat this several times to show him that when you point to yourself you say "I," and when you point to someone else you say "You."

It is all right if he does not learn to say "You" correctly right away. Just make sure to give him many chances to say "I am _____" to describe his behavior, and "You are _____," "He is _____," "She is _____" and "They are _____" to describe what other people are doing.

After the child learns to use a few pronouns you can start working on the next section, using opposites.

12. OPPOSITES (E10)

Opposites are words like "yes" and "no," or answers to questions like, "Daddy is a MAN; Mommy is a _____." Opposites are harder to learn than *naming* or *describing* things. Using *opposites* means that the child can really tell the *difference* between things. So do not expect him to learn opposites all at once. A little at a time is fine.

First, make sure the child can *name* or *describe* the objects you want him to learn the difference between. For example, make sure he can say "Dresser" when you say, "What is this?" and "Red" when you say, "What color is this?" Also make sure that he can say words like "yes" and "no." Then have him name the objects a few times: "This is a DRESSER . . . What is this?" . . . "Dresser." Then ask him, "Is this a DRESSER? . . . YES!"

Prompt him to imitate "Yes." And reward him for imitating your prompt ("YES"). Repeat the question several times and prompt him to say "Yes." Slowly *fade out* your prompt by saying "YES" in a softer voice, by waiting longer before you say "YES," and by saying only part of "YES" ("YE").

Have him answer the question with other objects, for example, "Is that a TABLE?" "Is that a BED?" "Is that a BOOK?" When he can say "Yes" correctly to many questions, start to teach him to answer "No." Use the objects he can already *name*, like dresser, bed, or book. Have him name the object a few times, for example, "DRESSER." Then ask him, "Is this a BED? . . . NO!" Prompt him to imitate "No." Repeat this several times until he will answer "No" correctly on his own. Do the same thing with other objects.

Once he knows how to say "No" and "Yes," go back and forth between different objects, for example, "Is this a TABLE?" . . . . . . "Yes"; "Is this a CHAIR?" . . . . . . "No"; "Is this a BOOK?" . . . . . . "Yes."

Next, you can teach him to answer questions with *opposites* in them, for example, "Fire is HOT and ice is COLD." You do not have to work on this full time. Just give the child some practice every few days.

First make sure that he knows the right answer. For example, tell him "Ice is COLD," and let him feel some ice. And make sure he knows that the right word to describe fire is "HOT." Then ask him the question, "Ice is cold and fire is . . .?" If he answers "Hot," reward him. If he does not answer "Hot," repeat the question and prompt him a few times.

Spread around the words "hot" and "cold" by having him point to or touch other things that are hot and cold. Have him tell you which things are hot and which things are cold. Once he can do this with three or four hot and cold objects, start working on another pair of opposites, such as "big"/"little," "up"/"down," or "man"/"woman." Use the same method as above.

The last kind of Functional Speech this chapter talks about is using "before" and "after." Make sure that the child can already name and describe many objects before you work on the next section.

13. WORDS ABOUT TIME:"BEFORE"/"AFTER"   (E11)

This section will help you to teach the child how to use and understand some basic words about *time*, for instance, "before" and "after." These are hard ideas to learn, so do not worry if it takes several weeks before the child even starts to be able to use the words correctly. The method for teaching "before" and "after" is just about the same as the methods for teaching the other kinds of functional speech.

One way to teach "before" and "after" is to have the child perform a small chain of simple tasks, for example, pointing to a red block and then pointing to a blue ball. While he is performing the tasks, *tell him* what he is doing: "You are pointing to the red block. FIRST you pointed to the red block. Now you are pointing to the blue ball. AFTER you pointed to the red block, you pointed to the blue ball." Have him repeat the same little chain a few times.

Then ask him, "What did you point to AFTER you pointed to the red block?" Wait a few seconds. If he does not give the correct answer, prompt him by *pointing* to the blue ball *and* by telling him, "You pointed to the BLUE BALL." Prompt him to imitate the answer ("BLUE BALL"). Repeat this several times.

Slowly fade out your prompts until he answers the question, "What did you point to AFTER you pointed to the red block?" by saying, "Blue ball," or "Pointed to blue ball," or "I pointed to the blue ball."

When the child can give the correct answer to one "after" question, do the same thing with other small chains of tasks, for example, pointing to your eye and then pointing to your nose, or bouncing a ball and then kicking a ball. Have him go through the chain several times, and tell him what he did *first* and what he did *after* that. Then ask him the "after" questions ("What did you do AFTER you bounced the ball?") and prompt him by telling him the answer ("KICKED the ball"). Slowly fade out the prompt.

Once the child can answer a few "after" questions, start working on "before." Teach this the same way you taught the word "after." Have him perform a small chain of simple tasks several times and tell him what he did *first* and what he did *after* that.

Then say, "First you pointed to the red block *(point to it with him).* AFTER you pointed to the red block, you pointed to the blue ball *(point to it with him).* What did you point to FIRST *(point to the red block)*? What did you point to BEFORE you pointed to the blue ball?" Prompt him to say, "Red block" by pointing to the red block and by saying, "RED BLOCK." Reward him for imitating the prompt.

Repeat this several times. Make sure that you prompt the child to point to or say the correct answer each time. Slowly fade out the prompt of *telling* him the answer. Instead, prompt him by *pointing.* Later, fade out the pointing prompt, too.

When he can answer one "before" and one "after" question, start to switch the tasks around, so that there is a different "before" and "after." Then add new tasks to the small chains, for example, jump up and down, kick a ball, and sit down. Still later, slowly expand the use of "before" and "after" to other activities during the day or week, for instance, where he went first (to school) and where he went after that (to the store). A large calendar will be a good teaching aid for this.

The last section is on handling special problems. Read it carefully.

14. HANDLING SPECIAL PROBLEMS

If the child starts to pay less and less attention, becomes fussy, leaves the table, or makes the same errors over and over, go to Chapter 7, "Handling Common Problems of Teaching," to find out what to do. Maybe the reward is not strong enough. Maybe the reward is being given too slowly. Maybe the child is sick of the same reward or bored with the task. Maybe he is being prompted too much or not enough. This section talks about a few special problems and the things you can do about them. The problems are (1) the child does not *use* the speech he knows how to use (in other words, he does not say what he knows how to say); (2) the child *parrots* or *echoes* what he hears instead of using Functional Speech (answering questions, asking for things, and so forth); and (3) the child does not use his Functional Speech in *many places* and with *many people*. These are items on the BES. Check the child's BES to see if he needs help with these items and, if so, what kind of help he needs.

Teaching the Child to Use the Speech He Knows How to Use   (E12)

Sometimes, even though you have worked with the child on a certain kind of Functional Speech (say, asking for things) and he has learned it well, when it comes time for him to ask for things around the house or school, he does not. Instead, he waves his arms, points, takes you by the hand, or waits until *you tell him* what to say—even though you just taught him how to ask.

There are a few things you can do to handle this. First of all, if the child uses *gestures* a great deal (waving, pointing, hand signals), do not reward these gestures by doing what the child is pointing for you to do.

If you have just taught the child how to ask to go outside, do not open the door if he points to the door for you to open it. Prompt him to ask you in the right way: "DON'T POINT. TELL me what you want. . . . Say, 'OPEN THE DOOR' (or 'OUT')." If the child *imitates* the prompt, reward him with praise and by opening the door. As the days go by, prompt him *less* and less, and open the door only when he asks more ON HIS OWN.

But do this only when the child has already learned enough Functional Speech that he can ask for what he wants (or at least try). Gestures are better than nothing; at least the child is not screaming and throwing tantrums to get what he wants. So start ignoring only the gestures that the child no longer needs to use, because he has already learned *how* to say what he wants.

Second, give the child some extra practice in saying the right words during sessions, so that, when you start ignoring his pointing and waving, he will be more likely to talk.

Third, use another child as a *Model*. Reread part of Section 4 above on how to use a model.

When a child starts pointing, waving, pushing, or pulling on you for something, have the model child come to you and say the right words (for example, "I wanna apple"). Praise the model child and give him an apple. If the first child imitates what the model said, reward him too. If he does not, prompt him by saying, "Okay, Jimmy, it's your turn to ask. ASK ME for an APPLE." If the first child now asks, even a little bit, reward him. If he still does not ask, *tell him* what to say: "ASK ME for an APPLE. . . . Say, 'I WANNA APPLE (or 'AAAPLE')." If the child imitates all or part of this prompt, reward him. As the days go by, hold out on the rewards until he asks more on his own.

Fourth, give the child *many, many chances* to use the speech he has learned. As soon as he can use a word, phrase, or sentence, *have him use it at the right time and place to answer questions* ("How are you?"), *to name things* ("What is this called?"), *to describe things* ("What is the boy doing?"), and *to ask for things* ("What do you want?"). Use Grandma's Law to teach him to *use* words like "go," "come," "ride," "eat," and "out" before you let him do these things. If you see him looking at something, have him *describe* what he sees ("What is the dog doing? . . . SITTING"); and when he answers (even if you have to prompt him), keep talking to him about it or let him go over to or touch what he talked about.

In other words, make sure tnat his speech is followed by things he likes. He has to find out that his speech will have an effect on the behavior of other people, and that people will do things for him when he uses speech. Also, *anytime he uses speech on his own, be sure to reward him, and not just with food.* Reward him *naturally* by talking to him, by showing him how happy you are, by letting him do what he wanted, or by repeating what he said.

HOW FAST A CHILD LEARNS FUNCTIONAL SPEECH AND HOW MUCH HE USES IT DEPENDS ON HOW MUCH HE IS REQUIRED TO USE IT.

Teaching the Child to Use Functional Speech Instead of Imitating, Parroting, or Echoing What He Hears   (E13)

Some children parrot or echo what you say to them instead of using speech in a functional way. If you ask such a child, "What is your name?" he echoes, "What is your name?" or "Name" instead of saying his name. Or if you ask, "What is this?" he parrots, "What is this?" instead of telling you. Sometimes a child parrots so much that he memorizes whole television commercials, nursery rhymes, and songs. But, when it is time to answer a question, he just imitates the question; and when it is time to ask for something on his own, he either says nothing or says something that does not make much sense. For example, if the child drops his ice cream cone, instead of saying, "I dropped my ice cream cone" in a sad voice, he may say, "Jimmy hurt his knee." Why would a child say, "Jimmy hurt his knee?" The answer might be that someone once said that to him when he fell and hurt his knee. So he is parroting what he heard many months ago, and using it to talk about what is happening to him now (feeling sad because he dropped his ice cream cone).

There are a few reasons why a child parrots instead of using his speech in a functional way: (1) he has been accidentally *rewarded* for parroting; (2) he does not know *what* to say at certain times (for instance, he does not know how to say, "I feel sad because I dropped my ice cream"); or (3) he does not know *when* to use his speech in a functional way. Here are some ways to *replace parroting* with Functional Speech.

First, you must teach the child *how* to use his speech. In other words, you must teach him *when it is his turn* to say something in a conversation. One way to do this is to work on simple naming and describing tasks. Make sure that the child knows how to say the right words. Then ask him, "What is this?" or "What do you see?" Tell him the answer *before* he gets a chance to imitate the question: "What is this? BALL." Reward him for imitating "Ball." If he starts to imitate the question, *interrupt* him *before* he gets very far:

PARENT OR TEACHER: "What is this?"
CHILD: "What is . . ."
PARENT OR TEACHER: "No! BALL" (or "What is this? BALL").

Then reward him for imitating "Ball." Make sure to use *strong* rewards.

If the child can *read*, the job is even easier. You can use story books with pictures in them or other materials that let the child read the answer to questions you ask. For example, show him a picture in a story book and talk about what you see. Then ask him a question: "What is the boy DOING?" and point to the lines he should read to answer your question: "The boy is swimming." When he reads the lines (and answers your question), reward him. Work on the same story for a few days. Then ask the child the *same* questions, but now prompt him to answer *without* reading, by *telling* him part of the answer: "The boy is. . . ." Reward him for finishing the answer: "Swimming."

Do this with many stories and other activities to teach the child *how* to answer questions.

Now, please reread the part of Section 3 above that is headed "What To Do If the Child Imitates Too Much."

Modeling is another way to teach the child *how* to use his speech in a functional way. Have the first child and the model child sit with you during snack time. Have a few different snacks in small pieces on a plate in your lap. Turn to the first child and ask, "Do you want a cookie?" If he starts to imitate the question, have the model child answer, "Yes!" Then make a big show and reward the model child. If the first child imitates what the model child said ("Yes"), hug him and give him a cookie, too.

Repeat this many times. The idea is to teach the child that *parroting the question gets nothing, while answering the question is rewarded.* After a while, do not reward the first child for just imitating the model child's answer. Reward him only if he answers *when it is his turn*. If he imitates the question when it is his turn, have the model child answer and reward the model child. Then give the first child another chance to answer.

You can use the same method in different settings. Instead of working with snacks, use pictures and story books. Just as before, ask the children a question. If the first child does not answer or imitates the question, *ignore it* and have the model child say the right answer. Reward the model child, and then give the first child another chance to answer the same question.

It is also important to teach the child *what* to say at certain times and places. If he does not know what to say, he may parrot something he said or heard many months or years ago. For example, if the child does not know how to say "Hello" when his daddy comes home, instead of saying, "Hello, Daddy," he may say, "Daddy's car. Daddy's car," because that is what he heard someone say years ago when his daddy drove up. So, if the child says things that do not make much sense at certain times, if he parrots certain things he said or heard months or years before, it is a good bet that he does not know the right thing to say at those times. You must teach him the right thing to say. This means spending some time during sessions teaching him how to say the right words and sentences. And it means prompting the child to use the right words and sentences when those certain times come up. For example, teach him how to say, "Hello, Daddy" during sessions. When his father comes home, *prompt* him to say or imitate, "Hello, Daddy" when his father walks in the door. And make sure his father gives him a big hug for this.

Of course, you cannot do this all at once. Pick a few times and places for which the child needs to learn the right speech: how to say "Hello," how to ask questions ("What is this called?"), how to say "No." When the child learns these, go on to others.

To sum up, the trick to replacing parroting is to (1) *quickly stop the child as soon as he starts to parrot* and (2) teach him the right way to talk by *telling him what to say*, having a *model child say the right thing*, and by *teaching him what to say beforehand*.

Teaching the Child to Use Functional Speech in Many Places and with Many People   (E14)

As we have said many times, a child's speech will not do him much good if he uses it only with you in the home or school. Nor will the child's speech spread out to other places and people by itself. *You have to help him to spread out his speech.*

First of all, when the child is fairly good at a certain kind of Functional Speech, start having *new* people work with him on it in the same place. At first, have a new person just sit in the same room with you and the child. Later, have the new person reward the child. Still later, have the new person ask the child more and more questions during the session. If the child becomes fussy or inattentive, or stops talking, *you* go back to working with him for a while and slowly fade the new person back in.

Also, work on speech in new places. Have the child *name, ask for, describe,* and *identify* things on the sidewalk, on the playground, in the store, and in a friend's house. Have him say "Hello" and "Goodbye" in other places. *Make sure to reward the child often, at first, when you are doing this.*

Second, it is important to teach the child the speech to use in different settings. If the child's problem behaviors have kept him from going many places, he is not likely to know the words to describe what he will find in them. He will not even know what to look for. So it is a good idea to *prepare* the child for new experiences by *acting them out.* Before a trip to the supermarket, show him pictures of supermarkets in magazines. Have him *describe* and *identify* what he sees in the pictures. Also, have him describe and identify grocery store items found around the home or school. Then, when you get to the supermarket, point the items out to him and have him *name* them. Let him take part in the activities by putting items in the shopping cart and carrying packages.

The same goes for trips to the doctor's or dentist's office. Show the child pictures of what he is likely to see: people in white coats, examining tables, chairs, and instruments. Better yet, let him handle toy or real instruments (stethoscope, tongue depressors, and so on). In this way, the child will be more likely to follow directions and to take part in new settings.

REFERENCES AND EXTRA READINGS

Baer, D. M., and Guess, D. "Receptive training of adjectival inflections in mental retardates." *Journal of Applied Behavior Analysis,* 1971, **4,** 129-139.

Barton, E. S. "Inappropriate speech in a severely retarded child: A case study in language conditioning and generalization." *Journal of Applied Behavior Analysis,* 1970, **3,** 299-307.

Buddenhagen, R. G. *Establishing Vocal Verbalizations in Mute Mongoloid Children.* Champaign, Ill.: Research Press, 1971.

Fineman, K. R. "Visual-color reinforcement in establishment of speech in an autistic child." *Perceptual and Motor Skills,* 1968, **26,** 761-762.

Guess, D., Sailor, W., Rutherford, G., and Baer, D. M. "An experimental analysis of linguistic development: The productive use of the plural morpheme." *Journal of Applied Behavior Analysis,* 1968, **1,** 297-306.

Guess, D. "A functional analysis of receptive language and functional speech." *Journal of Applied Behavior Analysis,* 1969, **2,** 55-64.

Guess, D., and Baer, D. M. "An analysis of individual differences in generalization between receptive and productive language in retarded children." *Journal of Applied Behavior Analysis*, 1973, **6**, 311-329.

Hartung, J. "A review of procedures to increase verbal and imitation skills and functional speech in autistic children." *Journal of Speech and Hearing Disorders*, 1970, **35**, 203-217.

Kastein, S., and Trace, B. *The Birth of Language*. Springfield, Ill.: Charles C Thomas, 1966.

Lovaas, O. I. "A program for the establishment of speech in psychotic children." In H. N. Sloane, Jr., and B. D. MacAulay (Eds.), *Operant Procedures in Remedial Speech and Language Training*. Boston: Houghton-Mifflin, 1968. Pp. 125-154.

Mann, R. A., and Baer, D. M. "The effects of receptive training on articulation." *Journal of Applied Behavior Analysis*, 1971, **4**, 291-298.

Marshall, N. R., and Hegrenes, J. R. "Programmed communication therapy for autistic mentally retarded children." *Journal of Speech and Hearing Disorders*, 1970, **35**, 70-83.

McReynolds, L. V. "Verbal sequence discrimination training for language impaired children." *Journal of Speech and Hearing Disorders*, 1967, **32**, 249-256.

Nelson, R. O., and Evans, I. M. "The combination of learning principles and speech therapy techniques in the treatment of non-communicating children." *Journal of Child Psychology and Psychiatry*, 1968, **9**, 111-124.

Risley, T. R., and Wolf, M. M. "Establishment of functional speech in echolalic children." In H. N. Sloane, Jr., and B. D. MacAulay (Eds.), *Operant Procedures in Remedial Speech and Language Training*. Boston: Houghton-Mifflin, 1968. Pp. 157-185.

Rubin, H., Bar, A., and Dwyer, J. H. "An experimental speech and language program for psychotic children." *Journal of Speech and Hearing Disorders*, 1967, **32**, 242-248.

Sailor, W. "Reinforcement and generalization of productive plural allomorphs in two retarded children." *Journal of Applied Behavior Analysis*, 1971, **4**, 305-310.

Sailor, W., and Taman, T. "Stimulus factors in the training of prepositional usage in three autistic children." *Journal of Applied Behavior Analysis*, 1972, **5**, 183-190.

Sapon, S. M. " 'Receptive' and 'expressive' language." Paper presented at the annual meeting of the American Psychological Association, Division 7, Chicago, Ill., 1965.

Sapon, S. M. "Shaping productive verbal behavior in a non-speaking child: A case report." Paper presented at the Seventeenth Annual Round Table Meeting on Linguistics and Language Studies, *Georgetown University Monograph Series*, No. 19, March 25, 1966.

Sapon, S. M., and Reeback, R. T. "Shaping vocal antecedents to productive verbal behavior in a nine year old mongoloid boy." *Reports From the Verbal Behavior Laboratory*. Rochester, N.Y.: University of Rochester, 1968.

Schell, R. E., Stark, J., and Giddan, J. J. "Development of language behavior in an autistic child." *Journal of Speech and Hearing Disorders*, 1967, **32**, 51-64.

Schumaker, J., and Sherman, J. A. "Training generative verb usage by imitation and reinforcement procedures." *Journal of Applied Behavior Analysis*, 1970, **3**, 273-287.

Skinner, B. F. *Verbal Behavior*. New York: Appleton-Century-Crofts, 1957.

Sulzbacher, S. I., and Costello, J. M. "A behavioral strategy for language training of a child with autistic behaviors." *Journal of Speech and Hearing Disorders*, 1970, **35**, 256-275.

Touchette, P. E., "Transfer of stimulus control: Measuring the moment of transfer." *Journal of the Experimental Analysis of Behavior*, 1971, **15**, 347-354.

Wolf, E., and Ruttenberg, B. A. "Communication therapy for the autistic child." *Journal of Speech and Hearing Disorders*, 1967, **32**, 331-335.

CHAPTER FOURTEEN

CHORES
and
SELF-HELP
SKILLS

1. WHAT THIS SKILL AREA IS ABOUT

Teaching a child *Chores and Self-Help* skills is just as important as teaching him Small Motor, Motor Imitation, Verbal Imitation, or Functional Speech skills. Here are some reasons why. First, when a child does a chore or self-care task, he is hooking up many smaller behaviors into a *chain*. Instead of just cooperating with a simple request (for example, picking up his hat), he may be (1) unscrewing the toothpaste cap; (2) rinsing his toothbrush; (3) squeezing some toothpaste onto the brush; (4) putting down the toothpaste; (5) moving the brush up and down and back and forth across his teeth; (6) rinsing his mouth and the brush; (7) screwing the cap back on the toothpaste; and (8) putting the toothbrush away. Learning to go through a whole *sequence* or *chain* like this will help the child to *organize* his behavior and to learn other *complex* behaviors.

Second, when a child learns to do chores and self-help tasks with more skill and on his own, it takes a burden off his parents, brothers and sisters, and teachers who might otherwise have had to do these things for him. At the same time, the child starts to help out—to take part—in family and classroom life. Third, chores and self-help tasks give the child more constructive ways to spend his time. And, fourth, often a child must already have certain Chore and Self-Help skills before he can get into a school. For example, some schools require that a child be toilet trained before they will accept him.

So we cannot say it often enough: *as soon as you can (and the child is ready), start teaching him to do chores and self-help tasks.*

2. PLANNING AND RUNNING TEACHING PROGRAMS IN THIS AREA

Is the Child Ready for This Area?

First of all, look at the Table of Basic Behaviors (Table 4-2) in Chapter 4. It shows you that before you start in this area the child should learn four skills:

(A1)　Spontaneous Eye Contact.
(A2)　Eye Contact on Request.
(A4)　Cooperates with Simple Spoken Requests.
(B14)　Looks at Objects, Parts of the Body, Face, Mouth.

Of course, if the child has already learned the other *basic behaviors,* such as Skill at Many Large Motor Activities (B13), Skill at Many Small Motor Activities (B21), Imitation of Large Motor Models (C1), Imitation of Small Motor Models (C2), and Imitation of Object Placements (C3), it will be easier for him to learn complex Chores and Self-Help skills. But it is *not* a good idea to wait until the child is an expert at Looking, Listening, and Moving or Motor Imitation before you start on Chores and Self-Help skills. *Get the child using the motor skills he has.* In fact, by working on chores and self-help tasks, you will give him more skill in the Looking, Listening, and Moving area. In other words, run teaching programs for Chores and Self-Help skills, Looking, Listening, and Moving, and Motor Imitation all at once.

What Behaviors Are in This Skill Area?

Skim over the section on Chores and Self-Help skills in the BES or BET.

You can see that behaviors in this skill area build on behaviors from earlier skill areas. For example, Doing More Complex Tasks and Chores (F2) builds on the child's skill at Cooperating with Simple Requests (A4), Large and Small Motor activities (B13, B21, B22), and Motor Imitation (C1, C2, C3).

Basic Teaching Methods

If you have worked on behaviors in earlier chapters, then you already have all the skills needed to teach Chores and Self-Help skills. There is really nothing new. But let us be businesslike and review some of the basic methods. Please reread the following:

1. "Tips on Teaching" in Section 1 of Chapter 10.
2. The list of steps to follow in Section 2 of Chapter 10.
3. "Increasing Skill at Small Motor Activities" in Section 3 of Chapter 10.
4. "Increasing the Amount of Time the Child Spends at Small Motor Activities" in Section 3 of Chapter 10.

Please do not go any further until you have reread them.

Here is a summary of methods and steps to follow.

1. *Set Up a Certain Time or Place for the Child to Do the Task.* You want the time or place to become a *signal* for him to do tasks on his own. A good time is *just before* a *high behavior* or *activity* is supposed to happen. For example, have the child set the table before mealtime; have him pick up his toys before a favorite TV program; have him brush his teeth after a meal and before he can go outside; or have him put away his clothes (or undress himself) before he can have a bath.

To help the child learn that a certain time or place is a *signal*, tell him what the time or place is, what the task is, and what the consequence will be. Grandma's Law will help you to put them all together. Just say, "Okay. 'It's SUPPER TIME. Let's SET THE TABLE. As soon as you (we) set the table, you (we) can EAT SUPPER." Then start teaching him to do the task.

2. *Break Down the Target Chore or Self-Help Task into Small Steps.* When you teach the task, start with the *last* step (if possible). When the child learns to do the last step, back up and teach him the second to last step. This is called *back-chaining.*

For example, let us say that making the bed has four steps: (1) pulling up the sheet; (2) pulling up the bedspread; (3) putting the pillow in the right spot; and (4) fluffing the pillow. The first day, *show* the child all the steps and *tell* him what you are doing. Unmake the bed and *prompt* him to go through the steps with you. The next day, show him all the steps again. Prompt him to repeat all the steps, but have him fluff the pillow (the *last* step) on his own. The idea is to teach him that he should fluff the pillow (Step 4) after the pillow is put in the right spot (Step 3). When he can fluff the pillow on his own, show him how to do all the steps, prompt him to do them, and have him put the pillow in the right spot (Step 3) *and* fluff the pillow (Step 4) by himself. In other words, you help him to do the first two steps, and he does the last two. When he can do the last two steps by himself, show him how to do the first step and have him do the last three steps more on his own. Keep this up until he is starting with the first step and going all the way through the task.

When you teach a task backwards, the child learns what the right order is; he stays close to the reward at the end of the task; and, when he starts the task, he does each next step better and better because he has had more practice on the later steps.

3. *Make Sure That the Child Is Looking at You Before You Show Him How to Do the Task or Give Him Any Directions.*

4. *Show Him (Model) and Tell Him How to Do the Task While He Is Watching.* "Look at the PILLOW. I FLUFF the pillow (pat, pat). That's right. See how I FLUFF the PILLOW. Now YOU do it. FLUFF the PILLOW."

5. *Prompt the Child by Telling Him What to Do.* "Put your hands ON TOP of the PILLOW." If necessary, put him through the *right motions.* If possible, *stand behind* the child when you are putting him through the motions. In that way, he will see his own movements rather than your hands and arms. *Fade out* your prompts as the child gets better at the task.

In fact, once the child can do all or at least part of the task very well, get him started and then *step away* a few feet and for a few seconds so that he can work by himself. When you come back, give the child a great deal of praise for working. As long as he keeps working well when you are gone, slowly increase how far away you are and how long you are gone.

6. *Use an Effective Reward.* Praise the child with enthusiasm ("Hey. Way to go! Great. You are PULLING UP THE SHEET"). Use tokens, too, for some tasks if you have a token system going (see Section 1 of Chapter 8). Remember to have the child do the task *just before* a favorite activity. In that way, he gets an Activity Reward besides the other rewards (praise, tokens) he is getting while he works.

At first, reward the child *very often* while he is working at a task. Also, reward other good behaviors that happen, for instance, looking at what he is doing, making correct movements, imitating your models when you show him what to do, or talking about the task. As he becomes more skilled at the task, slowly decrease your rewards until you are rewarding him for *finishing* the job well and are using mostly *natural Activity Rewards*.

7. *If the Child Makes a Mistake on Part of a Task, Have Him Back Up a Few Steps and Try Again*. Then prompt him to do those few steps correctly and in the right order. This is called *positive practice*. Do not overdo it. Do not have the child repeat the same few steps so often that he becomes bored or angry. Just have him try again once or twice, and prompt him to do them right. He will get more practice the next day.

8. *If the Child Keeps Making Mistakes, Stops Paying Attention, or Becomes Whiney, You May Have to Revise the Teaching Program*. Check into Chapters 7 and 15.

9. *When the Child Can Do Most of the Task By Himself, Add a New One to Work on at a Different Time or Place*. Also, have the child do the first task with other people and in new places.

Write the Teaching Program Plan and Run the Program

Now that we have talked about basic methods for teaching chores and self-help tasks, *pinpoint* the easiest one on the list in the BET that the child needs help with. Write a *teaching program plan* for it on a copy of Table 6-2 at the end of Chapter 6. Each day, keep track of the child's progress by noting (1) which steps he needs help with; (2) how much help he needs; (3) whether he started to do the task on his own; (4) how long he took to get started once you signaled him to start; and (5) in what places and with what other people he will do the task.

Remember: just because you are starting to work in this skill area, this does not mean that you should forget about the others. Keep working on harder Large and Small Motor activities and Motor Imitation. Use Verbal Imitation methods to teach the child how to say words that describe the task (for instance, "bed," "cover," "pillow," "sheet," "fluff," "pull"). And teach him to *use* the words in a functional way to describe what he is doing ("What are you doing?" . . . "Fluffing").

3. CHORES (F1 and F2)

There are two *basic behaviors* to work on in this section: Does Simple Tasks (F1); and Does More Complex Tasks and Chores on His Own, Often (F2).

Teaching the Child to Do Simple Tasks   (F1)

This behavior is very much like Cooperates with Simple Spoken Requests (A4) in the Learning Readiness area. The difference is that in the Learning Readiness area you were trying to increase cooperation with requests. Now you are teaching the child to do many simple tasks that are important to his family and school life. The idea is to teach him to do simple tasks that will be rewarded by *natural activities.*

Make yourself a long list of simple tasks for the child, for instance, picking up or putting away things from around the home or classroom; opening or closing drawers, windows, and doors; turning on or off the lights, the fan, the TV set, or the record player; putting trash in the wastebasket; taking out the trash; rinsing the dishes or cooking utensils; helping to cook (stirring, cracking eggs, pouring, carrying, or bringing things you ask for); loading or unloading the washing machine. During the day, ask the child to do simple tasks like these. When he does, reward him with plenty of praise and maybe even tokens. Be sure to also reward many of these tasks with *Activity Rewards* that the child gets when he has finished. For instance, after he loads the washing machine, he can start it or go outside.

After a while, the child may begin to enjoy doing certain tasks, such as washing dishes, helping you cook, or vacuuming the rug. If so, use these tasks as Activity Rewards for doing other tasks: "As soon as you pick up your clothes (new task), you can help me cook (task he likes)." Please read Section 5 of Chapter 9 to brush up on how to teach the child simple tasks.

Teaching the Child to Do More Complex Tasks and Chores on His Own, Often   (F2)

Teaching this behavior means two things: (1) helping the child to hook up or *chain* many smaller and simpler movements into the right order, so that they make up a more complex task or chore; and (2) getting his chore behavior under the *control* of *natural signals* (such as the sight of a full waste basket), so that he does chores more on his own. We have already talked about both of these.

CHAINING SIMPLER MOVEMENTS INTO A CHORE

Here we use *back-chaining.* Start the chore with a request or Grandma's Law. For example, when the child has finished eating but before he gets very far from the table, say, "Okay, it's time to help CLEAR the table" or, better, "As soon as you help CLEAR the table, you can watch 'Captain Kangaroo.'" For the first few days, show the child all the steps in clearing the table and prompt him through the motions: (1) putting all the silverware on one plate; (2) carrying the plates to the counter; and (3) carrying the glasses or cups to the counter. While you are showing and prompting him make sure that he is *watching* what he and you are doing, and use simple words to *describe* the steps. The next day, prompt him through all the steps as before, but have him do the *last* step (carrying one or two cups to the counter) on his own. Praise him while he is doing the last step. When he has finished, give him the Activity Reward as stated in Grandma's Law: "GREAT JOB. You helped to clear the table. Now you can watch 'Captain Kangaroo.'"

Still later, show him how to do the earlier steps as before, but when you reach the *last two* steps, have him do them more on his own. "The silverware is on this plate. Now what do you do? CARRY the PLATES to the COUNTER . . . VERY GOOD! And now we CARRY the CUPS . . . GOOD JOB." As the days go by, *fade out* even telling the child what to do in the last steps. Instead, if he still needs a prompt to get him to start the next step, *point* to what you want him to do (for instance, after he carries the plates, point to the cups). Or just say or whisper *part* of what he is supposed to do ("Now carry the . . . cu . . ."). Praise him as he goes through the steps and give him the Activity Reward when he is done.

Keep working backwards, a little at a time, teaching the child how to do the steps in the chore, and to do them in the right order. If he leaves out an important step, use *positive practice* by having him back up a few steps and try again, this time putting in all the steps in the right order.

When the child has learned to do the chore, it is fine if he does the steps in a little different order, as long as the job gets done well. In fact, you should reward him for being creative or more efficient. Just make sure to check on how well the job was done. Otherwise, he may get careless as the weeks go by.

If the child keeps making the same mistake, give him extra help on those steps at the right time in the chain.

GETTING CHORE BEHAVIOR UNDER NATURAL CONTROL

The idea is to have the child do his chores at the right times and places and about as often as is proper. At first, *you* may be signaling him when the right times and places are. Slowly, you want the right times and places to be the signals for him to get started on his chores. For example, at first when you were fixing a snack, you might have told the child, "As soon as you set the table, you can have your snack." So Grandma's Law was the signal that got him started. But as he becomes more skilled at setting the table, you want just the *sight* of you fixing the snack to be the signal for him to set the table.

Shifting from your statement ("As soon as you set the table, you can have your snack") to the more natural time and place signals is a matter of *adding new prompts* and then *fading them out*. Once the child can do the chore well when you tell him to, fade out telling him. Instead, say, "Okay, it's snack time. What do you do NOW?" or "What do you do BEFORE you eat your snack?" You can also use *gestures* to signal him, for instance, by *pointing* to the plates. As long as these signals and prompts are enough to get him started on the chore, keep fading them out. Instead of saying, "What do you do now?" just point to the plates or say, "Well?" Still later, fix the snack and *wait* to see what he will do when he *sees* the snack sitting on the table. If he starts to set the plates, give him plenty of praise. If he does not start to set the table by himself, give him part of a prompt by *pointing* to the plates. Do not let him sit down and eat until he sets the table.

4. SELF-HELP TASKS   (F3 through F9)

There are many self-help tasks that children usually learn. Some of the most important ones are these: Eating Properly with a Spoon, Fork, Knife, and Glass (or Cup) (F3); Undressing and Dressing (F4 and F5); Washing (F6); Brushing Teeth (F7); and Using the Toilet (F8). The goal is to teach the child to Do Many of These Self-Help Tasks on His Own, Often   (F9). Again, you already have the skills needed for teaching all of these self-help tasks. The next sections will give you some extra tips.

Self-Feeding or Eating with the Right Utensils   (F3)

Some children do not know how to use a fork, spoon, knife, and glass to feed themselves. They eat with their fingers or lick the food from the bowl or plate. Other children have some skill with utensils. For instance, they may be able to use a spoon, but they do not know how to use a fork to pick up or cut food. And some children know how to eat in the right way with utensils, but they have other problem behaviors, such as stealing food from another person's plate, leaving the table many times during a meal, licking food from the table, throwing tantrums during meals, eating only certain foods, or eating too fast or slow. Of course, children who do not know how to use utensils very well may also have the same problem behaviors.

Teaching a child to feed himself in the right way means (1) giving him *more skill* at using the right utensils; and (2) *keeping* his new self-feeding behavior *going* after he has learned how. There are three ways to give the child *more skill* as feeding himself in the right way.

1. *Telling* him how: "Hold the SPOON in your right hand. . . . That's it. Now DIP the spoon DOWN to the potatoes. . . . Good. Now PUSH the spoon IN."

2. *Showing* him how or *modeling*: "WATCH me. . . . Okay, PUSH the spoon IN like this. . . . That's right. See how I LIFT UP the spoon. . . . Now YOU LIFT UP the spoon."

3. *Moving* or *prompting* him through the right motions at the same time you are *telling* or *showing* him how (O'brien and Azrin, 1972).

On the other hand, *keeping* the child's self-feeding behavior going means *rewarding* him when he eats in the right way and *not* rewarding him when he does not (by telling him "No" and showing him what to do instead, by timing him out or removing his meal for a short time, or by stopping his hand before he finishes a wrong movement).

WHAT TO DO IF THE CHILD DOES NOT USE UTENSILS VERY WELL

If the child does not use any utensils very well but instead uses his fingers or licks food from the plate, it may be best to first teach him to eat with a *spoon*. Start with foods that are *mushy* and are not supposed to be eaten with fingers, like pudding, mashed potatoes, cereal, and thick soup. Stand *behind* the child and put the spoon in his hand. If he does not hold the spoon on his own, put your hand around his. Tell him, "HOLD the spoon. . . . Very good. You are HOLDING the spoon." Then tell him, "Now DIP the spoon into the potatoes," and move his arm so that the spoon dips into the food. If possible, clink the spoon against the bottom of the bowl when you dip it in. This sound will become a *learned reward* for the child when he dips the spoon deep enough into the food on his own. The sound will also become a *signal* for the next step, which is to lift the spoon to his mouth. If the child turns his head away and does not watch what he and you are doing, *stop* the movement just where it is and wait until he looks again, or tell him to look, before you resume the movement.

If the spoon does not pick up enough food, tell the child, "Now

PUSH the spoon IN," and move his hand and arm through the motion. Do not load the spoon too full, though. Then say, "Okay, now LIFT UP the spoon to your MOUTH." If necessary, move his arm so that the spoon is right in front of his mouth. Praise him. If he opens his mouth, see if he will move the spoon in by himself. If he does not move the spoon into his mouth, move it for him. If he does not even open his mouth, use your other hand to pull down his chin and *gently* open his mouth while you *slide* the spoon in.

Finally, move the child's arm so that the spoon lifts up and out, and the food is taken off the spoon by his upper lip or teeth. Praise him and start the second bite.

Repeat the chain for each bite, many times. Remember to tell the child what to do; use the *same, simple phrases;* move his arm and hand through the right motions; and praise him as he does the different motions in the chain. If the child gets restless, make the meals shorter (4 or 5 minutes) and have more meal sessions.

After a few days, you should be able to start *fading* your prompts. First of all, start fading them from the *back* of the chain. In other words, help the child to get the spoon up to his mouth, but fade out helping him to open his mouth and put the spoon in. When he has done the last step (opening his mouth or putting the spoon in) by himself three or four times in a row, fade out your prompt on the second to last step. This means helping him to load up the spoon, but only moving his arm *part* of the way to his mouth. As the days go by, keep backinging down the chain until the child can go through the whole chain by himself.

Second, fade out your prompts by holding the child's hand with *less and less pressure*. In other words, when you have moved his hand (and spoon) to his mouth, *relax* your grip a bit while he puts the spoon into his mouth. Later, just *lightly* touch his hand. Third, shift *where* you hold or touch him. At first you may be holding his hand. Later, hold his elbow, and, still later, just touch his shoulder to get him started. Also, fade out telling the child what to do at each step. Say less and less ("Dip. . . . Push. . . . Lift. . . . Open") and say it softer and softer.

If, after a few days of fading your prompts, you notice that the child is having trouble with one of the steps, give him a bit more prompting. For instance, *hold the bowl closer to his mouth so that the spoon does not have to travel very far*. Also, tell and show him what to do. Then fade out your prompts again. If the child tries to use his fingers, *stop* his hand *before* he can eat with his fingers. Say, "NO! Use the SPOON." And prompt him through the motions. Reward him with praise when he is eating in the right way. If the child repeats trying to use his fingers, *remove* his food for 30 seconds or so.

If the child already eats with a spoon, or you have just taught him to do so, but he cannot eat with a fork and knife, or drink with a cup or glass in the right way, teach him how by *telling, showing,* and *prompting.* At first, use just a few foods—one or two for the fork (bites of meat, sliced carrots, beets) and one or two for the spoon (pudding, apple sauce). Stand behind the child and a little to one side. Get him started by *telling* him to eat one of the foods with the right utensil: "Eat the MEAT. Use your FORK." If he does not reach for the fork, or if he reaches for the wrong utensil, gently stop him and *show* him how to hold the fork. Praise him if he picks up the fork. If he does not pick up the fork, *prompt* him to hold it and tell him how: "Now PICK UP the FORK. . . . That's it. Hold it at the BACK." Once he is holding the fork, tell him and prompt him, if necessary, to pick up a bite of meat: "Now PICK UP a bite of MEAT. MEAT (move his arm through the motions). That's good. Okay, now LIFT UP the fork to your MOUTH." *Show* him how to lift up the fork, and *prompt* him to do it. When the fork is in front of his mouth, prompt him to open his mouth by gently pulling down on his chin, and put the fork in. Then slide the fork up and out so that his upper lip or teeth pull the meat off the fork. Start the next bite. Remember: if the child looks away and stops paying attention, stop talking and prompting him. Wait until he is paying attention again.

After a few bites of one food, switch to a food that needs a spoon. Go through the same steps as before. Tell the child which food to eat and which utensil to use. Show him how and prompt him through the motions. Then switch to another food and utensil. For instance, prompt him to take a drink from his glass or cup, using one hand.

Slowly fade out telling, showing, and prompting. If the child reaches with his fingers or begins to make a mistake, gently *stop* him before he makes it, correct him ("Use your fork"), and prompt him to make the right movement with the right utensil. If he repeats the same mistake again, remove his plate for 30 seconds and give him extra prompting the next time.

Of course, this method will not work overnight. It may take 2 or 3 weeks before the child begins to use the spoon and fork with the right foods on his own. Take your time and look for just a little progress each week. It will add up to a big change before you know it.

WHAT TO DO IF THE CHILD KEEPS LEAVING THE TABLE

The easiest way to handle this behavior is to reward the child by talking to him, praising him while he is eating, or even giving him small amounts of his favorite foods every few minutes while he is sitting and eating the other foods. At the same time, let the *natural consequences* of leaving the table do their work. Ignore the child when he leaves the table. Make no effort to stop him. When mealtime is over, he gets no more to eat until the next meal. If he still leaves the table but just eats faster, remove his plate when he gets up and do not let him eat again until the next meal.

WHAT TO DO IF THE CHILD EATS ONLY CERTAIN FOODS

We all have foods we like and others we do not like. If the child refuses to eat a few foods, it is best to forget about them. But if the child will eat only a few foods—soft foods, very spicy foods—you can increase the number of different foods he will eat by using Grandma's Law and by fading new foods in.

First of all, you can use large bites of the child's favorite foods as rewards for eating small bites of foods he does not like: "As soon as you eat a bite of meat, you can have some mashed potatoes." Slowly, increase the amount of meat the child must eat before he gets to eat some potatoes. Second, you can mix small pieces of foods the child does not like with his potatoes. Slowly increase the amount of meat you mix in. At the same time, reward the child for taking a small bite of the meat and potato mixture with a bite of straight potato.

WHAT TO DO IF THE CHILD EATS TOO FAST OR TOO SLOW

If the child eats too fast and is making messes because of it (drooling, spilling), tell him and show him how to eat slowly. For instance, show him how to move his fork more slowly and talk to him between bites. Be sure to give plenty of praise when he takes a slower bite. If he keeps making messes because he is eating too fast, remove his plate for 30 seconds or so each time he makes a mess.

On the other hand, if he eats too slowly, so that everyone has been done for a half hour while he is still picking at his food, make sure to praise him whenever he eats a bit faster. Set up Grandma's Law so that he gets an Activity Reward when he is done: "As soon as you have finished eating, we can wrestle." Or set a kitchen timer for a *little less* time than it usually takes him to finish. Tell the child how many minutes he has and that you are taking away his plate when the bell rings. Of course, this goes for everyone. Then set the timer and let him see it.

Praise him for digging in. When the bell goes off, clear the table. *No* arguments and *no* snacks between meals. Slowly decrease the number of minutes you put on the timer until you are down to a reasonable amount of time.

Undressing (F4) and Dressing (F5)

As always, *tell* the child what to do, *show* him how, and *prompt* him through the right motions. Make sure that a big Activity Reward comes after undressing and dressing. For instance, as soon as the child is undressed, he can (have a bath, have a story read to him, wear his favorite pajamas). And as soon as he is dressed, he can (go outside, have breakfast).

In general, teach the child to undress and dress by himself by showing, telling, and prompting him through the whole chain, but have him do the last step more by himself (taking off his socks, putting on his shoes). It is a good idea to give the child *extra* practice on some of the hard steps, for instance, putting on or taking off his shirt, untying or tying his shoes. You can practice these steps a few times *during* the chain or at a special time. Notice that you can break down each step into even smaller ones. For example, you can break down putting on a shirt into (1) opening the shirt; (2) putting the arms and head through the holes; and (3) pulling the shirt down. So, just as for the whole task, you can teach a *hard step* by going in smaller steps, starting with the last one.

Washing and Drying Hands and Face (F6) and Brushing Teeth (F7)

These self-help tasks should be followed by strong, natural *Activity Rewards*. For example, when the child has washed his face or hands, he can eat his meal, go for a ride, or play with his favorite toys. And, when he has brushed his teeth after a meal, he can take a bath, have a bedtime story, or go outside and play. Here are some steps to follow when you teach these tasks.

Washing Hands	*Washing Face*	*Brushing Teeth*
1. Turn on the water.	1. Turn on water.	1. Unscrew toothpaste cap.
2. Pick up the soap.	2. Soak washcloth.	
3. Hold hands with soap under the water.	3. Spread out washcloth in one hand.	2. Rinse toothbrush.
	4. Pick up soap.	3. Squeeze toothpaste onto brush.

4. Rub hands to-
   gether; front and
   back.
5. Hold soapy hands
   under water.
6. Turn off water.
7. Dry hands.

5. Rub soap on wash-
   cloth.
6. Put down soap.
7. Wash face.
8. Put down wash-
   cloth.
9. Rinse face (cup
   water in hands).
10. Rinse washcloth.
11. Put away wash-
    cloth.
12. Turn off water.
13. Dry face.

4. Put down tooth-
   paste.
5. Move the brush
   up and down,
   back and forth,
   across the teeth.
6. Rinse the mouth
   and brush.
7. Screw the cap
   back on the tooth-
   paste.
8. Put the tooth-
   brush away.

Remember: help the child to do all the steps, but let him do the last one more on his own. As he masters the last step, have him do the second to last step more on his own. Try to correct a wrong movement *before* it goes very far. And give plenty of strong praise for correct movements.

Becoming Toilet Trained   (F8)

There are many reasons why a child may not be toilet trained. First, the signals he gets inside his body telling him that he has to go may not be hooked up to walking to the bathroom and going in the toilet. Second, going to the bathroom will be painful to the child if he is often consti-pated. Third, going to the bathroom happens so little anyway that the child does not have very many chances each day to learn how to use the toilet and be rewarded for it. And, fourth, the child may be rewarded for going in his pants, for example, if you holler at him or clean him up. So it is important to make sure that the child is not rewarded with at-tention or any other reward when he goes in his pants.

There are many ways to toilet-train children. Some children just need a few weeks during which they get a great deal of practice and many rewards for using the toilet in the right way. Other children may need a toilet training program that takes more time or that has more steps in it. If you have been trying to toilet-train a child for a long time without much success, do not give up. The methods we will talk about have worked well even with children and adults who were "severely retarded." Let us start with the method that has the fewest steps.

THE SIMPLEST METHOD

First of all, make sure that no one pays much attention to "accidents." Just set up a program that will teach the child to use the toilet, and let the program take care of "accidents." The child should, at first, get *strong* rewards for using the toilet. Several times a day, state Grandma's Law: "When you go in the toilet (potty), you get (candy, soda pop)." Also, if the child is learning to talk or already talks, tell him, "Tell (Mommy, Daddy, Teacher) when you have to go potty." Then set up a schedule for *checking* the child, *taking* him to the bathroom, and *rewarding* him for having dry pants or for going in the toilet (Madsen, 1966).

For example, every hour (and especially when the child gets up in the morning or gets up from a nap) check to see if he has dry pants. If he does, give him a great deal of praise for staying dry. Then tell him, "When you go in the toilet (potty), you get candy. Tell (Mommy, Daddy, Teacher) when you have to go." *In a little while* (5 or 10 minutes), if the child says he has to go, praise him and take him to the bathroom. Help him, if needed, to get undressed and to stand or sit in the right position. Reward him when he goes. If the child does not tell you he has to go within about 5 or 10 minutes after you checked and found him dry, take him anyway and again tell him, "When you go to the toilet (potty), you get _____." Help him to get undressed and to stand or sit in the right position. If the child goes, reward him with the candy. If he does not go, give him a small reward for just sitting or standing.

Each day, have him sit or stand *longer* and longer before he is rewarded. *If you take him to the bathroom often enough and have him sit or stand longer and longer, he is bound to go in the toilet sooner or later.* Then give him a big reward.

Once he starts going in the toilet when you take him, fade out the rewards for sitting or standing, and just reward him when he goes. Later, reward him with praise and once in a while with candy for going. Still later, fade out the candy and the praise.

"What do I do if the child has accidents at other times?" There are a few things you can do. First, you can just *ignore* it and make sure to take the child to the bathroom *more often* and to reward him *only* when he goes in the toilet. Second, you can give the child a *mild* scolding: "That's not big boy behavior. We DO NOT go in our pants. Go in the toilet." And, third, you can make going in the pants mildly unpleasant. Have the child clean up the floor and himself every time he does not go in the toilet. Or have the child rinse out his underpants and wear them wet for about a half hour. Reward him with praise and a change of clothes if he stays dry for that half hour.

THE CHAINING METHOD

This method (Mahoney, Van Wagenen, and Meyerson, 1971) has more steps and may take longer than the first method, but it is more likely to work with some children. The idea is to (1) teach the child all the *steps* in the chain of going to the bathroom; (2) give him lots of *practice* in going through the steps; (3) teach him to start the chain of going to the bathroom when he gets a *signal;* (4) *reward* him for going in the toilet; and (5) *mildly punish* him for not going in the toilet.

Here are the steps in the *chain* of going to the bathroom: (1) *walking* to the bathroom; (2) *pulling down* the pants or underpants; (3) *standing* in front of or *sitting* on the toilet; (4) *going* in the toilet; (5) *pulling up* the pants or underpants; and (6) *flushing* the toilet and *washing* the hands. Of course, the first four steps are the most important. Once the child has learned them, you can work more on the last two steps and add them to the chain.

Each day, for an hour or so, give the child practice on the *first three* steps of the chain: (1) *walking* to the bathroom; (2) *pulling down* the pants or underpants; and (3) *sitting* on or *standing* in front of the toilet. The reason for working on just these three steps at first is that, if the child is rewarded only when he goes in the toilet (Step 4), he will not be rewarded very often.

Start the chain of going to the bathroom with a *signal*: "Let's go potty." Walk with the child to the bathroom. Hold his hand if necessary, and reward him with praise and candy while he is walking. As the days go by, have him walk *faster,* start walking more *behind* him, and give him *less prompting* while he is walking. Later, reward him only when he gets to the bathroom by himself a few seconds after you give the signal.

When the child has learned the first step in the chain (walking to the bathroom on signal), add the second step (pulling down the pants or underpants). As before, start the chain with the signal ("Let's go potty"). When the child gets into the bathroom, tell him, "Pull DOWN your pants," and *prompt* him to pull down his pants or underpants while he is in front of the toilet. Use as little prompting as you can. Just *point* to his pants if that is enough. Or touch the waistband. Or put his hands on the waistband. As a last resort, hold his hands while you help him to pull down his pants by the waistband. Reward him after he has walked to the bathroom quickly on his own *and* has pulled down his pants. Pull up his pants after you reward him. Later, fade out your prompts by holding his hands with less pressure or by holding his upper arms instead of his hands. Work on this until he can pull his pants down by himself. Then add the third step to the chain (standing or sitting).

Again, start the chain with the *signal* ("Let's go potty"). Reward the child for walking to the bathroom and pulling down his pants. Then prompt him to sit on or stand in front of the toilet. Hold him for about 10 seconds and reward him. Slowly, increase the length of time the child stands or sits to about 30 seconds before you give the reward. Also, slowly fade out your holding prompts.

When the child can do all three of the steps on his own after you give the signal, start teaching him Step 4 (going in the toilet). To do this, have the child drink lots of water or juice during the day. You should know about how long it usually takes him before he needs to go to the bathroom after he has had a drink. When it is just about time for him to have to go, give the *signal* ("Let's go potty") and have him repeat the chain. If he goes in the toilet, reward him. If he does not go, let him return to what he was doing. If he then goes in his pants, *quickly give him the signal and a mild scolding* ('NO! Go to the POTTY") and have him repeat the chain again. If he goes in the toilet, reward him. If not, have him clean himself and change his clothes. Give him as little attention as you can when you are having him clean and change himself. Stay on this step for a few days or more.

When the child has learned to go in the toilet (Steps 1 through 4) when he is given the signal, start teaching him Step 5 (pulling up the pants or underpants). After the child has gone in the toilet, tell him, "Pull UP your PANTS." Again, give him as little prompting as you can. Point to his pants; touch the waistband; put his hands on the waistband to get him started; or hold his hands on the waistband while you help him to pull up his pants. Reward him after his pants are pulled up. Slowly fade out any prompts you were using.

At this time you can also teach him to flush the toilet and wash his hands before he leaves the bathroom.

The last part of this method is to get the chain under more *natural control*, that is, the signals the child gets inside his body. Up to now, you have waited until the child was just about ready to go after he had eaten or had a big drink. Then you gave him the signal to start the chain ("Let's go potty"). Now, you should be on the lookout for any signals from the child that he *feels* as if he has to go, for instance, straining, blushing, bending over, tugging at his pants, or making faces. That is the time to quickly give the signal ("Let's go potty"). Reward him for repeating the chain and going in the toilet. It is also a good idea to teach the child to say where he is going while he is walking to the bathroom ("Where are you going?" . . . "Potty"). Keep giving the child lots of liquids for a while and then slowly fade them out.

THE CRASH PROGRAM

The "crash" program gives the child a great deal of practice on all the steps of the chain in a short time. Instead of giving the child an hour-long session, this method (Azrin and Foxx, 1971) has the child stay in the bathroom near the toilet for about 8 hours. He leaves the area only to eat meals. As in the chaining method, give the child plenty of liquids. He should be placed and kept on the toilet for 20 minutes out of every half hour. He can get up if he goes before the 20 minutes are up. If he goes during the 20 minutes while he is sitting on the toilet, hug him, praise him, and give him a strong food reward, for instance, fruit or a liquid he likes. During the 10 minutes out of each half hour that the child is not sitting on the toilet, reward him every 5 minutes that he stays dry.

When it is time to get on the toilet, prompt the child to pull down his pants. As we said before, use as little prompting as is needed. After the child has been sitting for 20 minutes or has gone in the toilet, prompt him to pull up his pants and flush the toilet. Slowly fade out rewards for staying dry, and just reward going in the toilet.

If the child has "accidents" during the 10 minutes he is not on the toilet, scold him and have him clean himself up as well as the bathroom area. Give him as little attention as possible while he is doing this, but make sure that he cleans up.

When the "crash" program is over (which should be in less than a week), check the child during the day, especially before bedtime, when he gets up in the morning, and before meals, snacks, and special activities. If he has had an accident, he must clean himself and the area. He must also miss the snack or must wait for the meal or activity.

WHAT TO DO IF THE CHILD IS CONSTIPATED

If the child is constipated, going to the bathroom may be painful. Ease the constipation by having the child eat dried fruit. Liquid medication and glycerin suppositories will also help. If you use suppositories, slowly decrease their size as the child learns to use the toilet.

A FEW LAST TIPS

First, if you have other teaching programs going at the same time as toilet training, the child's training may take longer. So it may be a good idea to relax the other teaching programs for a little while. If you keep other teaching programs going, though, use *different rewards* in the different programs so that the child will be less likely to become satiated.

HOW TO KEEP TRACK OF THE CHILD'S PROGRESS IN TOILET TRAINING

One way to keep track is to count and chart the number of times the child has "accidents" and the number of times he uses the toilet each day.

Second, write down how well the child is doing at each of the steps in the chain of going to the bathroom. Write down what kinds of prompts the child needs, if any, or if he can do the step on his own. This will help you to plan what to do on the following days.

REFERENCES AND EXTRA READINGS

Azrin, N. H., and Foxx, R. M. "A rapid method of toilet training the institutionalized retarded." *Journal of Applied Behavior Analysis*, 1971, 4, 89-99.

Barton, E. S., Guess, D., Garcia, E., and Baer, D. M. "Improvement of retardates' mealtime behaviors by timeout procedures using multiple baseline techniques." *Journal of Applied Behavior Analysis*, 1970, 3, 77-84.

Bensberg, G. J., Colwell, C. N., and Cassel, R. H. "Teaching the profoundly retarded self-help activities by behavior shaping techniques." *American Journal of Mental Deficiency*, 1965, 69, 674-679.

Madsen, C. H., Jr., "Positive reinforcement in the toilet training of a normal child: A case report." In L. P. Ullmann and L. Krasner (Eds.), *Case Studies in Behavior Modification*. New York: Holt, Rinehart and Winston, 1966. Pp. 305-307.

Mahoney, K., Van Wagenen, R. K., and Meyerson, L. "Toilet training of normal and retarded children." *Journal of Applied Behavior Analysis*, 1971, 4, 173-181.

Marshall, G. R. "Toilet training an autistic eight-year-old through conditioning therapy: A case report." *Behaviour Research and Therapy*, 1966, 4, 242-245.

O'brien, F., and Azrin, N. H. "Developing proper mealtime behaviors of the institutionalized retarded." *Journal of Applied Behavior Analysis*, 1972, 5, 389-399.

O'brien, F., Bugle, C., and Azrin, N. H. "Training and maintaining a retarded child's proper eating." *Journal of Applied Behavior Analysis*, 1972, 5, 67-72.

CHAPTER FIFTEEN

Replacing
PROBLEM
BEHAVIORS

1. WHAT THIS SKILL AREA IS ABOUT

In the very first chapter we talked about the four ways in which any behavior can *change*: (1) it can be done with *more skill;* (2) it can be *increased* (done more often); (3) it can be done at a *certain time* or *place;* or (4) it can be *decreased* (done less often). So far, all of the chapters have been helping you to change a child's *good* behaviors in the first three ways—for instance, to speak, cooperate, play, and do chores with more skill, more often, and at the right time and place. We have hardly talked at all about behaviors you might want to *decrease,* for example, tantrums, whining, or getting into things. The reason is that you cannot just *get rid* of problem behaviors. You have to teach a child *good* behaviors to *replace* the problem ones.

And that is what you have been doing! You have been teaching a child the behavior skills that will help him to live with and learn from others. It is very likely that by now many of his problem behaviors have *decreased,* because you have started to *replace* them with *good* behaviors. The child is learning other, better ways to *earn rewards* (rewards like attention) and to *spend his time* (by playing and doing chores).

So Why Talk about Decreasing Problem Behaviors Now?

There are two reasons why we need to think about decreasing problem behaviors. First, *some problem behaviors may not be replaced or de-*

creased very fast. If a child has been throwing tantrums or moving his hands and fingers in strange ways for years, these behaviors may not go away during the first few months that you teach him speech or play skills. You yourself know how hard it is to stop a behavior you have been doing for a long time.

The point is that, even though these behaviors *will* decrease or *be replaced* by good behaviors in time, they may be very hard on you and the child now. Seeing and hearing a child throw tantrums is upsetting and probably wears you out. Also, his problem behaviors, for instance, head-banging and hitting, may be painful to him and others. Most important, the *problem behaviors he still does may be keeping him from learning good behaviors.*

The second reason why we have to think about decreasing problem behaviors is that a child may try *new* ones later on. For instance, just when you think you have decreased his *getting into things*, he may try some other undesirable way to get attention. And, unless you run very *attractive (rewarding)* sessions when you are working on the harder skills, like speech, a child may use disruptive behaviors to *get out of (escape)* the sessions with you.

For these reasons it is a good idea to find out what *controls (causes)* problem behaviors and what methods you can use to *keep them from happening* and to *replace* them when they do happen. In the next two sections we will talk about what the different kinds of problem behaviors *look like* and what *controls* them. By "control" we mean the kinds of *signals* that start a certain problem behavior and the kinds of *consequences* (rewards) that *keep it going strong.*

Keep in mind that *what controls a problem behavior is more important than what it looks like.* For example, a child's tantrums may all *look the same*, but they may be *controlled* by different *consequences.* Some of his tantrums may be controlled by a reward such as *attention* when you try to stop him, and other tantrums may be controlled by a reward such as *getting out of a teaching session,* because you stop the session. The point is that you may have to use different methods to decrease these two kinds of tantrums. Even though they *look the same*, they are *different behaviors* because they are *controlled by different consequences.*

2.   WHAT THE DIFFERENT KINDS OF PROBLEM BEHAVIORS LOOK LIKE

When we look at problem behaviors, we can see three kinds: *destructive* behavior, *getting into things*, and *strange* behavior. When you read about these behaviors on the following pages, try to figure out what might be *controlling* them.

Destructive Behavior

One kind of destructive behavior is *tantrums*. When a child throws a tantrum, he may hop up and down, yell or scream, throw himself on the floor, and kick or bang himself against tables, chairs, or walls. Tantrums are pretty hard for anyone to stand. If a parent or teacher tries to calm a child by holding him, what do you think the *consequence* is for the child? If you think he is being rewarded, you *may* be right. That is what is *controlling* his tantrums.

Another kind of destructive behavior is *aggression*. This may mean scratching, kicking, or hitting other people, throwing things like puzzle pieces or chairs, or biting. If a child does these things during a teaching session and the teacher or parent *stops* the session and lets the child go, is the child being rewarded by *getting out* of the session? Yes, he probably is. So his *aggressive* behavior is *controlled* by its *consequence;* it gets him out of the session, and aggressive behavior during sessions may increase.

Self-destructive behavior means that the child hits or bites himself, or bangs his head against the walls or on other objects like tables. Who can stand to see a child hurting himself? If a child bangs his head and his parents try to make him feel better by cuddling him, or try to stop him by talking to him, what is the *consequence* for the child? If you think it is *attention,* you are right! *Attention* is what is *controlling* the child's self-destructive behavior, at least in part.

Getting into Things

Getting into things is another kind of problem behavior. For example, the child may splash water all over the bathroom, climb onto the kitchen counters to get food out of the cupboards, keep taking food out of the refrigerator, strip the covers off chairs and beds, or take things out of closets and scatter them all over the room.

What might be the *signal* that gets a child *started* doing these things? Could it be that he is *bored* and has nothing better to do, or does not know how to spend his time in better ways? And what might be the *consequence* that keeps these behaviors going? No parent likes to see his child making a complete mess of the house. If the parent gives the child attention (by going after or yelling at him) when he gets into things, the child has found a rewarding way to spend his time, has he not? He has found out that when he makes messes he gets attention. Do you think attention could be the *consequence* that is *controlling* getting into things?

Strange Behavior

Strange behavior is the kind of problem behavior that usually happens most frequently. There are many kinds of strange behaviors. For example, a child may move his hands or fingers in front of his eyes; run up and down the hall many times a day; cover his ears or his head; flap his arms or hands; spin or flip lids, belts, and pieces of string; repeat little rituals over and over, for instance, at bedtime; or make noises and whine for no clear reason.

Sometimes strange behaviors happen so many times during the day that no one really pays much attention to them. What may be *controlling* such behaviors? Do you think they may be another way for the child to spend his time? If he does not know how to play, he may sit around the house spinning things or making noises. So just doing these things may be *rewarding* to the child. What must be done to decrease strange behaviors if the child uses them to spend his time? If you think that he needs to learn more constructive behaviors, such as doing chores and playing, you are right!

On the other hand, some behaviors are so irritating or embarrassing (as when a child moans or walks around with his tongue hanging out) that the parent or teacher may try to stop the behavior by telling the child, "Billy, don't stick your tongue out," or "For God's sake, stop that moaning!" As you know, trying to stop a strange behavior often means that the behavior is rewarded with attention, and so the attention keeps the strange behavior going strong. If attention is the rewarding consequence that is controlling a strange behavior, what should you do? You should not pay attention to the strange behavior any more (ignore it), and, instead, reward the child for a good behavior that can *replace* the strange behavior, for example, keeping his tongue in his mouth or not moaning for at least 10 minutes.

Now let us talk more about what *controls* problem behaviors.

3. WHAT CONTROLS PROBLEM BEHAVIORS?

As we said before, it is most important to find out what controls any problem behaviors a child may have. What are the *signals* that get him started? And what are the *consequences* that keep problem behaviors going strong?

Positive Rewards

One kind of *consequence* that makes problem behaviors strong is *positive rewards*, for example *attention*. Tantrums are pretty hard to watch and listen to. If you go over to a child, talk to him, or give him what he wants when he starts to throw a tantrum, *you* are using *get away* or *escape* behavior to stop his tantrum. If your escape behavior works (his tantrum stops for a while), *you* are being *rewarded* for trying to stop him. But when you try to stop him, you are also giving him *attention*. You may be *rewarding* his tantrum. So your *attention may be the consequence that is controlling his tantrums*. If he smiles or looks at you out of the corner of his eye, that is the *tip-off* that he is trying to get your attention.

Can you think of any other problem behaviors that may be rewarded by attention when you try to *escape* from them by talking to, yelling at, or going over to the child? Do you yell at him to get out of the cupboard or bathroom? Do you let him eat what he took out of the refrigerator or ride him around the block one more time to *avoid* a tantrum? If you do, you may be rewarding these behaviors. So *some problem behaviors are controlled by positive rewards, such as attention, food, and activities.*

Another way in which problem behaviors may get *positive rewards* is by *rewarding good behaviors too slowly.* For example, you might have a program to reward eye contact. But if the child makes eye contact and you wait too long (more than a few seconds) to reward him with food or praise, he may have already started some problem behavior, such as a strange noise or hand movement. Then you will have rewarded the problem behavior and not the eye contact. This is the reason why it is so important at first to reward good behaviors as fast as you can.

Or you might use *Grandma's Law* and tell the child, "As soon as you finish the puzzle, you can go outside." He finishes the puzzle, but before you open the door for him he starts to whine. If you let him out of the door for finishing the puzzle, you really will be rewarding him for whining. *It is very easy to reward the wrong behavior.* You have to keep on your toes to reward good behaviors fast and to make sure that you do not reward problem behaviors by accident.

Negative Rewards

Another kind of *consequence* that controls problem behavior is *negative rewards*. Just as *you* may use some *escape* behaviors to get away from or stop a child's problem behaviors, so the *child* may use his problem behaviors to *escape* or *avoid* teaching sessions or doing things you want him to do. If you are working on a hard skill area, like Verbal Imitation, and the child looks away from you, throws a tantrum, starts to whine, or leaves the table, and you *stop* the session, you have *rewarded* these problem behaviors. You have accidentally taught him to use them as *escape* behaviors.

Or during a session a child may flap his hands or make strange faces. If you end the session or stop giving him tasks to do because you think he is not paying attention or is in a "bad mood," you are accidentally rewarding him. Again, he is learning to use problem behaviors to *get away* or *escape*.

Does the child ever start to whine, fuss, or not pay attention to you just *before* you are going to have a teaching session? And do you figure that since he is not in a *good mood* you may as well put off the session? If this has ever happened, maybe you have rewarded him for using these behaviors to *avoid* sessions with you.

So *negative rewards* are another kind of *consequence* that *controls* problem behaviors. The child learns to *use* problem behaviors to *escape* or *avoid* doing or learning things.

Filling Time

Sometimes problem behaviors are the child's way of *filling* or *spending* his time. Everybody has to do something with his time. If a child does not *know how* to play or do chores, he may *get into things, make noises,* or *spin objects* just to have something to do. Can you imagine what it would be like if you had to stay in an empty room for about 4 days? In a few hours, with nothing better to do you would be making faces and looking at your hands too!

But the problem is that, if you give a child *attention* for these behaviors, you have *rewarded* him. It will start being fun for him to tease and get you upset. He knows what will make you look or come after him. Again, if he *smiles* when you give him attention, or *looks* at you out of the corner of his eye to see if you are looking at him, that is the tip-off that your attention is rewarding the behavior.

So problem behaviors that a child uses to fill time may be rewarded in two ways. These behaviors are rewarding *in themselves* because they give the child something to do. And if these same behaviors get you upset and you try to stop the child, he is also being rewarded with *attention*.

Summary of What Controls Problem Behaviors

To summarize, problem behaviors can be *controlled* by several kinds of *consequences*. If a child's problem behaviors get attention or get him what he wants, then they are being controlled by *positive rewards*. If some of a child's problem behaviors allow him to stall, avoid, or get out of doing what people want him to do, then these behaviors are being controlled by *negative rewards*. And some problem behaviors seem to be *rewarding* in *themselves*. A child may do some problem behaviors to fill time. And if he also gets attention for these behaviors, then he is getting positive rewards as well.

As for *signals* that control problem behaviors, anything that happens just *before* the child starts a problem behavior that is rewarded, will become a *signal* for that behavior. For example, you may find that a child throws tantrums only when certain people are around. It may be that he has learned that his tantrums will be rewarded only when those people are present. They are a *signal* for him to throw a tantrum.

Problem behaviors can also be *signaled* by a certain *time* of day. The child may have learned that at this time of day he is very likely to be rewarded. For instance, if you are more tired in the afternoon, you may be more likely then to try to stop him from *getting into things*.

Or you may find that a child *messes up* only certain things in the house or classroom. For example, he may bang only on the windows. If so, he has probably found out that he is more likely to be rewarded when he bangs on windows than on anything else, perhaps because you are afraid that he will break a window and get hurt. So windows are a *signal* for him to bang.

Can you think of any other signals that might start a child's problem behaviors? How about certain *places* you might take him, such as restaurants or supermarkets? Why is he more likely to throw tantrums in those places?

In the next section, Section 4, we will talk about methods for handling problem behaviors.

4. METHODS FOR HANDLING PROBLEM BEHAVIORS

There are two main ways to handle problem behaviors: (1) making it *less likely that they will happen;* and (2) *weakening* or *decreasing them in a more direct way.*

Making It Less Likely That Problem Behaviors Will Happen

Remember: some problem behaviors happen because the child does not know how to spend his time in better ways. Other problem behaviors happen because the child is trying to *escape* or *avoid* doing things people want him to do, for example, during sessions or on being asked to do a chore. So, to make it less likely that problem behaviors will happen, you have to *teach the child new and better ways to spend his time (playing, chores), and you have to make sure that the things you want him to do are rewarding.*

TEACHING NEW AND BETTER BEHAVIORS

We have said many times that you cannot just get rid of problem behaviors. You have to *replace* them with other behaviors that the child can be rewarded for doing instead. This is one reason why it is important to teach a child *Small* and *Large Motor activities.* He can use them during the day to *play,* for instance, with puzzles and toys, and in simple games with you and with other children. Chapter Ten, "Looking, Listening, and Moving," tells you how to teach many play activities.

It is also important to teach a child to do *chores* around the house and school, like sweeping, picking up clothes and toys, setting the table, making the bed, and even wiping and washing dishes. Chore skills will help him in many ways. They will let him take a real part in family and school life; they will give him a constructive way to spend his time; and they will help him to learn other kinds of tasks later on. Chapter Fourteen, "Chores and Self-Help Skills," tells you how to teach a child to do chores. You should use it to get him started on a program for learning chores.

To sum up, if you want to decrease problem behaviors, you must also teach the child *new* behaviors that will be rewarding to him, such as playing and doing chores. Once he has learned new behaviors and is being rewarded for doing them, he will be less likely to use his problem behaviors to get attention or to pass the time. So *you must always have programs in the home and school to teach him new play and chore behaviors.* You must also *give him many chances during the day to play and work at chores so that he can earn rewards.* In that way he will learn to *enjoy* playing and doing chores.

Have you ever gotten "sick" so that you would not have to go to work that day? Have you ever "blown your top" when you were tired of doing a hard or boring job? These were *escape* behaviors. If your teaching sessions are not rewarding (*attractive*) for a child, he will do the same thing. He will refuse to come to the table, will not do what you ask, will look away from you, leave the table, whine, or even throw tantrums.

Of course, you want to make it less likely that a child will do these things. Chapter Seven, "Handling Common Problems of Teaching," and Chapter Ten, "Looking, Listening, and Moving," tell you how to run attractive sessions that will keep a child working and learning at a fairly smooth pace. Let us review some of the ways to make your teaching sessions attractive.

1. *The less skill the child has at a task or the harder the task is, the more often he should be rewarded and the stronger the rewards should be.* For example, when you start working on a *new* skill, you should reward the child just about *every time* he does the task correctly or makes a good try.

2. *Make sure that the rewards are effective.* If praise by itself is not increasing the behavior as you want it to, try another and stronger reward, such as food or an Activity Reward (Grandma's Law). *Switch* to other rewards *before* the child becomes *satiated* or sick of the one you have been using.

3. *Switch to other tasks during a session before the child gets bored.* If he becomes bored with a certain task, switch to another one for a few days.

4. *Prompt the child to perform the correct movements.* He is being rewarded for correct movements or close tries. If he does not make any correct movements or close tries, he will not be rewarded. This will make him try other ways to get rewards (for example, by fighting with you), or it will make him use problem behaviors to *escape* from the session.

5. *When you start working on a new skill, you should be using a schedule of continuous rewards (rewarding the target behavior every time).* As the child becomes more skilled, you will be rewarding him less often (*Intermittent Schedule of rewards*). But do not move too fast from continuous to intermittent rewards, or else your sessions will be less rewarding for him. *Slowly move from continuous to intermittent rewards.*

And if the target behavior still decreases, *go back to rewarding him more often for a while.*

6. *If something stops the child from working and learning, make sure that it does not happen any more during sessions.* For instance, if loud noises keep the child from paying attention, try to get rid of such noises during sessions. Some children become angry and stop paying attention when you say things like, "No, that's wrong!" If the child is like this, be sure to correct him in a different way, for example, by saying, "Good try. Next time do it this way," and then prompt him.

So the two ways to make it less likely that problem behaviors will happen are: (1) teaching the child new and better ways to spend his time; and (2) making your teaching sessions attractive.

But sometimes a certain problem behavior happens so much, is so *strong,* or has been happening for so many years, that it keeps a child from learning new behaviors. For example, the child may throw tantrums every time you try to teach him something new. Or he may spend so much time spinning objects that he hardly pays attention during sessions. In other words, there are times when you have to *weaken* or *decrease* (*"put a stop to"*) *a problem behavior in a more direct way* so that you can teach the child new behaviors.

How to Weaken or Decrease Problem Behaviors in a More Direct Way

When you *increase* a *target behavior,* you set things up so that the child gets a *rewarding consequence* every time he performs the target behavior. But we are talking about ways to *decrease* behaviors. Remember the rule in Chapter 1 that says *"People stop doing what they are no longer rewarded for doing."* That rule tells us how to *decrease* behaviors. *We set things up so that the child does not get a rewarding consequence when he performs the problem behavior.* Instead, he gets a consequence that is no fun at all! Let us talk about the different methods (*consequences*) you can use to *decrease* problem behaviors. Try to think of ways you can use them to *decrease* any problem behaviors of a child you are working with.

IGNORING

Ignoring is probably the method most often used to decrease behaviors. It is the *easiest* for the parents or teacher to use, and it is also the easiest on the child. All *ignoring* means is that you set things up so the child is *never* rewarded for a certain problem behavior. You decide that from now on you will *ignore* it every time he performs the target problem behavior. *You simply act as though the behavior were not even happening.* You do not see or hear it.

Ignoring does not mean turning away from the child or covering your face. The child can *see you doing this.* He may *like* seeing you do this, and the problem behavior may stay strong because he is rewarded when you turn away from him. *Ignoring* means acting as though the problem behavior did not happen. You just go about your business.

Many people have used *ignoring* to decrease disruptive behaviors. A child that Carl Williams wrote about in an article (1966) always threw tantrums if left alone at bedtime. The father and mother would stay in the little girl's room to *avoid* having to hear her tantrum. But during the teaching program the child was put to bed in a nice way, and the parents left the room. If the little girl threw a tantrum, no one went back in to her. *In 7 days the child's bedtime tantrums were gone.*

Two men named Buchar and Lovaas (1968) wrote about the use of *ignoring* with a child who banged his head so badly that he had to be tied down all day long. They watched how people tried to stop the child from banging, and found that the child's head-banging was *controlled by the attention* he was getting. They told everyone to just stop paying attention to the child when he banged his head and to pay attention to him only when he was not. The child's head-banging decreased to almost nothing in 2 weeks.

Ignoring is also a good method to use for many of the minor strange behaviors the child may still have, for instance, blinking his eyes many times or making strange faces. It is best not to even notice them. Instead, go on with your business during sessions, and reward him for good behaviors instead throughout the day, for instance, keeping his eyes open or not making strange faces.

The beauty of ignoring is that many times the *natural consequences* of a problem behavior will decrease it. For example, if the child dawdles or leaves the table during meals, and you just ignore him and clear the table when you have finished eating, he will *naturally* get hungry. If done every day, this will often take care of dawdling and leaving the table. Or, if the child puts up a big fuss about getting dressed, and you ignore the fussing but do not let him eat breakfast *until* he is dressed, that will usually take care of fussing over getting dressed.

Of course, just because you ignore a problem behavior, this does not mean that it will decrease right away, or that it will "go away" by itself. When you first start to ignore a problem behavior that has often been rewarded, the behavior may even *increase* for a few days. It is as though the child does not believe he will no longer be rewarded for that behavior, and he tries even harder. For example, if he used to be rewarded for throwing tantrums, and suddenly no one seems to notice or care about his tantrums, he is likely to throw some real whoppers for a few days. If this happens, you have to stick to your guns and keep ignoring the problem behavior, because if you "give in" and pay attention to it, you will have rewarded the child for throwing worse tantrums.

Also, if you are ignoring a problem behavior, it will decrease faster if you are rewarding another behavior to *replace* it. In fact, unless you are replacing it with a good behavior, the problem behavior may not decrease at all. For example, when you start ignoring tantrums, you should also reward good behaviors that are the *opposite* of tantrums, such as sitting or working quietly, cooperating, or playing with others. In that way, the child learns other and better ways to get rewards.

TIME OUT

Time out usually means removing the child from wherever he is and putting him somewhere else ("out of action") for a little while *every* time he *starts* the target problem behavior. For example, if he is screaming, you would time him out by putting him in his room or in a special time out room as soon as the screaming starts, and leave him there for 10 minutes or so until the screaming stops.

It is very easy to abuse time out! Time out should not be used to stop a problem behavior when the behavior is really caused by something wrong in the teaching program, and not "something wrong" in the child. Before you use time out (1) try to replace the problem behavior with a good behavior; and (2) make sure that the teaching sessions are rewarding, that you are prompting enough, that the child is not bored, and that the task is easy enough. If you have tried these and the problem behavior is still going strong, then you might think about time out.

About the only other time to use time out occurs when the child's problem behaviors are hurting him or other people, and are happening so often that you can hardly teach him good behaviors to replace them. In that case, for about a week at the very beginning of a child's educational program, you might use time out for some problem behaviors, along with rewards for good behaviors, to get the problem behaviors under control.

The message is clear: *Time out should never be the usual way of teaching!* Always aim to *replace* problem behaviors with good behaviors. Think about using time out only when (1) you have first tried to replace a problem behavior by rewarding an opposite, good behavior; or (2) the child has so many problem behaviors that you cannot get his education started as long as they are so strong (happen so often).

If time out is used, you must be careful about a few things. First, you must not give the child *attention* while you are taking him to the time out room. You should take him quickly and firmly. Do not go into long speeches about why he is being timed out. If he gets timed out for a certain behavior every time it starts, he will soon learn why he is being timed out. Second, you must not let him out of time out until the problem behavior has stopped. For example, if you have timed out a child for screaming, do not let him out until he has stopped screaming.

Third, strange as it seems, it is possible for a child to like being timed out. He may *use* a problem behavior to get you to time him out just so that he can *escape* from a teaching session. Again, you must *make sure that sessions are very rewarding and that the child will be rewarded for good behaviors when he is out of the time out room.* And you must be sure that there is nothing much to do in the time out room.

A child can also get used to time out. This can happen for two reasons. First, you might have been using time out for too long. If you have been timing out the child for the same problem behavior for several weeks, and it has not decreased, he is probably used to time out by now. Find out why time out has not been working. Were you also rewarding good behaviors? Were teaching sessions attractive? Did you remember not to give the child attention while you were timing him out? *If time out does not decrease the behavior a good deal in about a week, try something else.*

A child can also get used to time out if you have been timing him out for a little longer each time. For example, if you time him out for 2 minutes the first time he throws a tantrum, 5 minutes the next time, 10 minutes the third time, and so on, it will not be long before he is in the time out room for an hour and time out is still not working! Again, find out why time out did not work sooner. Also, to keep a child from getting used to longer and longer time outs, *time him out for a long time from the very beginning.* In that way he will not like time out. Later, a time out of even a few minutes will be enough.

Finally, time out should be used *every time* the behavior happens, and as soon as it starts. Otherwise, the child will learn that he can "get away with" the behavior many times.

Two men named Risley and Wolf wrote about a different way of using time out (1967). Instead of removing the child, they left the room. Every time the child started throwing tantrums during sessions, they would go out and would come back to the room only when the child was quiet and ready to start working.

You can do this, too. When a disruptive behavior starts, set a timer on the table to ring in a few minutes, pick up all the food and materials, and leave the room (without saying anything). Come back when the timer rings. If the problem behavior starts up again after you have come back and started the session, set the timer again and leave the room with all the materials and rewards. Come back when the timer rings. If your sessions are *attractive* enough, if the rewards the child is missing because of the problem behavior are *strong* enough, and if he can *only* earn those rewards in sessions, this method will eventually work.

PUNISHMENT

There is too much punishment in the world already. Besides, most (maybe all) problem behaviors *can* and *should be* decreased by rewarding good behaviors to replace them. But sometimes a child's problem behaviors, for instance, head-banging, are causing him physical damage and may need to be decreased very fast. And sometimes, in anger, you may feel like punishing the child because his problem behaviors are very upsetting to you. For these reasons we must talk about punishment to show you how to use it right if you are going to use it at all, and to show you what the dangers are.

Punishment usually means that a problem behavior is followed by an *unpleasant consequence* that is strong enough to *quickly stop* the behavior and to keep it from happening very much in the future. For example, head-banging might be followed by a spanking. To be effective, the punishing consequence should:

FOLLOW THE PROBLEM BEHAVIOR EVERY TIME;
FOLLOW THE PROBLEM BEHAVIOR IMMEDIATELY (as soon as
it starts; not when you cannot stand it anymore); and
BE STRONG.

Let us be honest about it. Punishment works because it is unpleasant. The only reason we can see for using punishment is that, in the long run, the child's problem behavior is hurting him and others more than being punished hard a few times will hurt him. So you want to make sure that the punishment (if you are going to use it) works fast. It makes no sense to keep giving the child mild spankings that are not working.

Also, the punishment has to be given *immediately* after the target problem behavior starts. Otherwise, the child will learn that he can keep on with the behavior for a while before he will get punished. Finally, the punishment has to be given *every time*. If you punish the behavior only once in a while (when you cannot stand it any more!), the child will learn that he can safely do it five times or so before you get angry and he should stop.

There are also a few *dangers* to punishment. For example, it is easy for punishment to become a *signal for a reward!* If you punish the child and then hug him to make him feel better, *the problem behavior may increase!* He may start doing his problem behaviors just to get punished, because he is learning that punishment is followed by a reward. Of course you do not want this to happen. So make sure you do not give the child extra attention after you punish him. Wait a few minutes until he calms down by himself.

Second, *punishment seems to work best on behaviors which happen very often and without other people being involved.* For example, punishment works best on head-banging and tantrums which happen many times a day. Punishment does not work well at all on what you might call *misbehavior.* For example, it does not work well on inattention, leaving the table, or tantrums which happen just once in a while. So *it is best to use punishment to decrease problem behaviors which happen many, many times a day and which harm the child too much to wait for another method (like ignoring) to work.*

Third, it has been found that, even if punishment decreases a behavior in one place, the behavior may still happen in *other* places where the child was not punished. In other words, *punishment does not teach the child not to perform the behavior. It just teaches him when and where not to perform it.* So, if punishment is to be used, it has to be used *wherever and whenever the target problem behavior happens.*

Fourth (and this is most important), *punishment works best if the child is being rewarded for other behaviors* that can replace the problem behavior. If there is only one "game in town," that is the one people will play, even if they get punished for it. For this reason you must be teaching and rewarding the child for good behaviors when you use punishment, or else he will keep doing the behavior you are punishing.

THIS RULE APPLIES TO ALL THE OTHER METHODS, TOO.

The last thing we (or you) want is for you to start liking to use punishment. So try the other methods first. And, if you find that they do not work, or if you feel that the child's behavior is hurting him too much to wait for the other methods to work and you decide to use punishment, use it *immediately* after the behavior starts—before you get angry. If you wait until you are angry, you may start liking to use punishment because, for the moment, it will stop the behavior you cannot stand. But in the long run you will be using it more and more, and that is no way to run an educational program.

You can see that punishment is a risky business. There are other methods that may work just as fast as punishment, but that do not carry the risks that punishment does. Let us look at them now.

NEGATIVE PRACTICE

The idea behind *negative practice* is that the child gets so tired of doing the problem behavior that it decreases. Negative practice means prompting the child to do the problem behavior over and over again, very fast, for several sessions a day, until he is so sick of it that he tries to stop you from prompting him to do it. But you keep prompting him anyway for a few more sessions until he is completely sick of the behavior.

One child had been messing up the house for years. He always started by throwing pillows off the couch and worked his way to the bookcases, pictures, and bedspreads. So negative practice was used on pillow-throwing (the first behavior in the chain of messing up the house). For 4 days he had to throw pillows for hours on end. He had to throw them even when he wanted to stop. After that, he did not throw pillows (or mess up the house) any more.

As you can see, negative practice takes time and hard work. And *it does not teach the child what to do instead.* You still have to teach and reward the child for doing an opposite, good behavior. Otherwise, when you stop using negative practice, the child will go right back to the problem behavior. The next method, *positive practice* may work better.

POSITIVE PRACTICE

We talked about *positive practice* in many of the earlier chapters. It means having the child do a chain or part of a chain of good behaviors a few times in a row until he is closer to getting it right. This method can also be used to replace problem behaviors with good behaviors. In fact, positive practice seems to work very well on behaviors which a child may do very often during the day, behaviors which keep him from paying attention and learning.

Foxx and Azrin (1973) used positive practice to replace (1) mouthing of hands and objects; (2) hand-clapping; and (3) head-weaving. *Any time* a child started doing one of these behaviors, he was given a short positive practice session to replace the problem behavior with an opposite, good behavior.

For example, one child was always sticking objects (toys) in her mouth, and another was always putting her hand in her mouth. This is called *mouthing.* The opposite of putting dirty objects or dirty fingers in the mouth is to *clean* the mouth. So *every time* these children started mouthing, they were given a positive practice session on *cleaning.* The teacher said "No" in a firm voice and brushed the children's gums with a toothbrush soaked in an *unpleasant mouthwash.* The teacher prompted them to spit out the solution and then wiped their lips with a washcloth soaked in the same bad-tasting solution. The sessions lasted only *2 minutes*. But every time a child started mouthing, she was given a 2-minute session. How could the children *avoid* having these rather unpleasant sessions? By not putting things in their mouths.

Another child was always moving her head from side to side. This is called *head-weaving*. You can see that if a child does this a lot she will not be able to pay attention and learn good behaviors. What is the opposite of head-weaving? Of course, it is holding the head still and moving it only at the right time, for instance, when instructed to. So, whenever the child started head-weaving, she was given a *5-minute* positive practice session on holding her head still and moving it on command. Every time she started head-weaving, the teacher would use her hands to *restrain* the child's head. Then the teacher would tell the child to move her head in a certain position, for instance, "Head up." If the child did not move her head to the right position, the teacher moved it for her. The child was also required to *hold her head still* in that position for 15 seconds. If she moved it, the teacher again *restrained* her head. Slowly, the teacher faded out holding and moving the child's head. At first, the child did not mind the sessions. So the teacher *increased* the length of the positive practice sessions from 5 minutes to *15 minutes*. Then the child stopped liking the sessions and began to hold her head still to *avoid the sessions*.

Another child spent most of his time clapping his hands. The opposite of hand-clapping is holding the hands still and moving them when it is the right time, for instance when doing small motor activities or when told. So every time the child started clapping his hands he was given a *5-minute* session on keeping his hands still except when told. He was told to move his hands into different positions, one after the other (above the head, straight out in front, in his pockets, held together, and behind his back). And he was supposed to keep them there for 15 seconds. If he did not move his hands when told, the teacher moved them for him. If he did not hold them still for 15 seconds, the teacher held them still. Slowly, the teacher faded out her prompts until the child moved and held his hands still when told.

After these behaviors had been decreased and replaced by using positive practice sessions, the sessions were faded out and a *verbal warning* was given instead. The child was firmly told to *stop* doing the hand-clapping behavior if it happened. If the child did not stop or did the behavior again later that day, more positive practice sessions were given.

You can see how this method can be used on other problem behaviors. If the child messes up the house, *every time* he starts, and *as soon as* he starts, he could be given a 10-minute (or longer) positive practice session on cleaning the house. If he plays with water in the bathroom and splashes water all over, he could be made to clean up all the water, wipe the sink, tub, and toilet, and put the sponge and bucket away. Or, if the child opens a cereal box and pours the cereal all over the floor, you could have him clean up the floor with a broom and dustpan, put all the cereal boxes back in the pantry very neatly, take out the trash with the cereal in it, and put the broom and dustpan away.

In other words, as soon as the child starts a *strange* behavior or a behavior that *messes* things up, he is given a positive practice session *on the opposite* of the problem behavior. And during the session he is made to do the opposite, good behaviors so much or for so long that (1) he learns how to do the good behaviors; and (2) he stops doing the problem behavior so that he does not have to go through any more sessions. Because this method teaches the child good behaviors, and because it works about as fast as punishment, it is probably a better choice than punishment for most behaviors.

SATIATION

Remember what happens to a behavior when the child gets sick of (*satiated on*) the reward? The behavior decreases. You can use the same idea to decrease some problem behaviors. When you use satiation, you reward the child by letting him do the problem behavior. In other words, you can use the problem behavior as an *Activity Reward.*

For example, if the child runs into the bathroom to play in water every chance he gets, you could have him do simple tasks and then let him play in water. *If you reward him with water play many times, day after day, he may get sick of playing in water.* Or, if the child spends a lot of time rocking, you could have the child work in a session for a few minutes or do a simple task, and then (and *only* then) allow the child to rock in her favorite rocking place.

Note that this is Grandma's Law: "As soon as you (work these puzzles) you can rock in your chair." You can handle many problem behaviors this way: the child can do them, but only as a reward for doing a little of a good behavior first.

BEHAVIOR COST

An example of *behavior cost* is getting a fine for running a red light. *Something that we like (a reward) is taken away.* Behavior cost is a kind of punishment. You punish by taking away a reward. There are many ways it can be used. For example, if the child hits his sister, he might be fined five tokens. Or, if he throws a tantrum in the afternoon, he might not be allowed to watch his favorite TV program.

The problem with this method is that the child may try other, just as undesirable, behaviors to get back what you took away. He may whine or fight to get you to turn on the TV. So, *if you use behavior cost, you must be able to control the rewards you are taking away.* Since this is sometimes very hard to do, *it is better to try other methods first,* such as *time out or ignoring (plus rewarding an opposite, good behavior).*

ONE LAST WORD

No method works all by itself. You always have to be teaching the child other, better ways to gain rewards. If you are *ignoring* strange hand movements, you should be rewarding the child for using his hands correctly when he plays, or for at least keeping them in his lap when he does not have anything to do for the moment. If you are ignoring the way he makes messes with his food, you should be rewarding him for eating in a little neater way. If you are *timing him out* for throwing tantrums, you should be rewarding him for cooperating and for spending his time in constructive ways. If you are *punishing* head-banging, you should be rewarding him when he is sitting nicely or using his hands to play and do chores. *Always find an opposite, good behavior to reward— and reward it as often as you can.*

The next section, Section 5, tells you how to set up a program for replacing problem behaviors.

5. SETTING UP A PROGRAM FOR REPLACING PROBLEM BEHAVIORS

Just as you set up teaching programs to increase good target behaviors, such as eye contact or motor imitation, so you have to set up programs for replacing problem behaviors. In this section we will talk about the things to keep in mind when you decide to replace a problem behavior. Here are the questions you must answer.

What Is the Target Problem Behavior?

Just as you *pinpoint* target behaviors to *increase,* so you have to pinpoint target problem behaviors to replace and decrease. You must know exactly which behavior you are going to try to decrease with one or more of the methods we have talked about. For example, do you want to *decrease all* of the strange hand movements the child makes, or just the one he does the most? Reread Section 7 in Chapter 5, "Measuring Behavior," to recall how to *pinpoint* and *define* a target behavior.

How Often Does the Target Problem Behavior Happen?

Before you decide which method to use to replace a target problem behavior you pinpoint, you must take *baseline* counts of how often the behavior happens. This will give you some clues as to the right method to use. For example, *if the behavior happens only once in a while, there may be some special signal that starts it. So you may be able to decrease the behavior by making sure that the signal does not happen. Or you may teach the child something else to do when the signal happens.*

For example, when relatives come to the house, the child may do all kinds of strange things—noises and hand movements—when he is greeting them. In this case, it would be best to teach him a better way to say "Hello" (with *positive practice*).

On the other hand, if the behavior happens fairly often and does not seem to be started by some special signal, the child is probably being rewarded for it, at least once in a while (Intermittent Schedule), and he probably does not know a better way to get rewards. For example, the child may not know how to play, gets bored, starts messing up the cabinets, and finally gets attention.

Once you start a program to replace the target problem behavior, you must keep on *counting* it to see how well your program is working. You can count it in the same way as you would any other behavior—with a note pad and a pencil, a wrist counter, a calendar, or a stopwatch. For example, you might use a stopwatch to measure *how* long it takes before the child falls asleep at night. Sections 8 and 9 of Chapter 5 tell you how to *count* and *chart* behaviors. Keep in mind that, *if the behavior does not decrease very much in a few weeks, you should try another method to decrease it.*

How Long Has the Child Been Doing the Behavior?

This is the third question you should ask yourself before you pick a method to replace a problem behavior. If he has been doing it for a long time, he has probably been *rewarded on an intermittent schedule.*

For example, people might have given him attention for his tantrums every once in a while—when they were in a "bad mood" or were tired. *This means that it will take a long time for the behavior to decrease if you start to ignore it.* The reason is that, if the child has been rewarded only once in a while (Intermittent Schedule), he has never learned just when he will be rewarded. If you start to ignore this behavior now, he will keep trying to get attention anyway for a long time. So, *if he has been doing the behavior for a long time, it may be faster to use time out or positive practice.*

What Controls the Behavior?

We have already talked about the kinds of *signals* and *consequences* that control problem behaviors. It is important to find out just what it is that controls the problem behavior you pinpoint. This will help you to decide which method to use. Here are some rules that will help.

1. *If the behavior is controlled by positive rewards (like attention), you might first try to decrease the behavior by ignoring it.*
2. *If the behavior is controlled by negative rewards (the child uses the behavior to escape or avoid doing things people want him to do), you may be able to decrease the behavior by making your teaching sessions (or whatever it is you want him to do) more rewarding.*
3. *If the behavior seems to be the child's way of spending his time, you may be able to decrease the behavior by teaching him better ways to spend his time (and by ignoring the behavior or using time out, or, better, positive practice, when it does happen).*
4. *If you find out that the behavior usually happens at certain times or places (signals), you must make sure to never, never reward the behavior then or there. Instead, you must teach the child to do something else at those times or places.* For example, if he is always getting into the refrigerator, you should teach him to *ask* for food in front of the refrigerator. Or, if he usually throws tantrums in the supermarket, you should teach him to walk quietly and to put the cans in the shopping cart, rewarding him often.

This leads to the next question you must answer.

How Easily Can You Change What Is Controlling the Behavior?

It is one thing to find out what is controlling the problem behavior. It is another thing to be able to *change* whatever is controlling the behavior.

For example, if *attention* is what is controlling tantrums, you can easily stop giving a child attention when he throws tantrums. But what if *just being in the same room* with him rewards him for tantrums? Then *ignoring* the tantrums will not work. You will have to use a different method, for instance, *time out.*

Or what if the child starts to bite himself whenever an airplane flies over the house (*signal*)? You cannot stop airplanes from flying over your house. So you will have to use a different method, such as rewarding him for standing quietly. Or the child may spend too much time playing in water. You cannot remove water from the house. So you might try *satiation* or *negative practice.*

How Much Does the Behavior Hurt the Child?

Some problem behaviors do not really keep a child from learning good behaviors. For example, strange hand movements or face movements that do not happen too often will not keep him from learning Small Motor skills. They may bother you, but they are not hurting the child's education. So *it is best to just leave these behaviors alone. Ignore them and reward the child for other, good behaviors.* In that way, they will usually decrease without any trouble.

But some behaviors, like head-banging, are very painful for the child. And others, such as constant whining or tantrums, hurt him by keeping him from learning new behaviors. *You have to decide how much the behavior is hurting the child.* If it is hurting him a great deal, it may be best to decrease the behavior fast with *time out, positive practice,* or *punishment,* because *ignoring* the behavior may take too long.

Can the Child Do Other Behaviors?

This is the last question to ask yourself. Remember that you always have to be rewarding the child for other, good behaviors when you are trying to decrease a problem behavior. But how well and how often does he perform other behaviors? If the child does not have much skill at playing, doing chores, or following directions, you must *teach him.* Otherwise, there will not be any other good behaviors to reward.

Once you have answered the above questions, you are ready to start a program to replace the target problem behavior. Remember: *whatever method (consequence) you use (ignoring, positive practice, time out, punishment, behavior cost),* it is important that *the method be used immediately and every time the problem behavior happens.* If the target problem behavior does not decrease very much in about a week, *switch to another method.* And, finally, *always pinpoint other, good behaviors to reward.*

The next section, Section 6, gives you examples of programs parents and teachers have used to replace problem behaviors.

6. HOW OTHER PARENTS AND TEACHERS HAVE REPLACED PROBLEM BEHAVIORS

Many, many people have been using the methods we have talked about in this chapter. Here are some good examples.

Problem Behavior	What Parent or Teacher Did
Billy stays in the car when it pulls into the driveway.	Billy's father used to try to coax Billy out (*attention*). Now he says, "Okay, we are home." Then he just goes into the house (*ignoring*). Soon Billy gets tired of sitting in the hot car and goes into the house.
Sally rolls around in the mud every time her mother gets her nice and clean.	Sally's mother used to clean Sally up when the child got herself all muddy (*attention*). Then Sally's mother *made* Sally *stay* in the mud all day (*negative practice*). And she praised Sally other times when Sally kept herself clean. Now Sally does not roll in the mud.
Pete bites his hand and arms until they bleed.	Pete's parents could not stand to see him bite himself. So they used to hug and talk to him (*attention*). One week they decided to spank him very hard each time he bit himself (*punishment*) and to reward him when he did not bite himself for 10 minutes. In 5 days he did not bite himself any more.

Kim flaps her hands, makes noises, and looks at her fingers many times during teaching sessions.

Her teacher used to tell Kim to stop, but it did not work. Kim smiled when her teacher told her to stop. Now her teacher gives her a 5-minute *positive practice* session every time Kim starts flapping or looking at her hands. Kim must hold her hands still in different positions when her teacher tells her.

John started throwing tantrums during sessions.

At first John's mother used *time out*. It did not work. Then she started *rewarding* John more often and worked on easier tasks. His tantrums decreased.

Ginny whines and cries to get what she wants.

Ginny's father used to give in to her (positive rewards) because he could not stand the whining. Now he walks away as if he does not even hear it. He asks Ginny what she wants when she stops whining, and he gives her what she wants if she asks without whining.

Greg spends much of his time messing up the house by taking things out of closets, pantries, and drawers.

Greg's parents used to run after him to stop him (*attention*). Then they started teaching him to play instead. They also timed him out for 15 minutes every time he started to mess things up.

Jimmy spends half his time trying to get keys to play with.

Jimmy's parents used to let him have keys because they were tired of trying to talk him out of liking them. Then they decided to let him choose between playing with keys and having other Activity Rewards (such as watching TV or going for a ride). At first, Jimmy kept playing with keys. After about a week, though, he started giving up the keys and choosing the other activities.

7. PLANNING A PROGRAM TO REPLACE PROBLEM BEHAVIORS

Before you plan and write a program to replace a problem behavior, turn to the BES or BET to *pinpoint* the target problem behavior. You should have circled behaviors on the child's BET (or listed others on his BES) that need to be replaced and decreased. The best ones to start with are those which hurt the child the most, either physically or by keeping him from learning good behaviors.

Use Table 15-1 to help you plan the program. Write your plan in the spaces. Also, make copies of the blank table for future use. Use your answers to items G16 through G19 on the child's BES to help you pick the best method to use. Remember to count and chart the target problem behavior, using Table 6-3 and Figure 6-2 at the end of Chapter 6. Give the program about a week. If the problem behavior has not started to decrease a good deal in a week, take a hard look at your program. Are you rewarding opposite, good behaviors enough? Are teaching sessions attractive? Are you accidentally rewarding the problem behavior? Revise the program if necessary, and try again.

Table 15-1. Program Plan for Replacing Problem Behaviors

1. *Pinpoint* the target problem behavior for this teaching program. (Give name and number if it is on BET.)

2. *Define* the target problem behavior as *movements*. (Describe it as well as you can.)

3. *How often* does the behavior happen? (If it happens only once in a while, look for some *signal* that starts it off. If it happens many times, look for the *consequences* that may be controlling it. Take a *baseline* to find out how often it happens.)

4. *How long* has the child been doing the behavior? (If he has been doing it for a long time, it might take many days before *ignoring* will decrease it. Other methods, such as *time out* or *positive practice,* might work faster.)

5. What *controls* the behavior? (If the behavior is controlled by *attention,* *ignoring* the behavior may be the best method to try first. If the behavior

Table 15-1 (continued)

is *escape* or *avoidance* behavior—it gets the child out of doing what people want him to do—it would be best to make sessions more rewarding. If the child uses the behavior to *spend his time*, teach him better ways to do this, for example, playing and doing chores.)

6. Can you *change* what is controlling the behavior? (If you cannot remove the rewarding consequence, you might try *satiation, negative practice, or positive practice.*)

7. How much does the behavior *hurt* the child? (If he is causing himself pain or hurting his education, you might not have time to wait for *ignoring* to decrease the behavior. So you might use *time out, punishment, or positive practice.*)

8. Can the child do *other* behaviors? (If the child's skills in other areas are weak, you must teach him other skills so that he will have behaviors that he can be rewarded for doing instead of the problem behavior.)

9. What *consequence* or *method* will you use? (Ignoring? Time Out? Positive Practice? Satiation? Negative Practice? Behavior Cost? Punishment? Read your answers to items G16 through G19 on the BES to help you choose.)

10. *How often* and *where* will you use the method on the behavior?

11. *How, when,* and *where* will you count the behavior?

12. Which method will you *try next* if the first one does not work well enough?

13. Which *good* behaviors will you be rewarding as often as possible to *replace* the problem behavior? (Give their names and numbers if they are on the BET.)

REFERENCES AND EXTRA READINGS

Allen, K. E., and Harris, F. R. "Elimination of a child's excessive scratching by training the mother in reinforcement procedures." *Behaviour Research and Therapy,* 1966, 4, 79-84.

Azrin, N. H., and Holz, W. C. "Punishment." In W. K. Honig (Ed.), *Operant*

Behavior: Areas of Research and Application. New York: Appleton-Century-Crofts, 1966. Pp. 380-447.

Bostow, D. E., and Bailey, J. B. "Modification of severe disruptive and aggressive behavior using brief time out and reinforcement procedures." *Journal of Applied Behavior Analysis*, 1969, **2**, 31-37.

Buchar, B., and Lovaas, O. I. "Use of aversive stimulation in behavior modification." In M. R. Jones (Ed.), *Miami Symposium on the Prediction of Behavior, 1967: Aversive Stimulation*. Coral Gables, Fla.: University of Miami Press, 1968. Pp. 77-145.

Buchar, B., and Lovaas, O. I. "Operant procedures in behavior modification with children." In D. J. Levis (Ed.), *Learning Approaches to Therapeutic Behavior Change*. Chicago: Aldine, 1970. Pp. 36-64.

Carlson, C. S., Arnold, C. R., Becker, W. C., and Madsen, C. H. "The elimination of tantrum behavior of a child in an elementary classroom." *Behaviour Research and Therapy*, 1968. **6**, 117-119.

Church, R. M. "The varied effects of punishment on behavior." *Psychological Review*, 1963, **70**, 369-402.

Dunlap, K. *Habits: Their Making and Unmaking*. New York: Liveright, 1932.

Foxx, R. M., and Azrin, N. H. "The elimination of autistic self-stimulatory behavior by overcorrection." *Journal of Applied Behavior Analysis*, 1973, **6**, 1-14.

Gardner, W. I. "Use of punishment procedures with the severely retarded: A review." *American Journal of Mental Deficiency*, 1969, **74**, 86-103.

Koegel, R. L., and Covert, A. "The relationship of self-stimulation to learning in autistic children." *Journal of Applied Behavior Analysis*, 1972, **5**, 381-387.

Lovaas, O. I., and Simmons, J. Q. "Manipulation of self-destruction in three retarded children." *Journal of Applied Behavior Analysis*, 1969, **2**, 143-159.

Peterson, R. F., and Peterson, L. R. "Mark and his blanket: A study of self-destructive behavior in a retarded boy." Paper presented at a meeting of the Society for Research in Child Development, New York, 1967.

Risley, T. R., and Wolf, M. M. "Establishing functional speech in echolalic children." *Behaviour Research and Therapy*, 1967, **5**, 73-88.

Risley, T. R. "The effects and side effects of punishing the autistic behaviors of a deviant child." *Journal of Applied Behavior Analysis*, 1968, **1**, 21-35.

Sajwaj, T., Twardosz, S., and Burke, M. "Side effects of extinction procedures in a remedial preschool." *Journal of Applied Behavior Analysis*, 1972, **5**, 163-175.

Solomon, R. J. "Punishment." *American Psychologist*, 1964, **19**, 239-253.

Weisen, A. E., and Watson, W. E. "The elimination of attention-seeking behavior in a retarded child." *American Journal of Mental Deficiency*, 1967, **72**, 50-52.

White, G. D., Nielsen, G., and Johnson, S. M. "Time out duration and the suppression of deviant behavior in children." *Journal of Applied Behavior Analysis*, 1972, **5**, 111-120.

Williams, C. D. "The elimination of tantrum behavior by extinction procedures." In L. P. Ullmann and L. Krasner (Eds.), *Case Studies in Behavior Modification*. New York: Holt, Rinehart and Winston, 1966. Pp. 295-296.

Zimmerman, E. H., and Zimmerman, J. "The alteration of behavior in a special classroom situation." In L. P. Ullmann and L. Krasner (Eds.), *Case Studies in Behavior Modification*. New York: Holt, Rinehart and Winston, 1966. Pp. 328-330.

ANSWERS
to REVIEW QUESTIONS
on Chapters TWO,
THREE,
FOUR

CHAPTER 2: HOW PARENTS, TEACHERS, AND CHILDREN TEACH ONE ANOTHER

1. a. A bite of sugar-coated cereal. A *possible* reward. We say "possible" because the only way to tell if the cereal is really a reward is to keep giving it to Jimmy as a "reward" for making eye contact. If eye contact increases, then we can call the cereal a reward.
   b. Jimmy makes eye contact. His eyes "fix" on his mother's.
   c. Increase (as long as sugar-coated cereal is a reward). Behavior that is rewarded increases.
   d. Decrease. Behavior that is no longer rewarded decreases. Mother's behavior is giving food when Jimmy makes eye contact (her signal). If his eye contact does not increase, her food-giving behavior will not be rewarded and may decrease (unless she tries another method for increasing his eye contact).

2. a. Rewarding.

   Sandy whines→ Teacher gives→ Sandy stops→ Rewards teacher
                him what he   whining   for giving him
                wanted (rewards   what he wanted
                whining)

   b. Sandy is whining (see steps in *a* above).
   c. If you answered "Decrease," you are partly right. The teacher is

ignoring whining, but is she rewarding good behavior that can replace whining? Remember what we said in Chapter 1: "We must *replace* 'bad' behaviors with 'good' behaviors." If the teacher ignores Sandy's whining, it may decrease, but if she does not teach him better behaviors he can use, his whining will increase again. She must ignore whining *and* teach him to ask for what he wants.

d. In general, being near someone who has rewarded him for whining, for example, being near the teacher and the things she gives him when he whines for them.

3. a. Reward. The consequence for Mr. Blake when he takes out the trash is supper. The best way to find out if supper is a reward for Mr. Blake is to keep giving him supper after he takes out the trash. If his behavior of taking out the trash increases, then we can say that the supper is probably a reward.

b. To take out the trash (as long as supper is a reward).

c. Decrease. Behavior that is no longer rewarded decreases.

4. a. Billy's mother goes after him, talks to him, and takes him out of the kitchen: attention (a possible reward).

b. He is left alone: no attention, he is ignored. This may mean that playing is not rewarded.

c. Increase (if attention is a reward).

d. Decrease. If attention is a reward for Billy, then playing behavior is not being rewarded and will decrease.

e. When she sees or hears Billy messing up the kitchen.

f. He usually stops for a while. So, when she goes after him and he stops for a while, she is rewarded for going after him.

g. Increase. Behavior (going after Billy) that is rewarded (when he stops making a mess) increases.

5. a. Without talking to him, Billy's mother puts him in his room for 15 minutes. So messing up the kitchen is ignored (she does not talk to him about it). Putting Billy in his room so that he cannot get any rewards for a while is called "time out" (*time out* from any chance of rewards).

b. Decrease. Messing up the kitchen is no longer being rewarded, and, at the same time, playing behavior is being rewarded. So messing up the kitchen will be replaced by playing.

c. His mother goes over to him, talks to him, praises him, and hugs him: attention, possibly a reward.

d. Increase (as long as the consequences in c above are rewards).

e. When she sees or hears Billy starting to mess up the kitchen. This used to be a signal for her to give him attention.

f. When she sees or hears Billy starting to play. This used to be a signal to leave him alone (ignore playing).

g. Increase. If his mother enjoys seeing him play, then when his playing increases she will be rewarded for giving him attention when he plays.

h. It may decrease. If Billy's behavior of messing up the kitchen does not decrease, then his mother's behavior of putting him in his room when he messes up the kitchen (time out) will not be rewarded.

WHEN YOU HAVE ANSWERED THE QUESTIONS FOR CHAPTER 2 CORRECTLY, REWARD YOURSELF. THEN YOU CAN GO ON TO CHAPTER 3.

CHAPTER 3, SECTIONS 1 THROUGH 5: REWARDS

1. Have always been rewards for the person. Primary rewards are "born" rewards.
2. Only as long as a person has not had enough of them.
3. Decrease. Once a person has had enough of (is satiated on) a reward, it is *no longer* a reward. So the behavior is not being rewarded. Behavior that is no longer rewarded will decrease.
4. Followed.
5. *b*: Praise will become a learned reward when it is *followed* by something that is already a reward—going outside.
6. Can. You can become sick of being praised just as you can become sick of your favorite dessert.
7. Do not have value. We have to learn to be rewarded by them.
8. That he can *use* them to *buy* other rewards. Or that they are *followed* by things that are already rewards.
9. It is hard. If you become satiated on whatever you are buying with your General Reward, you can start to buy something else that you are not satiated on.
10. Reward him over and over for learning to do it.
11. There are four Grandma's Laws that can be made:
"As soon as you eat your spinach, you can go for a walk."
"As soon as you eat your spinach, you can eat your cherry pie."
"As soon as you do your chore, you can go for a walk."
"As soon as you do your chore, you can eat your cherry pie."
Note that the *high* behavior *follows* the *low* behavior.

12. A *lot* of a *high* behavior is supposed to follow a *little* of a *low* behavior.
13. As soon as Jimmy does a little of some *low* behavior, he can do a lot of reading. For example, as soon as he washes his face (*low* behavior), he can read (*high* behavior).
14. Control or have an effect on the scene around you.
15. Rewards.

WHEN YOU HAVE ANSWERED ALL THE QUESTIONS CORRECTLY, GIVE YOURSELF A NICE BREAK. THEN YOU CAN GO ON TO THE NEXT SECTIONS OF CHAPTER 3.

CHAPTER 3, SECTIONS 6 THROUGH 9: REWARDS

1. *a.* Strong reward, possibly a *Primary* Reward.
   b. Every time it happens.
2. Make sure that the child has not yet had enough of it. Also, make sure that the child does not get the reward for nothing. This does not mean that you starve the child. It simply means that he gets the reward only for a certain behavior. In other words, he does not get it for free.
3. Every time it happens.
4. *a.* Continuous Schedules of rewards and Primary Rewards are *unnatural.* Very few behaviors are rewarded this way in daily life. As long as the child's behavior gets Primary Rewards on a Continuous Schedule, his behavior is not "normal," even if it looks the same as anyone else's behavior. To be "normal," a behavior must *look* normal *and* be rewarded with usual (natural) rewards on a natural schedule.
   b. The child will become *satiated* quickly on Primary Rewards if a Continuous Schedule is used. The behavior will decrease. An Intermittent Schedule (in which the behavior is rewarded less often) will help to prevent satiation.
   c. When you are keeping three or four old behaviors going and trying to teach a new one at the same time, you will not have enough eyes and hands to see and reward all the behaviors every time they happen (Continuous Schedule).
5. Once in a while.
6. *a.* Times.
   b. Time.
   c. Stays the same after each reward.
   d. Changes after each reward.

7. Can figure out, because it is always the same.
8. Goes down after the reward and then up again as the reward gets closer. How do you feel and how hard do you work on Monday?
9. Cannot figure out, because it is never exactly the same.
10. Is steady, because the reward can come at any time.
11. Changing Schedules. They produce steadier behavior.
12. Has leveled off. If you cut down on the rewards when the behavior is increasing (is not strong yet), or when the behavior is decreasing (is getting weaker), it may decrease. Wait until it is strong (has increased and leveled off).
13. Slowly. If you cut down on the rewards too fast, many of the child's behaviors will be ignored. Behavior that is no longer rewarded decreases. If you cut down on rewards slowly, the child will hardly know the difference and his behavior will stay strong.
14. Getting an apple. How would you like it if you were cold and asked someone for his extra coat, and he said, "Good asking" but did not give you a coat?
15. Use his eye contact as a signal to go over to him or talk to him. In daily life, eye contact is often used as a signal that we want to make some kind of contact with another person. By going over to the child or talking to him, you are teaching him to use his eye contact in a natural way.
16. Natural or Activity Rewards. Of course, other kinds of rewards can also be used in Grandma's Law, for example, "As soon as you wash your face, you can eat supper" (Primary Reward). The point is that there are many *Activity* Rewards that can be used as *natural* rewards for behavior.
17. Closer. For example, you get out of bed, wash your face, get dressed, and eat breakfast (Primary Reward). Breakfast rewards *all* of the behaviors in the chain.
18. 1. Child makes eye contact with mother (natural signal to get her attention while he asks her).
    2. Child asks for ice cream cone.
    3. Child gets ice cream cone.

    1. Child sits and watches teacher (natural signal for her to notice and call on him).
    2. Child answers question.
    3. Child is given a token (reward for answering question, sitting, and paying attention).
19. What things are rewarding to the child.

WHEN YOU HAVE ANSWERED THE QUESTIONS CORRECTLY, REWARD YOURSELF. THEN GO BACK TO CHAPTER 3 FOR YOUR LAST WRITTEN ASSIGNMENT.

**CHAPTER 4, SECTION 4, STEPS 2, 3, AND 9 IN PLANNING AN
EDUCATIONAL PROGRAM**

1. First Skill Area to Work On: Learning Readiness Skills   (A)
   The child's BET says that he needs help on Cooperation with Simple
   Spoken Requests   (A4). The Table of Basic Behaviors (Table 4-2)
   says that this is a *basic behavior* for *all* the other skill areas farther
   down the skill sequence. So we must start with this behavior. It is in
   the Learning Readiness area.
2. First and Second Target Behaviors to Work on in Each Skill Area
   A.   Learning Readiness Skills
        First: Cooperates with Simple Spoken Requests   (A4)
        Second: Smiles at Others   (A7)
   B.   Looking, Listening, and Moving Skills
        First: Hops on One Foot   (B9)
        Second: Catches Ball   (B11)
   C.   Motor Imitation Skills
        First: Imitates Object Placements   (C3)
        Second: Plays Imitation Games   (C5)
   D.   Verbal Imitation Skills
        First: Imitates Phrases and Simple Sentences   (D10)
        Second: Imitates Verbal Models of Many People   (D11)
   E.   Functional Speech Skills
        First: Identifies and Describes   (E3)
        Second: Uses Phrases and Simple Sentences to Name, Ask, De-
               scribe, Answer Questions   (E6)
   F.   Chores and Self-Help Skills
        First: Does More Complex Tasks and Chores on His Own,
               Often   (F2)
        Second: Brushes His Teeth   (F7)
   G.   Problem Behaviors
        First: Throws Tantrums   (G3)
        Second: Hits, Bites, Kicks Others   (G4)

   The target behavior to work on first in each skill area was a behavior
that (1) the child needed help with (it was *circled* on the BET); and
(2) was *closest* to the *top* of the list for the skill area on the BET. The
target behavior to work on second was the *next* one down on the list on
the BET that the child needed help with. If you did not agree with an
answer, check Section 4 of Chapter 4. Then *go on to Part Two of the
assignment for Chapter 4.*

BEHAVIOR
EVALUATION
SCALE (BES)

INTRODUCTION

How Is the Behavior Evaluation Scale Put Together?

The Behavior Evaluation Scale (BES) has six *skill areas* of "good" behaviors to increase, teach the child to do better, or teach the child to do at the right time and place. Those skill areas are Learning Readiness; Looking, Listening, and Moving; Motor Imitation; Verbal Imitation; Functional Speech; and Chores and Self-Help skills. The behaviors in each area are listed from *easy to hard*, the way most children learn them. So, by following the list, a child's education will be a "normal" educational sequence. The Behavior Evaluation Scale also has an area for problem behaviors that may need to be replaced and decreased.

Each *skill area* has certain *basic behaviors*. They are the most important behaviors in a skill area and are the ones you are shooting for. The reason they are so important is that, if a child does not learn the basic behaviors in one skill area (say, Learning Readiness), he may never learn behaviors in harder skill areas (say, Functional Speech). Table 4-2 in Chapter 4 lists all the basic behaviors a child must learn *before* he can start in any of the skill areas.

Each skill area has a letter. For example, Learning Readiness is "A," and Looking, Listening, and Moving is "B." So the behaviors listed in the Learning Readiness area are numbered "A1," "A2," "A3," and so on, *starting with the easiest behavior* (A1) *and moving to the harder ones*

(A5, A7). The *basic* (most important) *behaviors* in each skill area have asterisks (**) in front of them and are written in CAPITAL LETTERS.

What Can the Behavior Evaluation Scale Do?

The Behavior Evaluation Scale will help you to plan a child's educational program. By answering the questions in the BES you will find out (1) *which* behaviors the child needs help with; and (2) *what kind* of help he needs (Does the behavior need to be increased? Done with more skill? Decreased? Done at the right time and place? Done with more people?). So the BES will tell you which behaviors to *start* with, which behaviors to move to *next*, and *what kind* of help the child needs with any behavior.

How Do I Use the BES to Plan a Child's Education?

First of all, after you have answered the questions in a skill area, go back and put a *circle* around the number of each and every item that the child needs help with. *Reward yourself* for doing a good job. When you have finished the whole BES, you will have many items circled, probably too many to remember. To help you to see just which behaviors the child needs help with in each Skill Area, we have a Behavior Evaluation Table. It is right after the BES, in Appendix 3. Take a look at it now. The Behavior Evaluation Table (BET) is a list of all the behaviors in each skill area of the BES. So, when you finish filling out the BES, turn to the BET. Then *take all the items you circled on the BES and circle them also on the BET*. For instance, if you circled item A1 on the BES, circle it on the BET. From then on, you will be able to see at a glance which behaviors to work on in each skill area. As you will learn from reading Chapter 4, the Skill Sequence Table (Table 4-1) tells you which skill areas to start with and which ones to move to next in the child's education.

How Do I Fill Out the Behavior Evaluation Scale?

The next sections of the Behavior Evaluation Scale have a number of items about children's behaviors. Under each item there will be a few statements or questions about the behavior in that item. These statements will be called *a, b, c,* and *d.* Read each item carefully and then put a small circle around the statements (or the statement) which best describe how the child does the behavior in that item. For example:

(B2)   The child's balance when walking or climbing is (circle one):
    a.   Better than average.
    b.   About average.
    ⓒ   Below average or clumsy.
Since the child's balance is "Below average or clumsy," he needs help
with this item, so B2 should be circled.

However, some of the *a*, *b*, and *c* statements or questions you will be
circling also have a few more choices for you to make. When an item
is followed by several *a*, *b*, and *c* statements, and each statement has several more choices after it, *put a circle* around the *a*, *b*, and *c* statements
which apply to the child's behavior *and underline* the extra choices in
parentheses which best apply to the statements you have circled. For
example, here is a *basic behavior* in the Learning Readiness area:

**(A1)   THE CHILD MAKES EYE CONTACT (LOOKS AT PEO-
        PLE'S EYES) *ON HIS OWN.* We call this SPONTANEOUS
        EYE CONTACT. (Circle as many as apply, and underline.)
        ⓐ   Child (often; sometimes; <u>rarely</u>; never) does this.
        ⓑ   Child holds his gaze for 5 seconds or so (often; once in a
            while; <u>makes eye contact for only a second</u>; does not make
            eye contact).
        ⓒ   Child (<u>often</u>; sometimes; rarely; never) "avoids" looking at
            a person's eyes by looking out of the corner of his eyes,
            looking away, or covering his eyes.
        ⓓ   Child (often; <u>sometimes</u>; rarely; never) seems to be "lost
            in thought" or not to notice or care that people are there.
        ⓔ   Child makes eye contact (anywhere and with anyone; in
            most places and with most people; <u>only in certain places
            or with certain people</u>; does not make eye contact yet).

Does the child need help with this item—A1? Yes, he does. In fact, he
needs help with all of the *a*, *b*, *c*, *d*, and *e* statements in the item. He
rarely makes eye contact; he holds his gaze for only a second; he often
avoids making eye contact; he sometimes seems to be "lost in thought";
and he makes eye contact only in certain places or with certain people.
(These statements were underlined in the parentheses.) So item A1
should be circled. *But an item should be circled even if the child needs
help with only one or two of the a, b, c, statements.* If the child's only
problem is that he sometimes seems to be "lost in thought," the item
should still be circled.

As much as possible, try to watch the child while he does the behavior
in an item before you answer the questions in the item. You may be able
to give the child a simple test to see how he does on some items. For

example, to see how well he picks up small objects (item B16), you might put a raisin in front of him on the table and watch how he picks it up. In other words, if necessary, spend a week watching and testing the child while you fill out the BES. For some items, though, you may have to use your memory or ask other people (parents, teachers) who have seen the child for a long time. A good rule to follow if you are not able to see a certain behavior for yourself, or if you have *any* doubt about whether or not the child needs help on it, is to *circle the item anyway—* as though he needed help. *Do not give the child the benefit of the doubt.* You can always teach another behavior if you find that the child really does not need help on an item you circled.

A. LEARNING READINESS SKILLS

By "Learning Readiness skills," we mean the skills which a child *must* have before he will learn anything in a teaching setting. Children who do not talk yet, imitate, or do chores or self-help tasks, and have many problem behaviors, are going to need help on Learning Readiness skills before anything else. Even children who can talk, play, and do chores may need help on some of the behaviors in this area, such as cooperating with simple requests.

The *basic behaviors* for the child to learn is this area are as follows:

SPONTANEOUS EYE CONTACT   (A1).
EYE CONTACT ON REQUEST   (A2).
COOPERATION with Simple Spoken Requests   (A4).
SITTING Long Enough to be Rewarded for Working at Simple Tasks (A5).

The behavior items in the following list start with the ones that are easiest for most children.

**(A1)   THE CHILD MAKES EYE CONTACT (LOOKS AT PEO-PLE'S EYES) *ON HIS OWN.* We call this SPONTANEOUS EYE CONTACT. (Circle as many as apply, and underline.)
  a. Child (often; sometimes; rarely; never) does this.
  b. Child holds his gaze for 5 seconds or so (often; once in a while; only makes eye contact for a second; does not make eye contact).
  c. Child (often; sometimes; rarely; never) "avoids" looking at a person's eyes by looking out of the corner of his eyes, looking away, or covering his eyes.

d. Child (often; sometimes; rarely; never) seems to be "lost in thought" or not to notice or care that people are there.

e. Child makes eye contact (anywhere and with anyone; in most places and with most people; only in certain places or with certain people; does not make eye contact yet).

(Pages 190 to 194 in Chapter 9 tell you how to teach the above behavior.)

**(A2)   THE CHILD MAKES EYE CONTACT (LOOKS AT PEOPLE'S EYES) when HE IS ASKED TO. We call this EYE CONTACT *ON REQUEST*. (Circle as many as apply, and underline.)

a. Child (often; sometimes; rarely; never) does this.

b. When asked to make eye contact ("Billy, look at me") the child usually (makes eye contact; turns his head away; covers his eyes; only looks out of the corner of his eye; seems not to hear or care). (Underline as many as apply.)

c. Child makes eye contact on request (anywhere and with anyone; in most places or with most people; only in certain places or with certain people; does not make eye contact yet).

(Pages 194 to 196 in Chapter 9 tell you how to teach the above behavior.)

(A3)   The child stops what he is doing, or turns around, or looks at the person who calls his name or tells him to do something. (Circle one.)

a. Child often or usually does this.

b. Child sometimes does this, but most of the time he seems not to hear or to be lost in thought.

c. Child rarely or never does this; almost always seems not to hear, not to care, or to be lost in thought.

**(A4)   THE CHILD *COOPERATES* WITH (FOLLOWS) *SIMPLE* SPOKEN REQUESTS, FOR EXAMPLE, TO CLOSE THE DOOR, HANG UP HIS COAT, SIT DOWN, PUT A PLATE ON THE TABLE. (Circle as many as apply, and underline.)

a. Child (often; sometimes; rarely; never) cooperates with simple spoken requests.

b. When child cooperates, it is usually with (a spoken request *all by itself*; a spoken request but only in *certain places*; a spoken request but only if *extra gestures*—body movements—are used to tell him what is wanted).

c. When child does not cooperate, it is usually because (he seems not to hear or to *notice* the request; he hears but does not seem to *understand* the request; he seems to want to *tease* by not doing it). (Underline as many as apply.)

    d. When child cooperates it is with (just about anyone; most people; only with certain people).

(Pages 197 to 198 in Chapter 9 tell you how to teach the above behavior.)

** (A5) THE CHILD SITS DOWN WITH PARENT OR TEACHER LONG ENOUGH TO EARN REWARDS BY WORKING AT SOME TASK (NO MATTER HOW SIMPLE). (Circle as many as apply, and underline.)

    a. Child (often; sometimes; rarely; never) sits down with someone to work at a task.

    b. If child will sit and work with someone, he *usually* will do it (on his *own*; only when he is *asked*; only when he is *made* to sit down).

    c. If child will sit and work with someone, he will stay sitting without being *forced* (for 30 minutes or more; for 15 to 30 minutes; for 5 to 15 minutes; for less than 5 minutes) before he becomes restless and tries to get up.

    d. Child will sit and work with (almost anyone; most people; only certain people; does not sit and work).

(Pages 199 to 203 in Chapter 9 tell you how to teach the above behavior.)

  (A6) The child comes over to (approaches) people. (Circle as many as apply, and underline.)

    a. Child (often; sometimes; rarely; never) does this *on his own.*

    b. If child comes to a person *on his own,* the reason is that (he wants the person to do something for him; he wants some loving; he wants to talk, play, or do something with the person). (Underline as many as apply.)

    c. Child (often; sometimes; rarely; never) does this when he is *asked to* (on request).

    d. Child comes over to (just about anyone; most people; only certain people; does not come to people yet).

The next two items will help you to find out if different things are rewards for the child, that is, if they will increase his behaviors.

  (A7) The child *smiles* at others. (Circle as many as apply, and underline.)

    a. Child smiles at others (often; sometimes; rarely; never) when he is *greeted* (for instance, "Hello, Billy. How are you today?").

b.   Child smiles at others (often; sometimes; rarely; never) when he is hugged or cuddled.

c.   Child smiles at others (often; sometimes; rarely; never) when he is being praised (for instance, "Oh, you did that so well!").

d.   Child smiles at others (often; sometimes; rarely; never) when he is annoying them or has made them angry.

(A8)   What does the child do when he is *praised* or *hugged* (possible Social Rewards) for something good he has just done? (Circle as many as apply, and underline.)

a.   He (often; sometimes; rarely; never) shows that he likes it by smiling, laughing, or hugging you back.

b.   He (often; sometimes; rarely; never) *repeats* doing what it was that you praised or hugged him for doing.

Note that, if praise and hugging *are not* Social Rewards for the child, you must make them learned rewards by praising and hugging him *just before* you give him something that is *already* a reward for him (see Chapter 3, Section 4).

Now that you have finished the items in the Learning Readiness skills area, take a break. When you come back, put a *circle* around the number of each item the child needs help with. Chapter 9 tells you how to teach the Basic Behaviors in this area.

B. LOOKING, LISTENING, AND MOVING SKILLS

The behaviors learned in this skill area will help the child in many ways. First, the *Large* and *Small Motor* skills he learns will give him more control of his body and will give him ways to spend his time constructively. Second, if you look at Table 4-2 you will see that *basic behaviors* from this area are needed before the child can work in harder skill areas like Motor Imitation, Verbal Imitation, Functional Speech, and Chores and Self-Help skills.

The *basic* (most important) *behaviors* to learn in this skill area are as follows:

SKILL at Many LARGE MOTOR ACTIVITIES; SPENDS MUCH TIME at Them   (B13).

LOOKING AT OBJECTS, Parts of the Body, Face, Mouth   (B14).

SKILL at Many SMALL MOTOR ACTIVITIES; SPENDS MUCH TIME at Them   (B21).

GOOD WORK HABITS, Such as Sitting, Listening, and Working at a Task   (B22).

POINTING or MATCHING by Name   (B23).

USING EYE CONTACT to Get NATURAL REWARDS   (B24).

The first section of this skill area is about *Large Motor activities* that the child can learn. Large Motor activities are those in which the child uses the large muscles and muscle groups in his arms, back, chest, legs, and belly. The following are examples of Large Motor activities that can be worked on. They are listed starting with the ones that are easiest for most children.

(B1)   The child can bend over and return to a standing position. (Circle one.)
    a.   Child does this without help (prompting).
    b.   Child does not do this well without help or is somewhat clumsy.

(B2)   The child's balance when walking or climbing is (circle one):
    a.   Better than average.
    b.   About average.
    c.   Below average or clumsy.

(B3)   The child can walk backwards. (Circle one.)
    a.   Child does this well by himself.
    b.   Child needs some help in doing this.
    c.   Child does not do this without a lot of help.

(B4)   The child can kick a ball forward. (Circle one.)
    a.   Child does this easily without help.
    b.   Child needs some help in doing this.
    c.   Child does not do this without a lot of help.

(B5)   The child throws a ball overhand. (Circle one.)
    a.   Child does this easily without help.
    b.   Child needs some help in doing this.
    c.   Child needs a lot of help to do this.

(B6)   The child jumps in place with both feet leaving the floor at once. (Circle one.)
    a.   Child does this easily without help.
    b.   Child attempts to jump, but is clumsy or does not get both feet off the ground at once.
    c.   Child does not or will not jump.

(B7)   The child balances on one foot for about 5 seconds. (Circle one.)

   a. Child does this without support.

   b. Child can balance on one foot, but for less than 5 seconds.

   c. Child needs support to balance on one foot.

 (B8) The child broad-jumps at least 8 inches with both feet at once. (Circle one.)

   a. Child does this without help.

   b. Child needs help in doing this but tries.

   c. Child does not or will not broad-jump even if you try to help.

 (B9) The child hops on one foot. (Circle one.)

   a. Child does this without help.

   b. Child needs help in doing this but tries.

   c. Child does not or will not do this even if you try to help.

 (B10) The child walks about eight steps by placing the heel of one foot in front of the toe of the other foot (like a tightrope walker). (Circle one.)

   a. Child does this without help.

   b. Child needs help in doing this but tries.

   c. Child does not or will not do this even if you try to help.

 (B11) The child catches a ball bounced to him from 3 feet away. (Circle one.)

   a. Child does this without help.

   b. Child needs help but tries.

   c. Child does not do this or try to do this even if you try to to help him.

 (B12) The child pedals a tricycle. (Circle as many as apply, and underline.)

   a. Child does this easily without help.

   b. Child needs some help but tries.

   c. Child does not do this or try to do this even if you try to help him.

   d. If child pedals a tricycle, he (spends a "normal" amount of time doing it; does it once in a while; rarely or never does it).

Now that you have seen the kinds of *Large Motor* activities that you can work on, and the amount of help the child needs with them, rate the child on the following *basic behavior.*

**(B13) THE CHILD HAS SKILL AT *MANY* LARGE MOTOR ACTIVITIES AND *SPENDS* MUCH OF HIS TIME AT THEM. (Circle as many as apply, and underline.)

   a. Child (has a great deal of coordination; has average co-ordination; is a bit clumsy; is very clumsy) at Large Motor activities.

   b. Child spends much of his time—several hours a day; some time—an hour or so—but not enough; a little time—maybe a half hour; almost no time) at proper Large Motor activities, such as pedaling a tricycle, playing on swings, playing catch.

   c. When you try to teach the child or get him to do Large Motor activities he usually (cooperates, pays attention, and tries; makes a half-hearted try and pays some attention; mostly ignores you; puts up a fuss).

   d. Child will use or learn Large Motor skills with (just about anyone; most anyone; only certain people; no one yet).

Note that the answer to *a* tells you how much *skill* the child has; *b* tells you how much to *increase* the behavior; *c* tells you if the child still needs to learn the basic *learning readiness skills* first; and *d* tells you if you must teach the child to work with others. Pages 209 to 211 of Chapter 10 tell you how to teach these Large Motor activities.

The next section in this skill area is about *Small Motor* activities that the child should become skilled at. These are activities in which the child uses the smaller muscles and muscle groups in his wrists, hands, and fingers, and carefully uses his eyes at the same time to see what he is doing. These are also activities that may be done at a table.

The first item is a *basic behavior* for this skill area.

**(B14) THE CHILD LOOKS AT OBJECTS, PARTS OF YOUR BODY (ARMS, HANDS), FACE, AND MOUTH WHEN YOU TELL HIM TO LOOK OR WHEN YOU POINT TO THEM. (Circle as many as apply, and underline.)

   a. Child does this (often; sometimes; rarely; never).

   b. Child needs (no prompting; a little prompting; a great deal of prompting) to get him to look at something.

   c. Child needs to look at (objects; parts of the body; eyes; mouth) more than he does. (Underline as many as apply.)

   d. When asked to look at something ("Tommy, look at my mouth"), the child usually (looks at it; turns his head away; covers his eyes; only looks out of the corner of his eye; seems not to hear or care).

    e. Child will usually look at things (with just about anyone; with most people; with only certain people; does not look at objects).

If the child needs help with this behavior, it will be important to increase his looking at things very early in his education. Pages 212 to 213 in Chapter Ten, "Looking, Listening, and Moving," tell you how.

The following items are examples of Small Motor activities you can work on with the child. They begin with the easiest ones.

(B15) The child moves objects from one hand to the other. (Circle one.)

    a. Child does this without the help of his mouth, his body, or the table.

    b. Child does this, but often with the help of his mouth, his body, or the table.

    c. Child does not move or rarely moves objects from one hand to the other.

(B16) The child picks up small objects (for instance, raisins or nuts) using the tip of his thumb and index finger from above. (Circle one.)

    a. Child usually picks up small objects in this way.

    b. Child picks up small objects rather awkwardly (for instance, by raking them).

    c. Child rarely or never tries to pick up small objects.

If you circled *b* or *c* in the above two items, the child may need a good deal of work with Small Motor skills. It would be best to start with very simple movements and tasks, such as picking up objects (for example, blocks, simple puzzles) and moving them to a certain place.

(B17) The child stacks blocks (or other small objects) either on his own or if asked, without help or physical prompting. (Circle one.)

    a. Child can build a tower of five to eight blocks without help.

    b. Child can build a tower of three to four blocks without help.

    c. Child can build a tower of two blocks without help.

    d. Child builds towers, but only if helped.

    e. Child rarely or never stacks blocks on his own. If helped or asked to do so, he fusses or does not pay much attention.

(B18) The child works simple puzzles (in which each piece is apart from the rest). (Circle one.)

    a. Child does this without help, seems interested, and looks at what he is doing.

    b. Child does this without help, but for only a short time; soon loses interest.

    c. Child tries to work puzzles and seems interested, but needs help.

    d. Child rarely or never works simple puzzles on his own. He fusses or is uninterested when you try to help or get him to work puzzles.

(B19) When you tell the child, "Make marks up and down *as I do*," the child imitates drawing a vertical line of more than 2 inches fairly well and without help. (Circle as many as apply.)

    a. Child does this.

    b. Child does this only if given help at the start (for instance, nudging his hand).

    c. Even if the child is helped, his line is awkward.

    d. Child rarely or never imitates drawing a vertical line and does not pay much attention when you tell him to make marks or when you help him.

(Chapter 11, "Motor Imitation," tells you how to teach this behavior.)

(B20) When you draw a circle for the child to see, give him a pencil and paper, and ask him to draw one like the one on the paper, he draws a closed figure that looks like a circle. (Circle one.)

    a. Child does this without help.

    b. Child needs a great deal of help in copying a circle, but he tries.

    c. Child seems uninterested or fusses when you tell him to copy the circle or try to help him.

(Chapter 11, "Motor Imitation," tells you how to teach this behavior.)

Now that you have looked at the child's skills at some Small Motor activities, rate the child on the *basic behavior* below.

**(B21) THE CHILD HAS SKILL AT *MANY* SMALL MOTOR AC-TIVITIES AND *SPENDS* A GOOD PART OF HIS TIME AT THEM. (Circle as many as apply, and underline.)

    a. Child (has a great deal of coordination; has average co-ordination; is a bit clumsy; is very clumsy) at Small Motor activities.

    b. Child spends (a good part of his time—several hours a day; some time—an hour or so—but not enough; a little time—maybe a half hour; almost no time) at proper Small

Motor activities, such as working puzzles, coloring, using toys or other objects to build things.

c. Child usually (cooperates and pays attention; makes a half-hearted try; often ignores you; puts up a fuss) when you try to teach him or get him to do Small Motor activities.

d. Child will usually do or learn small motor tasks with (just about anyone; most people; only certain people; no one as yet).

(Pages 213 to 217 of Chapter 10 tell you how to help the child with this basic behavior.)

On the basis of what you know of the child's Large and Small Motor skills and how he behaves when people try to teach him, rate him on the following few items, which are *basic behaviors* for this skill area.

**(B22) THE CHILD HAS *GOOD WORK HABITS* SUCH AS SITTING, LISTENING, AND WORKING AT A TASK, LESSON, OR ACTIVITY. (Circle as many as apply, and underline.)

a. Child will sit for a task, lesson, or activity without being forced (for 30 minutes or more; for 15 to 30 minutes; for 5 to 15 minutes; for less than 5 minutes) before he becomes restless and tries to get up.

b. While he is working at a task (for example, puzzles), the child (pays attention rather steadily; drifts off sometimes; drifts off a great deal; will not sit and work at a task).

c. Child (usually; sometimes; rarely; never) looks closely at what he is doing when he is working at some task.

d. Child (usually; sometimes; rarely; never) listens to directions.

e. Child has good work habits when working with (just about anyone; most people; only certain people; has no good work habits as yet).

If the child does not sit and work for at least 15 minutes, work steadily, and look at what he is doing, you will need to increase these behaviors, using pages 199 to 203 in Chapter 9 and pages 217 to 219 in Chapter 10. You should also teach the child to work with many people.

**(B23) THE CHILD IS LEARNING THE *NAMES* FOR THINGS. EVEN IF HE CANNOT SAY THE NAMES, HE CAN POINT TO THE OBJECTS OR MATCH THEM WHEN THEY

ARE NAMED. For example, if you show him a toy car and a toy dog and say, "Point to the dog," he will do it. And he will pick up a blue block when there are blue and red blocks on the table, and you say, "Pick up the blue one." (Circle as many as apply, and underline.)

a. Child can point to or match (more than thirty; twenty to thirty; ten to twenty; a few; no) things in this way.

b. Child needs (no prompting; a little prompting; a great deal of prompting) to point to or match things correctly.

c. When asked to point to or match something, the child usually (does it correctly; tries but makes some errors; makes so many errors you think he is faking or teasing; looks away or does not really try).

(Pages 219 to 221 in Chapter 10 tell you how to teach this behavior.)

The items in this section have to do with *Social Skills* the child will need to live and learn with others.

(B24)   THE CHILD MAKES EYE CONTACT IN ORDER TO GET NATURAL REWARDS. For instance, he will make eye contact as a signal for you to give him attention, to open the door, hand him a piece of a puzzle he is working, or get him a cookie. (Circle as many as apply, and underline.)

a. Child does this (often; sometimes; rarely; never).

b. Child needs (no prompting; a little prompting; a great deal of prompting) to get him to make eye contact before he is given natural rewards he wants.

c. Instead of making eye contact as a signal to get people to do things, the child (gets things he wants himself; pulls and pushes; whines or throws tantrums; covers his head; looks out of the corner of his eye; looks away). (Underline as many as apply.)

d. Child makes eye contact to get things from (just about anyone; most people; only certain people; no one yet).

Note that, once you have increased *spontaneous eye contact* and *eye contact on request* (Learning Readiness skills), you can begin to *require eye contact* before the child gets the natural rewards he wants. You should also teach the child to make eye contact with many people. Pages 221 to 222 in Chapter 10 "Looking, Listening, and Moving," tell you how.

(B25)   The child plays with or joins in activities with others (for instance, hide-and-seek or tag). This does not include fighting or simply playing near others. (Circle as many as apply, and underline.)

a. Child often joins in on his own without having to be asked.

b. Child joins in but usually only when he is asked to or helped.

c. Child rarely joins in and may fuss or ignore you when you try to get him to do so.

d. Child (plays with others; only plays near others; plays only by himself).

(B26)   The child works at or cooperates on a task with other children. For example, he helps to work a puzzle or put together a toy farm set. (Circle as many as apply, and underline.)

a. Child (often does this; sometimes does this; usually plays by himself; never does this).

b. Child needs (no prompting; a little prompting; a great deal of prompting) to do this.

c. Child cooperates on a task with (almost any child; most children; only certain children; does not cooperate on tasks yet).

(B27)   The child takes or waits his turn in activities. (Circle one.)

a. Child usually does this on his own.

b. Child will take or wait his turn but usually must be physically or verbally prompted.

c. Child does not pay much attention to waiting or taking his turn even if he is asked or prompted.

GOOD JOB. REWARD YOURSELF. When you come back, draw a circle around the number of EACH AND EVERY item in this skill area that the child needs help with.

C. MOTOR IMITATION SKILLS

Imitation is a skill that helps a child to learn many new behaviors fast. He learns by watching and then doing. By teaching the child to imitate, you can help him (1) to learn the harder Large and Small Motor activities listed earlier; (2) to learn the Chores and Self-Help tasks we will talk about later; and (3) to say sounds, words, and phrases (Verbal

Imitation). As you can see, Motor Imitation is very important to the child's education.

When a child imitates you, he is doing three things: (1) *watching* you show some *model* (for example, clapping hands together); *trying* to imitate or *repeat* the model right after you show it; and (3) getting *better* and better at imitating the model, that is, matching it. Answers to the following items will help you to find out what kinds of models the child can and cannot imitate and which part of imitation (watching, trying, getting better at imitating) he needs help with.

The *basic behaviors* in this skill area are as follows:

Imitating LARGE MOTOR MODELS   (C1).
Imitating SMALL MOTOR MODELS   (C2).
Imitating OBJECT PLACEMENTS   (C3).
Imitating MOUTH MOVEMENTS and POSITIONS   (C4).
Imitating Some Models EVEN IF NOT REWARDED   (C7).
Imitating Motor Models of MANY PEOPLE   (C10).

Before you go on, check Table 4-2 in Chapter 4. Notice which *basic behaviors* the child needs before he can work in this area. Behaviors such as Spontaneous Eye Contact   (A1), Eye Contact on Request   (A2), Cooperation   (A4), and Looking, Listening, and Moving skills   (B13, B14, B21, B22, and B24) are *musts*.

The first six items are about different kinds of models the child can learn to imitate.

** (C1)   THE CHILD CORRECTLY IMITATES (REPEATS) SIMPLE *LARGE* MOTOR MOVEMENTS (MODELS) SHOWN TO HIM, such as holding arms over his head, jumping, bending over, or swinging his leg (may be prompted by saying, "Do this"). (Circle as many as apply, and underline.)

   a. How many simple Large Motor models can the child correctly imitate? (just about any; more than ten; between five and ten; between one and five; none)

   b. Child (usually; sometimes; rarely; never) tries to imitate simple Large Motor movements.

   c. Child usually needs (no prompting; a little prompting; a great deal of prompting) to repeat the movements (models) he is shown.

   d. Child usually (cooperates and pays attention; makes a half-hearted try; ignores you; puts up a fuss) when you try to get him to imitate.

(Pages 228 to 232 in Chapter 11 tell you how to teach this behavior.)

** (C2)   THE CHILD CORRECTLY IMITATES (REPEATS) SIM-
          PLE *SMALL* MOTOR MOVEMENTS, for instance, touch-
          ing an object you are touching, tapping his fingers on the
          table, wiggling his nose, or clapping his hands (may be
          prompted by saying, "Do this"). (Circle as many as apply and
          underline.)
          a. How many simple Small Motor models can the child cor-
              rectly imitate? (just about any; more than ten; between
              five and ten; between one and five; none)
          b. Child (usually; sometimes; rarely; never) *tries* to imitate
              simple Small Motor movements.
          c. Child usually needs (no prompting; a little prompting; a
              great deal of prompting) to repeat the movements (mod-
              els) he is shown.
          d. Child usually (cooperates and pays attention; makes a
              half-hearted try; ignores you; puts up a fuss) when you
              try to get him to imitate.
(Pages 228 to 232 in Chapter 11 tell you how to teach this behavior.)
** (C3)   THE CHILD CORRECTLY IMITATES OR COPIES THE
          PLACEMENT OF OBJECTS, such as building a bridge of
          three blocks, putting a block on top of or inside a box, or
          putting a fork in the plate. The child is not following spoken
          directions; he is just copying what you did. (Circle as many
          as apply, and underline.)
          a. How many simple Object Placements can the child imi-
              tate? (just about any; more than five; a few; none)
          b. Child (usually; sometimes; rarely; never) *tries* to imitate
              simple Object Placements.
          c. Child usually needs (no prompting; a little prompting; a
              great deal of prompting) to repeat the Object Place-
              ments he is shown.
          d. Child usually (cooperates and pays attention; makes a
              half-hearted try; ignores you; puts up a fuss) when you
              try to get him to imitate Object Placements.
(Pages 228 to 233 in Chapter 11 tell you how to teach this behavior.)

    Note that the above three *basic behaviors* will help the child to learn
harder Small and Large Motor activities and also Chores and Self-Help
activities. The next *basic behavior* has to do with the imitation of *Mouth
Movements* and *Positions*. This will help the child to learn Verbal Imitation, because the correct imitation of sounds and words means that the
child makes a sound at the same time his mouth is in a certain position.

** (C4) THE CHILD CORRECTLY IMITATES MOVEMENTS OF THE MOUTH OR MOUTH POSITIONS, such as opening his mouth wide (as in the *Ah* sound), shutting his lips together (as in the *M* sound), putting his tongue out, wiggling his tongue, putting his lower lip between his teeth (as in the *F* sound). (Circle as many as apply, and underline.)

    a. How many Mouth Positions can the child correctly imitate (just about any; more than five; a few; none).

    b. Child (usually; sometimes; rarely; never) *tries* to imitate Mouth Positions.

    c. Child usually needs (no prompting; a little prompting; a great deal of prompting) to imitate the Mouth Positions he is shown.

    d. Child usually (cooperates and pays attention; makes a half-hearted try; ignores you; puts up a fuss) when you try to get him to imitate mouth positions.

(Pages 228 to 234 in Chapter 11 tell you how to teach this behavior.)

The next two items are not *basic behaviors* for this skill area, but they are skills to work toward.

    (C5) The child plays imitation games such as "pat-a-cake," "bye-bye," or "so big." (Circle as many as apply, and underline.)

        a. How many imitation games can the child play? (more than ten; five to ten; one or two; none)

        b. Child (usually; sometimes; rarely; never) *tries* to play imitation games.

        c. Child usually needs (no prompting; a little prompting; a great deal of prompting) to play imitation games.

        d. Child usually (cooperates and pays attention; makes a half-hearted try; ignores you; puts up a fuss) when you try to get him to play an imitation game.

    (C6) The child correctly imitates *complex* movements (Large and Small Motor movements together) shown to him, such as sweeping the floor or brushing his teeth (may be told, "Do this"). (Circle as many as apply, and underline.)

        a. How many complex movements can the child correctly imitate? (just about any; more than ten; between five and ten; a few; none).

        b. Child (usually; sometimes; rarely; never) tries to imitate complex movements.

        c. Child usually needs (no prompting; a little prompting; a great deal of prompting) to imitate complex movements.

    d. Child usually (cooperates and pays attention; makes a half-hearted try; ignores you; puts up a fuss) when you try to get him to imitate complex movements.

The last four items are about what is called "generalized imitation." This means that the child's imitation behavior is so *strong* that he will try to imitate almost anyone and anything. And he seems to be rewarded just by correctly imitating (matching) the model, as if he got a kick out of "doing like (Mommy, Daddy, brother, teacher)." This is also a behavior to shoot for, because the stronger the child's imitation behavior, the easier he will learn to imitate sounds, words, phrases, chores, and self-help tasks.

** (C7) THE CHILD CORRECTLY IMITATES OR TRIES TO IMITATE SOME MODELS EVEN IF HE IS NOT REWARDED FOR IT. (Underline.)

    a. How many different models will the child imitate or try to imitate even if he is not rewarded for it? (just about any; more than ten; between five and ten; a few; always needs to be rewarded; does not imitate).

(Pages 235 to 236 in Chapter 11 tell you how to teach this behavior.)

  (C8) On his own, the child places or moves his body like others. For instance, he gets up off the chair and lays down on the floor when he sees his brother do it, or he crosses his legs when he sees his mother do it. (Underline.)

    a. Child does this (often; sometimes; rarely; never really saw him do this).

  (C9) On his own, the child imitates you when you do chores and tasks, such as sweeping, dusting, wiping the table, or hammering. For example, if he sees you wiping a table or sweeping the floor, he either begins to do something that looks like what you are doing, he tries to get you to let him do it too, or he later does something like what you were doing. (Underline.)

    a. Child does this (often; sometimes; rarely; never really saw him do this).

The last item is another *basic behavior,* a very important one.

**(C10) THE CHILD IMITATES MOTOR MODELS OF MANY PEOPLE.

    a. Child will imitate Large Motor movements of (just about anyone; most people; only certain people; does not imitate these movements yet).

    b. Child will imitate Small Motor movements of (just about anyone; most people; only certain people; does not imitate these movements yet).

    c. Child imitates Object Placements by (just about anyone; most people; only certain people; does not imitate object placements).

    d. Child imitates Mouth Positions of (just about anyone; most people; only certain people; does not imitate mouth positions yet).

Note that, no matter how well or how often the child imitates, he must learn to imitate the behavior of many people—more people than just his parents or teachers. The more people he will imitate (other children, for example), the faster he will learn new behaviors. Pages 236 to 237 in Chapter 11, "Motor Imitation," tell you how to teach the child to imitate more people.

Now please go back over this skill area and put a circle around the number of each item the child needs help with.

D. VERBAL IMITATION SKILLS

A child learns to talk by watching and listening to what people say, by trying to repeat (imitate) what he sees and hears, and by being rewarded for good imitations. As time goes by, the child gets more practice (and becomes better and better) at imitating the talk of others. In other words, most (maybe all) of the sounds, words, phrases, and sentences a child learns to say are learned through *Verbal Imitation.* If a child does not know how to talk yet (does not know how to say or use words, phrases, and sentences), you will be using Verbal Imitation methods to teach him.

The *basic behaviors* to learn in this skill area are as follows:

MAKING MANY DIFFERENT SOUNDS on His Own, Often   (D3).
MAKING EYE CONTACT and a SOUND at the SAME TIME to GET THINGS   (D6).
IMITATING BASIC SOUNDS   (D7).
IMITATING SYLLABLES   (D8).

IMITATING SIMPLE WORDS   (D9).
IMITATING PHRASES and SIMPLE SENTENCES   (D10).
IMITATING the VERBAL MODELS Of MANY PEOPLE   (D11).

Before you read any more, look back at Table 4-2 in Chapter 4. Note which *basic behaviors* from other skill areas the child must learn *before* he can learn Verbal Imitation.

The first six items have to do with *easing* the child into Verbal Imitation. Items D3 and D6 are *musts* for this.

(D1) If the child does not say any words or says only a few words, does he pay attention to people who are talking in natural settings? For example, if his mother is alone with him in the kitchen and she is talking about what she is doing (*self-talk*), does the child look at her or make sounds along with her? (Underline.)

  a. Child (often; sometimes; rarely; never really) pays attention to the speech of others in this way.

  b. Child pays attention to the speech of (almost anyone; most people; only certain people; does not pay attention to speech yet).

The child will learn Verbal Imitation skills easier if he pays attention to the speech of others in natural settings. If he does not yet pay attention in this way, Chapter Twelve, "Verbal Imitation" tells you (in the section on *self-talk*) how to teach him to pay attention to the speech of others.

(D2) If the child uses no words or few words, it is important to know what *speech sounds* he can make. So spend a day listening to the child. In the space below, list all of the sounds the child makes *on his own*. We are not talking only about sounds he will imitate. Write down *any* speech sounds (except crying and other nonspeech noises) that he makes on his own. In listing sounds, write them as if they were in words. Section 5 of Chapter Twelve, "Verbal Imitation," shows you how to write sounds, for example, *Ah* as in "mama," *Ee* as in "bee," or *Uh* as in "up."

  a. Sounds heard the most often:

b.   Sounds heard once in a while:

c.   Sounds child used to make but does not any more:

Remember this list. You will need it when you start working on Verbal Imitation. The next item is a *basic behavior.*

** (D3)   THE CHILD MAKE *MANY DIFFERENT* SPEECH SOUNDS ON HIS OWN (OTHER THAN CRYING AND OTHER NONSPEECH NOISES), AND HE MAKES HIS SOUNDS *OFTEN.* (Circle as many as apply, and underline.)

a.   Child makes speech sounds on his own (often, sometimes; rarely; never).

b.   The number of different speech sounds the child uses *regularly* (most often) is (more than fifteen; between ten and fifteen; between five and ten; less than five). See the list you make for item D2.

Note that, if the child does not make speech sounds on his own very often, you will have to *increase* the number of times (how often) he makes sounds during the day by rewarding him *each* time he makes a sound. And, to teach him to make *different* sounds, you will have to reward him for making different sounds. We will talk about how to do this on pages 254 to 256 in Chapter 12.

(D4)   When the child makes sounds, *how* does he USUALLY do it? (Circle one.)

a.   His "bursts" of sounds usually have only one or two sounds in them. For instance, he goes *"Eeeeee"* or *"Ahhh-Yahhh."* And the bursts are pretty short.

b.   His bursts of sounds usually have several different sounds in them, as though he were *babbling.* For example, he goes *"BAh-BAh-BAh-GU-GU-DAh."* In other words, his sounds come out in fairly *long* streams having lots of different sounds in them.

c.   He makes both long and short bursts with different sounds. He seems to be listening or paying attention to the sounds he is making, especially when he makes a new one. He may even try to repeat a new sound he just made. He seems to be playing with his voice and the sounds he can make.

If you circled *a*, you want to move the child to *b* and *c*. In other words, you want to teach him to make long bursts with many sounds (*babbling*). You want him to *play* with his voice and listen to it. The chapter on Verbal Imitation tells you how to teach the child to make sounds in that way.

(D5)   If the child does not say words or says only a few words, does he make more sounds if you imitate his sounds? For example, if he is saying or has just said *"Eeee-Ahhh,"* and you repeat it to him, will he say *"Eeee-Ahhh"* again or perhaps another sound? (Underline.)

a.   Child (often; sometimes; rarely; never really) makes more sounds if you repeat his sounds along with him or after him.

Some children who do not imitate sounds or words yet will at least keep making sounds if you repeat back to them the sounds they make. It is as if they are rewarded by hearing someone else repeat the sounds they are making. This means they will probably learn Verbal Imitation more easily. The chapter on Verbal Imitation tells you how to increase the child's sounds by imitating the sounds he makes (see the section called "Imitating His Sounds").

** (D6)   THE CHILD MAKES EYE CONTACT AND A SOUND AT THE SAME TIME TO GET THINGS HE WANTS. For example, he comes up to a person, makes eye contact, and then makes a sound, as if he were trying to "tell" the person something or get the person to do something. (Circle as many as apply, and underline.)

a.   Child (often; sometimes; rarely; never) does this.

b.   If the child makes sounds in this way, how close to words are they? For example, does he say things like *"WAh"* for "water"? *"TAh-U"* for "Thank you"? *"Ow"* for "out"? Or *"BAh-BAh"* for "bye-bye"? Child uses (more than ten; between five and ten; three to five; one or two; no) sounds that are close to words.

c.   Child makes eye contact in this way, but not the sound with it.

d.   Child makes sounds in this way, but not eye contact with them.

e.   Child makes eye contact and sounds to get things from

(just about anyone; most people; only certain people; does not do this yet).

f. In the space below, please list the sounds the child uses more often to get things he wants.

Sound Child Uses   *What It Means*

_____   _____

If the child makes eye contact and a sound together (the two are *chained*), he may have the "idea" behind Functional Speech (that sounds are used to *control* the scene around a person). This may make it easier to teach him Verbal Imitation and Functional Speech. If he does not do this behavior yet, increase how often he makes eye contact and sounds. Then *require* him to do *both* before he gets what he wants. Page 257 to 258 in Chapter 12 tell you how to teach this behavior.

The next five items have to do with Verbal Imitation itself—the imitation of sounds, syllables, words, phrases, and sentences.

** (D7) THE CHILD IMITATES OR REPEATS *BASIC SOUNDS* THAT HE HEARS YOU SAY OR THAT YOU ASK HIM TO TO SAY. For instance, if you tell him, "Say '*M*'" or "Say '*Ee*,'" he will do it. (Circle as many as apply, and underline.)

    a. How many basic sounds does the child usually and correctly imitate in this way? (just about any sound; more than fifteen; between ten and fifteen; between five and ten; a few; none really).

    b. Of the basic sounds the child can imitate, how regularly or often will he imitate them? (just about every time; more than half the time; once in a while; does not imitate)

    c. Of the basic sounds the child imitates, how well does he usually imitate them? How close is his imitation to the basic sound model? (usually perfect imitations; usually very close; usually fairly close; not very close, but at least he makes some sound; does not try to imitate)

    d. Of the basic sounds the child imitates, how fast does his imitation follow the model? For example, if you say, "Say '*Ee,*'" how long does it take before he imitates or tries to? (usually imitates within a few seconds; usually imitates between 5 and 10 seconds later; usually says the sound later that day; may say the sound days later; does not imitate basic sounds)

e. How well does the child usually cooperate when you try to get him to imitate basic sounds? (pays attention and tries; pays attention sometimes and makes a half-hearted try; ignores you; puts up fuss; never tried to get him to imitate basic sounds).

f. In the space below, make a list of the basic sounds the child imitates well and often. Section 5 of Chapter 12 shows you how to write sounds.

(Pages 260 to 277 in Chapter 12 tell you how to teach basic sounds.)
** (D8) THE CHILD IMITATES OR REPEATS SYLLABLES (TWO OR MORE BASIC SOUNDS TOGETHER) THAT HE HEARS OR THAT YOU ASK HIM TO SAY. For example, the child imitates things like "*BEe,*" "*BAh,*" "*LU,*" "*MAw.*" (Circle as many as apply, and underline.)

a. How many syllables does the child usually and correctly imitate? (just about any syllable; more than fifteen; between ten and fifteen; between five and ten; a few; none really)

b. Of the syllables the child can imitate, how regularly or often will he imitate them? (just about every time; more than half the time; once in a while; does not imitate syllables)

c. Of the syllables the child imitates, how well does he usually imitate them? How close is his imitation to the syllable model? (usually perfect imitations; usually very close; usually fairly close; not very close, but at least he makes some sound; does not try to imitate syllables)

d. Of the syllables the child imitates, how fast does his imitation follow the model? How long does it take before he imitates it (usually imitates within a few seconds; usually imitates between 5 and 10 seconds later; usually says the syllable later that day; may say the syllable days later; does not imitate syllables)

e. How well does the child usually cooperate when you try

to get him to imitate syllables? (pays attention and tries; pays attention sometimes and makes a half-hearted try; ignores you; puts up a fuss; never tried to get him to imitate syllables)

f. In the space below, please list the syllables the child imitates well and often.

(Pages 277 to 281 in Chapter 12 tell you how to teach the child to imitate syllables.)

** (D9)   THE CHILD IMITATES OR REPEATS SIMPLE *WORDS* THAT HE HEARS OR THAT YOU ASK HIM TO SAY. For example, the child imitates words like "mama,' "bye," "eat," "more," "go," "me," "out," "cookie," "soda." (Circle as many as apply, and underline.)

a. How many simple words does the child usually and correctly imitate? (just about any simple word; more than thirty; between twenty and thirty; ten to twenty; between five and ten; a few; none really)

b. Of the simple words the child can imitate, how regularly or often will he imitate them? (just about every time; more than half the time; once in a while; does not imitate words)

c. Of the simple words the child can imitate, how well does he usually imitate them? How close is his imitation to the model? (usually perfect imitations; usually very close; usually fairly close; not very close, but at least he makes some sound; does not try to imitate words)

d. Of the simple words the child can imitate, how fast does his imitation follow the model? (usually imitates within a few seconds; usually imitates between 5 and 10 seconds later; usually says the word later that day; may say the word days later; does not imitate words)

e. How well does the child cooperate when you try to get him to imitate simple words? (pays attention and tries; pays attention sometimes and makes a half-hearted try; ignores you; puts up a fuss; never tried to get him to imitate words)

f. In the space below, please list the words the child imitates well and often.

(Pages 281 to 291 in Chapter 12 tell you how to teach the child to imitate words.)

****(D10) THE CHILD IMITATES OR REPEATS *PHRASES* AND
SIMPLE SENTENCES THAT HE HEARS OR THAT YOU
ASK HIM TO SAY.** For example, the child imitates phrases
and sentences like "Mama come," "More food," "Gimme a
cookie," "What's that?" "That's a ball." (Circle as many as
apply, and underline.)

   a. How many phrases or sentences does the child usually
   and correctly imitate? (just about any; more than thirty;
   between twenty and thirty; between ten and twenty; between five and ten; a few; none really)

   b. Of the phrases and sentences the child can imitate, how
   regularly or often will he imitate them? (just about every
   time; once in a while; does not imitate phrases or sentences).

   c. Of the phrases or sentences the child can imitate, how
   well does he usually imitate them? How close is his imitation to the model? (usually perfect imitations; usually
   very close; usually fairly close; not very close, but at least
   he makes some sounds or words; does not try to imitate
   phrases or sentences).

   d. Of the phrases or sentences the child can imitate, how
   fast does his imitation follow the model? (usually imitates within a few seconds; usually imitates between 5
   and 10 seconds later; usually says the phrase later that
   day; may say the phrase days later; does not imitate
   phrases or sentences).

   e. How well does the child cooperate when you try to get
   him to imitate phrases or sentences? (pays attention and
   tries; pays attention sometimes and makes a half-hearted
   try; ignores you; puts up a fuss; never tried to get him to
   imitate phrases or sentences).

   f. In the space below, please list the phrases and sentences
   the child imitates well and often.

(Pages 291 to 294 in Chapter 12 tell you how to teach the child to imitate phrases and simple sentences.)

The last item is another *basic behavior.* Again, it is a *must* that the child not only learn to imitate well, but also learn to imitate *many* people besides his parents and teachers, for example, his brothers and sisters, classmates, other teachers, and neighborhood friends.

**(D11)   THE CHILD IMITATES VERBAL MODELS OF MANY PEOPLE.

a.   Child will imitate basic sounds of (just about anyone; most people; only certain people; does not imitate basic sounds yet).

b.   Child will imitate syllables of (just about anyone; most people; only certain people; does not imitate syllables yet).

c.   Child will imitate simple words of (just about anyone; most people; only certain people; does not imitate simple words yet).

d.   Child will imitate phrases or simple sentences of (just about anyone; most people; only certain people; does not imitate phrases or simple sentences yet).

e.   Child uses sounds and "word-like" sounds to get things from (just about anyone; most people; only certain people; does not use sounds and "word-like" sounds to get things yet).

(Chapter 12 tells you how to teach this behavior.)

Now please circle the number of all items in this skill area that the child needs help with. Then take a long break and give yourself a big reward.

E.   FUNCTIONAL SPEECH

Verbal Imitation skills are very important. With them, the child learns *how* to say the basic sounds, syllables, words, phrases, and sentences that people use in everyday life. But knowing how to say things is not good enough by itself. The child must also learn the *meaning* of what he can say and learn *where* and *when* to say certain things. In other words, the child must *understand* what other people say (so that their speech will *control* or have an *effect* on him) and *use* words and phrases so that he can learn from others and have an effect on them. For this reason he must learn the *names* for objects and events in the scene around him, and he must learn how to *ask* for, *point out*, and *describe* things; *answer* questions; and use other kinds of Functional Speech.

Look back at Table 4-2 in Chapter 4. Notice the *basic behaviors* from other areas the child needs before he can start on Functional Speech.

The *basic behaviors* to learn in this skill area are as follows:

USES words to NAME objects or pictures   (E1).

USES words to ASK FOR things he wants   (E2).

IDENTIFIES and DESCRIBES what he sees and hears   (E3).

ANSWERS SIMPLE QUESTIONS   (E4).

Says "HELLO" and "GOODBYE" at the right time   (E5)

Uses PHRASES and SIMPLE SENTENCES to Name, Ask for, and Describe   (E6).

Identifies and Describes ONE AND MORE THAN ONE thing: PLURALS (E7).

Understands and uses PREPOSITIONS   (E8).

Understands and uses PRONOUNS   (E9).

Understands and uses OPPOSITES   (E10).

Answers questions and uses words about TIME ("BEFORE"/"AFTER") (E11).

USES the Functional Speech he knows how to use   (E12).

Uses Functional Speech instead of just imitating (ECHOING) or PARROTING   (E13).

Uses Functional Speech in MANY PLACES and with MANY PEOPLE (E14).

** (E1)   THE CHILD USES WORDS TO *NAME*, LABEL, OR CALL ATTENTION TO MANY OBJECTS, PERSONS, OR PICTURES. For example, he uses words like "egg," "cat," "house," "table," "chair," "tree," "apple," or "car" to tell you what these things are called or to answer you when you ask him, "What is this?" "What is this called?" or "This is a . . ." (Circle as many as apply, and underline.)

    a.   How many things does the child name *on his own*? (a normal number for his age; between thirty and fifty; between twenty and thirty; ten to twenty; just a few; does not name things on his own)

    b.   How many things does the child name *when asked*? (a normal number for his age; between thirty and fifty; between twenty and thirty; ten to twenty; just a few; does not name things when asked)

(Pages 307 to 311 in Chapter 13 tell you how to teach this behavior.)

** (E2)   THE CHILD USES WORDS TO *ASK FOR* MANY THINGS

HE WANTS, for example, a glass of water, music, help, a toy, or to go outside. In other words, how does the child ask you for something or tell you that he wants it? (Circle as many as apply, and underline.)

a. Child (usually; more than half the time; once in a while; never really) uses words to ask.

b. Child (usually; more than half the time; once in a while; never) cries and whines for what he wants.

c. Child (usually; more than half the time; once in a while; never) pulls and pushes.

d. Child (usually; more than half the time; once in a while; never) gets what he wants for himself.

e. Child (usually; more than half the time; once in a while; never) just makes sounds to tell people to get him what he wants.

f. If prompted or required to ask for what he wants, the child usually (will ask for it; cries, whines or tantrums instead; gets it himself; loses interest and walks away).

(Pages 312 to 314 in Chapter 13 tell you how to teach this behavior.)

The next item is like B23 in the Looking, Listening, and Moving skill area, but it is harder.

** (E3) THE CHILD IS LEARNING TO IDENTIFY (PICK OUT OR POINT TO) THINGS BY NAME AND TO DESCRIBE (TALK ABOUT) THINGS. FOR INSTANCE, HE CAN IDENTIFY AND DESCRIBE THINGS BY NAME, COLOR, SHAPE, AND SIZE. If you say, "Point to the picture of the house," "Point to the red circle," or "Show me the big ball" he can do it (*identify*). And if you ask him, "What color is the circle?" or "What do you see?" he can tell you (*describe*). (Circle as many as apply, and underline.)

a. How many objects can the child identify (point to) by name? (a normal number for his age; more than thirty; twenty to thirty; ten to twenty; a few; none really)

b. How well does the child identify objects by color? (very well; fairly well but needs some help; not very well and needs a lot of help; does not really know his colors)

c. How well does the child identify objects by size (big/little; big/bigger)? (very well; fairly well but needs some help; not very well and needs a lot of help; does not really know sizes)

d. When you try to teach the child to identify (point to)

things, he usually (is interested and tries; makes a half-hearted try but soon loses interest; hardly ever pays much attention; puts up a fuss)

e. How many objects or actions can the child describe with words? For example, can he tell you what things he sees in a picture (dog, house, tree) or what a person is doing (eating, sitting, running)? (a normal number for his age; more than thirty; twenty to thirty; ten to twenty; a few; none really)

f. How well does the child describe things by colors? Can he tell you what color something is? (can tell you the color of almost anything; uses a few color words well; uses a few color words correctly but only once in a while; does not really use color words)

g. How well does the child describe things with general size words (big/little; big/bigger/biggest)? (uses many size words correctly; uses a few size words correctly most of the time; uses a few size words correctly once in a while; does not really use size words)

h. When you try to teach the child to use words to describe or talk about things, he usually (is interested and tries; makes a half-hearted try but soon loses interest; hardly ever pays attention; puts up a fuss)

(Pages 318 to 325 in Chapter 13 tell you how to teach this behavior.)

The next kind of Functional Speech is an important part of carrying on conversations.

** (E4) THE CHILD USES WORDS TO *ANSWER SIMPLE QUES-TIONS* IN A CONVERSATION. For example, he can answer questions such as, "What is your name?" "How are you to-day?" "Where do you live?" or "How old are you?" (Underline.)

a. How does the child answer simple questions such as "How are you?" or "What is your name?" (usually answers them correctly; sometimes answers them correctly; answers them correctly once in a while; does not answer questions like this)

(See pages 325 to 326 in Chapter 13 on how to teach this behavior.)

** (E5) THE CHILD SAYS "HELLO" AND "GOODBYE" AT THE RIGHT TIME AND PLACE.

a. The child (usually; sometimes; once in a while; never really) does this.

  b. The child needs (no prompting; a little prompting; a great deal of prompting) to do this.

  c. When you try to get the child to say "Hello" or "Goodbye" he usually (says it; sometimes makes a half-hearted try; just ignores you; puts up a fuss)

(See pages 326 to 328 in Chapter 13 on how to teach this behavior.)

The next item has to do with using the kinds of Functional Speech talked about above in a more advanced way—in *phrases* and *sentences* rather than single words.

** (E6) THE CHILD USES PHRASES AND SIMPLE SENTENCES WHERE PROPER TO NAME, ASK FOR, OR DESCRIBE THINGS, AND TO ANSWER QUESTIONS. For instance, the child uses phrases and sentences such as "Want milk" or "I want milk," "That's a dog," "Gimme cookie" or "Give me a cookie," "Six years old" or "I'm six," "House and a car and a tree." (Circle as many as apply, and underline.)

  a. How many phrases or simple sentences does the child know how to use? (a normal number for his age; more than thirty; between twenty and thirty; between ten and twenty; a few; none really)

  b. How often does the child use his phrases or simple sentences when it is proper to do so? (most of the time; sometimes; once in a while; does not really use phrases or simple sentences).

  c. What does the child usually do when you try to prompt him to use a phrase or simple sentence? (he uses it or at least tries hard; he sometimes makes a half-hearted try; he often ignores you; he puts up a fuss)

(See pages 328 to 333 in Chapter 13 on how to teach this behavior.)

** (E7) THE CHILD IDENTIFIES AND DESCRIBES ONE AND MORE THAN ONE (PLURALS). For example, if you show the child a picture of one dog and another picture of two dogs, he will point to the right one, depending on whether you said, "Point to the do*g*" or "Point to the dog*s*." And he will put the right ending on a word to describe one thing (bloc*k*, bo*y*, glas*s*) or more than one thing (blocks, boys, glasses). (Circle as many as apply, and underline.)

  a. How much help does the child need in identifying (pointing to or picking out) one or more than one? (does this very well; needs a little help; needs a great deal of help; does not identify one and more than one)

  b. How much help does the child need in describing things

with the right plural ending (dog/dog*s*; block/block*s*; match/match*es*)? (does this very well; needs a little help; needs a great deal of help; does not really describe with plural endings)

(See pages 333 to 336 in Chapter 13.)

** (E8)   THE CHILD UNDERSTANDS AND USES PREPOSITIONS SUCH AS "ON," "IN," "UNDER," "NEXT TO," "OVER," "IN FRONT OF," "BEHIND." For example, he can correctly move or place objects when asked ("Put the block IN the box," "Put the book UNDER the table"). And he can *use* the right preposition to describe objects and events ("The penny is UNDER the box," "The box is ON the table"). (Circle as many as apply, and underline.)

    a. Child understands (all or most prepositions; two or three; none really).

    b. Child knows how to use correctly (all or most prepositions; two or three; none really).

    c. How often does the child correctly use prepositions when asked about things? (all or most of the time; about half the time; once in a while; does not use prepositions)

(See pages 336 to 337 in Chapter 13.)

** (E9)   THE CHILD UNDERSTANDS AND USES PRONOUNS SUCH AS "I," "ME," "YOU," "SHE," "HE," "IT," "THEY." For example, if you ask, "What is the dog doing?" he will say, "It (He) is eating." Or, if you ask, "Who is Billy?" the child will say "Me" or "I am." (Circle as many as apply, and underline.)

    a. Child understands (all or most pronouns; three or four; one or two; none really).

    b. Child knows how to use correctly (all or most pronouns; three or four; one or two; none really)

    c. How often does the child use the pronouns he understands when it is proper? (always or almost always; more than half the time; once in a while; never really)

(See pages 337 to 339 in Chapter 13.)

**(E10)   THE CHILD USES OPPOSITES. For example, he can answer some questions such as "Fire is HOT; ice is _____" or "Mother is a WOMAN; Dad is a _____." And he correctly uses "Yes" and "No" to answer questions like "Is this a book?" (Circle as many as apply, and underline.)

    a. How many questions such as "Mother is a woman; Dad is a _____"can the child answer? (many; five or so; one or two; none really) *b.* How often does the child correctly use "Yes" to answer questions such as "Is this a book?" or "Do you want a cookie?" (all or most of the time; about half the time; once in a while; never really)

    c. How often does the child correctly use "No" to answer questions such as "Is this a chair?" or "Do you want a ride?" (all or most of the time; about half the time; once in a while; never really).

(See pages 339 to 340 in Chapter 13.)

**(E11) CHILD CAN ANSWER QUESTIONS ABOUT TIME AND USES TIME WORDS ("BEFORE"/"AFTER") TO DESCRIBE EVENTS. For example, if you ask, "What did you point to AFTER you pointed to the red block?" or "Where did we go BEFORE we went to the store?" the child gives the right answer.

    a. How many simple "before"/"after" questions can the child answer correctly? (all or most; more than half; a few, none really)

    b. How often does the child describe events with "before"/ "after" words? (enough; needs a little work on this; needs a great deal of work on this; does not use "before"/"after" words to describe events)

(See pages 340 to 342 in Chapter 13.)

The next few items are about certain problems in learning or using Functional Speech. For examples, (1) the child does not use the speech he knows how to use; (2) the child parrots, repeats, or echoes speech he hears instead of using speech; or (3) the child uses his speech only in a few places or with a few people.

**(E12) THE CHILD *USES* THE FUNCTIONAL SPEECH HE IS ABLE OR *KNOWS HOW* TO USE. In other words, how much does the child *say* out of what he *can* say? (Circle as many as apply, and underline.)

    a. Child uses (about all the speech he knows; over half the speech he knows; says only a little of what he is able to say; can talk but hardly ever does; does not know how to talk yet).

    b. When you try to get the child to use the speech he knows how to use, he usually (cooperates or tries; makes a halfhearted try; ignores you; puts up a fuss).

    c. How often does the child use nonspeech gestures (point-

ing, noises, waving) instead of the speech he is able to
use? (all or most of the time; more than half the time,
gestures once in a while; uses speech, not gestures; uses
no gestures and no speech yet).

(See pages 342 to 344 in Chapter 13.)

**(E13)   THE CHILD USES SPEECH INSTEAD OF JUST ECHO-
ING OR PARROTING. For example, if you ask, "What is your
name?" does he tell you his name or does he repeat, "What is
your name?" or "Name?" Does he repeat television commercials right after or days after he hears them, over and over?
(Circle as many as apply, and underline.)

    a.   How much of the child's speech is echoing or parrot talk?
(all or most; more than half; some parroting but mostly
proper speech; no parroting, all normal speech; no speech
yet)

    b.   What does the child usually do when you try to get him to
say something or to answer a question without parroting?
(cooperates; ignores you and says nothing; keeps parroting
anyway; puts up a fuss)

(See pages 344 to 346 in Chapter 13.)

**(E14)   CHILD USES HIS FUNCTIONAL SPEECH IN MANY
PLACES AND WITH MANY PEOPLE. (Circle as many as
apply, and underline.)

    a.   Child uses his functional speech (with anyone or any-
where; in most places and with most persons, except for a
few; uses his speech only in a few places and with a few
persons; uses no speech yet).

    b.   In a new place or with a new person, the child (uses his
speech in the usual way; will talk after a while; will talk
with prompting; will not talk even if prompted; starts
to fuss or withdraw).

(See pages 346 to 347 in Chapter 13.)

Now go back and circle the items the child needs help with.

F.   CHORES AND SELF-HELP SKILLS

Chores and Self-Help skills are important for the child in several ways.
They teach him to do Small and Large Motor movements in long chains;

they give him skills that let him help out at home and school; they give him a feeling of success; they give him a good way to spend some of his time; and they may help him to get into and stay in certain schools.

There are three *basic behaviors* or goals to shoot for in this skill area:

Does SIMPLE TASKS (F1).
Does MORE COMPLEX TASKS and CHORES on his own, often (F2).
Does MANY SELF-HELP TASKS on his own, often (F9).

** (F1) THE CHILD HELPS IN THE HOME OR SCHOOL BY DOING SIMPLE TASKS such as bringing and putting away everyday objects. (Circle as many as apply, and underline.)

 a. Child (often; sometimes; rarely; never) does simple tasks on his own or pitches in when he sees others doing them.

 b. Child (often; sometimes; rarely; never) does simple tasks when asked.

 c. Child needs (no prompting or help; a little prompting; a great deal of prompting) when doing simple tasks.

 d. When you try to teach the child or get him to do a simple task, he usually (cooperates and pays attention; makes a half-hearted try; often just ignores you; puts up a fuss)

(See pages 352 to 355 in Chapter 14 on how to teach this behavior.)

**(F2) THE CHILD HELPS IN THE HOME OR SCHOOL BY DOING MORE COMPLEX TASKS AND CHORES (such as making beds, setting a table, cleaning the table, washing dishes, taking out the trash, putting all the chairs around the table) on his own, often. (Circle as many as apply, and underline.)

 a. Child (often; sometimes; rarely; never) does more complex chores on his own or pitches in when he sees others doing them.

 b. Child (often; sometimes; rarely; never) does complex tasks when asked.

 c. Child needs (no prompting or help; a little prompting; a great deal of prompting) when doing more complex chores.

 d. When you try to teach the child or get him to do a more complex chore, he usually (cooperates and pays attention; makes a half-hearted try; often just ignores you; puts up a fuss)

(See pages 355 to 357 in Chapter 14.)

The following are examples of *self-help tasks* that the child can be taught. They are listed starting with tasks that are easiest for most children.

(F3) The child feeds himself with the right utensils. (Circle as many as apply, and underline.)

    a. How many utensils does the child know how to feed himself with well? (spoon; fork; knife; cup or glass; none)

    b. Child (often; sometimes; rarely; never) feeds himself with the utensils he knows how to use.

    c. When you try to teach the child or get him to eat with the right utensils, he usually (cooperates and pays attention; makes a half-hearted try; often just ignores you; puts up a fuss).

    d. What other mealtime problems does the child have? (keeps leaving the table; eats only certain foods; east too fast or slow; none of these). (Underline as many as apply.)

(F4) The child can undress himself. (Circle as many as apply, and underline.)

    a. Child can take off (all or most of; a few pieces of; none of) his clothes by himself.

    b. How often does the child, by himself, take off the clothes he is able to? (always or almost always; about half the time; once in a while; never)

    c. Child needs (no help or prompting; a little prompting; a great deal of prompting) when taking off his clothes.

    d. When you try to teach or get the child to take off his clothes, he usually (cooperates and pays attention; makes a half-hearted try; just ignores you; puts up a fuss)

(F5) The child can dress himself. (Circle as many as apply, and underline.)

    a. Child can put on (all or most of; a few pieces of; none of) his clothes by himself.

    b. How often does the child, by himself, put on the clothes he is able to? (always or almost always; about half the time; once in a while; never)

    c. Child needs (no prompting; a little prompting; a great deal of prompting) when putting on his clothes.

    d. When you try to teach or get the child to put on his clothes, he usually (cooperates and pays attention; makes a half-hearted try; just ignores you; puts up a fuss)

(F6) The child washes and dries his face and hands. (Circle as many as apply, and underline.)

a. Child (often; sometimes; rarely; never) does this on his own.

b. Child needs (no help or prompting; a little prompting; a great deal of prompting) when doing this.

c. When you try to teach or get the child to do this, he usually (cooperates and pays attention; makes a half-hearted try; just ignores you; puts up a fuss).

(F7) The child brushes his teeth. (Circle as many as apply, and underline.)

a. Child (often; sometimes; rarely, never) brushes his teeth on his own.

b. Child needs (no help or prompting; a little prompting; a great deal of prompting) when brushing his teeth.

c. When you try to teach or get the child to brush his teeth, he usually (cooperates and pays attention; makes a half-hearted try; just ignores you; puts up a fuss).

(F8) The child is toilet trained. (Circle as many as apply, and underline.)

a. Child uses the toilet by himself and rarely or never has an "accident."

b. Child has an "accident" once in a while.

c. Child has many "accidents" and does not seem to know or care about using the toilet.

d. When you try to teach the child or get him to use the toilet, he usually (cooperates and pays attention; makes a half-hearted try; just ignores you; puts up a fuss).

Now that you have read the different self-help tasks, rate the child on the next *basic behavior.*

(F9) THE CHILD DOES MANY SELF-HELP TASKS (such as dressing, washing, and using the toilet) on his own, often. (Circle as many as apply, and underline.)

a. Child does (many; a few; really no) self-help tasks on his own.

b. Child needs (no prompting; a little prompting; a great deal of prompting) on his self-help tasks.

c. Child usually (cooperates and pays attention; makes a half-hearted try; ignores you; puts up a fuss) when you try to teach him or get him to do self-help tasks.

(See pages 357 to 368 in Chapter 14 on how to teach self-help skills.)

Fine. Now please take a minute to circle the items in this area that the child needs help with.

G. PROBLEM BEHAVIORS

So far, the Behavior Evaluation Scale has been about behaviors of the child that might need to be done with more skill (done better), increased (done more often or longer), or done at the right time and place. But children with learning and behavior problems often do things that simply should not be done, or they do some behaviors too often. It may be important to *replace* such behaviors because they may (1) keep a child from learning good behaviors; (2) keep him out of school or get him put out; and (3) be painful for him and others to live with. The following is a list of behaviors that may need to be replaced. The list has three sections: *Destructive Behaviors; Getting into Things;* and *Strange Behaviors.*

Destructive behavior is behavior that hurts the child or other people. Sometimes, destructive behavior is kept going because it is accidentally rewarded. The child gets attention or gets things he wants. And sometimes destructive behavior seems to be the child's way of spending his time, because he either does not know a better way or is not rewarded for spending his time in a better way. Keep in mind that you cannot just "get rid of" problem behaviors. You have to *replace* them, especially if the child does them because he does not know better ways to spend his time and energy. The following are examples of *destructive behaviors* that may need to be replaced.

(G1) The child bangs or hits his own head or face. (Circle as many as apply, and underline.)
- *a.* Child does this (often; sometimes; rarely; never).
- *b.* Child usually does this (when he is by himself; when he is with others; when alone and when with others.
- *c.* Child usually does this (when he does not seem to have anything better to do; when he is not given what he wants; for reasons that are unclear).

(G2) The child bites or scratches himself. (Circle as many as apply, and underline.)
- *a.* Child does this (often; sometimes; rarely; never).
- *b.* Child usually does this (when he is by himself; when he is with other people; when alone and when with others).
- *c.* Child usually does this (when he does not seem to have anything better to do; when he is not given what he wants; for reasons that are unclear).

(G3) The child throws tantrums (for instance, yells, jumps up and down, or throws and breaks things). (Circle as many as apply, and underline.)

    a. Child does this (often; sometimes; rarely; never).

    b. Child usually does this (when he is by himself; when he is with others; when alone and when with others).

    c. Child usually does this (when he does not seem to have anything better to do; when he is not given what he wants; for reasons that are unclear).

(G4) The child hits, bites, kicks, or scratches other people *(aggression)*. (Circle as many as apply, and underline.)

    a. Child does this (often; sometimes; rarely; never).

    b. Child usually does this (when he does not seem to have anything better to do; when he is not given what he wants; for reasons that are unclear).

(G5) Please use the space provided below to list and describe any other *destructive behaviors* of the child, how often they happen, and when and where they happen.

Behaviors	*How Often*	*When and Where They Happen*

Getting into things is another kind of problem behavior. Often, when children get into things (cabinets, water), the reason is that they do not know a better way to spend their time or are not rewarded for spending their time in better ways. The following item is on *getting into things*.

(G6) The child gets into or messes up things (for instance, empties packages and cabinets, scatters records and books, plays in bathroom water). (Circle as many as apply, and underline.)

    a. Child does this (often; sometimes; rarely; never).

    b. Child usually does this (when he is by himself; when he is with others; when alone and when with others).

    c. Child usually does this (when he does not seem to have anything better to do; when he is not given what he wants; for reasons that are unclear).

Strange behavior is the third kind of problem behavior. Like *getting into things*, some strange behaviors may be the child's way of spending his time. He may also do "strange" things because he is accidently rewarded for this behavior when people look at him or try to stop him. Anyway, one thing is sure; strange behavior puts the child in a bad light from the start. People may not give him a chance to learn because they think he must really be "sick" or because it is uncomfortable to watch him. The following are examples of *strange behaviors* that may need to be decreased and replaced.

(G7) The child rocks himself. (Circle as many as apply, and underline.)
  a. Child does this (often; sometimes; rarely; never).
  b. Child usually does this (when he is by himself; when he is with others; when alone and when with others).
  c. Child usually does this (when he does not seem to have anything better to do; when he is not given what he wants; for reasons that are unclear).

(G8) The child spins himself like a top. (Circle as many as apply, and underline.)
  a. Child does this (often; sometimes; rarely; never).
  b. Child usually does this (when he is by himself; when he is with others; when alone and when with others).
  c. Child usually does this (when he does not seem to have anything better to do; when he is not given what he wants; for reasons that are unclear).

(G9) The child spins things, such as lids, compacts, ashtrays. (Circle as many as apply, and underline.)
  a. Child does this (often; sometimes; rarely; never).
  b. Child usually does this (when he is by himself; when he is with others; when alone and when with others).
  c. Child usually does this (when he does not seem to have anything better to do; when he is not given what he wants; for reasons that are unclear).

(G10) The child looks closely (stares) at his fingers or at shiny objects. (Circle as many as apply, and underline.)
  a. Child does this (often; sometimes; rarely; never).
  b. Child usually does this (when he is by himself; when he is with others; when alone and when with others).
  c. Child usually does this (when he does not seem to have anything better to do; when he is not given what he wants; for reasons that are unclear).

(G11) The child flaps his hands or arms (maybe while jumping up and down or making sounds). (Circle as many as apply, and underline.)
  a. Child does this (often; sometimes; rarely; never).

b. Child usually does this (when he is by himself; when he is with others; when alone and when with others).

c. Child usually does this (when he does not seem to have anything better to do; when he is not given what he wants; for reasons that are unclear).

(G12) The child makes strange faces (tongue out, twisting his lips, closing his eyes tightly or opening them wide). (Circle as many as apply, and underline.)

a. Child does this (often; sometimes; rarely; never).

b. Child usually does this (when he is by himself; when he is with others; when alone and when with others).

c. Child usually does this (when he does not seem to have anything better to do; when he is not given what he wants; for reasons that are unclear).

(G13) The child holds himself in strange postures (hands or arms covering his head or eyes, covering his ears, twisting his head). (Circle as many as apply, and underline.)

a. Child does this (often; sometimes; rarely; never).

b. Child usually does this (when he is by himself; when he is with others; when alone and when with others).

c. Child usually does this (when he does not seem to have anything better to do; when he is not given what he wants; for reasons that are unclear).

(G14) The child performs or demands certain arrangements or rituals (lines up objects, wants furniture in one place, insists on same foods). (Circle as many as apply, and underline.)

a. Child has (five or more; three to five; one or two; no) ritual patterns.

b. Child demands or performs ritual patterns (often; sometimes; rarely; never).

c. Child usually does this (when he is by himself; when he is with others; when alone and with others).

d. Child usually does this (when he does not seem to have anything better to do; when he is not given what he wants; for reasons that are unclear).

(G15) In the space below, please list any other strange behaviors of the child, how often he does them, and when or where they happen.

Behaviors   *How Often*   *When and Where They Happen*

Before you pick a method to replace and decrease a problem behavior, it is a good idea to find out how the child reacts to certain consequences. If they have not decreased problem behaviors in the past, they may not have this effect now, either.

(G16)   What does the child do when he is *physically punished* for instance, spanked)? (Circle as many as apply, and underline.)

    a.   Child (often; sometimes; rarely; never) cries or shows discomfort.

    b.   Child (often; sometimes; rarely; never) goes back to what he was punished for doing.

    c.   Child (often; sometimes; rarely; never) smiles, laughs, grins, or teases, as if he liked getting you to physically punish him.

Note that, if spanking *is not* a punishment (does not decrease the behavior it follows) it may be because (1) the spanking is followed by a reward (talking to the child—"Poor baby. I'm sorry I had to spank you"—or cuddling him); (2) the spankings are not *hard* enough; (3) they are not given *fast* enough after the behavior; (4) a "good" behavior is not being rewarded to replace the "bad" behavior. (See Chapter 2 and Chapter 15.)

(G17)   What does the child do when he is *verbally punished* or scolded for something he is doing or has just done (for instance, "Stop that this instant!" or "That is a bad thing to do! Don't ever do that again!"). (Circle as many as apply, and underline.)

    a.   Child (often; sometimes; rarely; never) seems to show discomfort by pouting, frowning, or crying.

    b.   Child (often; sometimes; rarely; never) stops what he is doing.

    c.   Child (often; sometimes; rarely; never) goes back to what he was scolded for doing.

    d.   Child (often; sometimes; rarely; never) smiles, laughs, grins, or teases when he is scolded, as if he liked getting you to scold him.

If verbal "punishment" is not really punishment (does not decrease the behavior it follows), and, instead, the child smiles and teases afterward, does not stop the behavior, or does it again later, it may be because (1) the verbal "punishment" has not been backed up often enough by something that is *really* punishment; (2) the verbal "punishment" is followed by something that is rewarding (attention), or (3) the verbal "punishment" does not follow the behavior *fast* enough. (See Chapter 2 and Chapter 15.)

(G18) What does the child do when he is *timed out* (put in his room
       or isolated in some way for a "bad" behavior)? (Circle one.)
       a. Child is likely just to start the same behavior, or one like it,
             soon after the time out is over.
       b. Child is not likely to do the behavior for a while after the
             time out is over, but he will do it again in the future.
       c. Child is not likely to do that behavior very much any more,
             at least not around the person who times him out.
       b. Child is not timed out for "bad" behaviors.

Note that, if time out does not decrease the behavior it follows, it may
be because (1) the time out does not follow the behavior *fast* enough;
(2) it is not used *often enough* on that behavior; (3) the child is allowed
to come back while he is *still* fussing or tantrumming; or (4) the child is
not being rewarded for a behavior to replace the one he is being timed
out for. (See Chapter 2 and Chapter 15.)

(G19) What does the child do when a problem behavior is *ignored?*
       In other words, no one pays any attention or reacts in any way,
       as though the problem behavior was not seen or heard. (Circle
       one.)
       a. Child is likely to keep on doing the behavior, maybe even
             louder or longer, as though he were trying to get attention.
       b. Child is likely to stop doing the behavior after a while, but
             he will do it again in the future.
       c. If you keep ignoring the behavior day after day, the child
             is likely to do it less and less often.
       d. Child's problem behaviors are not usually ignored.

Note that ignoring *does not* mean that you turn away from the child.
It means that you act as if the behavior had not even happened. If you
turn away from him, you have reacted to his behavior, and this may be a
reward for him. He is *controlling* you. So, even though you think that
you are ignoring the problem behavior, you may be rewarding it. Also,
if the child keeps on with a problem behavior even though you are really
ignoring it, it may be that the behavior used to be rewarded on an *Intermittent Schedule.* Such a schedule makes the behavior harder to decrease
by ignoring.

There is only one *basic behavior* for this area:
**(G20) PROBLEM BEHAVIORS ARE BEING REPLACED WITH
          "GOOD" BEHAVIORS FROM OTHER SKILL AREAS.
In the same way that you will be setting up programs for teaching

good behaviors, you will be setting up programs for replacing and decreasing problem behaviors. Chapter Fifteen, "Replacing Problem Behaviors," tells you how to set up and run such programs.

EXCELLENT JOB! What you did was tiring, but it will make the job of teaching easier. Now you won't have to keep asking yourself, "What do I teach now?"

The last thing to do is to fill out the Behavior Evaluation Table (BET) in Appendix 3. That will take only a few minutes. Just *circle the same items on the BET that you circled on the BES.* From then on you will know which behaviors to help the child with. To find out *what kind* of help the child needs with a behavior, just come back to this BES and see how you answered the question for that behavior.

REFERENCES

This scale includes some of the behavioral items from the following sources:

Frankenburg, W. K., and Dodds, J. B. "The Denver developmental screening test." *Journal of Pediatrics*, 1967, **71**, 181-191.

Rimland, B. "Diagnostic check list for behavior-disturbed children (Form E-2)." In B. Rimland, *Infantile Autism*. New York: Appleton-Century-Crofts, 1964. Pp. 221-236.

BEHAVIOR
EVALUATION
TABLE (BET)

A. Learning Readiness Skills

** (A1) SPONTANEOUS EYE CONTACT

** (A2) EYE CONTACT ON RE-QUEST

(A3) Responds to his name

** (A4) COOPERATES WITH SIMPLE SPOKEN RE-QUESTS

** (A5) SITS TO WORK AT SOME TASK

(A6) Approaches others

(A7) Smiles at others

(A8) Responds to praise

B. Looking, Listening, and Moving Skills

Large Motor Skills

(B1) Bend and stand

(B2) Balance when walking

(B3) Walks backwards

(B4) Kicks ball

(B5) Throws ball

(B6) Jumps in place

(B7) Balances on one foot

(B8) Broad-jumps

(B9) Hops on one foot

(B10) Heel-toe walks

(B11) Catches ball

(B12) Pedals tricycle

** (B13) SKILL AT MANY LARGE MOTOR ACTIVITIES; SPENDS MUCH TIME AT THEM

Small Motor Skills

** (B14) LOOKS AT OBJECTS, PARTS OF THE BODY, FACE, MOUTH

(B15) Moves objects from one hand to the other

(B16) Picks up objects with thumb and index finger

(B17) Stacks blocks

(B18) Works simple puzzles

(B19) Imitates drawing line

(B20) Imitates drawing circle

** (B21) SKILL AT MANY SMALL MOTOR ACTIVITIES; SPENDS MUCH TIME

Behavior Evaluation Table (continued)

AT THEM

°° (B22) GOOD WORK HABITS, SUCH AS SITTING, LISTENING, AND WORKING AT A TASK

°° (B23) POINTS OR MATCHES BY NAME

Social Skills

°° (B24) USES EYE CONTACT TO GET NATURAL RE-WARDS

(B25) Plays with others

(B26) Cooperates on a task

(B27) Takes or waits his turn

C.   Motor Imitation Skills

Imitation of Movements

°° (C1) IMITATES LARGE MO-TOR MODELS

°° (C2) IMITATES SMALL MO-TOR MODELS

°° (C3) IMITATES OBJECT PLACEMENTS

°° (C4) IMITATES MOUTH MOVEMENTS AND PO-SITIONS

(C5) Plays imitation games

(C6) Imitates complex movements

Generalized Imitation

°° (C7) IMITATES SOME MOD-ELS EVEN IF NOT RE-WARDED

(C8) Moves body as others do on his own

(C9) Imitates chores or tasks on his own

°° (C10) IMITATES MOTOR MODELS OF MANY PEOPLE

D.   Verbal Imitation Skills

Easing into Verbal Imitation

(D1) Pays attention to the speech of others

(D2) List of sounds child makes

°° (D3) MAKES MANY DIFFER-ENT SOUNDS ON HIS OWN, OFTEN

(D4) How does the child make sounds?

(D5) Makes more sounds if you imitate him

°° (D6) MAKES EYE CONTACT AND A SOUND AT THE SAME TIME TO GET THINGS

Verbal Imitation

°° (D7) IMITATES BASIC SOUNDS

°° (D8) IMITATES SYLLABLES

°° (D9) IMITATES SIMPLE WORDS

°° (D10) IMITATES PHRASES AND SIMPLE SEN-TENCES

°° (D11) IMITATES VERBAL MODELS OF MANY PEOPLE

E.   Functional Speech

Kinds of Functional Speech

°° (E1) NAMES OBJECTS OR PICTURES

°° (E2) ASKS FOR THINGS HE WANTS

°° (E3) IDENTIFIES AND DE-SCRIBES WHAT HE SEES AND HEARS

°° (E4) ANSWERS SIMPLE QUESTIONS

°° (E5) SAYS "HELLO" AND "GOODBYE" COR-RECTLY

Behavior Evaluation Table (continued)

°° (E6) USES PHRASES AND SIMPLE SENTENCES TO NAME, ASK, DESCRIBE, ANSWER QUESTIONS

°° (E7) IDENTIFIES AND DESCRIBES ONE AND MORE THAN ONE (PLURALS)

°° (E8) UNDERSTANDS AND USES PREPOSITIONS

°° (E9) UNDERSTANDS AND USES PRONOUNS

°°(E10) UNDERSTANDS AND USES OPPOSITES

°°(E11) USES WORDS ABOUT TIME (BEFORE/AFTER)

Handling Special Problems

°°(E12) USES THE FUNCTIONAL SPEECH HE KNOWS HOW TO USE

°°(E13) USES FUNCTIONAL SPEECH INSTEAD OF ECHOING OR PARROTING

°°(E14) USES FUNCTIONAL SPEECH IN MANY PLACES AND WITH MANY PEOPLE

F.   Chores and Self-Help Skills

Chores

°° (F1) DOES SIMPLE TASKS

°° (F2) DOES MORE COMPLEX TASKS AND CHORES ON HIS OWN, OFTEN

Self-Help Tasks

(F3) Feeds himself with the right utensils

(F4) Undresses himself

(F5) Dresses himself

(F6) Washes and dries face and hands

(F7) Brushes his teeth

(F8) Toilet trained

°° (F9) DOES MANY SELF-HELP TASKS ON HIS OWN, OFTEN

G.   Problem Behaviors

Destructive Behaviors

(G1) Bangs head

(G2) Bites or scratches himself

(G3) Throws tantrums

(G4) Hits, bites, kicks others

(G5) List of destructive behaviors

Getting Into Things

(G6) Gets into or messes up things

Strange Behaviors

(G7) Rocks himself

(G8) Spins himself

(G9) Spins things

(G10) Stares at fingers or objects

(G11) Flaps hands or arms

(G12) Makes strange faces

(G13) Strange postures

(G14) Demands or does rituals

(G15) List of strange behaviors

Reaction to Certain Consequences

(G16) Physical punishment

(G17) Verbal punishment

(G18) Time out

(G19) Ignoring

°°(G20) PROBLEM BEHAVIORS ARE BEING REPLACED WITH GOOD BEHAVIORS FROM OTHER SKILL AREAS